With love,

To Brother Paul,

A...

...ll you...

In appre...

hove...

Cam...

C...

S0-BQL-860

97.08.

¡Viva Cristo Rey!

THE CRISTERO REBELLION AND THE CHURCH-STATE CONFLICT IN MEXICO

Texas Pan American Series

¡Viva Cristo Rey!

The Cristero Rebellion and the Church-State
Conflict in Mexico

By DAVID C. BAILEY

Novitiate Library
Mont La Salle
Napa, California

UNIVERSITY OF TEXAS PRESS, AUSTIN AND LONDON

14435

The Texas Pan American Series is published with the assistance of a revolving publication fund established by the Pan American Sulphur Company.

The publication of this book was assisted by a grant from the Andrew W. Mellon Foundation.

Bailey, David C   1930–
  Viva Cristo Rey!

  (Texas pan American series)
  Bibliography: p.
  1. Cristero Rebellion, 1926–1929. 2. Church and state in Mexico. I. Title. II. Title: The Cristero rebellion and the church-state conflict in Mexico.
F1234.B175   972.08'2   73-17119
ISBN 0-292-78700-6

Copyright © 1974 by David C. Bailey
All Rights Reserved
Printed in the United States of America
Composition by G&S Typesetters, Austin
Printing by The University of Texas Printing Division, Austin
Binding by Universal Bookbindery, San Antonio

To Don and Dot, and Sherry, Sandy, Scott, and Sindy

CONTENTS

ILLUSTRATIONS

PREFACE

Between 1926 and 1929 thousands of Mexicans fought and died in an attempt to overthrow the government of their country, a government which itself had come to power through violence. They were the Cristeros, so called because of their battle cry, *¡Viva Cristo Rey!*—Long live Christ the King! Their saga is the central focus of this book, but the Cristero rebellion's significance lies in its relation to two other conflicts broader in scope and implication than the warfare that devastated large areas of Mexico during those tragic years. The first was the longstanding enmity between Mexican Catholicism and the Mexican state, which in 1926 reached a climax that triggered insurrection. The second was the division within the Mexican church caused by the determination of Catholic militants to destroy the regime created by the 1910 revolution. These two conflicts, rather than military exploits, form the major part of this work. United States intervention in the struggle, official and unofficial, also receives detailed attention. It decisively influenced events, and I have tried to clarify the nature of that involvement.

I am indebted to a number of people who helped make this study possible. My deepest gratitude is to the late Charles C. Cumberland, in one of whose graduate courses my interest in the Mexican religious question was first aroused. I wish to thank Paul V. Murray of Mexico City, who provided leads on locating materials and allowed me to use his magnificent personal library. Antonio Ríus Facius, Mexico's foremost student of the Cristeros, made available a variety of items from his private files and contributed to my understanding by sharing his thoughts with me and reacting to mine.

Antonio Pompa y Pompa and his staff at the library of the Instituto Nacional de Antropología e Historia were unfailingly helpful in facilitating my work in their collection. Father Daniel Olmedo, S.J., of the Jesuit Casa de Estudios in Mexico City, kindly allowed me to consult the Mariano Cuevas library, so important to anyone who studies Mexican ecclesiastical history. The skilled personnel of the Foreign Affairs and Modern Military Records Divisions at the National Archives in Washington, D.C., helped make my research there both profitable and pleasant. Their Mexican counterparts in the Archivo General de la Nación were equally generous with their time and courtesy.

The directors and staffs of other repositories also deserve thanks. These include the Robert Frost Library at Amherst College, the archive of the state of Coahuila, the Biblioteca Nacional and Hemeroteca Nacional in Mexico City, the Catholic archives of Texas in Austin, the library of the University of Nuevo León in Monterrey, the Latin American Collection at the University of Texas, and the archives of the University of Notre Dame.

Many individuals in addition to those already mentioned supplied information or insights for which I am grateful. The names of all would fill pages, but special thanks must go to Felipe Brondo Alvarez, Father Bernard Doyon, O.M.I., Michael C. Meyer, the Most Reverend Luis Guízar Barragán, Jean A. Meyer, Sara Cooney, Lic. Salvador Reynoso, María Ana Murillo Peralta, and Father José Bravo Ugarte, S.J. Perhaps few of the people who helped will be completely satisfied with the result, but they deserve much of the credit for whatever merit it may have. The responsibility for the choice of data used and the conclusions reached is mine alone, and the shortcomings can be shared with no one else.

My friend Professor Joseph P. Hobbs read the manuscript with his expert and merciless editorial eye. Thanks to him it has less verbiage and more continuity than it would have otherwise.

I acknowledge with gratitude a Ford Foundation grant awarded under the auspices of the Latin American Studies Center at Michigan State University, as well as some timely financial assistance from the M.S.U. All-University Research Fund and the Faculty Research and Professional Development Fund at North Carolina State University.

D. C. B.

¡Viva Cristo Rey!

THE CRISTERO REBELLION AND THE CHURCH-STATE CONFLICT IN MEXICO

1. The Ancestry of a Conflict

THE MEN WHO CAME to America from Spain owed their identity as Spaniards to their religion. Moslem invaders from Africa overran Christian Iberia in the eighth century, and shortly thereafter the Christians began the long struggle of the Reconquest. In seven hundred years of intermittent warfare the intruders were gradually driven southward, while the Christians, although often at odds with each other over control of the redeemed territories, erected kingdoms that later joined to form a Spanish national state. The Reconquest was preeminently a religious crusade. Catholicism was the great constant in an otherwise disparate situation and gave the movement both its impetus and its dignity. When the long struggle ended in 1492 with the occupation of Granada, the victorious Catholic warriors did not even pause for breath before turning their eyes westward, in effect merely rechanneling energies that had been centuries in forming.

Crown and cross came to the New World together. A desire to spread the faith to pagan lands moved Queen Isabella to support

Columbus's plan, and from the first the monarchs of Castile and the leaders of expeditions appealed to missionary motives to justify exploration and conquest. There were other impulses, to be sure. The Catholic Sovereigns and their successors were keenly interested in gaining financially from such ventures and were always careful to secure a share of any profits. The conquistadors, on their part, pursued wealth and power with a hunger that drove them to cross uncharted seas and face a thousand dangers in unknown lands among often hostile native populations. Yet the desire for worldly gain never foreclosed spiritual considerations. Serving God while satisfying venal cravings presented no conflict to the Spaniards. On the contrary, the two passions were complementary in their make-up.[1]

In colonial Mexico, as in all of Spanish America, Catholicism was an integral part of every individual's life. Baptism conferred both spiritual and civil standing. The Church was responsible for education and for such social welfare and medical care as existed. It exercised primary authority in matters involving marriage and family stability. Even the innumerable fiestas with attendant bullfights and other revelry marked some saint's day or other Church feast. The priest comforted the dying with the sacraments, buried the dead in consecrated ground, and offered Mass for the repose of the souls of the departed. Although churchmen occasionally held high political office, Church and State were not synonymous. The situation was, rather, an extension of the medieval ideal of Christendom—human society leavened by a spiritual presence that men deemed essential to the proper functioning of the social order.

In the areas of Christian knowledge, belief, and conduct, the Church's record was uneven. The high caliber and dedication of the priests in the first decades after the conquest gave way as

---

[1] Scholarly works on the conquest and the colonial period which present reliable treatments of the Church's role include Clarence H. Haring, *The Spanish Empire in America*; Charles Gibson, *Spain in America*; and Robert Ricard, *La "conquête spirituelle" du Mexique*. The present summary is based on these studies except where otherwise indicated.

the years passed to something often less edifying. Clerical life settled into comfortable patterns frequently devoid of noticeable fervor, and laxity in morals apparently became widespread. Mexico ended its three-hundred-year colonial era a Catholic realm, but the substance of its spiritual life ranged from the intellectual sophistication found among some Creole city dwellers to a veneer of vaguely understood essentials, sometimes mixed with ancient pagan rites, in the mass of the subject Indian peoples.

The Church's presence had a vast influence on the economic life of the Mexican colony—greater, probably, than in other Spanish possessions in America. The impact was beneficial in some respects, less clearly so in others. Clergymen introduced industries and agricultural techniques that were in many instances a boon to the Indian population. On the other hand, land and money, often in the form of pious donations from the faithful, tended inexorably to accrue to the religious establishment. Civil authorities showed an early concern over the concentration of Church wealth. As early as 1535 the crown decreed that lands in Mexico could be bestowed on Spaniards only on condition that they not be alienated to any ecclesiastical body. In 1578 the municipal council of Mexico City urged enforcement of similar limitations, and in 1664 that body pleaded for a halt to the founding of new convents and monasteries, making reference to the financial burden imposed on the colony by the existence of mortmain lands and the need to maintain the burgeoning number of monastic houses. Although the extent of Church holdings in colonial Mexico has never been accurately determined, by 1700 it may have included 50 percent of the usable land. Yet, undeniably, this accumulation of wealth made possible certain kinds of economic growth. Religious orders and diocesan treasuries had cash available, and, functioning as credit banks, they provided most of the capital that fueled colonial economic enterprise.

If the religious presence enhanced social stability, it was also at times a source of friction. There were conflicts between missionaries and greedy conquistadors, and between humanitarian clergymen and holders of *encomiendas*.[2] There was also strife within the official Church itself—between regular and secular clergy and among the various orders, between clergymen born in the colony and those from Spain, and between the Inquisition and almost every other branch of Church officialdom. There were periodic disputes between Church and government over questions of jurisdiction—one celebrated clash early in the seventeenth century between the viceroy and the archbishop of Mexico plunged the capital into rioting and rocked the colony for weeks.[3]

Not only did the spiritual permeate the secular at all levels, but also the civil power wielded wide authority in ecclesiastical affairs. The crown's prerogatives were based on the "royal patronage," the *real patronato*, a body of concessions that the monarchs obtained from the pope shortly after the explorations began. These concessions gave the king control over all Church activities except clerical discipline and doctrine. The result was to make the Church in America an arm of the royal government. The crown nominated all occupants of ecclesiastical offices from the highest prelate to the sacristan in the local parish church. It controlled Church taxation and could dispose of at least a portion of the proceeds. Places of worship, rectories, convents, monasteries, schools, hospitals—any edifices connected with religious uses—could be built only with royal approval. The crown determined which clergymen and how many could go to America;

---

[2] An *encomienda* was a grant that entitled the holder to receive tribute from Indians living in a designated area. After 1551 it could be collected only in the form of produce or money, not labor, although the law was often violated.

[3] A minor government official, accused of misconduct, fled to a monastery for protection. The viceroy posted a watch at the building to prevent his escape, an act which the archbishop claimed violated the right of sanctuary. When the viceroy refused to remove the guard, the archbishop excommunicated him. The viceroy counterattacked by confiscating the archbishop's property and imposing a fine, whereupon the archbishop placed the city under an interdict. As street mobs howled opposition to the viceroy, the *audiencia*—the viceregal council—suspended him from office. Madrid recalled the viceroy and transferred the archbishop to another post. See Hubert Howe Bancroft, *History of Mexico*, III, 33–78.

it established and changed the boundaries of dioceses; and it reserved the right to veto publication and enforcement of papal edicts in the colonies. In return for these formidable powers, the king had the responsibility of providing for the conversion and protection of the millions of indigenous inhabitants of the new lands, tasks that would have been far beyond the human capabilities of the papacy.

This paradoxical position of the Church—a powerful presence but in most matters subordinate to the State—must be kept in mind in any evaluation of its role. Beyond question, the Church must be credited with much that was good, both spiritual and material. If unworthy clerics sometimes compromised an institution that should have stood for justice and humanity more often than it did, the Church did restrain some of the worst excesses of exploitation by avaricious Spanish colonials, and it provided for the defenseless native a shield that otherwise might have been totally lacking. The Church was a mainstay of the stability that made it possible for Spain to dominate for three centuries an area remote from Europe and larger than the mother country, but it also nurtured priests like Miguel Hidalgo, José María Morelos, and Mariano Matamoros, whose sympathy for the oppressed, translated into deeds, heralded the end of Spanish rule. The pluses and minuses can be debated; what is certain is that the Church's place in society became the subject of bitter conflict as independent Mexico groped for an accommodation with the modern age.

Mexico began national life in the world of the French Revolution. Beliefs and institutions that had been the soul and body of European civilization for a thousand years were crumbling before an onslaught that left no part of the past unchallenged. The philosophers of the Enlightenment had insisted that man's ills stemmed from his dependence on irrational and outmoded forms. Their disciples moved to destroy those impediments to felicity so that mankind might build its own heaven on earth. Plans for the new rationalist millennium did not go unchallenged. Forces of tradition fought to turn back the assault. In most western countries liberals and conservatives battled throughout the nineteenth century, and in Mexico the struggle was exceptionally vicious and long-lived. The reasons for this are far from clear, but in part they reflected general weaknesses in postindependent Mexican society. With no experience in self-rule, with little precedent for compromising differences, with a stunted economy that the war for independence rendered even less viable, Mexicans were ill prepared for nationhood. Even the basic form of government was not decided upon for nearly fifty years, until the fall of Maximilian's empire ended the debate over monarchy versus republic. Irreconcilable differences wracked the nation for over a century on the more fundamental questions of man's place in society and the State's obligations to its people.

From the first, the issue was the colonial past, which, despite Mexico's political separation from Spain, remained very much intact. Men divided over whether Mexico should reject that past or build upon it. And no institution bequeathed by Spain was more firmly imbedded in the new nation's life than the Catholic Church, which quickly found itself inextricably involved in nearly every contention that separated Mexicans into hostile factions.

Even though the Church had served Spain, the revolt against Spanish rule in 1810 entailed no attack on the Church. Both royalists and rebels seized on religion to support their stands, and clergymen were prominent in both camps. Hidalgo and Morelos were only the most eminent of a host of lower clergy who rebelled against Spanish authority in the name of social justice and political freedom. The higher clergy bent all their efforts to aiding the royal cause, which, they insisted, was also the cause of religious orthodoxy. Only after the hated liberalism seemed to have triumphed in Spain itself in 1820 did they switch sides and welcome Agustín de Iturbide's drive for independence as the best way to preserve Mexico from the heresy of secularism. In 1821 Mexico gained independence on the basis of Iturbide's Three Guarantees, the first of which was the preservation of Catholicism as the national religion.

Although the Church had official standing in the new nation, problems involving its relation to the State quickly came to the surface. Most immediately perplexing was the matter of the *real patronato*. Did the prerogatives of the Spanish crown in ecclesiastical matters pass automatically to the government of Mexico? Many claimed they did; others, notably the clergy, insisted they did not. Some political leaders suggested asking Rome for a reaffirmation of the old privileges or, if necessary, a new concession. Others proceeded as though the matter were not negotiable. The Senate in 1826 declared that Catholicism, as the State religion, was under the protection of the civil authority and that therefore the government had the rights of *patronato*. The dispute waxed warm for several years, and not until the accession of the conciliatory Pope Gregory XVI in 1831 did matters move to more normal levels. The Holy See recognized Mexico's independence and appointed bishops to the vacant sees; but the *patronato* question, and with it the whole issue of Church-State relations, remained unresolved.[4]

The *patronato* controversy was related to a more basic phenomenon that appeared in the 1820's and soon became a central feature of the Mexican scene: anticlericalism. Anticlericalism, in Mexico as elsewhere, was a natural concomitant of Enlightenment liberalism. It was rooted in the conviction that the Church, or the clergy —the distinction was seldom carefully made—was an impediment to natural virtue. Man could perfect himself by use of reason; clericalism corrupted him by insisting upon mindless acceptance of dogmas, superstitions, and irrational rules. Moreover, Church and clergy, allied as they were to archaic political institutions and often occupying a place of great economic power, constituted an implac-

---

[4] The old standard sources on Church-State relations in Mexico since independence are Wilfrid Hardy Calcott's two volumes, *Church and State in Mexico, 1822–1857* and *Liberalism in Mexico, 1857–1929*. Charles C. Cumberland, *Mexico: The Struggle for Modernity*, contains an excellent general treatment of the subject woven into the larger story. On the early years of the Church-State conflict see Martín Quirarte, *El problema religioso en México*, pp. 147–191. *Historia moderna de México*, ed. Daniel Cosío Villegas, especially vol. 4, *El porfiriato: La vida social*, by Moisés González Navarro, contains much valuable information on the Church in the era of Porfirio Díaz. With exceptions noted, the information presented here comes from these works.

able enemy of social progress. Anticlericalism was widespread in Catholic Europe before the end of the eighteenth century, and its Mexican variety, although different in some respects, was an extension of this same movement: Voltaire and lesser figures of like bent were read and applauded in Mexico.[5] Rarely did eighteenth- and nineteenth-century anticlericalism, outside France at any rate, entail a denial of the supernatural or a desire to abolish the Church. But all liberals agreed that lines must be drawn between religious and secular spheres and that many functions claimed by the Church as its proper domain belonged instead to the civil authority. They insisted most especially that the State must curb and regulate the clergy's economic activities.

By 1824, when the Mexican republic was established, a liberal anticlerical party had formed, and many of its early luminaries were clergymen. Most prominent were Fray Servando Teresa de Mier, Miguel Ramos Arizpe, and particularly José María Luis Mora, whom later generations would dub the father of Mexican liberalism. None of them were antireligious in the abstract, but all of them advocated curtailment of the Church's traditional social prerogatives and proclaimed the supremacy of the civil power in all but devotional matters.[6]

To Mexican liberals the most hated enemy was special privilege—whether clerical, military, or economic—which absolved certain classes of Mexicans from accountability to society as a whole. Mora urged the abolition of *fueros*—corporate immunities, which in the case of the clergy included the right to be subject to a separate system of justice even in purely secular matters. He also preached strict vigilance over the Church's financial activities, restrictions on its economic holdings (which he described as vast and pernicious), and the suppression of male monastic orders (which he branded a social and economic blight). Education, Mora insist-

[5] An intelligible summary of the origins and nature of anticlericalism is found in Crane Brinton, *Ideas and Men: The Story of Western Thought*, especially in chapters 10 and 11.

[6] Mora by the end of his life seems to have abandoned the practice of religion and moved to agnosticism.

ed, must be secular; Church-run schools were in principle and in practice inimical to the welfare of the nation.[7]

Opposition to the liberals solidified rapidly. The scholar and statesman Lucas Alamán, probably the greatest intellect of Mexico's first half-century of nationhood, denounced the liberal program as a blueprint for disaster. Alamán argued that Mexico's well-being depended on fealty to her Hispanic and Catholic traditions. Although he was critical of certain aspects of Spanish colonial rule, such as the stifling of trade and agriculture and the relegation of Creoles to an inferior position, he defended the legacy of a privileged status for Catholicism in society. Religion's precise role could vary according to circumstances, but only the Church's pervasive influence could ensure individual honesty and integrity, and only the Catholic faith could provide the cement for national unity. If Mora set the tone for a century of anticlerical thought, Alamán elaborated a point of view that provided generations of Mexican conservatives with some of their strongest arguments.[8]

The liberals had their first chance to translate their doctrines into national policy in 1833. That year Antonio López de Santa Anna, who had just reached the presidency for the first time, retired to his plantation at Jalapa, leaving the government in the hands of his liberal vice-president, Valentín Gómez Farías. There followed a whirlwind of dramatic official activity, much of it directed at the Church. Liberal decrees poured forth. One prohibited clergymen from preaching on any subject not strictly spiritual; another secularized the entire educational system; still others ended civil enforcement of the payment of Church tithes and the observance of religious vows. The government confiscated various Church properties and began a survey to determine the value of

[7] José María Luis Mora, *Obras sueltas*, pp. 55–65; idem, *México y sus revoluciones*, I, 239–240.

[8] Alamán's ideas are contained mainly in his *Historia de Méjico desde los primeros movimientos que prepararon su independencia en el año de 1808, hasta la época presente* and *Disertaciones sobre la historia de la república mejicana, desde la época de la conquista . . . hasta la independencia.* For a good capsule summary of his views see Charles A. Hale, *Mexican Liberalism in the Age of Mora*, especially pp. 16–21.

all ecclesiastical holdings, with the apparent intention of moving to wholesale seizure. But the liberals had overreached themselves. There was a virulent adverse reaction, and the government's attempts to suppress it only heightened the furor. In 1834 Santa Anna decided that the liberal cause was a losing proposition. He resumed personal control in Mexico City, expelled Gómez Farías and his cohorts, and nullified most of their work. But it was the end only of a brief first round.

Twenty years passed before the liberals had another opportunity.[9] After the debacle of the thirties they retrenched, while the Church establishment, thoroughly alarmed, moved to a position of intransigent political conservatism. Government after government stumbled through political instability and financial chaos. The nadir was the disastrous war with the United States, which cost Mexico half her national territory and brought the nation to the brink of dissolution. Then, in 1854, a revolt began which toppled the conservative regime and brought to power a new generation of liberals. They undertook to rule and reform a country that was perilously close to collapse. Although more cautious than their predecessors of 1833, they were no less convinced that fundamental change was imperative, and as they set to work the status of the Church was high on their list of concerns. Between 1855 and 1857, when a new constitution was adopted, they enacted a series of measures designed to settle once and for all the place of organized religion in Mexican society. The Church's spiritual activities did not concern them; their target was its economic and political power. They forced the Church to divest itself of all real estate except temples of worship. They abolished *fueros* and drew lines between ecclesiastical and secular jurisdictions by requiring civil registry of births, deaths, and marriages, and by granting freedom of education. They removed cemeteries from the clergy's control.

The promulgation of the Constitution of 1857 triggered armed rebellion, supported by Catholic leaders. The government, headed

---

[9] Gómez Farías served briefly as president during the war with the United States. He demanded a loan from the Church—a faux pas which led to his resignation when the archbishop of Mexico, pleading lack of funds, refused him.

by Benito Juárez, waged three years of bloody warfare against the conservative insurgents before gaining the upper hand. During the dark days of that conflict, Juárez, from his temporary capital at Veracruz, struck at his clerical enemies with a string of drastic measures—the Laws of Reform. These edicts separated Church and State, nationalized all Church realty, outlawed tithing, barred public officeholders from attending religious services in any official capacity, abolished male monastic orders, forbade female orders to accept new members, made civil marriage obligatory, and legalized divorce.

Juárez re-established his government in Mexico City at the beginning of 1861, but the conservatives, refusing to accept defeat, turned to Europe for aid. Reviving the old dream of a Mexican monarchy, they offered a crown to Maximilian of Hapsburg, who, with the military backing of the adventuring Napoleon III of France, arrived in Mexico in 1864. Juárez again took to the road as a refugee president, this time to the desolate regions of the north. With growing popular support, plus the crucial advantage of U.S. recognition of his regime, he directed a guerrilla war against the intruders that ended in 1867 when Maximilian, abandoned by the French, was captured and shot at Querétaro. Juárez, at last victorious over all his adversaries, domestic and foreign, lay and clerical, re-entered the capital in July. He resumed control of a broken and exhausted nation, still confident that the liberal vision could lead Mexico to prosperity and happiness.

The clerical conservatives withdrew in silence, submitting to the unavoidable but in no way reconciled to it. There was a final, abortive attempt at resistance in 1873, when Juárez's successor, Sebastián Lerdo de Tejada, incorporated the hated Laws of Reform into the constitution. Peasant bands backed by local clergy rose in Michoacán, Jalisco, Querétaro, Guanajuato, and the state of México. The violence ended in 1877, when Porfirio Díaz seized power and, as part of his over-all policy of national pacification, soon made his first gestures toward conciliation with the Church.

The Church's status during the thirty-four years of Díaz's rule was ambivalent. The constitutional restrictions remained, and the

government was always careful to avoid appearing openly friendly
to Catholicism. But there was a gradual relaxation of official zeal
for enforcing the anticlerical laws, and by the 1890's the Church
enjoyed considerable freedom and was showing outward signs of
vigor. New dioceses were established, Catholic schools operated in
many parts of the country, and some of the old bitterness seemed
to be fading on both sides. But while the de facto truce removed
Catholic apprehensions regarding the survival of the faith in Mexico, the possibility that Catholicism might re-enter national life in
a public way seemed as remote to Catholics as it was unpalatable
to liberals. And no one could foresee that a re-entry would come in
the form of Catholic leaders promoting social reform.

On May 15, 1891, Pope Leo XIII, the eighty-one–year–old pontiff who had succeeded the conservative Pius IX, issued the encyclical letter *Rerum Novarum*. Coming only twenty-seven years after
the *Syllabus of Errors*, in which Pius had seemed to condemn most
of the trends in the world since the Enlightenment, the pronouncement had an impact possibly greater than that of any other papal
document of modern times.[10]

The Pope called for the application of Christian principles to the
solution of the world's social ills and, specifically, for Catholics to
aid in solving the problems of the working class. The task must be
undertaken within the framework of Christian teachings regarding
the nature of man and society if true reform were to be realized.
Surveying the condition of the laboring class, Leo pointed out that
workers were no longer protected by the ancient guilds or by the
moral authority of religion; such evils as usury and unbridled
greed had reduced the masses to near slavery. He condemned the
evils of child labor; he insisted that particularly exhausting work,
such as that performed by miners, demanded shorter hours; he
asserted that women must not be put in the position of having to
work in occupations that damaged their dignity or weakened the

---

10 An English translation of the encyclical letter is in Etienne Gilson, ed.,
The Church Speaks to the Modern World: The Social Teachings of Leo XIII,
pp. 205–240.

cohesion of the family; he defended the right of workers to organize and bargain with employers; and he advised Catholic workingmen to form their own unions, guided by Christian precepts of responsibility to God and society. At the same time, he rejected the Marxist prescription for change: socialism was wrong because it denied the right of private ownership, which was a natural right. He condemned class struggle as un-Christian and destructive of the ends of man.

The State, Leo insisted, had the obligation to uphold impartially the rights of all but must show special solicitude for the weak, and its first duty was to protect unfortunate workers from greedy men who used them as mere instruments to make money. He pledged that the Church would cooperate fully in the task and said that the efficacy of her intervention would be in proportion to her liberty of action in secular society. He summoned every minister of religion to "bring to the struggle the full energy of his mind and all his power of endurance."

The encyclical attracted little immediate attention in Mexico. Although it was printed there the same year it was issued, the first serious comment on it did not come until March, 1895, when the lecturer and journalist Trinidad Sánchez Santos analyzed and praised the document.[11] Further attention to the new orientation came the same year with the publication of *Colección de documentos eclesiásticos de Guadalajara*, which included a letter from Leo to the archbishop of Taragona, Spain, recommending the calling of Catholic congresses to deal with religious and social matters, the publication of newspapers upholding the Catholic view of society, and the establishment of worker associations.[12] Other Mexican Catholic spokesmen now came forward. José de Jesús Cuevas criticized *hacendados* for treating their cattle better than their peons; he also decried the low wages paid to industrial laborers.

[11] See Octaviano Márquez, ed., *Obras selectas de Don Trinidad Sánchez Santos*, I, 99–101.
[12] Alicia Olivera Sedano, *Aspectos del conflicto religioso de 1926 a 1929: Sus antecedentes y consecuencias*, pp. 32–33.

The bishop of Chilapa urged the wealthy to revive the lay apostolate by aiding Indian missions. The bishop of Colima pressed for the creation of Catholic labor unions in Mexico.[13]

In 1903 the first Mexican Catholic congress met at Puebla. It was a gathering that set the tone for a decade of intense Catholic social effort.[14] The delegates recommended the creation of worker organizations which, in addition to furthering the spiritual development of their members, would work to diffuse technical knowledge to improve their material well-being. A young Jalisco attorney, Miguel Palomar y Vizcarra, proposed the establishment of credit cooperatives. The assembly resolved that landowners should provide schools, medical care, and other social insurance for rural laborers. A second Catholic congress, held in Morelia the following year, was devoted primarily to spiritual matters, but the delegates also debated social issues. They demanded primary education for the working class; the setting up of schools of agriculture, arts, and trades; creation of worker, employer, and craft guild associations; and a campaign against unjust and fraudulent labor contracts. The third congress, which was also the first Mexican eucharistic congress, convened in Guadalajara in 1908. It reaffirmed the work of the two previous ones and added resolutions urging employers to deal with employees as human equals, to respect the Sunday day of rest, to provide schools for workers and their children, and to pay laborers a just wage, in currency instead of company scrip. The last congress, which met in Oaxaca in 1909, took as its main theme the plight of the Indian. Delegates called for efforts to improve public health and to combat alcoholism and concubinage, and they recommended shorter work days for persons working at high altitudes or in unhealthful surroundings.

Paralleling the general Catholic congresses, agricultural congresses gathered at Tulancingo in 1904 and 1905 and at Zamora

---

[13] Cosío Villegas, ed., *Historia moderna*, IV, 364.

[14] The work of the Catholic congresses and related efforts are summarized in Cosío Villegas, ed., *Historia moderna*, IV, 266–273, and Olivera Sedano,

in 1906. They addressed themselves to problems peculiar to the *campesino* and included discussions of ways to better the material and moral life of the rural populace. As Catholic interest in reform grew, various "Social Weeks" designed to dramatize social problems were observed in different parts of the country between 1908 and 1912.

Concrete action stemming from the congresses began to appear before 1910, the most significant being the establishment of the Catholic Worker Circles. By 1911 there were more than twenty-five locals with a total membership of between eight and nine thousand, and that year the movement was strengthened by the formation of the Confederation of Catholic Workers of the Mexican Republic. The confederation's second national convention, in January, 1913, was attended by delegates from fifty locals representing over fifteen thousand members.

A new phase of the Catholic resurgence began in 1909 when at the Oaxaca congress José Refugio Galindo succeeded in launching an organization devoted to the implementation of Catholic social principles. Taking the name Operarios Guadalupanos, it attracted numerous clergy and laymen, who in several annual gatherings elaborated plans for formal Catholic participation in Mexican political life.

The desirability of Catholic involvement in politics was implicit in *Rerum Novarum*, but Mexican Catholics were reluctant at first to take the step. The Díaz dictatorship placed no legal restrictions on Catholic political activity, but one of the unspoken terms of the Díaz-Church standoff was that Catholics as such would remain silent politically. Then, in 1908, the aged dictator announced that Mexico had progressed to the point at which a loyal political opposition was feasible and that, in fact, he would personally guarantee its right to function. Almost immediately small groups of various persuasions began to emerge, and late in the summer of

---

Aspectos del conflicto religioso, pp. 34–40. Puebla was not, strictly speaking, the first Catholic congress in Mexico. One met in 1885, but its object was exclusively devotional. Catholic writers commonly refer to Puebla as the first.

1909 Gabriel Fernández Somellera organized the National Catholic Circle as a preliminary step to Catholic political action.[15] Planning was well advanced when Francisco I. Madero initiated his revolt against Díaz the following year.

Madero was obviously sincere in his desire to see democracy become a reality in Mexico, and Catholic leaders were eager to participate. During the first months of 1911 both the National Catholic Circle and the Operarios Guadalupanos debated strategy. In the spring, a few weeks before Díaz fled into exile, the archbishop of Mexico called leaders of both organizations together and on May 5 they founded the National Catholic party.[16] The party convention, meeting in Mexico City that summer, voted to support Madero for the presidency.

The party's program showed how dramatically Mexican Catholic thinking had changed in fifty years. It pledged the party to work for reform "on the constitutional basis of religious freedom" and to ensure that democratic, republican institutions, especially free suffrage, would become a fact in Mexico. It affirmed the principle of nonre-election of state and federal executives. It demanded freedom of education as a natural right. The cornerstone of the program was the furtherance of Catholic social aims. The party would apply Christian principles to the problems of the worker and of the agricultural and industrial sectors in general, insisting that those principles were the only ones that could effectively better the living conditions of the working class without impairing the rights of capital. Although somewhat distrustful of Madero's mild liberalism, the party found him acceptable as a humanitarian free of anticlerical prejudice and a national hero. It would build a base from which to elect a candidate of its own at a later time. The delegates did, however, balk at Madero's choice for the vice-presi-

---

[15] Karl M. Schmitt, "Catholic Adjustment to the Secular State," *Catholic Historical Review* 47 (July 1962): 201.

[16] Olivera Sedano, *Aspectos del conflicto religioso*, p. 45; Miguel Palomar y Vizcarra, *El caso ejemplar mexicano*, p. 136. Palomar y Vizcarra, who was close to the event, believed the archbishop acted to forestall an attempt by Porfirio Díaz to rally Catholics to the defense of his embattled regime.

dency—José María Pino Suárez, whom they deemed too liberal
—and instead backed the Catholic Francisco León de la Barra, who
headed the interim government after Díaz's departure. The party
placed special emphasis on the establishment of credit institutions
for agriculture and small business in order to end the evils of usury
and promote economic growth.[17] In a telegram to the convention, Madero welcomed the party's founding as a concrete mani-
festation of the new freedom Mexico had gained. He lauded the
ideals expressed in the platform and praised the delegates for their
civic-mindedness and their desire to cooperate for the common
good.[18]

The party's record during the two years from 1911 to 1913 was
impressive. It elected twenty-nine federal deputies, four senators,
and governors in Jalisco, Zacatecas, Querétaro, and the state of
México. In Jalisco and Zacatecas it won control of the legislatures
and proceeded to enact a considerable part of its program. The
effort in Jalisco was especially noteworthy. Laws were passed
granting civil personality to syndical institutions and exempting
credit cooperatives from state and local taxes; other legislation established proportional party representation in the state, provided
for worker accident insurance based on employer responsibility,
and required that workers be given a holiday on Sundays.[19]

The final years of the Díaz reign and the short Madero period
that followed witnessed the appearance of a new orientation in
Mexican Catholicism. If practical results were still few by 1913,
it was nevertheless clear that the lethargy and timidity that had
dominated religious life since the time of Juárez were giving way
to forces committed to change. Catholic reformers were rising to
positions of influence. They could look back with satisfaction on
the ten years that had elapsed since the Puebla congress. The new
leaders were determined that Catholicism would again play a central role in Mexican public life, not as the defender of a discredited
past but as an agent of progress.

[17] Palomar y Vizcarra, *El caso ejemplar mexicano*, p. 136.
[18] Olivera Sedano, *Aspectos del conflicto religioso*, p. 46.
[19] Ibid., pp. 48–49.

Admittedly, it was little more than a beginning. Many Mexicans were ignorant of the new horizons or indifferent to them. The overwhelming majority of the nation was nominally Catholic, as it had been since the conquest, but Catholicism for most was the priest who conducted services in the local church (attended with some regularity by women and children, less often by men) and whose ministrations dignified such important events as birth, marriage, and death. The Church as a national or international institution was a hazy concept, and attempts to add a new dimension to the traditional religious presence were either puzzling or suspect. Some of the poor and illiterate joined Catholic labor or social action groups, but many more of them would join the revolutionary armies.

For that matter, many Catholics from more sophisticated levels of society paid slight heed to the new directions. Even the clergy were not unanimously enthusiastic. The Holy See's policy, after the turn of the century, of filling important sees with prelates who showed leadership in the progressive movement had not brought all the hierarchy to the side of reform. Some bishops were totally dedicated to it, but others maintained a studied determination to limit their pastoral concerns to spiritual duties, strictly interpreted; still others gave minimal, perfunctory support to Catholic social and political programs.[20]

Nevertheless, a start had been made. Whether in another generation the new Catholicism might have become a force capable of regenerating Mexico can never be known. Natural attrition would undoubtedly have lessened the influence of the old Church establishment, while new leadership would have accelerated the movement's growth. But a drastic turn of events in 1913 made the question moot.

Enlightened Catholics had not been the only Mexicans urging change during the first decade of the twentieth century. Despite the stagnation of the Díaz years, the liberal tradition of Mora, Gómez Farías, and Juárez remained alive; and, as the dictatorship

[20] See Palomar y Vizcarra, *El caso ejemplar mexicano*, p. 138.

foundered, the liberal movement underwent a marked resurgence. A radical wing, represented by men like the Flores Magón brothers and Antonio Díaz Soto y Gama, demanded major surgery on the body politic. Others, like Madero, believed it was possible to solve Mexico's problems by more gradual approaches. But probably none of the moderates and few of the radicals recognized, any more than the Catholics, how critical and urgent were the ills they wanted to remedy. By 1910 the political and social framework that held Mexican society together had weakened to the breaking point, and the desperation and frustration of millions of Mexicans had reached explosive levels.

Madero inspired many Mexicans with his call for a national rebirth, but he was confronted by opposition that blocked him at every step and then crushed him.[21] From the moment he entered office he was attacked from both right and left, the former plotting assiduously to remove him and return to the discipline and order of the days of Don Porfirio, the latter demanding drastic reforms that the cautious Madero refused to accept. Even the Catholics, who at first supported him, reversed themselves in the hope of discrediting his administration to further their own political aims. Madero's allies, although numerous, remained too disorganized to provide a solid base of support. The end came in February, 1913, in a violent coup d'état engineered by military chiefs. On February 9, units of the federal army in Mexico City rebelled. Twelve days later, after being forced to resign, the president and the vice-president were murdered by their captors.

Madero's fall swept Mexico into one of the most thoroughgoing revolutions the modern world has known—a revolution in which religion became a central issue. The irony of the new conflict between Church and State was that the Mexican Church of 1913 was different from the colonial Church. The old Church had appeared to be the willing handmaiden of reaction. The new Church, independent of the State and caught up in the winds of change of *Re-*

[21] On Madero's administration and overthrow see Charles C. Cumberland, *Mexican Revolution: Genesis under Madero.*

rum Novarum, was on its way to becoming an instrument for social reform. Yet many revolutionary leaders were as convinced as their liberal fathers had been that Mexican Catholicism was a congenital enemy of progress. By the same token, the new Catholic leaders, like the old, were certain that a liberal secular State was a perversion of true Mexicanism and a foe of basic human values. Two forces that wanted many of the same things for Mexico reverted to old certainties that precluded cooperation. The final showdown would come more than a decade after Madero's demise, but the events of February, 1913, generated the melee that led to it.

The seizure of power by Victoriano Huerta aroused rabid opposition. Under the leadership of Venustiano Carranza, governor of Coahuila, liberal forces mobilized to dislodge the usurper. These new revolutionists, the Constitutionalists, declared total war on all who failed to join them. The Church was a target from the start, when revolutionary leaders accused the clergy of abetting Madero's overthrow and allying with Huerta. Catholics denied the charges and later pointed to instances where Huerta directed his oppressive tactics at them; but Carranza's partisans, who could cite cases that seemed to show collusion between the tyrant and Catholics, remained convinced that the counterrevolutionary reaction had Church support.[22] By the summer of 1913 there was a virulent reemergence of the animosities that had existed between Mexican liberalism and Catholicism for nearly a century.

The new anticlericalism stemmed from the same philosophical premises as that of earlier times, but its manifestations were more diverse. Carranza himself, for example, although angered by what he believed to be Catholic friendship for his enemies, was never enthusiastic about moves to impose severe and permanent limitations on Church and clergy. He saw no objection, for instance, to Catholics maintaining their own educational system. But others, like Antonio I. Villarreal and Adalberto Tejeda, were not only hos-

---

[22] See Michael C. Meyer, *Huerta: A Political Portrait*, pp. 167–170. Meyer concludes that the Constitutionalists' charges were unjustified initially but that their assault on the Church eventually drove Catholics closer to Huerta.

tile to Catholic influence in Mexican public life but also anxious to "liberate" Mexicans from even a personal and private reliance on religion. Still others, like Alvaro Obregón, tended to be pragmatic on the subject—sometimes moderate, sometimes harsh, depending on circumstances.

But as the revolutionary chaos spread, Catholic clergymen and lay leaders had little interest in trying to distinguish among varieties of anticlericalism. By mid-1914, revolutionists were seizing ecclesiastical holdings; jailing or exiling bishops, priests, and nuns; and harassing Catholics in countless other ways. To many it appeared that the revolution intended nothing less than the extermination of the Church in Mexico.

In December, 1916, representatives of the Constitutionalist movement, which had triumphed over Huerta and beaten back revolt in its own ranks, assembled at Querétaro to revise the Constitution of 1857. After two months of intense and often tumultuous deliberation, the convention produced a document that retained most of the earlier charter but included enough significant changes to be considered a new basic law: the Constitution of 1917. Among its more extraordinary provisions were those relating to religion.

Juridical personality was denied to "religious institutions known as churches," and the federal government was empowered to "exercise in matters of religious worship and external discipline such intervention as by law authorized" (Article 130). Public worship outside the confines of Church buildings was banned (Article 24). Monastic vows were prohibited and monastic orders outlawed (Article 5). Religious bodies were denied the right to acquire, hold, or administer real property or loans made on such property; all real estate held by religious institutions, either directly or through third parties (church buildings, bishops' residences, seminaries, convents, schools, hospitals, orphanages, and so forth), was declared national property, and "presumptive proof" would be sufficient to establish that such property was in fact religious owned (Article 27). The federal government was empowered to decide which church edifices might continue to be used for worship; churches could be erected in the future only with prior government approval and would immediately become the property of the nation (Articles 27, 130).

Ministers of religions were henceforth to be considered members of a profession and as such subject to civil regulation, and only native-born Mexicans could function as clergymen (Article 130). State legislatures were given the power to determine the maximum number of clergy that might function in their states. Clergymen were forbidden, in either public or private gatherings, to criticize the fundamental laws of the nation, public officials, or the government in general; they were denied the right to vote, hold public office, or assemble for political purposes (Article 130). Periodical publications which could be deemed religious by title, by policy, or "merely by their general tendencies" were forbidden to comment in any way on public affairs or even to print information on the activities of officials or private citizens as these related to public affairs (Article 130). Political parties bearing names that indicated a religious affiliation were outlawed (Article 130). All elementary education, public or private, was required to be secular, and religious associations or clergymen were prohibited from establishing or directing elementary schools (Article 3). Trial by jury was denied in cases arising from violations of Article 130—which included most of the constitutional provisions relating to religion (Article 130).[23]

Some of the stipulations reaffirmed earlier laws. The ban on monastic vows had existed since the time of the Reform, as had legislation depriving the Church of the right to own or administer real estate—although the precise meaning of the prohibition had been somewhat in doubt, and the new constitution clarified the point.[24] The Mexican state for nearly a century had intervened in

[23] The Spanish text of the constitution is in numerous collections. An English translation may be found in the March, 1917, issue of the *Annals of the American Academy of Political and Social Science*.

[24] The Constitution of 1857 prohibited the Church from owning any real property except buildings devoted to worship. The Reform Law of July 12, 1859, confiscated even these. In 1873 the Laws of Reform became part of the constitution, but in 1874 a decree stipulated that religious bodies could acquire

religious matters which had a civil implication. Obligatory civil marriage, secular control of cemeteries, the proscription on worship outside church buildings, and other items had been legal requirements for many years.

But the new charter went beyond previous legislation. By denying juridical personality to churches, it closed the question of separation of Church and State; henceforth the Church had no legal existence. Public nonreligious schools had existed since the time of Juárez; now all primary education would be secular. The clergy had previously been subject to certain restrictions, such as not being allowed to preach opposition to the law; the new charter denied them any voice whatever in public affairs and, moreover, empowered the civil authority to regulate the clerical "profession" and even to determine how many individuals might practice it. Formal Catholic political involvement was ended. Even Catholic participation in public matters via the printed word was severely restricted. In effect, religion in Mexico found itself in much the same relationship to the State that it had been under the old *real patronato*—subject to the civil authority in all things save doctrine and private devotion. But the new *patronato* subordinated it to a State whose attitude was aggressively secular and from whose decisions there could be no appeal.

The new constitution appeared after nearly four years of religious strife. In most parts of the country Catholic worship either had ceased entirely or was subject to the whims of local revolutionary chieftains. Hundreds of clergymen had fled Mexico or been expelled. And now the nightmare seemed to have been capped by the work of the Querétaro convention. In April, 1917, members of the Mexican episcopate issued a formal protest from exile in the United States. The new charter, they asserted, sanctioned and formalized religious persecution; it injured the rights of the

---

no property *except* buildings for public worship and annexes strictly necessary for auxiliary purposes; it added, however, that the nation had direct control (*dominio*) over such buildings, which had to be registered with civil authorities as places of worship. Texts of the laws relating to religion are in J. Pérez Lugo, *La cuestión religiosa en México.*

Church, of Mexican society, and of individual Catholics; it proclaimed "principles contrary to the truths taught by Jesus Christ." The bishops assailed the restrictions as unjust and tyrannical. The hierarchy, they insisted, did not seek political power; it was committed to bettering the condition of the poor, and it supported the establishment of democracy in Mexico. They appealed for an atmosphere of toleration, in which the Church would use its moral authority to aid the government in its task of promoting the national welfare.[25]

It is unlikely that the bishops expected their words to alter matters, and indeed they did not. The lines were drawn, and there was little doubt on anyone's part that more trouble lay ahead. It remained only to be seen when and how it would come.

[25] "Protesta que hacen los prelados mexicanos que suscriben, con ocasión de la constitución política de los Estados Unidos Mexicanos publicada en Querétaro el día cinco de febrero de mil novecientos diecisiete." Enclosure no. 1 in U.S. Consul John R. Silliman, Guadalajara, to SecState, August 8, 1917, Department of State Records, National Archives, Record Group 59, 812.404/152. Hereafter records in the National Archives are indicated by the symbol NA, followed by the record group (RG) number.

2. A New and Fertile Bloom

THE YEARS 1913 TO 1924 saw a steady growth of Catholic opposition to the revolution. It progressed from scattered efforts of Mexican Catholics to defend the Church during the turbulence of the teens to pervasive hostility that later eclipsed tentative moves by both the revolutionary regime and the Holy See toward conciliation.

Much of the spirit and leadership of the Catholic antirevolutionary challenge came from an elite phalanx of young Catholics first organized in 1911. In the spring of that year, during the last hectic weeks of the Díaz reign, a group of students in Mexico City calling themselves the Jaime Balmes Student Philosophical Society met regularly to discuss ways to strengthen religious life in Mexico. Apparently their immediate goal was to form a national organization to counter the growing influence of the YMCA, whose proselytizing efforts, fortified by an appealing athletic program, were making inroads among young Catholics in the capital and elsewhere.[1] But the bright young enthusiasts were ready to undertake more exalted tasks as well.

The founding of the National Catholic party widened their horizons. They decided to become a student auxiliary to the movement. Party President Fernández Somellera welcomed their offer of assistance and made rooms at the headquarters of the National Catholic Circle available for meetings. On August 9 the reconstituted organization, named the League of Catholic Students (Liga de Estudiantes Católicos), was formally established. Its stated goals were to aid the Catholic party and to rally Catholic students throughout the country for the purpose of promoting moral betterment. The program also called for the establishment of youth centers to attract young people away from places of vice and evil; in these centers students would instruct workingmen in their rights and duties. The archbishop of Mexico, informed of the *liga*'s founding, sent congratulations and pledged his cooperation. The *liga* immediately plunged into the political campaign then in progress, with public demonstrations supporting the candidacies of Francisco Madero and Francisco Léon de la Barra.[2]

In the months that followed, the *liga* opened centers in the states of Oaxaca, Hidalgo, México, Zacatecas, Jalisco, Michoacán, Querétaro, Veracruz, and Yucatán. But recruitment was slow, and late in 1912 the leaders decided to seek expert help. They invited the Jesuit priest Carlos María de Heredia to become their adviser. He had attracted considerable notice by a series of brilliant lectures he was giving to another Catholic youth group, the Congregaciones Marianas. Father de Heredia accepted the invitation and immediately undertook a reorganization of the *liga*. First he recommended that it withdraw from political activity and concentrate on the spiritual, intellectual, physical, and social development of the membership. Next he formulated a program that included obligatory religious indoctrination for members and training in journalism, public speaking, and propaganda techniques. He also brought

[1] Antonio Ríus Facius, *La juventud católica y la revolución Mejicana, 1910–1925*, p. 27.
[2] Ibid., pp. 27–29.

the *liga* into contact with the Association of Catholic Women, which he had recently organized at the archbishop's request and which he now persuaded to provide adequate headquarters for the *liga*'s Mexico City chapter. In February, 1913, only a few days before the coup that overthrew Madero, the Catholic Student Center, equipped with gymnasium, library, game rooms, a large meeting hall, and study areas, was dedicated in downtown Mexico City.[3] The distinguished group of clergy and laymen who attended the ceremonies could scarcely have anticipated the destiny of the organization they were helping to inaugurate. Its youthful, eager spirit was evident, but only later did it assume the orientation that would involve it in one of the most dramatic episodes of Mexico's history.

The particular dynamism that came to characterize the new movement was largely the work of a French Jesuit priest, Father Bernard Bergöend, who in 1907 became a professor of philosophy at the Jesuit Institute of San José in Guadalajara.[4] Father Bergöend's two chief interests, social problems and young people, found fertile soil in his adopted country. In 1907 he organized a program for laborers in Guadalajara that combined spiritual exercises with courses of instruction designed to identify and train Catholic worker leaders. His efforts brought him into contact with Miguel Palomar y Vizcarra, Luis B. de la Mora, and other members of the Operarios Guadalupanos, to whom Father Bergöend urged the need for Catholic political activity. At their request he drafted a memorandum on the subject. Many of his proposals were later incorporated into the program of the National Catholic party.[5]

In 1911 the Jesuit turned his full attention to the role of Catholic youth in Mexican society. The prospects, he admitted, were discouraging; his work with students had convinced him that most young Mexicans were devoid of ideals for either their religion or

[3] Ibid., pp. 31–36.

[4] Ibid., p. 19; Andrés Barquín y Ruiz, *Luis Segura Vilchis*, p. 75.

[5] Ríus Facius, *La juventud católica*, p. 20; Andrés Barquín y Ruiz [pseud. Joaquín Blanco Gil], *El clamor de la sangre*, p. 336.

their country; almost nothing in their education had prepared
them to participate in national affairs; indifference was common
among all but a very few. What was needed, he decided, was an
organization that would undertake a strident spiritual and civic
formation of the young, with the object of mobilizing them for total commitment to the task of building a Christian social order in
Mexico. Convinced that time was too valuable to be lost in experi-
mentation, the priest decided to pattern his new organization after
the Association Catholique de la Jeunesse Française, already flour-
ishing in France with a record of achievement that had led Leo
XIII to praise it as a prime force in the French Catholic resurgence.[6]

In October, 1912, with permission of his superiors, Father Bergöend moved to Mexico City to pursue his goal. There he was introduced to the officers of the Catholic Student Center by one of
its leaders, Manuel de la Peza, and made a most favorable impression. It was a propitious moment: Father de Heredia had been
transferred to the United States, and the center was looking for a
new adviser. At the officers' request, Archbishop José Mora y del
Río made the appointment, which Father Bergöend eagerly accepted. He saw in the *liga* a ready-made vehicle for implementing
his plans.[7]

The priest assumed his new post on March 9, 1913. In a carefully prepared address to the center's leaders, he expounded his views
on the evils besetting Mexico. The State, he said, had excluded
God from the laws, from the schools, and from public life, and the
result was hatred leading to the revolutionary chaos that had erupted. National salvation, he insisted, would come only through the
painstaking work of men who would infuse a new vitality into national life. Catholic youth was eminently suited for the mission,
but it lacked unity and a clear understanding of modern tactics. It
must prepare itself. Prodigies could be accomplished for Mexico

---

[6] Andrés Barquín y Ruiz, *Bernardo Bergöend, S.J.*, pp. 80–81.
[7] Ríus Facius, *La juventud católica*, pp. 42–43; Barquín y Ruiz, *Luis Segura Vilchis*, p. 75.

by a youth who would "work as one for God, Fatherland, and people to the limits of sacrifice."[8]

Father Bergöend proposed that the Catholic Student Center become the nucleus of a new body, the Catholic Association of Mexican Youth. The general statutes that Father Bergöend drafted for the ACJM (the association came to be commonly known by the initials of its Spanish name, Asociación Católica de la Juventud Mexicana) described the organization as a self-governing Catholic lay body. Its relationship to Church authority, however, was carefully spelled out: each chapter was required to have an ecclesiastical adviser appointed by the bishop of the diocese where it operated; the bishop would exercise "vigilance" over its internal government and general activities and "jurisdiction" over its religious actions and those related to faith and morals. The association's purpose would be to prepare Catholics for the task of infusing Christian principles of charity and justice into all the functions of secular society. It would abstain from political involvement, although individual members had an "imperative duty" to defend political and religious freedom, even in the field of elective politics. The entire program, Father Bergöend said, was contained in three words: piety, study, action.[9]

The center's directors were enthusiastic, yet it was several months before the project was approved. *Liga* chapters in various parts of Mexico had to be contacted. Some agreed to affiliate, but others objected to the change, and not until the Congregaciones Marianas agreed to collaborate was the ACJM formally constituted, on August 12, 1913.[10]

Growth was slow at first. The appalling conditions in the country during 1914 and 1915, when the revolutionary strife was at its peak, forced suspension of most recruitment work. The savage fighting and near anarchy in many regions often made communications impossible. Meanwhile, the Catholic Student Center in

[8] Barquín y Ruiz, *Luis Segura Vilchis*, pp. 75–77.
[9] Ríus Facius, *La juventud católica*, pp. 43–46.
[10] Ibid., pp. 46–49.

Mexico City functioned as the temporary executive committee of the association.[11]

In 1916, with the country relatively calm, the outlook brightened for the ACJM. A highly successful organizational campaign in Guadalajara, directed by the center's representative, Luis Beltrán, led to the establishment there of a strong chapter that incorporated a number of already existing Catholic cultural and recreational groups. During the next few months, under the leadership of the young attorney Pedro Vázquez Cisneros, of Efraín González Luna, and of one who would soon emerge as the paladin of the movement in the west, Anacleto González Flores, the ACJM spread rapidly across Jalisco. Throughout 1917 and 1918 national membership burgeoned. Chapters sprang up in Colima, Aguascalientes, Guanajuato, Zacatecas, San Luis Potosí, Nuevo León, and Tamaulipas.[12]

By the end of 1918 enlistments had increased to the point that the Catholic Student Center moved to relinquish its position of temporary executive, and the following year a central committee made up of delegates elected from each regional unit assumed national control under the presidency of René Capistrán Garza, the head of the Mexico City Student Center. Capistrán Garza was the most prominent of the core of bright, earnest young men who rose to leadership positions. Intelligent, handsome, well versed in the humanities, and with considerable talent for oratory and debate, this young zealot—he was only twenty-two years old—would hold undisputed command of the association for the next decade.[13]

Although the task of defending the Church was implicit in the conception of the ACJM, there is no evidence that either Father Bergöend or the student leaders at first considered violence to be an appropriate weapon. Combat would be in the realm of ideas. But the anticlerical assault of the Constitutionalists led the ACJM to intervene directly and physically to defend Catholic interests. Sometimes it protected clergymen and church buildings from the excesses of the revolutionists; at other times it mobilized its mem-

[11] Ibid., pp. 78–95.
[12] Ibid., pp. 101–103, 109–117.
[13] Ibid., pp. 117–118.

bers to equal or outdo their adversaries in propaganda work and street demonstrations—actions that resulted in (and sometimes provoked) pitched battles. The ACJM's idealistic young adherents were by no means averse to such confrontations. Motivated by convictions that were both deeply religious and stridently patriotic, with an esprit de corps that had about it a large measure of the romantic, they relished the role of Christian warriors. Odds were a stimulus, and the possibility that they might be overwhelmed by events was beyond their calculations.

One young recruit, Heriberto Navarrete, described the ACJM in Guadalajara, which he joined in 1920 at the age of seventeen. The study circle to which he belonged had around sixteen members, all of them students in *preparatoria* (i.e., preparing to enter the university). This group, together with some fifteen others like it, made up the *central local*, whose headquarters building was rapidly becoming a first-rate facility complete with recreational facilities, library, and chapel. The member circles, each named for some famous Catholic—O'Connell, Kettler, Mun, Pasteur, Iturbide—held weekly meetings, attended by ecclesiastical and lay advisers. Sessions were devoted to the study of Catholic apologetics, with a strong emphasis on sociology. Navarrete recalled the spirit of militancy and sacrifice that dominated the gatherings: "Sunday after Sunday, in our typically informal morning meetings, we listened to studies and accounts of the lives of these [for whom the circles were named] and other Christian champions of all peoples in all eras. Thus we learned, little by little, that man's life on earth is a fierce battle and those who live it best are those who are the most warlike, who master themselves and then throw themselves against the army of evil to conquer by dying, and leave to their children the inestimable legacy of heroic example."[14]

The ACJM seldom shrank from a fight. When Alvaro Obregón jailed a large portion of the Mexico City clergy in 1915 for refusing

[14] Heriberto Navarrete, *"Por Dios y Por la Patria": Memorias de mi participación en la defensa de la libertad de conciencia y culto durante la persecución religiosa en México de 1926 a 1929*, pp. 26–30. All translations from the Spanish are by the author.

him a sizable financial contribution, the Catholic Student Center organized a protest march that ended in a riot when Catholics and revolutionists clashed. Several of the center's members, among them Capistrán Garza, were jailed.[15] The Jalisco contingents had their first taste of direct action in the summer of 1917, when the state government, irked at the archbishop of Guadalajara's public criticism of the new constitution, closed a number of churches and arrested parish priests who had read the archbishop's protest from their pulpits. The ACJM led street demonstrations and battled police. A year later it helped spearhead a campaign against a decree by the state of Jalisco limiting the number of priests and requiring clergymen to register with civil authorities. After a struggle that saw the cessation of all public worship, a mass boycott by Catholics of business establishments, and the expulsion of the archbishop from Mexico, the government rescinded the edict. The archbishop, who was accompanied out of the country by a guard of ACJM members, returned later in the year; he brought with him authorization from Rome, which he had requested, to confer on ACJM leader Pedro Vázquez Cisneros and lay adviser Miguel Palomar y Vizcarra the papal distinctions of Knights of the Order of Saint Gregory.[16]

After 1917, religious strife was local and isolated, if occasionally intense. Venustiano Carranza, as president, showed no disposition to badger the Church and did not enforce most of the constitutional provisions on religion. He had never been a partisan of extreme anticlericalism, and, moreover, he had to deal with other problems, foreign and domestic, that he considered vastly more important. Alvaro Obregón, who became president in 1920, saw matters in essentially the same light.

Obregón's accession initiated a period of relative stability and order in Mexico after a decade of bloodshed. A Sonora rancher who

[15] Ríus Facius, *La juventud católica*, pp. 87–88.

[16] Ibid., pp. 106–108, 125–134. An outspoken advocate of Catholic social principles, Palomar y Vizcarra had been a key figure in the Catholic congresses, a leader of the Catholic party in the Jalisco legislature, and a member of the faculty of the Escuela Libre de Derecho in Guadalajara.

had fought for Madero, Obregón rallied to Carranza after the "apostle's" fall. His abilities led to a rapid rise in the Constitutionalist movement, and late in 1913 he became commander of the Army Corps of the Northwest. The series of defeats he dealt Pancho Villa in the spring and summer of 1915 saved the Constitutionalist cause and confirmed him as a paragon of the revolution. His popularity with the insurgent army's rank and file, coupled with an instinct for personal survival in a milieu of treachery, made it possible for him to challenge Carranza for supremacy. When Carranza attempted to impose the relatively unknown Manuel Bonillas as his successor, Obregón, in league with Adolfo de la Huerta and Plutarco Elías Calles, rose in revolt. Carranza fled Mexico City and was killed in the mountains to the east. After a six-month interim during which de la Huerta served as president while elections were held, Obregón took office on December 1, 1920.[17]

In power, Obregón pursued a policy of national conciliation in order to consolidate the revolution. A consummate manipulator of men and events, he combined a well-enunciated revolutionary idealism with a flexible approach to realities. He preferred to achieve his ends through persuasion but was capable of direct and even brutal tactics. His handling of the complex problem of foreign investments in Mexico, particularly those involving U.S. and British petroleum interests, resulted in an easing of tensions that had threatened to bring armed intervention. By concluding an agreement with the United States government—the Bucareli Accords— he won American recognition of his regime, a vital factor in his ability to survive a rebellion launched by de la Huerta late in 1923.[18] Obregón would leave office the following year the undisputed master of revolutionary Mexico.

In religious matters Obregón followed a course usually devoid of extreme measures. While he was always quick to check any

[17] On the events of 1920 see José Vasconcelos, ed., *La caída de Carranza*; Rubén Romero et al., *Obregón: aspectos de su vida*; and John W. F. Dulles, *Yesterday in Mexico: A Chronicle of the Revolution, 1919–1936.*

[18] The negotiations leading to U.S. recognition of Obregón's government are studied in detail in C. Dennis Ignasias, "Reluctant Recognition: The United States and the Recognition of Alvaro Obregón of Mexico, 1920–1924."

move by Catholics that smacked of a challenge, like Carranza he
left in abeyance most of the anticlerical laws, and in public pro-
nouncements he refrained from the caustic rhetoric that had
marked his references to the clergy earlier in his revolutionary
career.

The prospect of religious peace was welcome to the Vatican,
which had been forced to give increasing attention to Mexican matters since 1913. The ugly situation that developed after the outbreak of the Constitutionalist revolt caused much anxiety in Rome,
and in 1917 Pope Benedict XV seconded the Mexican hierarchy in
its protest against the new constitution's religious clauses.[19] But by
1920 Rome clearly hoped to bring about a relaxation of tensions.
Obregón appeared to be of like mind. After the new apostolic delegate, Archbishop Ernesto Filippi, arrived in Mexico in 1921, there
were exchanges of letters between him and Obregón which showed
evidences of good will on both sides.[20] When Pius XI informed
Obregón of his elevation to the papacy in 1922, the president sent
him a courteous note of thanks.[21]

But if the mood in Rome and in the Obregón administration was
conciliatory, that among the majority of Catholic leaders in Mexico was not. To them Alvaro Obregón remained the persecutor,
who, during the dark days of 1914 and 1915, had imprisoned clergymen and nuns, seized churches and convents, closed Catholic
schools, and slandered the priesthood, and who in 1917 had abetted
and probably directed the clique that wrote the hated Querétaro
constitution. To trust such a man now, they believed, was worse
than futile; and to acquiesce in the permanency of the revolution
would mean to write off a generation of Catholic effort and possibly
to accept the eventual death of Mexican Catholicism.

Certain events during Obregón's administration seemed to justify the Catholics' fears. In February, 1921, a dynamite charge

[19] The text of the pope's letter supporting the bishops is printed in *The Southern Messenger* (San Antonio, Texas), July 26, 1917.

[20] See, for example, Filippi to Obregón, December 30, 1921; Obregón to
Filippi, January 2, 1922; Filippi to Obregón, June 3, 1922; Archivo General de
la Nación, "Archivo de los Presidentes, Obregón-Calles," 438-F-1.

[21] Lagarde Memorandum. In NA, RG 59, 812.404/867½.

was detonated at the door of the archbishop's palace in Mexico City, and in June another bomb damaged the archepiscopal residence in Guadalajara.[22] On November 14 of the same year, a bomb hidden in a floral offering exploded inside the Basilica of Guadalupe in Mexico City, only a few feet from the image of the Virgin, the most venerated object of Catholic devotion in Mexico. Church leaders believed that the person responsible was one Juan M. Esponda, a member of Obregón's staff.[23] On January 11, 1923, on a hill called El Cubilete, near Guanajuato, Catholics dedicated a monument to Christ the King. Leading figures in the episcopate, led by Apostolic Delegate Filippi, officiated at the impressive ceremony. Church authorities later insisted that the function did not violate the legal prohibition against outdoor public worship.[24] Obregón, however, chose to view the matter as a deliberate provocation. Filippi was expelled from Mexico, and formal charges (later dropped) were brought against several Mexican bishops.[25] A eucharistic congress held in Mexico City in 1924 provoked another incident, which Catholic spokesmen labeled a clear example of persecution. Midway through the week-long proceedings, some of which were of at least a semipublic nature, Obregón dispersed the congress and consigned the matter to the attorney general for action. Foreign clergymen involved were deported and government employees who had participated were fired.[26] Collisions between

[22] Ríus Facius, *La juventud católica*, p. 167.

[23] Witnesses said that, immediately after the explosion, soldiers surrounded the presumed culprit, who was taken to the offices of the municipal president of Mexico City. He was ordered to stand trial, but a court dismissed charges for lack of evidence. The image was unharmed, although the high altar was badly damaged. See Ríus Facius, *La juventud católica*, p. 179; Eduardo Iglesias, S.J., and Rafael Martínez del Campo, S.J. [pseud. Aquiles P. Moctezuma], *El conflicto religioso de 1926: Sus orígenes, su desarrollo, su solución*, I, 282–283.

[24] Their legal logic was dubious. Article 24, paragraph 2, of the constitution says: "Every religious act of public worship shall be held strictly within the churches . . ."

[25] Leopoldo Ruiz y Flores, *Recuerdo de recuerdos*, pp. 81–82; Alicia Olivera Sedano, *Aspectos del conflicto religioso de 1926 a 1929: Sus antecedentes y consecuencias*, pp. 90–92.

[26] Olivera Sedano, *Aspectos del conflicto religioso*, p. 93; Iglesias and Martínez del Campo [pseud. Moctezuma], *El conflicto religioso*, I, 293–294.

militant Catholics and radical revolutionists became increasingly frequent. In Guadalajara, ACJM centers were periodically sacked by street bands—and sometimes by police.[27] In Mexico City an exchange between members of the progovernment General Confederation of Labor and the ACJM on May Day, 1922, ended in the looting of the Catholic Student Center while law officers reportedly looked on.[28] There were similar clashes in Michoacán, Veracruz, Zacatecas, and elsewhere. The fact that such occurrences were sporadic and considerably less violent than they had been in the teens, and that on occasion Obregón rebuked the revolutionary extremists, was of little consequence; Catholic activists were convinced that they represented a pattern of calculated harassment encouraged by the government.[29]

But despite the sometimes painful news from Mexico, Rome was determined to seek a workable arrangement. Late in 1924 Pietro Cardinal Gasparri, the Vatican secretary of state, exchanged letters with the Mexican secretary of foreign relations, Aarón Sáenz. The Mexican government agreed to allow an apostolic delegate to reside in Mexico and promised that in case of difficulties it would ask Rome to recall its emissary rather than resort to unilateral expulsion as in the Filippi case. The Holy See declared its intention to fill vacant Mexican sees with churchmen who were not involved in politics and who promised to work exclusively for the spiritual welfare of the people.[30] If the practical abandonment of Mexican social (and political) Catholicism was the price for the survival of Catholic spirituality, Rome was willing to pay it. The understanding made no mention of laws; so long as they remained only a theo-

27 Navarrete, *Por Dios*, p. 30.

28 Ríus Facius, *La juventud católica*, pp. 202–203.

29 On Obregón's disapproval of local harassment of Catholics, see Obregón to Governor of Veracruz, May 2, 1923, SP.D. 22; Obregón to Ricardo Vargas, May 2, 1923, SP.D. 23; Archivo General de la Nación, "Archivo de los Presidentes, Obregón-Calles," 438-0-6.

30 Texts of the letters are in Elizabeth Ann Rice, *The Diplomatic Relations between the United States and Mexico, as Affected by the Struggle for Religious Liberty in Mexico, 1925–1929*, pp. 199–201.

retical danger to the Church's freedom to care for souls, Church and State could live in peace.

Mexican Catholic militants saw matters quite differently. There could be no compromise with the godless revolution. Anti-revolutionary bellicosity dominated the ACJM's first national convention in 1922. René Capistrán Garza, in a rousing address to the delegates, described the challenge facing Mexican Catholics and youth in particular as nothing less than one of reversing the course of Mexico's history. The work of de-Christianization begun by Juárez and continued by the Díaz dictatorship, he said, had driven religion from public life, and the evil and corruption spewed forth by the revolution were the result. The liberals wanted a people without God, and they got bandit hordes; they wanted a country without a religion or a history, a society without ethics, and they got disaster. Only Providence, he said, had averted perdition: amid the terrifying collapse there had sprung into being an armed and dedicated Catholic youth, and with it, "as if surging from the depths of the national soul, as a new and fertile bloom from the roots of the Fatherland, Christian civilization with all the luxuriance of its eternal youth, rising above the ruins that seemed to have demolished it forever." Mexico, he vowed, would save herself, and in the struggle the ACJM would be the guiding force if it did not depart from the spirit of Christ. The association's formative period was over, he declared; mature and ready, the ACJM would move forward to its goal.[31]

Other Catholic organizations, some new, others already well established, intensified their labors, and opposition to the revolution was implicit in most of their activities. The Union of Catholic

[31] "El Primer Consejo Nacional de la Asociación Católica de la Juventud Mexicana," *El Archivo Social*, no. 92, copy in the Archive of the National League for the Defense of Religious Liberty, first part. The league archive was microfilmed in 1961. The bulk of the documents is in two groups, both of which contain data on Catholic activities between 1902 and 1937. Materials cited from these will be designated LA-1 and LA-2. Also in the collection is an unnumbered roll of film with a variety of miscellaneous items; this will be referred to as LA-3.

Women held its first national convention in November, 1922, and devoted its main attention to education. The women called for repeal of the constitutional ban on religious primary education and for the right of parents to determine the kind of schooling their children would receive.[32]

By the early twenties there was a galaxy of mature and competent Catholic lay leaders. One of them in particular exemplified the determination of the new Catholic generation not to abandon the field to the revolution, which Obregón and others were determined to make perpetual in Mexico.

Anacleto González Flores was born July 13, 1888, in the town of Tepatitlán, in the part of Jalisco known as Los Altos.[33] He was one of twelve children of parents who earned a frugal but respectable living as proprietors of a small tool shop. Young "Cleto," stoop-shouldered and solemn, was nicknamed "Camel."[34] Although reared in a staunchly Catholic family, his religious fervor was only average until he was seventeen, when a priest from Guadalajara preached a mission that changed his life. His conversion was total and final. He became a lifelong daily communicant, and his acts of charity became legendary. His particular passions were teaching catechism to children and visiting the sick—people would later recall seeing him go each afternoon to the home of an elderly shut-in to pray the Angelus with her.

In 1908 he entered the seminary at San Juan de los Lagos, where he remained for five years until, reaching the decision that he had no calling to the priesthood, he left to find fulfillment elsewhere. Forced to prepare for some kind of career, he studied law while earning a precarious living teaching history and literature in private schools. But his burning interest was Catholic action. While a student at San Juan, he had spent his vacations recruiting mem-

[32] El Archivo Social, no. 93, LA-1.

[33] Los Altos extends from near Guadalajara east to the Guanajuato border and from the area of Encarnación de Díaz and Lagos in the northern part of the state south to Atotonilco el Alto. It is hilly upland country well suited to agriculture and with a heavy concentration of population.

[34] With exceptions noted, this précis of González Flores's career comes from Antonio Gómez Robledo, Anacleto González Flores: El Maestro, pp. 25–167.

bers for the National Catholic party in Jalisco, and now he moved to involve himself in a whole host of lay activities. Sleeping little, he found time to conduct catechism classes, usually among the poor, and to do organizational work among laborers; he counseled study groups of young Catholics; he established or collaborated in founding five newspapers in Guadalajara before 1924.[35] When the ACJM was organized, González Flores found in it all that he wished to do with his life. He became the embodiment of the association in Jalisco—the ideal of the young, the mentor of Catholic students, and the awe of action-minded Catholics of all ages. "Camel" became "Maestro," the sobriquet that followed him to his grave. In 1922, already thirty-six years old, he took his law degree, making an unheard-of perfect score on the professional examinations. Eight months later he was married, in the chapel of the ACJM headquarters in Guadalajara.

A master of words, printed and spoken, and possessed of a keen and balanced intellect, González Flores became a major spokesman for Catholic activism. More temperate and less given to florid oratory than Capistrán Garza, he propounded his views in a flow of books and articles after 1918. His arguments always dwelt on two major themes: rejection of the ideology of secularism and the need for a structured, Christian social order grounded in human charity. He mistrusted democracy. A healthy society, he believed, must be an organism of order and authority in which an aristocracy of talent imbued with spiritual values provides the motor. He never rejected the possibility that political democracy might eventually work, but he came to believe that it was at best premature to promote it in a Mexico infected by secularism. Individual spiritual and moral regeneration must precede enfranchisement; otherwise the masses would elect impious demagogues to office, and the result would be to perpetuate the "revolutionary disease" of the modern age, whose manifestations he described as spiritual unrest, economic bankruptcy, moral degradation, and religious persecution.

González Flores's political philosophy was at variance with that

---

[35] Andrés Barquín y Ruiz, *Los mártires de Cristo Rey*, I, 231–232.

held by other important Catholics. The men who emerged from the Catholic congresses to lead the Catholic party wanted political democracy implemented at once. In a different milieu the issue could have been divisive, but in the climate of growing Catholic fear of the revolution it was never joined. There was a common enemy. All Catholic activists could agree with González Flores that the revolutionists were usurpers bent on demolishing Mexico's ancient Catholic foundations in order to impose a malignant and alien despotism.[36]

The Maestro preached resistance, not by violence, which he always abhorred, but by individual sacrifice and collective civil disobedience. Violence, he taught, begot only more violence, ending in tyranny. The spirit of Mohandas Gandhi, whom he studied and admired, was evident in his approach. Personal heroism, reaching to martyrdom, he urged as a powerful and practical weapon: "The martyr," he once wrote, "is a necessity so that freedom will not perish in the world." Like other militants, he was impressed by the experience of Ireland. He recalled the success of Daniel O'Connell, who overcame the indifference and cowardice of influential Catholics to win the hearts of a whole people.

González Flores saw in the ACJM a core, a nerve center; but he recognized that this was not enough. An organization was needed that would reach all Catholics. The answer he provided was the Unión Popular. Although it was tightly governed, with a chain of command that reached from the top to the city-block level, the UP was open to all, and its formal program was minimal. The objective was Catholic unity and education—to infuse into the Mexican masses an awareness of the need for Catholic action at every level of public life. Although the UP grew slowly at first, it eventually attracted broad popular support in Jalisco, and by 1924 its official organ, *Gládium*, was being distributed to some eighty thousand persons weekly.[37]

[36] Anacleto González Flores, *El plebiscito de los mártires*, pp. 97–99.

[37] Navarrete, *Por Dios*, pp. 36–37, 88–91. The Unión Popular remained predominantly a Jalisco organization. Branches were established in other states, but

Besides forming social and educational groups, engaging in propaganda activities, and in some cases taking to the streets to fight revolutionists, Catholics also attempted to regroup politically. The National Catholic party had disappeared by 1917, but its survivors attempted to operate under other auspices. In 1920 the National Republican party was hastily formed at a convention in which Catholics predominated. Rafael Ceniceros y Villarreal, who had been governor of Zacatecas in the days of the National Catholic party, was chosen party chairman, and the ACJM was well represented by such figures as Capistrán Garza, Luis Beltrán, and Fernando Díez de Urdanivia. The party nominated one-time Constitutionalist Alfredo Robles Domínguez for president and adopted a platform that called for revocation of the 1917 constitution. In the September elections Obregón and his supporters swept the field, and the eight-week-old party dissolved. Capistrán Garza, one of its congressional candidates, was among those defeated, and he joined others in leveling charges of fraud at the winners.[38] In 1924 Capistrán Garza again failed of election to congress as a candidate of the movement that supported Angel Flores's unsuccessful bid for the presidency.[39]

Frustrated politically, some Catholics were ready to abandon words for guns. A number of them—none, apparently, of the top echelons—threw in their lot with Adolfo de la Huerta in 1923. The revolt's failure served only to consolidate Obregón's power and prestige.

By 1924, as Alvaro Obregón prepared to turn over the presidency to a successor, it appeared that the revolution was achieving a degree of permanence. Catholic hostility toward it, although uncoordinated and largely ineffectual, had also assumed a kind of institutionalized existence. The positive programs inspired by the Catholic congresses had not been abandoned; in fact they underwent a cer-

---

they seem to have been absorbed by the National League for Religious Defense after 1925.

[38] Ríus Facius, *La juventud católica*, pp. 147–152.
[39] Barquín y Ruiz, *Luis Segura Vilchis*, p. 101.

tain rejuvenation after 1920, notably in attempts to organize workers into Catholic trade unions;[40] but the main thrust of Catholic effort had shifted to opposing the revolution. To Catholic leaders it
was obvious that, if the revolution prevailed, Catholicism stood no
chance of becoming a guiding force in Mexican social and political
development. Moreover, they believed it entirely possible that the
regime sooner or later would apply the constitution's religious provisions so harshly as to hound the Church into extinction.

How to confront the menace was a matter of considerable debate
not only among Catholic lay leaders but also among the clergy.
Most of the eight archbishops and twenty-six bishops who ruled the
Mexican church in 1924 did not share Rome's predilections for
accommodation, but they were far from agreement on what their
corporate position should be.[41] They were united only in their
antipathy to the revolution; their approaches to dealing with the
revolutionary state ran the gamut from a desire to avoid conflict if
possible to a combative stance capable of approving armed resistance.

The primate, seventy-year-old Archbishop José Mora y del Río,
was a veteran of the chaotic teens when, like many of the others, he
had spent several years in exile. He was in declining health and
took an increasingly reduced part in day-to-day ecclesiastical affairs; but his ardent nature and his appetite for political maneuver-
ing would still find room for exercise in the few years left to him.

The most vigorous spokesman for the intransigents was the
archbishop of Guadalajara, Francisco Orozco y Jiménez. Of tower-
ing intellect, with a capacity for command and a personal presence
that was almost hypnotic, he was a living symbol of opposition to

[40] In 1920 the bishops appealed for an intensification of Catholic social action
and organized a Mexican Social Secretariat. A Catholic workers' congress in
Guadalajara in 1922 drew over 1,300 delegates representing some 80,000 union
members; from it emerged the Catholic Confederation of Labor (Ríus Facius,
La juventud católica, pp. 242–246; Francisco Orozco y Jiménez, *Memorándum*,
p. 4). Most Catholic social and syndical activity, of course, carried an implication of antirevolutionary sentiment, since it competed with parallel programs
promoted by the government.

[41] For incisive and generally unflattering comments on the Mexican episcopate in the early 1920's, see the Lagarde Memorandum.

the revolution. Already exiled from Mexico three times and more than once a refugee in his own archdiocese, he was lionized by Catholic activists, especially the ACJM, which he supported without reserve. On several occasions Rome had administered reproofs to him for his tactics—apparently without much effect.[42] Yet his aggressiveness was sometimes coupled with discretion, an attribute not shared by some of his fellow militants in the hierarchy.

At least as contentious, and less cautious, was José María González Valencia, the youthful, restless archbishop of Durango. By nature outspoken and at times overconfident of his ability to control events, he would welcome a showdown with the Church's enemies. So would Juan de Herrera of Monterrey, José de Jesús Manríquez y Zárate of Huejutla, Vicente Castellanos of Tulancingo, and Leopoldo Lara y Torres of Tacámbaro.

A more temperate position still predominated in the episcopate in 1924, although it was losing ground. Pedro Vera y Zuria of Puebla, Antonio Guízar Valencia of Chihuahua, Francisco Banegas Galván of Querétaro, Manuel Fulcheri of Zamora, and others still hoped peace was possible and were not eager for confrontation, although they did not hide their dislike of the regime.

Two prelates not yet clearly identified with a particular point of view were destined for decisive and emotional roles in the storm about to break. Leopoldo Ruiz y Flores, archbishop of Morelia, was an eminent theologian and energetic administrator who had made his archdiocese one of the best in Mexico. He had also, in his twenty-four years in the episcopate, shown a remarkable capacity for adapting to changing circumstances. Before the revolution he was on friendly personal terms with Porfirio Díaz. After 1910 he ingratiated himself with Francisco Madero. Although no friend of the revolution, he had emerged from the 1913–1917 time of troubles with a lack of rancor uncharacteristic of most of his colleagues. His flexibility and his aversion to extreme stands would involve

<hr>

[42] See Filippi to Obregón, June 3, 1922, Archivo General de la Nación, "Archivo de los Presidentes, Obregón-Calles," 438-F-L; also, Lagarde Memorandum.

him in bitter contentions as he moved into situations where compromise was, to many, another word for deviousness, or worse.

Destined for a meteoric rise in the ranks of the episcopate was the Jesuit Pascual Díaz, who in 1924 was just completing his second year in the hierarchy as bishop of the relatively unimportant see of Tabasco. Agile, perceptive, with an unusual ability to gain the confidence of persons of diverse viewpoints, he would quickly assume a pivotal position in Church affairs and would become the most controversial Mexican churchman of modern times.

The Holy See in 1924 surveyed the Mexican scene with an apprehension that soon approached despair. Confronted by growing intransigence on the part of the bishops and the burgeoning antirevolutionary hostility of Catholic activists, it found its policy of conciliation a hard one to follow. The bishops, in their *ad limita* visits to Rome,[43] kept up a steady flow of invective against the revolutionary governments and were little impressed by Cardinal Gasparri's counsels of patience. Yet the Vatican held its course. When, to the outrage of the Mexicans, Filippi was expelled, it protested but kept channels open by leaving a subordinate in charge of the Apostolic Delegation in Mexico City. Even Obregón's dispersal of the eucharistic congress did not impede the Gasparri-Sáenz exchange, announced shortly afterward.[44] At the same time, Rome refrained from trying to impose a uniform stance vis-à-vis the revolutionary regime. With the future clouded, with the bishops divided, with Mexican passions so high that the possibility of schism could not be ignored, and with the conviction that time and dialogue offered the only hope for some eventual solution, the Holy See chose to operate in low key and await developments. A new turn of events came after the election of 1924.

[43] Canon law requires bishops to make a report in person to the Holy See every five years regarding conditions in their dioceses and their own stewardship.

[44] According to the Lagarde Memorandum, the bishops had insisted on Filippi's presence at El Cubilete, and the Vatican realized that the delegate had behaved improperly by going. Lagarde also suspected that Rome was not enthusiastic about the holding of a eucharistic congress, which might serve to heighten tensions.

3. Of Men and Laws

THE HOPES OF THOSE who sought a peaceful accommodation between the revolution and Mexican Catholicism were dashed during the presidency of Plutarco Elías Calles. The rising tide of Catholic militancy had increased the likelihood of open combat, and Catholic obstinacy was matched by the attitude of Obregón's hand-picked successor, who assumed office on December 1, 1924.

Calles's rise to power paralleled Obregón's in many ways.[1] Like Obregón, he was from Sonora and of lower-middle-class anteced-ents. His early years, however, were marked by bad luck mixed with reports of irregular conduct. He attended normal school in Hermosillo and taught for a time. He was fired from his teaching position after parents complained of his personal behavior. His uncle arranged his appointment as city treasurer in Guaymas; he was dismissed when shortages in his department were discovered. He then took work as a bartender, followed by brief and unsuccess-

[1] On Calles's early life, see James A. Magner, *Men of Mexico*, pp. 520–524.

ful periods of employment in hotel management, farming, and milling (the hotel burned down, the farm went into bankruptcy, and the milling business failed). But his talents were not suited to the world of middle-class respectability. His *métier* was revolution.

Calles had been involved in radical causes since his student days and sympathized with opponents of the Díaz dictatorship, including promoters of the anarchist newspaper *Regeneración*. Díaz's fall in 1911 opened the way to a new life for Calles. He was an early Madero partisan and in 1912 was given the job of chief of police in Agua Prieta. He seldom tolerated dissent. Once, when a laborer shouted "Down with Madero!" in public, Calles ordered him hanged by barbed wire from a railroad bridge. In 1913 he joined Carranza's Constitutionalist army. His military record was not as spectacular as that of Obregón, under whom he served for a time, but it was creditable enough, and he rose to the rank of divisional general. During Carranza's tenure he was governor of Sonora and then secretary of industry, commerce, and labor in the national cabinet, and in Obregón's administration he held the top post of secretary of *gobernación*.[2]

Calles possessed neither Obregón's reflective temperament nor his agility in handling people and problems. His revolutionary dedication, however, was beyond question and was backed by an iron will and inexhaustible drive. Stubborn by nature, he was implacable in pursuit of a goal and direct to the point of bluntness in his tactics. As president he had few intimates and rarely gave his confidence to anyone—closest to him were his two personal secretaries, "Chole," an efficient and mysterious girl who was utterly devoted to him, and Fernando Torreblanca, who had been Obregón's secretary and was married to one of Calles's daughters.[3]

Calles's political support varied from Obregón's in one important

[2] Ibid. The Ministry of Gobernación is somewhat equivalent to the U.S. Department of the Interior but has vastly greater jurisdiction, including authority over matters involving religion.

[3] Consul General Alexander Weddell, Mexico City, to SecState, March 3, 1925, NA, RG 59, 812.00/27508.

way that augured ill for Catholics. Obregón, in the final year of his presidency, had sought to counterbalance the growing power of Luis N. Morones and his labor federation, the CROM, by giving encouragement to agricultural syndicates and their political arm, the National Agrarian party. The CROM and its political arm, the *laboristas*, eager to strengthen their power in national affairs, gravitated to Calles and worked day and night to help elect him. In gratitude, the new president named Morones to the cabinet, and in his administration the CROM enjoyed favored treatment in both patronage and policy formulation.[4] Since the CROM, which included hard-core revolutionary extremists, represented the far-left hue of anticlericalism, Catholics could expect little official benevolence.

Calles's stated views on the religious question were not significantly different from Obregón's. Both insisted that they were not opposed to religion but only to its misuse at the hands of intriguing and meddling clergymen. Both were determined that the Church, if it must function in Mexico, should do so only under conditions laid down by the revolutionary governments they headed. Both probably believed that the religious problem would one day be resolved. But while Obregón evidently saw the solution as longterm and evolutionary, with time on the side of the revolution, Calles was less patient. Whether the religious crisis that came during his administration stemmed from a determination on his part to force matters to a showdown—the revolution, after all, was over a decade old, and Catholic opposition to it was increasing rather than decreasing—or whether it sprang from an atmosphere in which passions could no longer be contained, is difficult to determine. What is clear is that actions of the government rather than the Church heralded the end of the relative calm that had marked Obregón's term of office.

Within a few weeks after Calles became president, an unmistakable change in official moods appeared. On January 30, 1925, the state of Tabasco limited the number of priests in the state to six (one for each thirty thousand inhabitants).[5] On February 8 the

---

[4] Robert E. Scott, *Mexican Government in Transition*, pp. 119–120.
[5] *El Universal*, February 18, 1925.

state of México sent a circular to municipal authorities in regard to the approaching Holy Week observances, reminding them that Article 24 of the constitution required that religious rites be held only within church precincts.[6] Six days later Calles pointed out to the governments of all the states that it was their duty to exercise strict vigilance over the clergy's activities; he noted that local governments had the responsibility to see that priests did not exceed their proper functions and to ensure that there be no more than a sufficient number of them to conduct worship.[7] There were other indications of a hardening of official attitudes, which the press was quick to note. The Mexico City daily *Excélsior* for February 18 cited the jailing of a clergyman for wearing distinctive garb and the closing of a seminary as examples of "recrudescent Jacobinism." Such incidents, said the *Excélsior* editorial, represented a national regression: "Are we perhaps so free of problems that we need to revive the religious warfare that has stained three-quarters of the past century with blood?"[8]

An indication of the eventual answer to *Excélsior*'s question soon appeared. Around 8:00 P.M. on Saturday, February 21, 1925, some one hundred armed men entered the church of La Soledad in one of Mexico City's working-class districts. They ejected the sacristans and several worshipers and announced to the astonished pastor, Father Alejandro Silva, that they were taking over the building. The priest and his two assistants were hurried out without even being given time to get their hats. A few minutes later, escorted by another armed group, an elderly clergyman arrived at La Soledad and to those present proclaimed himself "Patriarch of the Mexican Catholic Church." The "Patriarch" was Joaquín Pérez, a seventy-three–year–old priest whose long life had included some unpriestly detours. He had been a Freemason and after the start of the revolution had abandoned the altar for a time to accept an officer's commission in Carranza's army. He was joined in his

---

6 *Excélsior*, February 20, 1925.
7 *El Universal*, February 15, 1925.
8 *Excélsior*, February 18, 1925.

new venture at La Soledad by a Spanish-born cleric, Manuel
Monge, likewise of shaky sacerdotal reputation.[9]

The following day was quiet at La Soledad. A number of the intruders, calling themselves "Knights of the Order of Guadalupe,"
stood guard around the building. But word of the goings-on spread
through the quarter, and trouble came Monday morning. When
Father Monge appeared to begin the 11:00 A.M. Mass, angry pa-
rishioners in the church rushed forward and attacked him. He fled
to the sacristy, where he was soon joined by Pérez, who had tried
briefly to calm the assailants. A general riot developed and it was
midafternoon before mounted police and firemen using high-pres-
sure hoses managed to disperse the mob, which had grown to over
a thousand persons. Many were injured, with one death reported.
Pérez and Monge, who had barricaded themselves in the rec-
tory, sent an urgent appeal to Calles for protection. The president
promptly assured them that the necessary orders had been given.[10]

Although the bizarre incident appeared on the face of it to be
the work of a handful of religious renegades, some Mexicans suspected that it had wider implications. For, on the same afternoon,
other "Knights" had attempted to seize the church of Santo Tomás
la Palma (they failed because a sacristan managed to bar the doors
in time).[11] The next morning Gilberto Valenzuela, Calles's secretary of *gobernación*, issued a statement. He said the government
was completely neutral in the controversy and that it would not
tolerate ministers of one creed using force to take over buildings belonging to the nation which had been entrusted to ministers of another creed. But then he added a comment that did much to con-

[9] Ibid., February 24, 1925; Antonio Ríus Facius, *La juventud católica y la
revolución mejicana, 1910–1925*, pp. 275–276; Eduardo Iglesias, S.J., and Rafael
Martínez del Campo, S.J. [pseud. Aquiles P. Moctezuma], *El conflicto religioso
de 1926: Sus orígenes, su desarrollo, su solución*, II, 309; Weddell to SecState,
March 3, 1925, annex B, NA, RG 59, 812.00/27508. Weddell's report of the incident stated that Monge joined Pérez after it was discovered that Monge had
been living with a woman. There was also an unconfirmed report that he had a
police record in Spain.

[10] *Excélsior*, February 24, 1925; Ríus Facius, *La juventud católica*, p. 276;
Rafael Ceniceros y Villarreal, "Historia de la L.N.D.R."

[11] *Excélsior*, February 24, 1925.

firm Catholic suspicions: "The members of the Mexican church [i.e., the Pérez group] must not resort to censurable methods to obtain what the authorities are prepared to grant them provided they seek it peacefully and comply with the requirements of the law."[12] *Excélsior* charged what many Catholics were already certain of: the intrusions of the "Mexican church" had occurred, it said editorially on February 24, with the support of "certain authorities"; the case did not involve a religious schism properly so-called but rather a new outbreak of persecution against the Catholic church.[13]

Excélsior was correct regarding official involvement in the Soledad-Pérez affair. Several times in the days before the seizure of La Soledad, Pérez and CROM leader Morones had held extended talks. With Calles's approval, Morones pledged all-out CROM support for the operation, the object being to promote creation of a "church" that would support the revolution and replace or at least offset the influence of the Catholic church in Mexico.[14]

The ruckus agitated the country for weeks. Stories circulated that the government, or at any rate men in high office, were behind the schism. The "Knights of Guadalupe," some said, were actually police officers; according to other reports, they were CROM members.[15] There were assaults on other churches in Mexico City and elsewhere, provoking riots that left a number of dead and injured.[16]

[12] Ibid.

[13] Ibid.

[14] In a speech four years later Valenzuela told the story of the government's part in the matter. He said he opposed the scheme, told Calles that a bad precedent was being set, and persuaded him to order the schismatics expelled from La Soledad, but that Calles countermanded the order before it was carried out. See Iglesias and Martínez del Campo [pseud. Moctezuma], *El conflicto religioso*, II, 311–312. The U.S. consul general in his March 3, 1925, report (NA, RG 59, 812.00/27508) told of the Morones-Pérez interviews. Ernest Lagarde in his Memorandum (NA, RG 59, 812.404/867½) also recorded the official involvement and added that government emissaries tried unsuccessfully to persuade a visiting Eastern Orthodox prelate to consecrate Pérez an archbishop.

[15] Weddell to SecState, March 3, 1925, annex B, NA, RG 59, 812.00/27508.

[16] Alicia Olivera Sedano, *Aspectos del conflicto religioso de 1926 a 1929: Sus antecedentes y consecuencias*, p. 105.

But the government gradually abandoned efforts to promote the new sect.

On March 14 it was revealed that Calles had ordered La Soledad closed and that the building would be converted into a public library. Soon afterward he gave the Pérez sect the use of the more centrally located Corpus Christi Church, which had not been used for religious purposes for many years.[17] Father Monge did not join the move. On March 2 he published a statement in *El Universal* abjuring his affiliation with the schismatic movement and announcing his submission to lawful Church authority.[18]

There were lessons in the Soledad incident for both radical revolutionists and Catholic militants, although evidently neither learned them. To the rabid anticlericals it should have been a reminder that Catholic resistance could have a broad popular dimension when anyone tried to tamper with religious observances at local levels. There had been occasions dating back to 1913 when ordinary people had lashed back at attempts to abuse clergymen or desecrate places of worship, and Soledad showed that the same spirit was still alive. But Catholic leaders determined to combat the revolution should have found little encouragement in the affair. The working-class people who collected at La Soledad to fight the schismatics and police were not opposing the revolution per se. They knew nothing of the official involvement. They, or others like them, had fought in the revolutionary armies. Many of them no doubt sympathized with the revolution's objectives. They rioted when intruders laid hands on *their* priest and invaded *their* parish church, but few of them were concerned over quarrels among bishops, politicians, and young Catholic intellectuals. They were not ready to join a Catholic antigovernment crusade.

Practical results of the attempt to engineer a schism were few. No more than five or six parishes went over to the Pérez clique, and these only briefly. The archbishop of Mexico excommunicated those involved, but neither he nor the rest of the clergy had reason

<hr />

[17] Ibid., pp. 104–105; Iglesias and Martínez del Campo [pseud. Moctezuma], *El conflicto religioso*, II, 309.

[18] *El Universal*, March 2, 1925.

to believe that the schismatics would attract many followers. The movement gradually waned as the months passed.[19]

But the affair aroused panic among Catholic activists. ACJM contingents mounted an around-the-clock vigil at the Basilica of Guadalupe to stave off any attack.[20] Hastily organized "defense leagues" appeared.[21] The Catholic newspaper *El Obrero* on March 1 declared that open religious persecution was under way throughout Mexico.[22] Most Catholic leaders agreed; the issue was no longer the capacity of religion to reform Mexican life, but the survival of the Church itself.

Fear led to action and brought Catholic lay militancy to full maturation. For several years leaders had pondered the creation of a national Catholic defense organization, and the Soledad affair brought one into existence.[23] Miguel Palomar y Vizcarra, Luis G. Bustos, and René Capistrán Garza invited representatives of major Catholic lay societies to meet on March 9 for the purpose.[24]

On the appointed evening nineteen men gathered at the Knights of Columbus hall on Melchor Ocampo Street in Mexico City.[25] Palomar y Vizcarra chaired the session, which began with the presentation of a "Program-Manifesto of the National League for Religious Defense," drafted by the three initiators of the meeting.

[19] See Lagarde Memorandum.

[20] Andrés Barquín y Ruiz and Giovanni Hoyois, *La tragédie mexicaine: Sous l'ombre d'Obregon*, pp. 24–25; Ríus Facius, *La juventud católica*, p. 279.

[21] Typical was the Liga Católica Popular Potosina, sponsored by the bishop of San Luis Potosí. Its propaganda leaflets deplored the schism and called on Catholics to unite to defend their rights by legal and peaceful means. Copies of its handbills are in LA-1.

[22] *El Obrero* (Guadalajara), March 1, 1925. The constitutional ban on religious periodicals that discussed public affairs had not been enforced, and a variety of them flourished after 1920.

[23] See Miguel Palomar y Vizcarra, *El caso ejemplar mexicano*, p. 143. Father Bergöend in 1918 formulated the first plan for such a body.

[24] "Cómo nació la Liga, su escudo y su lema," *David* 5, no. 109 (August 22, 1961): 198–199; Palomar y Vizcarra, *El caso ejemplar mexicano*, p. 143.

[25] Represented were the Knights of Columbus, the National Catholic Confederation of Labor, the ACJM, the Union of Mexican Women, the Mexican Nocturnal Adoration Society, the Labor Federation of the Archdiocese of Mexico, and the Congregación Mariana de Jóvenes (minutes of the meeting of the Liga Nacional de Defensa Religiosa [LNDR], March 9, 1925, LA-1).

The document's tenor was combative and urgent: "We must unite, therefore, concerting all our forces, so that in due time, and as one, we can make an effort that is energetic, tenacious, supreme, and irresistible, which will uproot once and for all from the Constitution all its injustices of whatever kind and all its tyrannies whatever their origin. Only thus will we have freedom and receive justice; and it is precisely for this purpose that the National League for Religious Defense is established."[26]

The manifesto described the league as "a legal association, civic in character, whose aim is to win religious freedom and all the freedoms that derive from it in the social and economic order." It added that the episcopate was not involved in the league's organization and activities and that, although the league did not wish to operate entirely independent of the hierarchy's counsel, it would assume full responsibility for its actions. Its program, said the manifesto, was neither "a call to arms nor an irrelevant demand: it is only a synthesis of just and proper claims to which Mexicans are entitled in order to be able to live as Catholics, and which no one, in a democratic republic, can question." The league would pursue its goals by constitutional means and "those required by the common good." In the discussion that followed, Ramón Ruiz Rueda of the ACJM asked Capistrán Garza whether the methods employed by the league would be exclusively legal. Capistrán Garza was deliberately vague: he replied that, as stated in the document, the means "will be constitutional and 'those required by the common good.' "[27]

In subsequent meetings during March the delegates made minor changes in the wording of the manifesto and program and completed an organizational structure. The league would be governed by a three-man executive committee, named by a general convention that would meet at least once a year. At the March 17 meeting the delegates, who had constituted themselves a provisional general convention, elected an executive committee. Chosen were

26 Ibid.
27 Ibid.

Rafael Ceniceros y Villarreal, Luis G. Bustos, and Capistrán Garza.[28]

On March 24 a telegram was read to the convention from the Unión Popular in Jalisco, pledging its adherence, and by the end of the month reports arrived from various parts of the country announcing the establishment of league committees.[29] The Central Committee of the ACJM ordered its locals throughout Mexico— nearly a hundred in number—to take the initiative in organizing league committees, and ACJM members were soon occupying many of the leadership posts in these.[30]

Government reaction came swiftly. The day after the league's birth was reported in the Mexico City newspapers, together with excerpts from the manifesto,[31] the secretary of *gobernación* referred the matter to the attorney general on grounds of probable sedition.[32] On March 24 Valenzuela sent telegrams to all state governors and chiefs of military operations, instructing them to be vigilant in view of the new organization's "seditious" program.[33] The next day, however, he announced that, having seen the complete text of the manifesto, he was withholding action; the manifesto, he stated, was ambivalent—a mixture of statements both bellicose and legal. The government, he said, would await developments.[34]

Organizational work proceeded through the spring. On June 26 the Executive Committee reported a membership of 36,000, with all parts of Mexico represented except Sonora, Campeche, and the territory of Quintana Roo. Guanajuato led with 8,600 members. At the same meeting, Executive Committee aide Manuel de la Peza announced that a representative of the National Catholic Welfare Conference of the United States was in Mexico City to study the religious situation and was asking the league for data;

28 Ibid., March 12, 1925; March 17, 1925.
29 Ibid., March 24, 1925; April 1, 1925.
30 Barquín y Ruiz and Hoyois, *La tragédie mexicaine*, p. 16.
31 *El Universal*, March 21, 1925.
32 Ibid., March 23, 1925.
33 Ibid., March 25, 1925.
34 Ibid., March 26, 1925.

at Capistrán Garza's suggestion, the convention instructed de la Peza to cooperate with the visitor.[35]

While the Catholic laity girded for the fray, attempts by a new apostolic delegate to bring peace were shunted aside. The agreement concluded between Obregón and the Holy See late in 1924 had cleared the way for the appointment of a new delegate, the first since Filippi's expulsion. On December 18, 1924, Pius XI named to the post the Franciscan Serafín Cimino, who soon afterward was consecrated titular archbishop of Cyrene.[36] He arrived in Mexico City on April 1, 1925, determined to be a peacemaker. He began by announcing that he would respect Mexican laws, and in a letter to the Mexican bishops he said that in accordance with his instructions he would limit his activities to matters involving the spiritual well-being of Mexican Catholics.[37] But it was quickly brought home to Cimino that the spirit of 1924 had been buried by events of recent weeks. Two days after he arrived, José de Jesús Manríquez y Zárate, bishop of Huejutla, addressed a pastoral letter to his diocese that expressed the increasingly dominant mood. The Church in Mexico, he said—not quite accurately—had tried to overcome prejudice "with prudent silence and resignation," but the adversary had not responded to this approach. Was it advisable to continue the same stance? Obviously not; the Church, he insisted, could not submit to civil intervention in ecclesiastical affairs: ". . . laws, whether constitutional, organic, or any other kind, which are contrary to divine or ecclesiastical laws, are null and void." While the use of physical force by the faithful to repel the aggression was illicit, he continued,

[35] Minutes of the meeting of the LNDR, June 26, 1925, LA-1. The National Catholic Welfare Conference (since 1967, the United States Catholic Conference) was established in 1919 by the American Catholic hierarchy with the approval of the Holy See. It is headed by an administrative board of bishops, elected by the episcopate at large. Although no individual bishop is bound by its decisions, the conference serves as a national secretariat for the hierarchy, coordinating a wide array of Catholic activities and in general acting as a spokesman for Catholic interests in the United States.

[36] José Bravo Ugarte, *Diócesis y obispos de la iglesia mexicana (1519–1965)*, p. 109.

[37] Lagarde Memorandum.

Catholics must remain firm, with the dignified spirit of Christian martyrs. The archbishop of Mexico, asked by reporters for his reaction to the bishop of Huejutla's pastoral, replied that it did no more than express Church doctrine.[38]

Cimino had been forewarned in Rome of the intransigence of many of the Mexican clergy, but he found them even more unyielding than he had expected. He clashed almost immediately with some of the bishops over what they considered his timidity and his reluctance to take an energetic stand against the government's actions. The government, in turn, was antipathetic to the archbishop. In a brusque interview, Valenzuela warned him that his continued presence depended on careful compliance with the requirements of the constitution.[39]

On May 15 Cimino left for Denver, Colorado, reportedly for reasons of health. Several weeks later, when he applied to the Mexican Embassy in Washington for permission to re-enter Mexico, he was told that President Calles opposed his return. After spending several months more in the United States, trying to keep in touch with Mexican affairs, he resigned.[40]

Summer brought more trouble. In July the state of Jalisco closed two seminaries, the action touching off protests and street violence.[41] In August the Chihuahua legislature voted to discharge two state employees because of their membership in the Knights of Columbus, and a federal judge in Ciudad Juárez, citing constitutional prohibitions, ordered that an orphan asylum and a home for the aged, both operated by religious orders, be transferred to government control.[42] Also in August, Calles made a significant change in his cabinet: he replaced Gilberto Valenzuela as secretary of *gobernación* with Adalberto Tejeda. Valenzuela had been consid-

[38] Ríus Facius, *La juventud católica*, pp. 301–302.

[39] Lagarde Memorandum.

[40] Ibid.; Bravo Ugarte, *Diócesis y obispos*, p. 109. Monsignor Tito Crespi remained in charge of the Apostolic Delegation in Mexico City.

[41] Consul Dudley G. Dwyre, Guadalajara, to SecState, July 28, 1925, NA, RG 59, 812.404/267.

[42] Consul Thomas McEnelly, Chihuahua, to SecState, August 18, 1925, NA, RG 59, 812.404/269.

ered relatively evenminded on the religious question; Tejeda was known to be adamantly anticlerical.[43]

By the autumn of 1925 the Vatican was receiving urgent cries of alarm from both clergy and laity in Mexico. In September, Palomar y Vizcarra and Gabriel Fernández Somellera were in Rome to report on the work of the National League for Religious Defense and to warn that, unless something were done to change conditions, the people, "victims of violence and immorality," might abandon the faith altogether.[44]

A few weeks later the Mexican episcopate sent Archbishop González Valencia of Durango and Bishop de la Mora of San Luis Potosí to review matters with Vatican officials. Their reception was cool. Cardinal Gasparri feared that the Church in Mexico would be the loser in any head-on collision with the government; despite the intense expositions of the two prelates, he still leaned toward moderation—a position also favored by other members of the Curia with knowledge of Mexican affairs.[45] The episcopal emissaries laid their case before the pope on November 12. The Mexican bishops, they said, were disheartened at reports that the Holy See was displeased with them, adding that any misunderstanding was apparently due to rumors that the bishops had mixed in partisan politics. They recalled the deplorable legal position of the Mexican church, which could become far worse when the constitutional provisions were activated by enabling legislation—a step which, they claimed, the national congress was preparing to take. The danger to the Church, they asserted, was heightened by the character and background of Mexico's current masters—men raised in surroundings hostile to religion, arrogant drege of the *plebe* motivated by lust for personal power, men whose word could not be trusted. The bishops reminded Pius of the events of the last five years—the bombings, the Filippi case, the suppression of the eucharistic congress, the government-backed schism, the closing of seminaries,

---

[43] Lagarde described Tejeda as "one of the most implacable and malignant enemies of the Catholic religion" (Lagarde Memorandum).

[44] Memorandum to Pope Pius XI, September 18, 1925, LA-1.

[45] Lagarde Memorandum.

the efforts of "socialist and Bolshevik propaganda" to force Catholics into "red" unions. Protests, petitions, demonstrations, even recourse to the electoral process had all been tried in vain. The only remedy lay in strong Catholic organization, which was being promoted but had been developing slowly. They begged the pontiff to give advice and orders, which, they assured him, the faithful would hasten to obey.[46]

Rome would not be hurried, but the endless barrage of doleful news and urgent advice was having its effect. On February 2, 1926, the pope directed an encyclical letter to the Mexican episcopate, stating his position and providing guidelines. The pronouncement did not close doors to a conciliation between Church and State, but it was a strong indictment of the revolutionary government's anticlerical policies: the laws, said the pontiff, were wicked, unreasonable, and unnecessary—"they do not seem to merit even the name of laws"—and their enforcement by officials hostile to the Church had oppressed Catholics. He recalled that his predecessor, Benedict XV, had praised the bishops for their protest against the 1917 constitution, and he said that he now ratified and made his own the same sentiment. He expressed fear that, if government oppression continued to intensify, Catholics would lose their rights as citizens, and the work of the Christian ministry itself would die. At the same time, he carefully limited the range of response to the injustices. He did not explicitly demand a change in the laws, and, moreover, he drew a line between what Mexicans could and could not do to oppose them: ". . . in the present sad state of affairs, it is supremely necessary, venerable brothers, that you, together with the whole clergy and every organization of Catholics, most studiously hold yourselves aloof from every kind of political party so that you will not give the enemies of the Catholic faith the pretext to contend that your religion is bound up with any political party or faction . . ."[47] On the other hand, he went on, the faithful could not be forbidden to exercise

---

[46] González Valencia and de la Mora to Pius XI, November 12, 1925, LA-1.

[47] English text in *New York Times*, April 20, 1926. The letter was not made public by the Mexican hierarchy until mid-April.

the civic rights and duties that were the property of other citizens. The only sure and wise course to follow, he concluded, was that of "Catholic action."[48] He did not specify what form this might take in the situation at hand.

Matters in Mexico had indeed worsened. Late in October, 1925, the state of Tabasco in effect ended Catholic worship by ordering enforcement of a law which provided that only clergymen who were married and over forty years of age could exercise the ministry.[49] In January, Chiapas authorities decreed that baptisms and religious marriage ceremonies could be performed only after proofs of civil registry or civil marriage were presented. A bill was introduced in the Hidalgo legislature to limit the number of priests in the state to sixty. In Jalisco and Colima, officials closed numerous seminaries and other Catholic schools.[50]

Reaction to these measures had important consequences. On November 4, Archbishop Mora y del Río publicly condemned the Tabasco decree,[51] and two days later he sent a telegram to Washington giving details of the Tabasco situation to Father John J. Burke, executive secretary of the National Catholic Welfare Conference.[52] It was the beginning of a contact between the Mexican church and the U.S. hierarchy that would become increasingly complex and, from the viewpoint of both, decidedly double-edged. The occasion also marked the start of relations between the NCWC and the U.S. State Department concerning the Mexican religious question: Father Burke forwarded a copy of the archbishop's telegram to the department the following day.[53]

[48] Ibid.

[49] Jesús García Gutiérrez [pseud. Félix Navarrete], ed., *La persecución religiosa en Méjico desde el punto de vista jurídico: Colección de leyes y decretos relativos a la reducción de sacerdotes*, pp. 335–336.

[50] *El Universal*, January 19, 1926.

[51] Ibid., November 5, 1925.

[52] Burke, a Paulist Father, had been editor of *Catholic World* in the teens. During World War I he organized the Chaplains' Aid Association, and after the war it was at his initiative that the NCWC was founded. See John Tracy Ellis, *American Catholicism*, pp. 138–139.

[53] Burke to Franklin M. Gunther, Chief, Division of Mexican Affairs, November 7, 1925, NA, RG 59, 812.404/271.

The bishops in both Chiapas and Hidalgo refused to comply with the new regulations. State authorities in Hidalgo summoned Manríquez y Zárate to appear in court, but he refused on grounds that civil officials had no jurisdiction in purely ecclesiastical matters. On January 19 Mora y del Río released a statement denouncing the actions of state governments in Hidalgo, Chiapas, Colima, and Jalisco, adding that the clergy could not obey stipulations that contravened religious freedom. He said a collective protest was being readied and would be published on February 1.[54]

El Universal for February 4, 1926, carried the following story on page 1:

His Grace the Archbishop of Mexico has made the following statement, dictated by him, to our reporter, Mr. Ignacio Monroy:

"The doctrine of the Church is unchangeable, because it is divinely revealed truth. The protest which we, the Mexican prelates, formulated against the Constitution of 1917 regarding the articles which are opposed to religious freedom and dogmas, remains firm. It has not been moderated, but strengthened, because it derives from Church doctrine. The information which *El Universal* printed on January 27 to the effect that a campaign will be undertaken against the laws that are unjust and contrary to Natural Law is perfectly true. The Episcopate, Clergy, and Catholics do not recognize, and will combat, Articles 3, 5, 27, and 130 of the present Constitution. We cannot for any reason change this position without betraying our Faith and our Religion."[55]

Monroy had been assigned to interview the archbishop regarding

---

[54] *El Universal*, January 19, 1926. Although the statement indicated that some kind of formal remonstrance was being prepared, it is not clear whether Mora y del Río meant that it would entail republishing the bishops' 1917 protest or that it would be in the form of some new indictment. Nothing appeared on February 1. League members released copies of the old protest on the seventh, but the sources do not indicate whether this was done by direction of the hierarchy. Iglesias and Martínez del Campo [pseud. Moctezuma], in *El conflicto religioso*, II, 326, say the bishops did not order it; José González [pseud. Luis C. Balderrama], in *El clero y el gobierno de México: Apuntes para la historia de la crisis en 1926*, I, 37, says they did. Neither cites his source. No other collective episcopal protest appeared, although it is possible that the furor over the archbishop's February 4 statement caused a change in plans.

[55] *El Universal*, February 4, 1926.

a report that the hierarchy would soon initiate steps to obtain repeal of the offending legislation, and to get his views on the religious situation in general.[56] The reaction to Monroy's story was
spectacular. On Sunday, February 7, copies of the bishops' 1917
protest against the constitution appeared on the streets of Mexico
City, distributed by workers of the National League for Religious
Defense, and the next day, the Ministry of Gobernación consigned
the statement of the archbishop as well as the printed protest to
the attorney general for legal action. Catholic sources pointed out
that the document in circulation was nine years old, not current,[57]
but the government decided to treat the entire affair as a calculated
challenge and struck back fast: on the evening of February 10
many Spanish-born priests in Mexico City were rounded up; they
were sent to Veracruz the next day for deportation.[58]

On the eleventh Mora y del Río issued another statement to the
papers. He said he had been surprised to see that he was quoted
in the press as having said that the clergy would combat certain
constitutional articles—a thing which was "very far from our
minds, and could lend itself to wrong interpretations, since we are
aware of the way in which to initiate constitutional reforms." The
religious questions that had occupied the attention of the press
during the past week, he asserted, did not have the quality of time-
liness that had been given them, since what was involved was
nothing more than a repetition of statements from a document
published by the episcopate in 1917.[59] El Universal, in an accompanying comment, said that although the archbishop's words did
not contradict categorically the February 4 report, it was nevertheless possible that reporter Monroy might not have proceeded "with
all exactitude," and that the paper was investigating.[60]

Despite the archbishop's clarification, the government did not

[56] Iglesias and Martínez del Campo [pseud. Moctezuma], *El conflicto
religioso*, II, 324.

[57] *El Universal*, February 8, 1926; February 9, 1926; February 10, 1926.

[58] *Excélsior*, February 11, 1926.

[59] *El Universal*, February 12, 1926.

[60] Ibid.

drop the matter. Expulsion of foreign clergy continued, and Gobernación announced that Article 130 would soon be strictly enforced.[61] On February 13, officials from the attorney general's office
interrogated the archbishop at his residence.[62] The aged prelate
reiterated his claim that he had been misquoted and misinterpreted. Six days later the judge with jurisdiction in the case ruled that
there was no cause to proceed, and on February 24 the press reported that all charges had been dismissed.[63] As for Monroy, the
Syndicate of Editors, which had undertaken an investigation at
the request of El Universal, concluded that he should be fired but
given three months' pay plus one for each year of service with the
paper.[64]

The incident had even more serious consequences. Whether the
result of irresponsible journalism, a deliberate move by the clergy
to exacerbate an already tense atmosphere, or the unintentional
mistake of an elderly and infirm man, it pushed events toward a
climax. Whether or not the Calles government needed an additional justification for moving hard and quickly on the whole Church
issue, it now had one. On February 17 Tejeda announced that the
constitutional prohibition on the activities of foreign clergy (Article 130) was now in force and that, in conformity with the Laws
of Reform, the government had ordered the closing of convents
and monasteries throughout Mexico. He added that investigations
were underway regarding primary schools directed by religious
corporations, with a view to insuring compliance with Article 3.[65]

The official fusillade was now in high gear, and Catholic reaction
was predictably vigorous. The first collision came in Mexico City.
On February 18 Gobernación notified the clergy in charge of the
Sagrada Familia Church that, pursuant to the constitution, they

[61] Sheffield to SecState, February 12, 1926, NA, RG 59, 812.404/287.
[62] El Universal, February 14, 1926.
[63] Alfonso Toro, La iglesia y el estado en México, pp. 402–404; González
[pseud. Balderrama], El clero y el gobierno de México, I, 44; Excélsior, February 24, 1926.
[64] González [pseud. Balderrama], El clero y gobierno de México, I, 43.
[65] Excélsior, February 18, 1926.

must apply for permission to use the building for public worship. The order was ignored, and when government agents closed the church to inventory it preliminary to seizure, there was a three-hour street battle between police and around two thousand protesters, some of whom tried to march on the Ministry of Gobernación. Reports placed casualties at seven dead and sixteen injured.[66] Tejeda told newsmen that the riot was the work of "mindless fanatics, rebellious to the law," and stemmed from the clergy's refusal to heed a government directive. He added that three other churches in the capital had been closed for the same reason.[67]

In the last week of February, 1926, Calles urged state governors to take immediate steps to enforce the constitutional articles on religion. These had been in existence for nine years, he noted, but for a variety of reasons had remained largely a dead letter. The recent difficulties, he asserted, would have been avoided had the laws been applied in the first place.[68] In a speech to a Labor party convention on March 5, the president linked the religious problem to the revolution's efforts to build a new Mexico. What was involved, he told the delegates, was a struggle against prejudices of the past, "that past which I strongly wish to see liquidated." Public opinion, he concluded, was not the wailing of sacristans or the *pujidos*[69] of the overpious.[70] Reactionary pressures, he promised, would not sway the government: "As long as I am President of the Republic, the Constitution of 1917 will be obeyed."[71]

The government crackdown rolled forward, its intensity varying from place to place, depending on the zeal of local officials and public reaction. By the middle of March, two hundred foreign born

---

[66] Ibid., February 24, 1926; Sheffield to SecState, February 23, 1926, NA, RG 59, 812.404/294 and 812.404/295, and February 26, NA, RG 59, 812.404/324.

[67] *Excélsior*, February 24, 1926.

[68] *El Universal*, February 24, 1926.

[69] Roughly equivalent to "bitching." An earthy term meaning cramps or breaking of wind.

[70] *Excélsior*, March 6, 1926. The paper called the speech "vehement" and "sensational."

[71] Ibid.

priests had been sent out of the country and eighty-three convents
and monasteries closed. More than a hundred church schools had
been forced to suspend operations after mid-February, although
many reopened after modifying their programs or otherwise satisfying authorities.[72]

Moves to limit the number of priests aroused strident opposition,
but here too there was great variance in enforcement and reaction.
In Puebla, Querétaro, Michoacán, and San Luis Potosí, Church and
civil authorities reached understandings, although only after rather
serious confrontations in the two latter states.[73] In Michoacán,
Archbishop Ruiz y Flores suspended public worship, and the resulting public uproar brought the government to a workable compromise.[74] In the city of San Luis Potosí there was a street battle,
with police firing on protesters, when the government announced
plans to thin the ranks of the clergy, but within a few days the
bishop and the state officials agreed to a settlement that left ten
churches open with one priest in each.[75] In Tamaulipas a crowd
gathered at the government palace in Victoria when it was reported
that the state was about to reduce the number of clergymen. Officials assured the throng that the legislature would not meet to
consider such a setup, and the demonstrators disbanded—whereupon the deputies hurriedly assembled and passed a law limiting
to twelve the number of priests who could exercise the ministry
in the state.[76]

In some parts of the country, action against clergymen led to
both bloodshed and irreconcilable breaks between ecclesiastical and
civil authorities. The Colima legislature passed a law cutting the
number of priests in the state from sixty-five to twenty-two. On
April 8, the day the law took effect, several persons were killed in

[72] Ibid., March 15, 1926.
[73] Lagarde Memorandum.
[74] Leopoldo Ruiz y Flores, *Recuerdo de recuerdos*, p. 83.
[75] Weddell to SecState, March 20, 1926, NA, RG 59, 812.404/399; Consul
William W. Early, San Luis Potosí, to Sheffield, March 26, 1926, NA, RG 59,
812.404/409.
[76] Consul Charles A. Bay, Tampico, to SecState, March 12, 1926, NA, RG 59,
812.404/593.

a riot, and the bishop suspended public worship.[77] No settlement was reached, and it would be over three years before the priests returned to the churches. In Nayarit, official attempts to enforce a decree excluding foreign clergy set off an explosion that nearly overthrew the state government. In an act of bravado, state Secretary of Gobernación Rafael Sánchez entered the cathedral in Tepic on February 28 during services and, brandishing a pistol, ordered the officiating Spanish priest to leave the building. Sánchez was immediately set upon by enraged worshipers and was rescued, badly beaten and unconscious, only by the strenuous efforts of a few peaceful members of the congregation. The same day, the president of the chamber of deputies and a colleague attempted a similar move in a nearby village; their bodies were found riddled with bullet holes and stab wounds. The following Monday, as angry mobs surged through the streets of Tepic, the governor, to save his own life, signed a statement promising to make no further attempt to enforce the decree. In neighboring Sinaloa, the governor told the U.S. consul that he would take no action whatever unless the national government forced him to do so.[78]

The deterioration of Church-State relations was also reflected in the brief and unhappy experience of the apostolic delegate who succeeded Cimino, and who arrived in Mexico City March 5, the same day Calles delivered his *pujido* speech to the labor convention. He was Archbishop George Caruana, a native of Malta and a naturalized U.S. citizen who had been a Navy chaplain during the war and later had served as bishop of Puerto Rico. Rome's choice of him for the difficult Mexican assignment was due in part to his success in mediating a Church-government conflict in Guatemala several years before. Caruana's American citizenship may also have been a factor—the Vatican was not unmindful of Washington's sensitivity to Mexican treatment of U.S. nationals.[79] It was an imaginative move, but it proved to be worse than useless.

[77] Consul William P. Blocker, Mazatlán, to SecState, August 16, 1926, NA, RG 59, 812.404/593.
[78] Ibid., March 9, 1926, NA, RG 59, 812.404/374.
[79] Lagarde Memorandum.

Caruana had little faith in his prospects for success; he even suspected that the sending of a delegate at the time was a mistake.[80]
Watching with growing hopelessness the advance of the government's anticlerical drive, yet mindful of Rome's desire for peace,
he took no decisive public steps. In private contacts with the bishops, however, he supported resistance. Convinced that matters
were worsening and aware of the need for unity in the Mexican
hierarchy, he recommended and obtained the establishment of a
special Episcopal Committee, presided over by the archbishop of
Mexico and including the archbishops of Morelia, Guadalajara,
and Puebla, as well as any other bishops who might at any time
be in Mexico City.[81] His other contribution was polemical: at his
request the National League for Religious Defense changed its
name to the National League for the Defense of Religious Liberty
(Liga Nacional Defensora de la Libertad Religiosa) [LNDLR].[82]

If Caruana's tenure was quiet, his departure was not. On May 12
the government ordered him to leave Mexico, charging that he had
entered the country with falsified immigration papers and that he
had broken the law by functioning as a clergyman while there. He
categorically denied the accusations in a statement to the press four
days later, just before departing for the United States.[83] The ensuing controversy served only to worsen the situation.[84]

[80] Lagarde Memorandum; Weddell to SecState, March [April?] 1, 1926, NA
RG 59, 812.404/416.

[81] Wilfrid Parsons, S.J., *Mexican Martyrdom*, p. 19; Alberto María Carreño,
El arzobispo de México, excmo. Sr. Dr. D. Pascual Díaz y el conflicto religioso,
pp. 16–17; Lagarde Memorandum.

[82] Minutes of the General Convention, May 5, 1926, LA-1.

[83] *Excélsior*, May 17, 1926.

[84] The government produced what it said was a photostatic copy of Caruana's
entrance papers, on which his occupation was given as "teacher." Catholic sources branded the photostat a forgery. U.S. Consul General Weddell, who investigated the matter, said Caruana's passport gave his occupation as clergyman. He
surmised that the archbishop had passed immigration by the inadvertence of a
local agent who did not realize who he was (see Weddell to SecState, April 9,
1926, NA, RG 59, 812.00/27756). The U.S. ambassador was certain that Caruana
had taken part in no religious ceremony and had broken no law, and that "the
government had no justifiable grounds for expelling him" (Sheffield to Kellogg,
personal, July 9, 1926, NA, RG 59, 812.404/513½). Apparently the government

Despite the growing religious turmoil, the Mexican episcopate in the spring of 1926 was still disunited regarding the form its opposition to the government should take. Pascual Díaz, whose influence had grown since his election as secretary of the new Episcopal Committee, favored vigorous resistance and was becoming the spokesman for those who opposed temporization. Ruiz y Flores, de la Mora, and others preferred a legalistic tack, appealing to the constitution's guarantees of individual rights while at the same time urging repeal of the objectionable articles.[85] Already on the battle line were Manríquez y Zárate, whose March pastoral calling for disobedience to the anticlerical laws had led to his arrest,[86] and Lara y Torres of Tacámbaro. The latter, in an open letter to Calles in March, flailed the government and reaffirmed his adherence to the bishops' 1917 protest—"which we are prepared to seal with our blood."[87] He stopped short of advocating insurrection, however; in a letter to his diocese announcing that he was suspending public worship he warned that it was not permissible to resort to rebellion to recover rights.[88] A middle-of-the-road position still seemed to dominate in April; a collective pastoral letter released by the hierarchy on April 21 urged Catholics to work by lawful means to reform the constitution.[89]

Meanwhile, the LNDLR intensified its organizational efforts and worked to establish sole title to leadership of the Catholic defense. In March it asked the episcopate to "declare that it considers the

did not know of Caruana's appointment until he was already in Mexico City. It seems unlikely that Calles, after having refused to allow Cimino to return the year before, would have agreed to admit a new delegate. Both Kellogg and Sheffield tried to dissuade the Mexican government from expelling the archbishop (see *New York Times*, May 18, 1926).

[85] Lagarde Memorandum.

[86] Iglesias and Martínez del Campo [pseud. Moctezuma], *El conflicto religioso*, II, 344.

[87] "Memorial dirigido por el Primer Obispo de Tacámbaro, Dr. D. Leopoldo Lara y Torres, al Sr. Presidente de la República . . . ," March 16, 1926, in *Documentos para la historia de la persecución religiosa en México*, by Leopoldo Lara y Torres, pp. 91–92.

[88] Ibid., p. 115.

[89] Carta Pastoral Colectiva, April 21, 1926, LA-1.

League's work its own [and] that it order all Catholics to work with it."[90] The bishops evidently were unwilling to go that far, but they did, in their April pastoral letter, urge Catholics to join organizations "which teach the people, in theory and in practice, their rights and obligations as citizens and [which] organize the nation for the defense of religious freedom."[91] The league correctly pointed out to its members that it was the organization that met the bishops' criteria.[92]

The Mexican government, while endeavoring to deal with internal opposition, was anxious to forestall adverse reaction by its powerful neighbor over its handling of the religious issue. In a conversation with U.S. Ambassador James R. Sheffield on February 12, Secretary of Foreign Relations Aarón Sáenz brought up the subject and told the ambassador that the government's stern measures were due to its awareness that the clergy and Catholic organizations were affiliated with movements seeking to destroy the government's authority—he did not elaborate—and that the government had been forced to act "almost against its will." Sheffield reported to the State Department that he merely listened to Sáenz and then told him that he was "of course unable to discuss such a purely internal matter as this general religious question."[93]

Washington was watching events closely but limiting its concern to incidents involving American citizens in Mexico. On February 18 Secretary of State Frank Kellogg wired Sheffield asking for information on reports that American-run schools had been closed. He appreciated, he said, the delicacy of questioning the Mexicans on actions clearly within their rights, but he hoped the ambassador would use his good offices where indicated in order to prevent the closing of schools and the deportation of Americans.[94]

[90] Memorándum para el Ilmo. y R. Sr. Obispo Dr. D. Pascual Díaz, March 23, 1926, LA-1.
[91] Carta Pastoral Colectiva, April 21, 1926.
[92] League pamphlet, dated April 30, 1926, LA-1.
[93] Sheffield to SecState, February 18, 1926, NA, RG 59, 812.404/302.
[94] Kellogg to Sheffield, February 18, 1926, NA, RG 59, 812.404/282.

As in other "purely internal" Mexican matters, however, Washington was finding it difficult to keep hands off the religious controversy. The intensification of the Church-State battle in February led to a rapid and increasingly complicated American involvement. The prime stimulus was pressure from American Catholics. On the same day that Kellogg asked Sheffield to help Americans affected by the conflict, Archbishop Michael Curley of Baltimore stated publicly that the United States should accept broader responsibilities. The prelate criticized the State Department for its apparent indifference to the deplorable situation in Mexico, saying that religion had been assaulted there since the time of Pancho Villa and Carranza, and yet the United States continued to extend diplomatic recognition.[95] Soon afterward, Curley urged the U.S. Knights of Columbus to take positive action at their March meeting in Philadelphia on behalf of their fellow Catholics in Mexico.[96]

To the league's leaders in Mexico City, Archbishop Curley's statements suggested interesting possibilities. In March two representatives, Carlos Blanco and José Tercero, arrived in Baltimore. They carried with them, besides their league credentials, a letter endorsing their mission signed by Mora y del Río. Curley received them cordially and gave them a letter of introduction to Father Burke in Washington.[97] Blanco and Tercero presented to Burke a memorandum proposing the formation of a joint U.S.-Mexican committee to promote defense of Catholic interests in Mexico. Specifically, the committee would collect funds to wage a publicity campaign. Father Burke was receptive, commenting that such a group might help arouse American public opinion and counteract false information in both the U.S. and the Mexican presses. As for direct financial aid to Mexican Catholics, he told the visitors

[95] *New York Times*, February 19, 1926.

[96] Antonio J. López Ortega, *Las naciones extranjeras y la persecución religiosa*, pp. 6–7.

[97] "Anotación a la carta del R. P. Burke, dirigida al Lic. Ceniceros y Villarreal, con fecha 6 de marzo de 1926," signed by Miguel Palomar y Vizcarra and dated February 21, 1941, LA-1.

that was outside the field of operations of the National Catholic Welfare Conference but that he would present the matter to the American Board of Home Missions. All three agreed that any propaganda would stress that there was no intention to foment U.S. intervention in Mexico; to give such an impression, Father Burke pointed out, would only hurt the Church there. Finally, the priest promised to discuss the entire matter with the NCWC's administrative board and solicit its approval.[98]

The propaganda battle had already begun. The *New York Times* of February 21 carried a letter to the editor from Mexican Consul General Arturo M. Elías, who told *Times* readers that Mexico's Catholic clergy, unlike their patriotic and public-spirited American counterparts, "have consistently fought the constituted authorities, neglected their spiritual mission, and been the uncompromising foe of all progress—spiritual, political and social."[99] Adalberto Tejeda, in an interview given to a *Times* reporter in Mexico City a week later, said the clergy had kept the Indians in ignorance, stymied progressive agricultural methods, and undermined national unity ever since Mexico became a nation.[100] Beginning in March, more American bishops were heard from. Arthur Drossaerts of San Antonio blasted the Mexican government, which he said was taking its cue from Soviet Russia: "There is no blinking the fact," Drossaerts thundered, "that Mr. Calles, and Morones and Tejeda and his other confreres are aiming to war against God and Christ, all their protests to the contrary notwithstanding." One wondered, he added, how the United States, which did not recognize Soviet Russia, could keep an ambassador in "Soviet Mexico."[101] Archbishop Curley, his sense of outrage mounting, said in a statement widely reported in the Catholic press in April that the United States was providing Calles with weapons used to tram-

98 Burke to Ceniceros y Villarreal, March 27, 1926, LA-1. Apparently no committee was ever established.

99 *New York Times*, February 21, 1926.

100 Ibid., February 28, 1926.

101 *The Southern Messenger*, San Antonio, Texas, March 11, 1926.

ple religion and that Calles and his minions would not last a month if Washington would stop aiding his "Bolshevik regime."[102]

The administration was also under fire from closer to home. On February 19 Congressman Benjamin Fairchild (R., N.Y.) introduced a resolution asking for a full State Department report concerning the expulsion of American religious and other alleged outrages.[103] In March Congressman John Boylan (D., N.Y.) urged President Coolidge to sever diplomatic relations with Calles. He charged that the Mexican government was operating under a constitution "at variance with international honor," as demonstrated by its exclusion of American clergymen and its actions against American property.[104]

On April 15 the Administrative Board of the NCWC addressed a letter to President Coolidge. It expressed "indignation and horror" at the situation in Mexico and criticized American policy. In 1916, the board members told the president, the United States had recognized Carranza's revolutionary government only after Carranza promised to respect the religious rights of Mexicans—a promise that had not been kept. "As American citizens, believing in the principle of religious freedom, we shall continue to raise our voices in protest until the intolerable conditions which exist in our sister republic have been remedied."[105]

The administration decided it was time to offer a defense. On April 21 Kellogg called Father Burke to the State Department. He pointed out (correctly) that Carranza had never given the United States any guarantees on religious questions.[106] Franklin M. Gunther, chief of the division of Mexican affairs, after further talks with the priest, managed to persuade him that in view of the letter's inaccuracies it would be a mistake for the NCWC to make it

[102] Cited in Andrés Barquín y Ruiz [pseud. Joaquín Blanco Gil], *El clamor de la sangre*, pp. 136–137.

[103] *New York Times*, February 20, 1926.

[104] *New York Times*, March 5, 1926.

[105] NCWC to Coolidge, April 15, 1926, NA, RG 59, 812.404/413.

[106] "Memorandum of interview had by Father Burke and Father Lyons with the Secretary of State in connection with the letter to the President dated April 15, 1926 . . . ," April 21, 1926, NA, RG 59, 812.404/502.

public. Following a conference on May 14 with Burke and William
F. Montavon, head of the NCWC's legal department, Gunther reported that Burke now seemed to understand that the U.S. government had done all it could under the circumstances.[107]

Although the NCWC suspended for the time being its jabs at the
State Department, its friendship with the National League for the
Defense of Religious Liberty became close to the point of intimacy
during the spring and summer. Dozens of letters shuttled between
Washington and Mexico City, carrying encouragement to the
Mexicans and detailed reports on the religious situation to the
Americans.[108] The league was highly pleased. It welcomed the pros-
pect of favorable publicity in the United States, and it was con-
vinced that large sums of money from American church sources
would soon be forthcoming.[109]

While the State Department maneuvered to avoid criticism, and
while both the Calles regime and its Catholic enemies hardened
their stands, the Vatican anguished over the Mexican problem. In
April, Pius XI ordered public prayers for Mexico in the churches
of Rome—a step which, the French ambassador to the Holy See
noted, was traditionally taken only in circumstances that were
considered extremely grave; the last time it had been done, he recalled, was in 1920, when Warsaw was in danger of capture by
Soviet armies. Rome also put out a feeler for worldly succor. In
June the papal legate to the eucharistic congress in Chicago inti-
mated during a visit with Coolidge that the Vatican hoped the
United States would use its influence to save Mexico.[110] Rome

[107] Memorandum, Gunther to Kellogg, May 14, 1926, NA, RG 59, 812.404/
464.

[108] Most of the correspondence on the NCWC side was carried on by Montavon, who was fluent in Spanish; the league's letters were written by various
persons, including Ceniceros y Villarreal, Palomar y Vizcarra, Ramón Ruiz
Rueda, and Carlos Blanco. Copies are in LA-1.

[109] Minutes of the General Convention, May 3, 1926; "Anotación a la carta
del R. P. Burke . . ."; LA-1. Palomar y Vizcarra said the league "was led to
believe" that the American Board of Home Missions had millions of dollars
available—implying that he thought the league would receive financial support
from that source.

[110] Lagarde Memorandum.

wanted peace, but not at any price. In a letter to the Mexican hierarchy on June 14 the pope urged patience but also firmness. He said that unfortunately he had received no news of an improvement in the religious situation, and his only course was to encourage the prelates to persevere in defending the faith, now so gravely threatened in Mexico.[111]

As summer began it was obvious that conciliation was almost hopeless. Positions had stiffened into cold intransigence, and compromise had few supporters. Any new provocation from one side or the other could push matters over the edge.

[111] *Excélsior*, July 25, 1926.

4. "Mexico Needs a Tradition of Blood"

ON JULY 2, 1926, the government made public the text of a decree signed by Calles on June 14. The decree consisted of thirty-three articles which specified the application of the constitutional provisions relating to religion and spelled out penalties for infractions, whether committed by private citizens or by officials who failed to enforce the law. Many of the constitutional precepts had already been invoked in varying degrees by state and federal authorities, especially since early 1925; now, however, they were to be uniformly enforced on a nation-wide basis and backed by severe sanctions. The new law would take effect July 31.[1] Dedi-

[1] "Ley que reforma el código penal para el distrito y territorios federales, sobre delitos del fuero común, y para toda la República sobre delitos contra la federación," Mexico, *Diario Oficial* 37, no. 2 (July 2, 1926): 1–4. In most instances constitutional provisions are put in force by the passage of enabling legislation (*reglamentación*). In this case Calles achieved the same result by the device of reforming the penal code, which Congress in January had authorized him to do by decree. Congress later enacted legislation implementing the constitution's religious articles.

cated revolutionists applauded; at last, after nine years, the anti-clerical articles would be fully implemented. But to Catholic militants the "Calles Law" was the cocking of a pistol pointed straight at the Church.

Upon receipt of the news, the Episcopal Committee went into permanent and secret session. All the bishops were shocked, but a majority at first favored a wait-and-see approach, hoping that some way might be found to deflect the blow or possibly to negotiate some tolerable accommodation.[2] Most of the committee's discussions centered on section 19 of the decree, which required priests in charge of churches to register with the government. Some bishops expressed the opinion that the stipulation, although admittedly menacing, was not per se contrary to canon law; but others argued that it jeopardized episcopal control of the Church in Mexico by enabling the government to appoint and dismiss priests at will—a legal vehicle for achieving what the heavy-handed Pérez schism of the previous year had failed to do. The only possible response, they insisted, was to halt public worship immediately throughout the country.[3]

Debate waxed warm. Rafael Guízar Valencia, bishop of Veracruz, opposed a clerical strike. He agreed that the law was unjust and could not be obeyed, but he insisted that the priests must remain in the churches; if they were ejected, others should replace them, thus peacefully defying the government until public opinion forced it to back down.[4] Leopoldo Ruiz y Flores also doubted that suspending worship was the best weapon.[5] The bishops of Cuernavaca and Zamora favored an attempt at conciliation. Pascual Díaz leaned in that direction, although unenthusiastically.[6]

[2] Memorándum del Excmo. Sr. Francisco Orozco y Jiménez, Arzobispo de Guadalajara, México," *David* 7, no. 155 (June 1965): 168; Lagarde Memorandum, NA, RG 59, 812.404/867½.

[3] Lagarde Memorandum.

[4] Eduardo J. Correa, *Mons. Rafael Guízar Valencia: El obispo santo, 1878–1938*, p. 103.

[5] Alberto María Carreño, *El arzobispo de México, excmo. Sr. D. Pascual Díaz y el conflicto religioso*, p. 112.

[6] Lagarde Memorandum.

Strong for resistance were Orozco y Jiménez of Guadalajara and González Valencia of Durango.[7] Monsignor Tito Crespi, the chargé of the Apostolic Delegation, sided with the conciliators, insisting on the need for compromise; he feared that great spiritual damage would result from lack of regular priestly ministrations.[8]

The Vatican followed the bishops' deliberations with acute anxiety. Cardinal Gasparri, informed by Crespi of the divisions among the prelates, was himself uncertain of the best course. Although inclined to oppose precipitous steps, he refrained from trying to dictate a solution, desiring only that the bishops unite on some responsible stand.[9]

Meanwhile, the Directive Committee of the LNDLR,[10] unaware of the anguished attempts of the bishops to hammer out a course of action, formulated its own strategy for combatting the "Calles Law." The directors recalled the effectiveness of the boycott in Jalisco in 1918. They believed that the league could achieve success by the same method on a national scale. The committee decided to call a nation-wide economic boycott to bring the government to terms. In order to obtain maximum impact, the leaders decided, they needed official Church support, and for this purpose the directors requested an audience with the Episcopal Committee. They were received at the archepiscopal residence on July 7 by Mora y del Río, Pascual Díaz, and several other prelates. When they had stated the purpose of their visit, Mora y del Río, after a brief pause, asked them to put their request in writing and promised an answer in the near future.[11]

As the debate in the Episcopal Committee ground on, the moderate viewpoint lost ground. Díaz, followed by others, moved to

[7] Ibid.; Andrés Barquín y Ruiz, *José María González Valencia: Arzobispo de Durango*, pp. 26–29; "Memorándum del Excmo. Sr. Francisco Orozco y Jiménez," p. 168.

[8] Lagarde Memorandum.

[9] Ibid.

[10] By the middle of 1926 the three-man governing body of the league styled itself the Directive Committee (Comité Directivo) rather than Executive Committee.

[11] Rafael Ceniceros y Villarreal, "Historia de la L.N.D.R."

a hardline position, and on the evening of July 11 the balance swung to the proponents of strong resistance. The bishops voted to stop all public worship throughout Mexico and to inform Rome that, unless they received instructions to the contrary, the order would become effective August 1.[12]

On July 14 the Episcopal Committee informed the league that it endorsed the boycott, both because of its objectives and because of the "ordered and peaceful form" the measure would take: "We are with you in this work of recovering just rights, and we earnestly recommend to our clergy and faithful their most active cooperation in so laudable an undertaking."[13] Two days later the league released its boycott proclamation and began a massive propaganda campaign to win public support. It urged Mexicans to abstain from purchasing anything except basic necessities, curtail their use of public and private vehicles, limit consumption of electricity, and refrain from all amusements and recreation. It also instructed parents to refuse to send their children to nonreligious schools.[14] *El Imparcial* of July 17 carried the text of the boycott appeal; the other Mexico City dailies did not, either then or later.[15] On July 22 the

[12] Lagarde Memorandum; Walter Lippmann, "The Church and State in Mexico: American Mediation," *Foreign Affairs* 8 (January 1930): 191. Francisco Orozco y Jiménez (*Memorándum*, p. 68) said the decision to suspend worship subject to papal approval was unanimous but did not say whether unanimity was achieved on July 11 or some days later. Carreño (*El arzobispo de México*, p. 112) says the bishops who favored suspension acted on absolute assurances given them by the league that it would overthrow the government within two or three months, the implication being that halting worship would help the league accomplish this. Carreño does not say whether the government was to be brought down by the boycott only or by armed action. There is no evidence that the league leaders were planning a revolt in July. Carreño's references to matters involving the league must be used with caution, because he was keenly interested in branding the league as irresponsible and incompetent and in defending the motives and actions of Pascual Díaz.

[13] Mora y del Río and Díaz to Ceniceros y Villarreal, Bustos, and Capistrán Garza, July 14, 1926. Copy in possession of Antonio Ríus Facius.

[14] League Bulletin 2-A, July 14, 1926, LA-1.

[15] *El Imparcial*, July 17, 1926. *El Universal* said only that the league had ordered a "program of social-economic action"; *Excélsior* printed no news of any kind on the subject. In later stories regarding the arrest of league leaders, both papers made only vague references to a document which they said the govern-

three members of the Directive Committee were arrested at the league offices on Donceles Street[16] and interned in the military prison of Santiago Tlaltelolco.[17] Alternates previously selected with such an eventuality in mind took their places. These in turn were taken into custody and interrogated. By the end of July, however, all had been freed and, with the exception of Capistrán Garza, had gone into hiding.[18]

As events rushed toward a final rupture, Rome decided to make one last attempt to reconcile the Mexican church and state. The Holy See instructed Crespi to make a formal approach to the government. With French Chargé d'Affaires Ernest Lagarde acting as intermediary, Crespi asked for an interview with Tejeda. They met on July 23, with Lagarde present. Gasparri had directed Crespi to inform the government that the Holy See agreed with the bishops that the laws were unjust and prejudicial and to urge that their application be postponed or moderated in the interest of peace. The seasoned Vatican diplomat did his best; he even confided to Tejeda that the pope was aware of the need for reform among the Mexican clergy. But Tejeda was unyielding; modification or suspension was not to be considered—although he did tell Crespi that the registration of priests was for administrative purposes only and had no further object, and that the bishops, as citizens, could initiate steps to amend the constitution. Visibly agitated over the crisis at hand, Tejeda said he hoped Rome would invite Catholics to use legal methods to advance their interests.[19]

The formal break came quickly. The Episcopal Committee had already sent a courier to Havana to deliver to Caruana a communi-

---

ment considered seditious. The reluctance to comment was understandable: Gobernación had forbidden newspapers to comment on the "Calles Law" on grounds that any newspaper doing so would be violating the constitutional prohibition on publications that manifested religious tendencies. See *New York Times*, July 24, 1926.

[16] Ruiz Rueda to Montavon, July 23, 1926, LA-1; *Excélsior*, July 23, 1926.

[17] *Excélsior*, July 24, 1926.

[18] Ibid., July 25, 1926; *El Universal*, July 22, 1926; August 1, 1926; Ceniceros y Villarreal, "Historia."

[19] Lagarde Memorandum.

cation telling of its decision. The June 14 decree, the bishops stated, made it impossible for the Church to function in accordance with the sacred canons. They added that they believed suspending worship would serve to arouse the public to work, by legal means, to obtain repeal of the anti-Catholic laws.[20] On July 24 the Episcopal Committee issued a pastoral letter announcing its intention to withdraw the clergy from the churches. The letter specified that the country was not being placed under an interdict, which would have prohibited almost all priestly ministrations. But Catholic devotional life requiring the mediation of a priest—the Mass and administration of the sacraments—would have to be carried on outside church buildings.[21] Three days later the Holy See, informed of Crespi's failure to obtain a satisfactory response from the government, condemned the "Calles Law" outright and informed Caruana that it approved not only the suspension of public worship but also the closing of the churches.[22]

Plutarco Elías Calles watched the deteriorating situation with apparent equanimity coupled with grim determination to hold his course. He told a crowd that met his train in Monterrey on July 19 that he would do his duty on the religious question even if it meant having to employ extreme methods; he repeated his *pujido* remark of March, this time applying it to the pope.[23] On July 29, repre-

[20] Carreño, *El arzobispo de México*, pp. 118–121. Carreño cites the archives of the Episcopal Committee, to which he had access. See also Lagarde Memorandum.

[21] *Excélsior*, July 25, 1926. The law of course prohibited public worship anywhere except in the churches. Thus, for example, for people to gather at a private home to hear Mass was illegal, and hundreds of arrests were made during the three years worship was suspended.

[22] Lagarde Memorandum; Díaz to Gasparri, August 12, 1926, cited in Carreño, *El arzobispo de México*, pp. 121–124. Díaz told Gasparri that the bishops had decided the closing of the churches was unnecessary and that, moreover, such a move could have been taken as a provocation to rebellion.

[23] Sheffield to SecState, July 21, 1926, NA, RG 59, 812.404/523. Sheffield said that a member of the *Excélsior* staff told him the newspaper was embarrassed to print the word but had done so and indicated that it was a direct quote (see *Excélsior*, July 20, 1926). The ambassador reported that "a Mexican close to the Administration" said the president had become so violent on the religious question that he lost control of himself when it came up in his presence, be-

sentatives of CROM locals in the capital called at the National Palace to pledge support for the government's stand. "Let the lines be drawn," their address proclaimed. "We are ready to offer our blood to save the Revolution." Responding, Calles agreed that the struggle had transcendent implications; it would decide whether the revolution or the reaction would prevail. The clergy, he said, had thrown down the gauntlet in February, and the revolution had no choice but to pick it up: ". . . we are compelled to it; it is the struggle of darkness against light."[24]

The same day, the government ordered Monsignor Crespi to leave the country. On July 31, deeply disheartened and with forebodings of disaster for the faith in Mexico, he boarded a train to the United States.[25] The next morning, Sunday, August 1, for the first time in more than four centuries, no priest mounted the altar of a Mexican church for morning Mass.

The cessation of public worship and the abandonment of the churches by the clergy transpired in some cases in an orderly fashion; in others, not. As provided by law, the buildings passed to the control of local citizens' committees (*juntas de vecinos* or *juntas vecinales*) named by municipal authorities. Most of the churches were closed for a day or two while government agents completed inventories but reopened as soon as possible, on specific orders from Gobernación.[26] In Chihuahua all churches were closed on July 31 but open on August 2. There were no disorders, although troops patrolled the state capital and searched vehicles entering the city for firearms.[27] In Guerrero the towns were quiet, but there were

coming livid and pounding the table (Sheffield to SecState, July 20, 1926, NA, RG 59, 812.404/578).

[24] *Excélsior*, July 30, 1926.

[25] Lagarde Memorandum.

[26] See Manuel Pérez Treviño to Tejeda, July 31, 1926, and Tejeda to Pérez Treviño, August 4, 1926, State of Coahuila Archives, *legajo* 36, *expediente* 6, 1926.

[27] Thomas McEnelly, Chihuahua, to SecState, August 2, 1926, NA, RG 59, 812.404/545, and August 4, NA, RG 59, 812.404/561.

rumors of unrest in rural areas.[28] The west coast in general remained peaceful. In Sinaloa, authorities consulted with the clergy regarding the make-up of the *juntas*.[29] Transfer of the churches in Veracruz was accomplished without difficulty, and the populace for the most part seemed relatively unconcerned.[30] There were disturbances in Mexico City: police fired on communicants who refused to leave the San Rafael Church, wounding nine of them, and women on the roof hurled stones down on the officers. A crowd of irate Catholics assaulted Attorney General Romeo Ortega and his assistants, who were attempting to close the Santa Catarina parish buildings. Fire trucks rushed about the city dispersing gatherings at other churches.[31]

In some areas there was even more serious trouble. When government agents in Guadalajara tried to take possession of the churches, street fighting erupted and left many dead and wounded; hundreds were jailed; by mid-August public resistance had stiffened, and the authorities held only one church in the entire city. In outlying areas of Jalisco, officials generally abandoned attempts to occupy churches; in some districts they simply announced that committees named by Church authorities to care for the buildings were also the government *juntas*.[32] In Torreón on August 1 two demonstrators were killed and eight injured in a

[28] Harry K. Pangburn, Acapulco, to SecState, July 31, 1926, NA, RG 59, 812.404/545.

[29] William P. Blocker, Mazatlán, to SecState, August 6, 1926, NA, RG 59, 812.404/581.

[30] Willys Myers, Veracruz, to SecState, September 1, 1926, NA, RG 59, 812.404/640.

[31] *New York Times*, July 31, 1926.

[32] Consul Dudley G. Dwyre, Guadalajara, to SecState, August 2, 1926, NA, RG 59, 812.404/546; August 6, NA, RG 59, 812.404/560; August 18, NA, RG 59, 812.404/591. Dwyre said between 18 and 40 persons were reported killed in Guadalajara. Orozco y Jiménez told a *New York Times* correspondent on August 13 that 43 federal troops had been killed or wounded and 5 Catholics killed; he said he understood that the soldiers had fired into the air—hence the light civilian casualties. The archbishop added that 390 persons had been arrested but were being released a few at a time (*New York Times*, August 14, 1926).

fracas finally quelled by federal troops.[33] Archbishop Ruiz y Flores returned to Mexico City from Morelia with the news that there had been bloodshed in northern Michoacán and southern Guanajuato. At Sahuayo, he reported, the populace had refused to let police take over the churches; troops were ordered to the scene and an all-day battle left an estimated fifty dead. The archbishop added that two priests and thirty-seven other Catholics were executed in the region on August 1 and 2 on charges of fomenting rebellion.[34]

The impact of the league's boycott was as uneven as the reaction to the suspension of worship. In Chihuahua and down the west coast only a small part of the population observed it, and except in the cities of Manzanillo and Colima it had little effect.[35] In the city of Veracruz, grocery sales declined for a few days. In Jalapa, Córdoba, and Orizaba, the effect was more marked but was not considered serious.[36] The success of the boycott generally paralleled the intensity of popular reaction against the transfer of churches to government control. In Jalisco it was devastatingly effective: spending plummeted, and by the end of the first week of August the streets of Guadalajara were almost empty of private cars.[37] Gládium, the Unión Popular newspaper, waged a massive blacklisting campaign against progovernment merchants.[38] Torreón and Saltillo partially observed the boycott during August and September.[39] but border towns like Piedras Negras and Mexicali all but ig-

[33] Consul Bartley F. Yost, Torreón, to SecState, August 2, 1926, NA, RG 59, 812.404/547.

[34] New York Times, August 12, 1926.

[35] McEnelly, Chihuahua, to SecState, August 4, 1926, NA, RG 59, 812.404/561; Blocker, Mazatlán, to SecState, August 6, NA, RG 59, 812.404/581; Earl Eaton, Manzanillo, to SecState, September 20, NA, RG 59, 812.404/668.

[36] Myers, Veracruz, to SecState, September 1, 1926, NA, RG 59, 812.404/640.

[37] Dwyre, Guadalajara, to SecState, August 6, 1926, NA, RG 59, 812.404/560.

[38] Heriberto Navarrete, "Por Dios y Por la Patria": Memorias de mi participación en la defensa de la libertad de conciencia y culto durante la persecución religiosa en México de 1926 a 1929, p. 110.

[39] Yost, Torreón, to SecState, August 19, 1926, NA, RG 59, 812.404/599; Consul Thomas S. Horn, Saltillo, to SecState, September 10, 1926, NA, RG 59, 812.404/658.

nored it.[40] By October—earlier in some parts of the country—it was clear that the boycott was dissipating. U.S. Consul David J. D. Myers in Durango suggested one reason: he commented in September that, although there had been a decline in the purchase of luxury items, "the great mass of the people . . . are unable to reduce their purchases to any appreciable extent as they have never been able to buy more than the basic necessities of life."[41] Probably just as important were apathy and lack of organization; it was obvious that the careful management and strong public support that had produced success in Jalisco, both in 1918 and in the present case, were not duplicated in most parts of Mexico.

During the first days of August the government was jittery over the possibility of widespread civil strife. On July 30 and 31, police arrested many league officers in various parts of the country. In Mexico City some seventy league workers, most of them ACJM members, caught distributing propaganda, were jailed.[42] Gobernación had warned the press not to comment editorially on the "Calles Law,"[43] and after August 1 the intimidated Mexico City press ceased editorial comment on religious matters and did not mention the disturbances. In Guadalajara, authorities ordered papers to print only news given out by official spokesmen.[44] The news media did report in detail, however, a series of public debates held early in August between league spokesmen, headed by Capistrán Garza, and defenders of the government—an encounter that occasioned high public excitement but provided nothing more than a recap of positions already well publicized.[45]

Although the violence of early August was isolated and spon-

[40] Consul Harry Leonard, Piedras Negras, to SecState, September 10, 1926, NA, RG 59, 812.404/647; Consul Frank Bohr, Mexicali, to SecState, September 9, 1926, NA, RG 59, 812.404/653.

[41] Myers, Durango, to SecState, September 8, 1926, NA, RG 59, 812.404/645. Ceniceros y Villarreal ("Historia") says the boycott had the immediate effect of sharply increasing league membership.

[42] Ruiz Rueda to Montavon, August 6, 1926, LA-1.

[43] New York Times, July 24, 1926.

[44] Dwyre, Guadalajara, to SecState, August 6, 1926, NA, RG 59, 812.404/560.

[45] See El Universal, August 3, 4, 5, 7, and 10, 1926.

taneous, the government was correct in not dismissing the possibility of concerted Catholic resistance. The league had never ruled out a resort to arms, and speculation that it might come had been on the minds and even the lips of some members throughout the spring and summer. As early as April, for instance, there had been informal talk along such lines at a regional league meeting in Saltillo, where a few young men active in the ACJM had begun quietly to accumulate ammunition.[46] The first step in the direction of armed action, however, was more oblique than direct. A few days after the suspension of worship, league leaders received word that Gen. Enrique Estrada, Obregón's secretary of war and marine, who had backed de la Huerta and fled to the United States when the rebellion collapsed, was preparing to enter Mexico with an armed force. They decided to send Capistrán Garza to offer Estrada support in exchange for a pledge to respect Catholic interests once he gained power. On August 14 Capistrán Garza left Mexico City for Laredo in disguise, and two days later he crossed into Texas. He arrived on the American side of the Rio Grande at 3:00 P.M.; at 7:00, extras appeared on the Laredo streets with the news that U.S. authorities in California had taken Estrada and his band into custody and charged them with violating the neutrality laws.[47] The collapse of the project postponed by only a few weeks what many league militants had come to believe was inevitable.

On September 19 league representatives from various parts of the country met in Mexico City. Their formal discussions dealt with problems of coordination and morale, but insurrection was on the minds of most of them. After the final session delegates from Chihuahua told league President Ceniceros y Villarreal that Catholics in that state and elsewhere were ready to rise. If the league would command the crusade, they would follow; if not, they would proceed alone. Ceniceros was receptive, although he expressed concern over whether adequate means were available for such an un-

[46] Interview with Felipe Brondo Alvarez, Saltillo, June, 1968.

[47] Antonio Ríus Facius, *Méjico cristero: Historia de la ACJM, 1925 a 1931*, pp. 107–108. The *New York Times* of August 17, 1926, reported that 174 men were rounded up near San Diego and their weapons and ammunition seized.

dertaking. He agreed to lay the matter before the Directive Committee.[48] But unlike the Chihuahuenses, other Catholics had not waited for directions from Mexico City; the directors pondered a decision, knowing that rebellion was already a fact.

On the evening of Saturday, August 14, two automobiles drove into the little hill town of Chalchihuites in the state of Zacatecas. Each carried five or six federal soldiers of Gen. Eulogio Ortiz's command. The officer in charge, Lt. Blas Maldonato, carried orders to apprehend various persons in connection with a reported conspiracy against the government.[49] The parish priest, Father Luis Batis, was the first arrested. He denied involvement in any plot; meetings held at his house, he said, had been routine gatherings of ACJM members and Catholic Workers. While the interrogation continued, the lieutenant rounded up other individuals whose names appeared on his list, and by dawn some twenty-two had been brought in. All were questioned and released except the priest and three young men: Manuel Morales, president of the local Catholic Workers, David Roldán, ACJM president, and Salvador Lara, an active ACJM worker, all of them prominent in the LNDLR's Chalchihuites chapter.

By the middle of the morning a crowd filled the plaza. At 10:30 the soldiers emerged from the municipal building with the four prisoners; they entered the cars—a third had been acquired—and started slowly out of town through the hostile onlookers. On the out-

---

[48] Ceniceros y Villarreal, "Historia."

[49] There is no significant disagreement in the various reports of the Chalchihuites affair. The present account is based on a hand-written, semiliterate, unsigned document in LA-1, entitled "Noticia pormenoriada de los acontecimientos que se desarroyaron [sic] en Chalchihuites, Zacatecas, la noche del 14 y la mañana del 15 de agosto de 1926," dated Chalchihuites, August 30, 1926. For the backgrounds of the principals involved, see Ríus Facius, Méjico cristero, pp. 95–97. Details are also given in Myers, Durango, to SecState, September 8, 1926, NA, RG 59, 812.404/645, and Ceniceros y Villarreal, "Historia." There was evidently some substance to the charge that a plot was afoot in the state—as early as March a young ACJM member in Valparaíso was trying to organize an armed rising there—although there is no evidence that persons in Chalchihuites were involved. See "Origen del movimiento católico libertador de México," undated and unsigned manuscript in LA-1.

skirts a group of *campesinos* stopped them. The lieutenant showed them his orders; there was a small scuffle, then the cars drove on, the *campesinos* following. A short distance down the road, Maldonato ordered a halt and told the prisoners to get out. Father Batis sensed what was happening; he told the soldiers to shoot him if they had to, but to spare the rest. The plea was ignored, and, seeing that they were about to die, all four shouted "¡VIVA CRISTO REY!"— Long live Christ the King! The priest and Morales fell on the spot. The other two were walked a few paces along the road and also shot. The cars then drove off at high speed. Maldonato later reported that he executed the captives to keep them from being rescued by the pursuers.

The men who had stopped the soldiers outside the town were led by Pedro Quintanar, a native of the nearby town of Valparaíso. Quintanar, a person of some local prominence, had served under de la Huerta in 1923 and 1924, reaching the rank of colonel. He was a religious man and an active member of the Catholic Workers. On August 14 he was in Chalchihuites on business, and after the troops arrived he decided on the spur of the moment to take a hand in things. When he discovered the bodies of the captives, he returned to the town with his followers. There Quintanar told the crowd he was going into rebellion. He and his men then seized the funds in the municipal treasury and rode off toward the Jalisco border.[50]

On August 22 and 23, members of Catholic Workers locals from the Peñitas Ranch and the Peña Blanca Hacienda near Valparaíso rose in arms. Since the appearance of the "Calles Law" in July, plans had been in the making for a general insurrection in the region, to be joined by men from a number of rural communities. At the designated time, however, most were still unprepared, and the handful that did respond found themselves isolated and had to flee. Led by Basilio Pinedo, they headed in the direction of Huejuquilla, Jalisco.[51]

---

[50] "Origen del movimiento católico"; Ríus Facius, *Méjico cristero*, p. 100.

[51] "Origen del movimiento católico"; "Boletín de las operaciones del grupo

Quintanar meanwhile had conferred with Aurelio R. Acevedo, ACJM leader in Valparaíso, and together they had mapped out a plan of action, to begin after suitable preparation. But news of the rising led by Pinedo decided them to make an immediate move; after consulting with Pinedo and other individuals in the settlements around Huejuquilla, they decided to take the town. At 11:00 A.M. on August 29, to shouts of "¡VIVA CRISTO REY!" Quintanar and thirty men occupied Huejuquilla without firing a shot. An hour later, as church bells pealed, Pinedo and his men arrived. At 1:00, other men were seen approaching. These proved to be a federal force, fifty-two hand-picked soldiers of General Ortiz's command, sent to round up clergymen and others suspected of seditious activities. Unaware of Quintanar's presence, the troops entered Huejuquilla to be met by a barrage of bullets. After a battle that lasted until late in the evening, the federals, who had lost nearly half their men, retreated.[52] But six days later, as a large government force composed of regulars and *agraristas*[53] personally led by Ortiz came up, the rebels, badly outnumbered, abandoned the town.[54] A few weeks later, pursued by Ortiz, hungry and demoralized, they disbanded. Quintanar accepted an amnesty and returned to his ranch, where he waited for a more favorable opportunity.[55]

The leader of another rising in September was Luis Navarro Origel, a prominent small landowner in Pénjamo, Guanajuato. Renowned for his personal piety and civic dedication—he served an exemplary term as mayor—he had also since 1925 directed LNDLR organizational activities in his region.[56] Calles's religious

---

libertador de Huejuquilla el Alto al mando del Sr. General D. Pedro Quintanar," LA-3. The latter is a typewritten chronicle, unsigned, covering the period August–December, 1926.

[52] "Boletín de las operaciones del grupo libertador."

[53] Ranchers and agricultural laborers belonging to syndicates sponsored or protected by the government.

[54] "Boletín de las operaciones del grupo libertador"; "Origen del movimiento católico."

[55] Ríus Facius, *Méjico cristero*, p. 102.

[56] Ibid., pp. 125–126; Alfonso Trueba [pseud. Martín Chowell], *Luis Navarro Origel: El primer cristero*, pp. 5–77.

policies had troubled him to the point of desperation, and in September, around the time the league convention met in Mexico City, he informed the Directive Committee that he intended to lead armed action. On September 28 he assumed command of a small group of irregulars, who for a few weeks acquitted themselves well. Pénjamo was taken, and in the first days of October the band held its own in encounters with government forces. But it suffered a bad defeat at the village of Corralejo, and Navarro decided to transfer operations to the mountains of Michoacán, better suited to guerrilla warfare than the gentle terrain of the Bajío.[57]

There were other outbreaks of violence in the weeks following the suspension of public worship. They were isolated, uncoordinated, and in most cases small scale, although a few involved fairly large numbers of men—Trinidad Mora in Durango led a force of almost three hundred when he fought government troops near Santiago Bayacora on September 29.[58]

A truce between the Church and government would probably have averted violence, and in fact a move in that direction came within hours after religious services ceased. In a statement to an Associated Press correspondent on August 1, the Episcopal Committee said it was willing to restore worship for a reasonable period if during that time the government would suspend enforcement of the objectionable statutes and hold a national plebiscite on the religious laws.[59] Calles immediately rejected the proposal, and Díaz, speaking for the committee, countered that the government would have to revoke or withhold enforcement of the laws before the bishops would enter into negotiations.[60] On the tenth the Vatican daily *Osservatore Romano* agreed that no parleys were possible so long as the antireligious legislation remained in effect.[61]

[57] Trueba [pseud. Chowell], *Luis Navarro Origel*, pp. 87–91. The Bajío is the alluvial plain of the Lerma River, a rich agricultural area in which are located the cities of León, Celaya, Irapuato, and Guanajuato.

[58] "Santiago Bayacora, Durango: Memorias de Francisco Campos," *David* 2, no. 33 (April 22, 1955): 130–132.

[59] *New York Times*, August 2, 1926.

[60] Ibid., August 3, 1926; August 4, 1926.

[61] Ibid., August 11, 1926.

The bishops put forward another feeler on August 16, in the form of a letter to the president. It asked for reform of the laws and expressed a desire for a peaceful resolution of differences.[62] In a reply three days later Calles noted that although the constitution denied legal existence to churches as such, individuals were perfectly at liberty to seek constitutional change through proper channels. The bishops promptly voted to accept Calles's invitation; they would petition Congress.[63]

Two days later, August 21, Ruiz y Flores and Díaz conferred with Calles. The meeting was arranged by Eduardo Mestre Ghigliazza, a government official trusted and respected by both the president and the episcopate.[64] The two prelates emerged from the conference very happy, telling Mestre that the president had been patient, courteous, and reasonable.[65] The three then drafted a statement saying that, it being understood that the registration of priests was a formality and in no way entailed government intervention in matters of Church doctrine, there was hope that public worship would soon resume. The Episcopal Committee decided that, if Calles endorsed the statement, it would recommend to Rome that the priests return to their duties.[66] Several hours later they learned

[62] El Universal, August 17, 1926. Lagarde (Memorandum) said the bishops' desire for a truce was motivated by their fear that the Church's material interests were in danger and that the lower clergy, deprived of a regular income, might disobey the episcopate and return to the churches.

[63] El Universal, August 20, 1926, and August 21, 1926; Esperanza Velázquez Bringas, ed., Méjico ante el mundo: Ideología del Presidente Plutarco Elías Calles, n.p.

[64] "Outline of statement of Lic. Mestre made in conversation with Ambassador Morrow on October 8, 1928," Dwight Morrow Papers. Attorney General Romeo Ortega and Finance Minister Alberto Pani were also involved in setting up the meeting. Mestre was head of Beneficencia Pública. See Carreño, El arzobispo de México, p. 114.

[65] "Outline of statement of Lic. Mestre." Mestre's account conflicts with both Carreño (p. 135) and Lagarde (Memorandum), who said that the session was stormy and ended with Calles saying the episcopate had only two choices: an appeal to Congress or an appeal to arms. In view of the fact that the negotiation proceeded to near agreement during the next few hours, Mestre's version is probably correct.

[66] "Outline of statement of Lic. Mestre"; Carreño, El arzobispo de México, pp. 137–138.

that the president had given his approval,[67] and Díaz told newsmen that the bishops expected divine worship would soon resume while Catholics pursued their ultimate goal of obtaining an adjustment in the laws.[68]

The papers on the next day reported the meeting and its outcome. Calles, interviewed by *El Universal*, acknowledged that he had met with the bishops but denied having made any agreement with the Church or having changed his position on the religious question: "When the priests reoccupy the churches, they will be subject to the laws."[69] His words did not contradict the assurances he had given the bishops, but some of them interpreted them as a sign that he meant to ignore his pledges[70] and began to back away from further consideration of a truce.

Within hours, news of the exchange reached Rome, where it caused consternation. The Vatican in July had abandoned hope of persuading the government to moderate its stand and had endorsed the bishops' decision not to compromise. On August 11 the *Osservatore Romano* had branded the "Calles Law" tyrannical and its application Nero-like. Three days later Gasparri had sent a circular letter to diplomats accredited to the Holy See and to Vatican representatives abroad, calling attention to the Mexican government's anti-Catholic policies and enclosing copies of the *Osservatore* article.[71] Now the bishops appeared to be caving in. Gasparri demanded an immediate explanation. Mora y del Río answered that no understanding would be reached that violated Rome's instructions.[72] Late on the twenty-third the bishops received a cable from Caruana in Havana, who told them not to accept Calles's assurances.[73] A majority of the bishops thereupon voted not to favor re-

[67] "Outline of statement of Lic. Mestre."

[68] *El Universal*, August 22, 1926.

[69] *El Universal*, August 22, 1926; "Outline of statement of Lic. Mestre."

[70] "Outline of statement of Lic. Mestre."

[71] Miguel Palomar y Vizcarra, *El caso ejemplar mexicano*, pp. 164–166.

[72] Rublee Memorandum, Dwight Morrow Papers; Lagarde Memorandum; *New York Times*, August 28, 1926. The instructions were presumably to the effect that the offensive laws must be suspended as a condition for a settlement.

[73] Rublee Memorandum.

sumption of worship after all, and the next morning Díaz told the press that the situation remained the same as before the talks.[74] On the twenty-sixth he told reporters that worship would not resume until the anticlerical laws were removed and the constitutional articles violating freedom of conscience were amended.[75]

Several days later Calles expressed to Lagarde his exasperation at the collapse of the negotiations. He had thought a settlement possible, he said, and he blamed Rome for sabotaging the peace efforts. He asserted he would never again tolerate having a papal delegate in Mexico. He would not give an inch; his stand had been firm but just. When the French diplomat ventured an opinion that the Vatican had not provoked the conflict but on the contrary had tried to find a basis for agreement, and when he pointed out that certain bishops preferred a moderate position, Calles launched into a tirade against the Mexican clergy. The absence of public worship in Mexico, he concluded, was highly desirable, since it would hasten the country's de-Christianization. Lagarde reported that Calles appeared obsessed with his obligation to uphold the constitution and viewed the religious problem in an "apocalyptical and mystical spirit."[76] Tejeda told the Frenchman two days later that religion was an "immoral business" that needed regulating in the public interest.[77]

The Vatican was not alone in its dismay over the peace talks. The LNDLR, which likewise had not been consulted, was apprehensive that there might be in the offing some "incomplete, insecure, and dangerous settlement."[78]

Despite scant prospects for success, the Episcopal Committee proceeded with its decision to approach Congress. On September 7 the hierarchy submitted a petition requesting reform of Articles 3, 5, 24, 27, and 130 of the Constitution of 1917. A few days later Con-

[74] "Outline of statement of Lic. Mestre"; *El Universal*, August 24, 1926.

[75] *New York Times*, August 27, 1926.

[76] Lagarde Memorandum.

[77] Arthur Bliss Lane to SecState, August 25, 1926, NA, RG 59, 812.404/604. Lane, who was at this time First Secretary of the U.S. Embassy in Mexico City, was repeating a comment made to him by Lagarde.

[78] Ceniceros y Villarreal, "Historia."

gress received a "memorial" bearing some two million signatures, gathered throughout Mexico principally by league workers, which seconded the demand for constitutional revision.[79] On the twenty-third the chamber of deputies rejected the bishops' petition by a vote of 171 to 1 on grounds that the prelates, by conspiring with a foreign power (the Vatican) to disobey the constitution, had lost their rights as citizens to petition.[80]

The bishops' personal situation, as autumn began, was becoming precarious. Many of them had remained in Mexico City after July to participate in the deliberations of the Episcopal Committee—a situation the government preferred since it made it easier to keep an eye on them; in fact, steps were taken to move all the prelates to the capital. In September police arrested the bishop of Saltillo and brought him to Mexico City.[81] Others, like the bishop of Huajuapan, went voluntarily to avoid the indignity of arrest.[82] (In Mexico City, the prelates were required to appear periodically at the Ministry of Gobernación but were otherwise free to move about.) Orozco y Jiménez of Guadalajara was handled with special circumspection. In October federal authorities asked Pascual Díaz to persuade the archbishop to come to the capital voluntarily, and on the twenty-fourth a Jesuit priest arrived in Guadalajara to deliver the message. The archbishop, who had already learned that agents were in the city with instructions to arrest him if necessary, decided not to go. The next day he dictated a letter to his archdiocese saying that orders were out for his apprehension and that

---

[79] Alicia Olivera Sedano, *Aspectos del conflicto religioso de 1926 a 1929: Sus antecedentes y consecuencias*, pp. 122–123; Ceniceros y Villarreal, "Historia."

[80] *El Universal*, September 24, 1926; Eduardo Iglesias, S.J., and Rafael Martínez del Campo, S.J. [pseud. Aquiles P. Moctezuma], *El conflicto religioso de 1926: Sus orígenes, su desarrollo, su solución*, II, 411.

[81] Jesús María Dávila, Saltillo, to José Luis Orozco [José Tello], November 25, 1926, LA-1. Dávila was the LNDLR delegate in Coahuila; Orozco was secretary to the Directive Committee. After 1926 the league's correspondence commonly used code names for security reasons. Fortunately for the researcher, Palomar y Vizcarra later identified most of the important aliases in marginal notations to the documents. I have used the real names unless there is doubt as to the identity.

[82] *New York Times*, October 22, 1926.

inasmuch as he would have no assurance of safety if arrested, he was going into hiding. He left Guadalajara immediately for an undisclosed part of Jalisco.[83]

Late in September—the exact date is uncertain—the LNDLR decided to lead the incipient rebellion. The Directive Committee, after lengthy discussion, resolved that a resort to arms was justified and proceeded to try to gain command of the situation.[84] It established a Special War Committee, headed by Jalisco businessman Bartolomé Ontiveros on an interim basis until a qualified military man could be designated.[85] The leadership struggled throughout October to get information on the number and size of the brushfire risings, and made numerous attempts to coordinate them and to persuade potential insurgents to act.[86] But by the end of the month it was clear that the desultory armed operations, although they had spread to ten states,[87] had been no more effective than the boycott in bringing the government to its knees. Only the application of organized military force backed by substantial material resources and broad popular support could succeed. A master strategy to mobilize all elements of the Catholic resistance was needed, and to that task the leadership turned its total attention. During days of intensive work the directors, assisted by the Jesuit priests Alfredo Méndez Medina and Rafael Martínez del Campo, hammered out details of a campaign to bring down the government. They estab-

[83] "Memorándum del Excmo. Sr. Francisco Orozco y Jiménez," *David* 7, no. 155 (June 1965): 168; Consul Dayle C. McDonough, Guadalajara, to SecState, November 17, 1926, NA, RG 59, 812.404/708.

[84] Ceniceros y Villarreal, "Historia." Capistrán Garza said the directors made their decision around the end of September. See "Informe del Sr. Don René Capistrán Garza a los Ilustrísimos y Reverendísimos señores Arzobispos y Obispos Mexicanos, reunidos en San Antonio, Texas," November 14, 1928, LA-1. Other sources are silent on the point. From the first, special care was taken to term the uprising an "armed movement," or "armed defense," never a rebellion.

[85] Ceniceros y Villarreal, "Historia."

[86] See, for example, Felipe Brondo Alvarez, Memoirs, 1932.

[87] A report to Congress from the president's office in November said religious rebels had been active since August in Michoacán, Jalisco, Guanajuato, Durango, Zacatecas, Guerrero, Oaxaca, San Luis Potosí, and Veracruz (*El Universal*, November 26, 1926; see also Blocker, Mazatlán, to SecState, October 2, 1926, NA, RG 59, 812.404/679).

lished a military command structure and named committees to raise funds. There was extended debate on some points, but the leaders had little difficulty deciding on a supreme leader for the movement. Ceniceros y Villarreal proposed René Capistrán Garza, and agreement was unanimous. He was the obvious choice. Defects he had, to be sure—the most serious, Ceniceros thought, was an irritating tendency to be lackadaisical at times—but these were outweighed by his great popularity and prestige, his oratorical gifts, his proven integrity, both personal and public, and the unshakable firmness of his convictions.[88]

One concern of the Directive Committee overshadowed all others: the imperative need to clarify the armed movement's relationship to the Church. The attitude of the episcopate, they knew, could mean the difference between success and failure. A formal understanding was essential, and to that end the directors requested a meeting with the bishops.

On Friday, November 26, the league leaders were received by the Episcopal Committee. Ruiz y Flores presided in the absence of Mora y del Río, who was ill. Also present were Pascual Díaz and eight or ten other prelates.[89] Ceniceros y Villarreal read a manifesto. It said that, all legal and peaceful means having been exhausted, the people had begun spontaneously to take up arms to defend their basic liberties and that the league, after careful consideration, had decided to assume leadership of the movement. Inasmuch as the die was already cast, any rift, however slight, in the united action that the episcopate and the league had carried on in the civic field would be prejudicial. The league therefore asked the bishops to acquiesce in their plan and in their choice of a leader. Prospects of success were good, the statement continued. A Catholic crusade would not face U.S. opposition because, providentially, the revolutionary regime had become inimical to American interests. Moreover, Mexicans were ready; never before had

[88] Ceniceros y Villarreal, "Historia."

[89] "Apuntes para la historia," statement signed by Luis Bustos, May 4, 1929; Palomar y Vizcarra to González Valencia, December 3, 1926; LA-1.

the "collective conscience" been better prepared for armed resistance.

The manifesto's appeal for an episcopal endorsement was almost
coercive: the bishops, it stated, could not condemn the movement,
which was both irreversible and a matter of legitimate self-defense.
To oppose it would corrupt it and would create a sentiment of popular displeasure toward the hierarchy. The league asked the bishops to form the consciences of the faithful, insofar as possible, "in
the sense that it is a matter of a lawful, laudable, meritorious act
of legitimate armed defense." It also asked the hierarchy to provide field chaplains and to sponsor an appeal to wealthy Catholics
for funds, so that "at least once in their lives they will understand
their obligation to contribute." Following Ceniceros y Villarreal's
presentation, Luis G. Bustos, second vice-president of the Directive
Committee, presented details of the league's plan of action, beginning with the announcement that Capistrán Garza had agreed to
command the movement. The plan stipulated that a provisional
government, to be constituted in due time, would replace the Calles
regime.[90]

Ruiz y Flores said that the Episcopal Committee wanted time to
consider the matter. He asked for a copy of the memorial read by
Ceniceros y Villarreal; the plan of action, he said, was political
and not within the bishops' legitimate area of concern. All the
prelates agreed to hold the information presented in strictest secrecy.[91]

Four days later the league directors were summoned to meet
with Ruiz y Flores and Díaz. Ruiz presented the answer of the
Episcopal Committee. He said that the bishops who had been present on November 26, as well as Mora y del Río, had with two reservations approved the memorial. Church doctrine, he stated,

[90] Sworn statement, dated Mexico City, May 13, 1929, signed by Ceniceros y
Villarreal, Palomar y Vizcarra, Méndez Medina, and Martínez del Campo;
Palomar y Vizcarra to González Valencia, December 3, 1926; LA-1. A copy of
the statement read to the bishops by Ceniceros y Villarreal is in LA-1.

[91] Sworn statement of May 13, 1929 (see above); Palomar y Vizcarra to
González Valencia, December 3, 1926.

taught that it was lawful to resort to force when peaceful attempts to combat tyranny had proven sterile. He added that prudence demanded that an uprising have probability of success. The reservations were, first, that the bishops had no canonical faculties for assigning chaplains, although they would grant permission to priests who wished to minister to men in the field. Secondly, regarding an appeal to the wealthy, the bishops deemed such a step on their part to be dangerous, difficult, and in practice impossible.[92]

The league was delighted. Palomar y Vizcarra wrote enthusiastically to González Valencia: "You can well imagine our satisfaction at the success achieved. There is nothing more to ask for . . ." except perhaps, he added, permission to sell the sacred vessels of the Church to raise money.[93]

Did the Mexican episcopate in November, 1926, support the "armed defense"? The question would be passionately argued in years ahead. Clearly, the Episcopal Committee did not condemn the resort to arms. It limited itself to stating traditional Catholic teaching on the subject and made no attempt to apply this to the case at hand, thereby implying that in the bishops' opinion armed action was justified. Ceniceros y Villarreal later said that the bishops did not provoke, sustain, or finance the rebellion but that once it was in progress they "approved it implicitly." Some Catholics, he added, had hoped for a categorical approval, "but this was not to be expected."[94] Leopoldo Lara y Torres, bishop of Tacámbaro and a strong partisan of the league and of the rebellion, did not draw so fine a distinction; he wrote later that the league, seeing itself compelled to undertake armed action, consulted the bishops, "and its undertaking was approved by the Episcopal Committee, without our having committed ourselves to take a direct part in

[92] Ibid.; Leopoldo Ruiz y Flores, *Recuerdo de recuerdos*, p. 85.

[93] Palomar y Vizcarra to González Valencia, December 3, 1926, LA-1. Palomar was mildly sarcastic about the wealthy escaping an episcopal call for money. Both Palomar and Father Méndez Medina reported that their reception by Ruiz y Flores and Díaz was warm and amiable and that the two bishops indicated positive satisfaction with the league's stance. See Méndez Medina's annotation to the statement of Ceniceros y Villarreal et al. of May 13, 1929, LA-1.

[94] Ceniceros y Villarreal, "Historia."

that action"—a statement which, oddly enough, Alberto María Carreño, later an opponent of the league, cited as proof that the Episcopate was not connected with (*ajeno a*) the rebellion.[95]

It is understandable that the bishops did not forbid the resort to arms on doctrinal grounds; they could not. On the other hand, had they chosen to do so, they might have exercised their pastoral prerogative of counsel to advise against it—as at least one prelate who was not present at the November meeting did: Francisco Orozco y Jiménez sent a trusted aide, Father José Garibi Rivera, to Mexico City to tell the committee that he was absolutely opposed to any Catholic armed movement.[96] But if the bishops had no theological grounds for objecting to armed resistance, they had ample grounds for forbidding the league to be a part of it. Pope Pius XI, in his apostolic letter of February 2, 1926, had ordered the clergy and Catholic associations to "abstain absolutely from any participation in political factions." The pope had not rescinded the directive. He had approved suspension of worship and denounced the offensive legislation, but he had not changed in his determination to keep official Catholic opposition at the level of nonviolent pressure and moral suasion. How had the bishops interpreted "political" action? In their collective pastoral of April 21, 1926, they defined it as "any activity related to the temporal government of the nation." They urged Catholics to participate in civic groups dedicated to the defense of religious liberty, "keeping themselves, however, outside of and above any party."[97] The league was undoubtedly a Catholic association; it was also by November, 1926, a political party, or faction, within the meaning of the papal admonition and the bishops' own definition, since the purpose of the rebellion it proposed to lead was to substitute one political regime for another.

Why, then, did the bishops not forbid the league to proceed?

---

[95] Carreño, *El arzobispo de México*, pp. 197–198.

[96] Ruiz y Flores, *Recuerdo*, p. 96; "Memorándum del Excmo. Sr. Francisco Orozco y Jiménez." It is not known whether Garibi Rivera arrived before or after the bishops' meetings with the directors.

[97] Cited in Carreño, *El arzobispo de México*, pp. 22–26.

For one thing, most of them undoubtedly favored the appeal to force, believing that if it succeeded it would save the Church and vindicate a generation of Catholic effort in Mexico. Moreover, a militant, aggressive lay leadership had taken matters into its own hands and had presented the bishops with a *fait accompli*. The ultimate showdown was at hand, and, even if the bishops had disliked the course being taken, to forbid it would have meant the tearing to shreds of Catholic morale at a time when the Church in Mexico was caught up in the most dangerous crisis it had ever known. This the prelates would not do. Instead, they took a position that left the hierarchy technically above the resort to arms while at the same time wishing it well.

The league had at least some grounds for believing that the United States might not protect Calles from his foes. American Catholic concern over the Mexican crisis increased sharply during the summer of 1926. The first week of August, the Supreme Council of the Knights of Columbus at its annual meeting in Philadelphia adopted a resolution criticizing the Coolidge administration for continuing to recognize Calles and for maintaining the arms embargo (imposed in 1924 during the de la Huerta rebellion), which in effect prohibited shipments to any Mexicans except the government.[98] The Knights had hoped to present their resolution to Coolidge in person, but the president's office told newsmen on August 10 that, in keeping with his hands-off policy regarding the religious difficulties in Mexico, the president had declined to grant the interview.[99]

Kellogg summoned Supreme Knight James Flaherty to the State Department for a personal conversation. He told him it was unjust to say that the United States had helped create or was sustaining the incumbent Mexican government or that Washington approved of its policies. He said the United States could not protest Calles's handling of an internal problem unless American interests were at issue. As for the embargo, Kellogg told him that at "a proper and

[98] James Flaherty to Kellogg, August 6, 1926, NA, RG 59, 812.404/638. The text of the resolution is in the *New York Times* for August 6, 1926.
[99] *New York Times*, August 11, 1926.

appropriate time" the United States expected to lift it. Flaherty finally agreed that the Knights' resolution was to a considerable extent unjustified and promised to take up the matter again with the Supreme Council. With the Knights mollified, Coolidge received Flaherty and a delegation on September 1. The Knights of Columbus leader told reporters afterward that the Knights were not asking for American intervention, an end to the embargo, or withdrawal of diplomatic recognition, but only for "sympathetic action in any way that can be done by the government properly within international law."[100]

Unknown to the Knights, however, the State Department's concern over the Mexican Church-State conflict had not been as limited as Coolidge and Kellogg implied. To begin with, its own chief agent in Mexico was siding with the administration's critics. Ambassador Sheffield was not a Catholic, but his aversion to the revolutionary regime made him a natural sympathizer with its opponents. On July 22 he addressed a remarkable memorandum to Kellogg in which he urged a reassessment of the U.S. attitude on the subject: "It is at least open to question as to whether our moral leadership of the Christian world for freedom to worship God in accord with the dictates of the individual conscience would not be jeopardized if we refused to take notice of so drastic and abhorrent a decree [the 'Calles Law'] aimed at all religion." He added that Latin American opinion should be considered, in view of the predominance of Catholicism in that part of the world. Sheffield did not conceal his disgust; it was not surprising, he said, that Americans had questioned continued recognition of a government capable of writing such a law. The United States, upon whose aid and support the Calles government depended in large part for its existence, had some degree of moral responsibility for the actions of Mexico's rulers.[101]

Whether influenced by Sheffield's views or not, the State Department decided to direct an official frown at Calles. At about the same time the Knights of Columbus were protesting, and probably before

[100] *New York Times*, September 2, 1926.
[101] Sheffield to SecState, July 22, 1926, NA, RG 59, 812.404/524.

he spoke with Flaherty, Kellogg instructed Sheffield to address a note to the Mexican Ministry of Foreign Relations saying that the U.S. government "regrets to observe that the [Calles] Law as a whole appears to contravene the principle of freedom of religious worship which prevails in the United States, has been productive of most satisfactory results in this country, and is in accord with the liberal spirit of the age."[102]

The Knights of Columbus were not the only American Catholics who sympathized publicly with the Church cause in Mexico. The bishops of the United States, at their annual meeting in September on the campus of Catholic University in Washington, D.C., drafted a message to the episcopate and laity of Mexico. American Catholics, they said, were watching with sympathy the struggle of the Mexican church against tyranny. They praised the example of courage and firmness the Mexicans were giving in their fight for religious and civil liberty and pledged that "with God's blessing, we shall be with you to the end and to victory."[103]

Would words turn into something tangible? What would U.S. Catholics do in the event of a Mexican Catholic rebellion; and, more importantly, what would be the stance of the American government? No one could say for certain as the summer of 1926 ended, but the National League for the Defense of Religious Liberty would count heavily on financial help from the first and at least neutrality from the second.

The first test came in the fall. Capistrán Garza, joined in Texas by three ACJM friends, Ramón and Luis Ruiz Rueda and José Gaxiola, set out on a cross-country tour to raise funds. In addition to a credential from the Directive Committee, he carried a letter from Mora y del Río addressed to the American Catholic hierarchy. It introduced him in laudatory terms, entrusting him with "representing us before the Catholic Hierarchy and American people"

---

102 Kellogg to Sheffield, NA, RG 59, 812.404/509. The dispatch is undated but was probably sent after July 22, since Sheffield would hardly have launched his complaint to Washington of that date in the terms he used if he had already had authority to remonstrate.

103 New York Times, September 16, 1926.

and asking the bishops to accord him "favorable and beneficent assistance."[104]

The four anticipated great success; Eamon de Valera had successfully appealed to American Catholics for aid against Ireland's oppressors, and they would do the same on behalf of Mexico. But at their first stop, Corpus Christi, the bishop rebuffed them with the comment that people in his diocese didn't like Mexicans. In Galveston the bishop took a ten-dollar bill from his wallet and gave it to René, ending the interview. Houston, Dallas, and Little Rock were much the same—they got twenty, thirty, fifty dollars. Sleeping outdoors at night and eating as little as possible in order to economize, they believed the northern states would be different —de Valera had succeeded there. The archbishop of St. Louis was outraged over conditions in Mexico as described by Capistrán Garza; he gave one hundred dollars. At the next seven stops—East St. Louis, Indianapolis, Dayton, Columbus, Pittsburgh, Altoona, and Harrisburg—they got even less. In Columbus the bishop expelled them from his residence without even hearing them out. In New York, without warm clothing, they nearly froze. Friends said Boston was promising. They went. There, Cardinal O'Connell examined their credentials carefully and listened without interrupting. Then, in a fatherly tone, he urged René to suffer patiently the trials God was sending and told him to urge those who had commissioned him to do likewise. He advised René to get out of the whole business, to look for a job; he would be happy to give him a letter of introduction to the Massachusetts Knights of Columbus, who might be able to help him find work.[105]

The Knights of Columbus were already the object of league at-

---

[104] Ramón Ruiz Rueda to Palomar y Vizcarra, October 1, 1945, LA-1; Ríus Facius, *Méjico cristero*, p. 118. Copies of the two credentials are in LA-1.

[105] Ruiz Rueda to Palomar y Vizcarra, October 1, 1945; "Informe que presenta Manuel de la Peza a la comisión de Prelados Residentes en Roma que representa al Episcopado Mexicano ante la Santa Sede," Rome, August 5, 1927; LA-1. Evidently Capistrán Garza's efforts among the U.S. bishops produced slightly better results by December. He later told Father Wilfrid Parsons, S.J., that he collected $3,260 from various prelates. See Parsons to Díaz, February 1, 1928 [1929?], quoted in Carreño, *El arzobispo de México*, p. 267.

tention. Their often stated sympathy for the plight of Catholics in Mexico indicated they might be an important source of financial help, and contacts were pressed. Mora y del Río lent his support; on November 1 he wrote to Supreme Knight Flaherty, referring to the credential he had given to Capistrán Garza and saying that, in view of the Knights' noble efforts on behalf of Mexico, he hoped they would consider the credential as directed especially to them "in the sense that Mr. René Capistrán Garza is, among the laity, the sole representative from us and of Mexican Catholic interests in [the United States]."[106]

But if the primate thought his letter might help open a flow of money to the league, he was due for a disappointment. Four days after he signed the letter, Flaherty stated publicly that the million dollars raised by the Knights was for relief work among exiled Mexican religious and for propaganda purposes. He specifically denied that the organization was helping instigate rebellion in Mexico.[107] The league continued to press its case, writing to Flaherty early in December that it was intensifying its campaign for religious freedom and urgently needed $500,000. It noted that Pius XI had recently praised the league in an encyclical letter.[108] But the Knights had backed off. They would not help finance a "campaign" that they suspected entailed insurrection. The league would have to look for help in other quarters.[109]

Despite its sanguine statement to the bishops about the official American attitude being tolerant of a move to oust Calles, the

---

[106] Ruiz Rueda to Palomar y Vizcarra, October 1, 1945, LA-1.

[107] *New York Times*, November 6, 1926. The Knights of Columbus August convention had directed the Supreme Council to raise $1 million through membership assessment for purposes of waging a publicity campaign on the subject of freedom both in the United States and south of the border (*New York Times*, August 6, 1926).

[108] Directive Committee to Flaherty, December 8, 1926, LA-1. The encyclical was the pope's *Iniquis Afflictisque* of November 18, 1926, in which he praised the faith and steadfastness of the Mexican clergy and various Catholic associations, including the LNDLR.

[109] Apparently no Knights of Columbus money went into the rebellion, or if it did the amount was inconsequential. Certainly the league, after December, shifted its fund-raising efforts to other targets.

league was apprehensive over the matter. The directors decided to take Ambassador Sheffield into their confidence. In a memorandum sent to the embassy on December 8, they informed Sheffield that an armed rising was being readied and asked the help of the United States: specifically, suspension of all current agreements with the Calles regime; denial of all aid, military included, to Calles or to any faction except the one headed by the league; accreditation of a U.S. representative to the movement; a benevolent attitude toward a league effort to negotiate a loan in the United States; an offer of protection to the Mexican bishops in view of the expected intensification of the persecution; recognition of belligerency; and, at an appropriate time, the granting of recognition to a provisional government. The league also expressed readiness to negotiate a treaty with the the U.S. government.[110]

The appeal came to nought. Although Sheffield's personal inclination may well have been to treat the approach sympathetically, he must have realized that the prospects were nil that Washington would seriously consider such a proposal. In forwarding it to the State Department, he said that it was "of course supplied to me entirely spontaneously, and I made clear to my informant that I was not in a position to discuss matters of this sort."[111]

Also, by the middle of December it was evident that chances for help from the U.S. Catholic hierarchy had evaporated. On December 12, the feast of the Virgin of Guadalupe, the American bishops issued a pastoral letter on the Mexican religious situation. Expressing strong disapproval of Calles's policies and urging Americans to pray for alleviation of the persecution, the prelates nevertheless specifically ruled out the use of force by the Church: ". . . the weapons of men are not for her . . . She has prayer."[112] Prayer was

[110] Ceniceros y Villarreal, "Historia"; "Memorándum al Embajador Sheffield, enviado por conducto del Sr. Manuel Amor, por el Comité Directivo de la L.N.D.L.R.," December 8, 1926, LA-1.

[111] Sheffield to SecState, December 10, 1926. A carbon copy of the telegram and the memorandum are in the post records of the Mexico City Embassy, NA, RG 84, 840.4. I have not found copies in the State Department records.

[112] *Pastoral Letter of the Catholic Episcopate of the United States on the Religious Situation in Mexico, December, 1926*.

welcome, but the league had hoped devoutly for tangible assistance as well.

Thus, possibilities of aid from official sources in the United States, governmental or ecclesiastical, vanished precisely at the time the league was approaching the eve of battle.

The Mexican community in the United States, however, offered a leader and proposed a timetable for the rebellion. The prospective leader was José Gándara, a young resident of El Paso, Texas, who appeared in Mexico City in the autumn to inform the league directors that he and other Catholics in the Texas city had formed a revolutionary *junta* to work for Calles's overthrow. After a fruitless trip to Europe in search of funds, Gándara returned to Mexico City in December. He told the Directive Committee that the El Paso *junta* was readying an attack on Ciudad Juárez for January 1. The directors at length agreed to designate that date for launching risings throughout Mexico. They rejected Gándara's request to be named supreme head of the movement, explaining that Capistrán Garza had already been designated. In reporting the whole matter to René, Ceniceros y Villarreal included a word of caution. Gándara, he said, had some good qualities but was too impulsive and ignorant to be a good leader; the directors feared he might cause problems. But Gándara's talent for making a good first impression neutralized the league president's advice. Capistrán Garza, after meeting the young enthusiast later in December, appointed him military chief of the rebellion.[113]

The league marched forward with an act of faith that somehow things would come right. Preparations inside Mexico mounted during the final weeks of 1926. Efforts were made to revive the boycott as an auxiliary to the military effort,[114] but results were insignificant. The league intensified its propaganda effort, all of it designed to mobilize public opinion and much of it hinting at re-

---

[113] Ríus Facius, *Méjico cristero*, pp. 140–142; Ceniceros y Villarreal, "Historia."

[114] See, for example, the bulletin issued by the league's regional delegation for the state of Nuevo León, December, 1926, LA-1.

volt. A league bulletin dated December 1 said that for the government to deprive Catholics of legal means to defend themselves and to persecute them for defending their religion was not only unjust; it excited them to tumult "and even to open armed rebellion."[115] On the twenty-first the league published an open letter to the Mexican army. It said the national military had a duty not to act against the people and that the armed forces, made up almost entirely of Catholics, should not abet the persecutory Calles government.[116]

Another league bulletin on December 24 sought to tie the episcopate firmly and publicly to the revolt about to begin. It reprinted a letter from the league asking the Episcopal Committee for an opinion on the obligation of Catholics to follow the norms of conduct laid down by the league for the purpose of securing religious freedom. The answer, signed by Pascual Díaz on the sixteenth, did not mention the league, nor did it refer to armed action, but its intent was unmistakable: Catholics, it said, had "the imperative duty . . . in these solemn moments, to come together, to discipline themselves in order to obtain by means of the formidable power of association that which isolated efforts will never be able to achieve."[117]

During the last week of December, league leaders throughout the country received copies of a formal call to arms signed by Capistrán Garza. In ringing words the proclamation excoriated "the implacable rule of a regime of armed bandits over a defenseless, honorable, patriotic population. . . . Destruction of religious and political liberty, of freedom of education, labor, and press; denial of God and the creation of an atheistic youth; destruction of private property through plunder; socialization of the national strength; ruin of the free worker by means of radical organiza-

[115] LNDLR Bulletin No. 16, copy in possession of Antonio Ríus Facius. This bulletin, along with two others, was distributed in Mexico City December 4 by being released from balloons in various parts of the capital (Weddell to Sec-State, December 7, 1926, NA, RG 59, 812.404/727).

[116] Copy in LA-1.

[117] Copies in possession of Antonio Ríus Facius.

tions; repudiation of international obligations: such is, in substance, the monstrous program of the present regime. In a word, the deliberate and systematic destruction of the Mexican nationality." The proclamation appealed to "the sacred right of defense," which justified "the necessity of destroying forever the vicious rule of faction in order to create a national government":

> The hour of battle has sounded!
> The hour of victory belongs to God![118]

In the final days of 1926, league agents fanned out from Mexico City, their mission being to mobilize every Catholic contingent possible for the January move. Jalisco was crucial, and there the league's position was complicated by the existence of Anacleto González Flores's powerful Unión Popular. The league had not attempted to replace the UP; rather, it had settled for an alliance whereby the UP retained its identity and became at the same time the regional league organization, as the Unión Popular de Jalisco-LNDLR. Gonzáles Flores was both UP president and league delegate. The Directive Committee in Mexico City did not, it realized, have unquestioned authority in the arrangement. González Flores often told intimates that, if the directors should take a course that seemed unwise, the UP would be under no obligation to follow.[119]

The Maestro's views on violence were well known, and his opposition could sink the entire effort in the west. The Directive Committee therefore sent Bartolomé Ontiveros, chief of the Special War Committee, to Jalisco with instructions to insure the UP's adherence.[120] The mission was successful. González Flores decided that to refuse his cooperation not only would impair the uprising's chances, but also would split the UP and cripple its capacity for even the civic action he had designed it to perform. He agreed to support the call to arms and to summon a meeting of UP leaders to second his decision.

---

[118] René Capistrán Garza, "A la Nación," LA-1.
[119] Navarrete, *Por Dios*, pp. 98–100.
[120] Ceniceros y Villarreal, "Historia."

The Maestro tried briefly to keep the UP formally separate from the rebellion. He named Heriberto Navarrete to assume immediate direction of the UP and a young engineer, Salvador Cuéllar, to organize the armed action with the cooperation of local chiefs who could and would join. González Flores would be the only link between the two spheres of activity. But it was futile. No one wanted to be left out of the action.[121] The day after he gave permission for Navarrete and other UP officers to join the coming fight, he met with a group of close associates, all of them veterans of the ACJM like himself, whom he summoned to his hiding place, a house on San Felipe Street. The Maestro took them to the roof terrace for greater privacy. He told them that their position as militant Catholics had led them, perhaps without their realizing it, to the juncture at hand. The LNDLR, he said, had launched itself into revolution, and he hoped its intuition had been correct. He had decided that duty required him to stand with the league, and he would devote to the effort everything he was and everything he had. He wanted posterity to know that the Unión Popular was never meant to be an agent of civil war; and the UP was too important "to lose in an adventure in which we are going to be left alone." Nevertheless, events were driving them all to the battlefield, and those who were determined to go should understand what was involved:

I know only too well that what is beginning now for us is a Calvary. We must be ready to take up and carry our crosses. . . . I, who am here responsible for the decision of all, feel a sacred obligation not to deceive anyone. If one of you should ask me what sacrifice I am asking of

---

[121] Navarrete, *Por Dios*, pp. 120–123. González Flores's wish to keep the UP out of the conflict may have been strengthened by a communication sent him by Francisco Orozco y Jiménez. The archbishop, in hiding since October, had heard rumors that military action was planned and wrote to the Maestro saying that under no circumstances was he to involve the UP in any armed movement, since the aim of the organization was purely civic and social. He later said that his instructions were not followed "because the Directive Center [i.e., the Directive Committee in Mexico City] gave other instructions, and I, far away and in hiding, could not exercise a more important influence" ("Memorándum del Excmo. Sr. Francisco Orozco y Jiménez," pp. 168–169).

you in order to seal the pact we are going to celebrate, I will tell you in two words: *your blood*. If you want to proceed, stop dreaming of places of honor, military triumphs, braid, luster, victories, and authority over others. Mexico needs a tradition of blood in order to cement its free life of tomorrow. For that work my life is available, and for that tradition I ask yours.[122]

122 Navarrete, *Por Dios*, pp. 123–125.

5. *Cristo Rey* and Capistrán Garza

DURING THE FIRST WEEKS of 1927, rebellion flared in a dozen Mexican states. What had been since August mostly a rash of piddling raids in remote areas now burgeoned into serious fighting, even though the rebellion's chief, Capistrán Garza, remained out of the country. Thousands of men who would be called Cristeros[1] flung themselves into combat for the final, desperate showdown in Mexico's long epic of religious strife.

Only a few rebel units went into action on New Year's Day, the date set by the LNDLR. Close synchronization was impossible. In the west, which would be the scene of the hardest fighting for the next thirty months, most of the risings began several days later; the leaders in Guadalajara, adjusting the timetable to their own

[1] The term "Cristero" was not commonly used until near the end of the rebellion in 1929.

exigencies, designated January 5 to 7 for the start of the movement in Jalisco and adjacent states.[2] From the first, effective control was loose; the order of battle amounted to little more than urging local *jefes* to gather men and arms and take the field. Several rebel chiefs in the Guadalajara jurisdiction, nevertheless, were under motion on January 1. That afternoon around forty *rancheros* led by Miguel Hernández assembled in the plaza at San Julián, Jalisco, where they received the blessing of the parish priest and then rode into the hills. The next morning they took San Miguel el Alto, which was defended by a handful of police and local officials, but evacuated before a federal regiment arrived.[3] Another band seized San Francisco del Rincón on the second, while still another attacked the larger town of San Juan de los Lagos.[4]

During the next two weeks Catholic insurgents fell on dozens of Jalisco towns and villages. Most of the action was in Los Altos, east and north of Guadalajara, where mounted rebels ranged the countryside and, by the third week of January, controlled sizeable rural areas.[5]

In neighboring Zacatecas, José María Gutiérrez and Marcial Murillo, with a few dozen followers, rose at Jalpa, seventy miles north of Guadalajara, on January 2. They captured the head of the municipal militia and disarmed the constabulary at the city

[2] Heriberto Navarrete, *"Por Dios y Por la Patria": Memorias de mi participación en la defensa de la libertad de conciencia y culto durante la persecución religiosa en México de 1926 a 1929*, p. 123. For a comprehensive survey of military operations during the rebellion, see Jean A. Meyer, "La Christiade: Société et idéologie dans le Mexique contemporain, 1926–1929."

[3] Antonio Ríus Facius, *Méjico cristero: Historia de la ACJM, 1925 a 1931*, p. 145. *Excélsior* for January 6 carried an account of the attack as reported by the chief of military operations in Jalisco, but there was no mention of the religious tie-in. This was usual in press accounts of the rebellion.

[4] José Dolores Pérez, *La persecución religiosa de Calles en León, Gto.*, p. 12; Alicia Olivera Sedano, *Aspectos del conflicto religioso de 1926 a 1929: Sus antecedentes y consecuencias*, p. 158.

[5] "Informe sobre los grupos levantados en armas o comprometidos a hacerlo, a fines de 1926 y principios de 1927, con los nombres de sus jefes," January 8, 1927, LA-1; Olivera Sedano, p. 158; *Excélsior*, January 12, 1927; January 18, 1927; January 20, 1927.

hall. Then Capistrán Garza's manifesto was read to a crowd assembled in the plaza. That evening two other rebel leaders arrived with around sixty men, most of them mounted and armed. The populace was warmly enthusiastic; not a shot had been fired. On the ninth, the Jalpa Cristeros (now styling themselves the "Libre de Jalpa" Regiment) fought their first battle. One hundred forty-five strong (although nearly half were without guns), they defeated a federal force of equal size near Tepechitlán, just west of Jalpa, in an engagement that lasted over five hours.[6] On the eighteenth they attacked Nochistlán, southeast of Jalpa on the Jalisco border. They were at the point of overwhelming the defenders when their ammunition gave out, forcing them to withdraw.[7]

Pedro Quintanar was also on the move. Assembling around ninety men, he sallied forth from Huejuquilla in the extreme north of Jalisco on January 4 for a whirlwind campaign of hit-and-run forays against mining towns in southern Zacatecas. Two weeks later he returned to his home base, only to be driven out before the end of the month by federal troops and armed agrarians, who established a firm occupation of the town.[8]

The risings in northern Zacatecas and Coahuila were brief, dramatic, and abortive. Preparations had begun in October, presided over by Antonio Acuña Rodríguez, ACJM leader and LNDLR delegate in Saltillo, and Maj. Manuel Silva, a federal army officer sympathetic to the Catholic cause. Their plan was to attack simultaneously Saltillo and Parras in Coahuila and Concepción del Oro in Zacatecas.[9] Manpower and materials were still scarce when the LNDLR's order for the January rising came, but the conspirators agreed to comply. They believed that their operation was part of a

---

[6] "Informe general de los hechos de armas del Regimiento 'Libre de Jalpa' que se rindió a la 'Liga Nacional Defensora de la Libertad Religiosa' desde el principio del movimiento a la fecha," June 5, 1928, signed by José María Gutiérrez, LA-1.

[7] Rafael Ceniceros y Villarreal, "Historia de la L.N.D.R."

[8] Ríus Facius, *Méjico cristero*, p. 147.

[9] Ibid., pp. 148–149; Felipe Brondo Alvarez, Memoirs; Olivera Sedano, *Aspectos del conflicto religioso*, p. 168.

highly coordinated national movement and that they would have to sustain it for a few days at most. Only later did they learn that theirs was the only important effort undertaken in northern Mexico.[10]

Led by Silva and Felipe Brondo Alvarez, a Saltillo ACJM stalwart and special representative of the LNDLR War Committee, two dozen rebels overpowered a small federal garrison to capture Concepción del Oro in the early hours of January 1. Some one hundred additional area men now joined them, but late in the afternoon word came that a trainload of federals was en route from Saltillo. Persons charged with the responsibility for interrupting communications had neglected to cut a telephone line, and news of the Cristero strike had got out. The rebels withdrew hastily to the north, but government troops found their trail and by the end of January had dispersed them. Silva died in the final action.[11]

The attack on Parras fared no better. At dawn on January 3, some two hundred Cristeros swept into the town to shouts of "¡VIVA CRISTO REY!" and "¡VIVA CAPISTRÁN GARZA!" The core of the force was thirty-five ACJM members; the rest were Catholic laborers from Parras and nearby *rancherías*, plus a few Knights of Columbus. They sacked the government offices and jailed local officials and CROM leaders.[12] Care had been taken to destroy railroad bridges and cut communications, but news of the attack somehow reached Torreón, and the next day government troops got through and retook the town.[13] The Cristeros, whose numbers had risen to around four hundred, fled to the sierra. Those with horses rode south into Zacatecas. The rest scattered in small bands, some of

[10] Interview with Felipe Brondo Alvarez, Saltillo, June, 1968; Brondo Alvarez, Memoirs.

[11] Interview with Felipe Brondo Alvarez, Saltillo, June, 1968.

[12] Angel Rodó to Governor Manuel Pérez Treviño, January 4, 1927; Felipe Flores to Pérez Treviño, January 4, 1927; Juan Martínez Negrete to Pérez Treviño, January 3, 1927; in State of Coahuila Archives, *leg.* 4, *exp.* 1/21, 1927.

[13] Angel Prado to Pérez Treviño, January 3, 1927; M. S. Mayagoitia to Chief of Operations and Governor of Coahuila, January 4, 1927; in State of Coahuila Archives, *leg.* 4, *exp.* 1/21, 1927.

1. Apostolic Delegate Serafín Cimino, *left*, and Archbishop José Mora y del Río, *right*.

2. Firemen dispersing rioters at La Soledad Church in Mexico City, February, 1925.

4 José María González Valencia, archbishop of Durango.

3 René Capistrán Garza

6. José de Jesús Manríquez y Zárate, bishop of Huejutla.

5. Francisco Orozco y Jiménez, archbishop of Guadalajara.

7. Cristeros attending a field mass.

8. Madre Conchita and José de León Toral during their trial, November, 1928.

9. Father Miguel Pro, S.J., moments before his execution, November, 1927.

10. Pascual Díaz, *left*, and Leopoldo Ruiz y Flores, *right*, leaving the National Palace, June 21, 1929.

11. Provisional President Emilio Portes Gil.

12. Ambassador Dwight W. Morrow, *left*, and President Plutarco Elías Calles, *right*.

them to be hunted down and killed by the federals over the next several weeks.[14]

The assault on Saltillo never materialized. Acuña assembled a band of ACJM companions and ranch hands in the nearby Sierra de Arteaga to storm the town, but the number mustered—less than a hundred—was clearly inadequate, and he abandoned the scheme. The authorities, however, learned of the conspiracy and sent units from the Saltillo garrison in pursuit. They caught up with the rebels at the village of Huamuchil and routed them. Most managed to escape, but Acuña was captured and shot after refusing, under torture, to disclose information regarding the rebellion.[15]

Plans for armed action in the Federal District were completed at a meeting of several dozen ACJM members in Mexico City on December 28. Manuel Bonilla, one of its organizers, announced that Manuel Reyes, a former officer in Zapata's army, would command the uprising. Reyes was a disciple of Sister Concepción Acevedo de la Llata, a cloistered Capuchin nun from Querétaro. "Madre Conchita," as she was familiarly known, was the superior of a group of religious living in the capital and was attracting attention among Catholics for her charitable work and spiritual zeal; a large and diverse circle of followers attended her holy-hour services and conferences.[16] Less widely known was her involvement in the insurrection about to begin.

On December 31 most of the new Cristeros attended Mass at Madre Conchita's convent. The nun gave Bonilla a Mexican flag to which were affixed medallions representing the Sacred Heart of Jesus and the Virgin of Guadalupe. The next day the rebels rendezvoused with Reyes and a handful of armed men in the

---

[14] A. Mendizo to Pérez Treviño, January 10, 1927, in State of Coahuila Archives, *leg.* 4, *exp.* 1/21, 1927; "Los Cristeros de Parras, Coahuila: La verdad sobre los fusilamientos de 1927," *David* 2, no. 30 (January 22, 1955): 81–82; Ríus Facius, *Méjico cristero*, pp. 151–152.

[15] Olivera Sedano, *Aspectos del conflicto religioso*, pp. 168–169; Ríus Facius, *Méjico cristero*, pp. 148–151.

[16] Olivera Sedano, *Aspectos del conflicto religioso*, pp. 172–174; Ríus Facius, *Méjico cristero*, pp. 187–188.

mountains south of the city. Bonilla read Capistrán Garza's manifesto to the group, and Reyes swore to support it. On January 2
they reached Ajusco, between Mexico City and Cuernavaca, where
they commandeered horses and weapons. But their movement died
aborning. Two days later a squad of federal soldiers surprised them
and killed at least five of them. The rest fortified themselves in less
accessible terrain, but a month later local agrarians, organized
into "social-defense" units, dislodged and scattered them. Bonilla
was captured and shot near Toluca; Reyes also fell into government hands and was publicly executed in the same city in August.
The few who escaped meanwhile straggled back to Mexico City.[17]

The chief of the Cristeros in the small Pacific coast state of Colima was twenty-six–year–old Dionisio Eduardo Ochoa, an ex-sem-
inarian and ACJM leader whose antigovernment-propaganda activities had so irked authorities that he prudently moved to Guadalajara in 1925 to complete his education. While in Colima for the
1926 Christmas holidays, he received a message from Guadalajara
directing him and his friend Rafael Sánchez to initiate a rising in
January. They agreed but decided it would be suicidal to try to
organize anything substantial under the noses of the government
in the state capital. Instead they withdrew with a few friends to
the slopes of the Volcano of Colima on the Jalisco border, a remote
area where a movement might develop without threat of immediate extinction. There, at a settlement called Caucentla, Ochoa assumed sole command. He paid a brief visit to González Flores in
Guadalajara and then began commissioning Catholic leaders from
various parts of Colima to raise and lead bands.[18]

By the end of January a sizable force was mobilized in Colima,
and on the twenty-third the Caucentla garrison repulsed an attack
by sixty mounted state gendarmes. A week later Ochoa's men
badly mauled a regiment led by Gen. Jesús Ferreira, federal chief
of operations in Jalisco, who had rushed to the scene after restoring

17 Ceniceros y Villarreal, "Historia"; Olivera Sedano, *Aspectos del conflicto religioso*, pp. 174–176; Ríus Facius, *Méjico cristero*, pp. 188–199.
18 Enrique de Jesús Ochoa [pseud. Spectator], *Los cristeros del Volcán de Colima*, I, 107–154.

momentary calm in his state. The commander of federal forces in Colima was likewise unsuccessful; after suffering heavy losses in an assault on the Caucentla redoubt, he withdrew to the city of Colima, where accounts of the rebel successes were spreading despite official denials.[19]

There were other Cristero bands in the field in January, in Oaxaca, Guerrero, the state of México, Michoacán, Querétaro, Guanajuato, Aguascalientes, Tamaulipas, San Luis Potosí, and Durango.[20] Much of the action was relatively insignificant, but some rebel columns created considerable havoc. In Durango, a Cristero force captured Mesquital, fifty miles from the state capital, as well as a number of smaller towns, which they held for several days; the same unit grew to around four hundred men and bested at least one federal regiment in open battle.[21] Two contingents, however, were conspicuously absent from the January fighting: the attack on Ciudad Juárez promised by José Gándara never transpired, and Chihuahua remained at peace.[22]

The LNDLR had hoped that the January risings would trigger a massive popular revolt that would overwhelm the Calles government, but this did not happen. In some parts of central and western Mexico there was all-out support for the rebels, although this was usually limited to rural regions. In urban areas generally, and almost everywhere in the north and extreme southeast, the populace was indifferent or at least quiet. The Cristeros of northern Zacatecas and Coahuila dispersed, and, except for a few minor flareups, those areas gave the government no further trouble. Cristeros in the immediate area of Mexico City reappeared from time to time, although they never established stable control over a particular locality. Bands that were occasionally large made life un-

---

[19] Ibid., pp. 162–174.

[20] "Informe sobre los grupos levantados en armas . . . ," LA-1; *Excélsior*, January 12, 1927.

[21] "Informe sobre los grupos levantados en armas"; Ceniceros y Villarreal, "Historia."

[22] The would-be rebels in Chihuahua may have been intimidated by the explicit opposition of Archbishop Antonio Guízar Valencia (see Meyer, "La Christiade," II, 512).

pleasant for federal troops in Puebla and Oaxaca during the next two years. But at the end of January there was a lull almost everywhere; even in Jalisco, government forces were retaking a number of towns.[23] The 64,000-man federal army[24] remained loyal to the government.

On the other hand, the men who had gambled on the rebellion succeeding had more than a few reasons not to despair. More than three thousand men had answered the call to arms,[25] and the majority did not give up after the initial reverses. Large areas of Jalisco remained in rebel hands, and in parts of Guanajuato, Michoacán, Querétaro, and Colima, government control was nominal as January closed. The few weeks of intense activity were followed by a lull that some interpreted as a collapse; in fact, it was a respite during which the Cristeros regrouped and deepened their determination to carry on. In Colima there was not even a slowdown; the movement gained steadily from the moment of its inception.

Just as encouraging to the rebels was the fact that a cluster of promising field leaders had emerged in January. Most were middle class, intensely Catholic, and young—like Lauro Rocha, a nineteen-year-old medical student from Guadalajara, ACJM militant, and close friend of González Flores, who in a few weeks had shown military ability of a high order.[26] Some of the new chiefs were untutored men of the land—like Victoriano Ramírez, a Jalisco *ranchero* with a reputation for gallantry, lady-chasing, and brawling. His nickname,"El Catorce" (Fourteen), came from an incident in which he killed fourteen pursuers after escaping from the San Miguel el Alto jail, where he was being held on a charge of killing a man in a fight. When the Cristeros rose, Victoriano, insisting on his staunch loyalty to the Church, rushed to join them. Within days he was at the head of an impressively ferocious band that

[23] *Excélsior*, January 18, 1927; January 20, 1927.
[24] G-2 report, no. 1334, January 18, 1927, from Lt. Col. Edward Davis, U.S. military attaché, Mexico City, to Military Intelligence Division of the War Department General Staff, NA, RG 165.
[25] See ibid.
[26] See "Datos biográficos del General Lauro Rocha G.," *David* 7, no. 157 (August 22, 1965): 207–208.

would alternately thrill and scandalize the Catholic leadership.[27] There were also priests, for example, Fathers José Reyes Vega and Aristeo Pedroza, both of whom quickly exhibited extraordinary military talents and later rose to top commands in the movement.

The Cristeros had not won in the early weeks of 1927, but the Calles goverment had on its hands a far more formidable contest than it imagined.

The rebellion had begun without the presence in Mexico of its Supreme Chief. René Capistrán Garza was in the United States. What were his plans? No one in Mexico knew exactly, and as the fighting mounted during the first week of January, the LNDLR directors became anxious. On the eighth they wired him a report on the military situation and told him they hoped he and the others in the United States would act soon.[28] On the twelfth they sent another message, asking when he proposed to enter Mexico. They also wanted to know when and where he would issue his manifesto—which, they said, had already been shown to a few select persons (they were obviously unaware that it was being read and sworn to all over the country). They also expressed concern over the attitude of the U.S. government and asked what success he had had on that score.[29] The manifesto finally appeared officially on the twelfth, in El Paso, Texas, but the league learned of it only from a brief item in the Mexico City press.[30] By the nineteenth, still with no direct word, the committee was desperate; they had heard nothing from Capistrán Garza since December, they wired; he had promised to keep them informed but had failed to do so: "We believe the matter wo have on our hands merits your heeding what is not mere curiosity."[31] Indirect word came on the twenty-fourth, when Capistrán Garza issued a "War Bulletin" from El Paso to

[27] Navarrete, *Por Dios*, pp. 183–186.

[28] Directive Committee to Capistrán Garza, January 8, 1927, LA-1.

[29] Ibid., January 12, 1927.

[30] *Excélsior*, January 13, 1927. The press mentioned that "a manifesto" signed by Capistrán Garza and Gándara had been issued in El Paso but refrained from reporting its contents.

[31] Directive Committee to Capistrán Garza, January 19, 1927, LA-1. Most of the league correspondence coming to Mexico City by mail after 1926 was ad-

some key leaders of the rebellion. It gave a general overview of the military situation in Mexico and said that organization would be completed when he entered the republic.[32]

On February 9, when the initial uprisings were substantially over, Capistrán Garza finally reported to the Directive Committee. He indicated clearly what he believed his chief contribution to victory would be: U.S. policy and U.S. money were the decisive ingredients, and his most urgent task was to marshal both behind the effort. He had just been in Washington, he said, summoned by Mr. William F. Buckley, president of the Patempec Oil Company, with whom he was on excellent terms and who was the chief figure in a group interested in financing the movement. He had also addressed to the U.S. government a memorandum which, he told the directors, had been presented at a cabinet meeting. It asked for a formal promise that belligerency would be recognized as soon as a place on the border was taken—this was the only condition imposed by the prospective financial backers. He was in touch with the State Department, which had told him that the matter would be decided by early March at the latest (the financiers believed the reply would be satisfactory).[33] The donors, he reported, would transfer $30,000 within a week, and after the way was cleared for the total arrangement he would have an advance of $200,000, which would make it possible for him to launch an attack across the border. He mentioned Tamaulipas as a likely target. Things had been going slowly, he admitted, but seemed to be on firm ground. The situation of the men fighting in Mexico was lamentable, he said, but their task was to maintain a state of war throughout the country until the blow on the border came; that, although it might be slightly delayed, would signal the destruction of Calles.

---

dressed to fictitious names at convenient pick-up places. Early in 1927 the Directive Committee received its mail in care of "J. C. Price" at the Hotel Cosmos on San Juan de Letrán.

[32] "Boletín de Guerra No. 3," LA-1.

[33] The extent of Capistrán Garza's contact with U.S. officialdom is unclear. Apparently he or his agents approached State Department officials, who expressed polite interest but made no commitments—although the Mexicans, grasping at straws, might have interpreted matters otherwise.

As for the projected attack on Ciudad Juárez, he said both he and the league had been miserably deceived. There had been nothing to back Gándara's promises. He had ended all collaboration with Gándara and had managed with great effort practicallly to eliminate him from all matters, although he would have to be watched; Gándara was presently in New York or Washington. He closed with the information that he had sent an aide, Jenaro Núñez, to New York to act as his go-between with Pascual Díaz, who had just arrived.[34]

Pascual Díaz, bishop of Tabasco and secretary of the Episcopal Committee, had been arrested in Mexico City on January 10, together with five other bishops, on charges of conducting public religious ceremonies at the committee's offices.[35] All had been released except Díaz, whom the government had accused of being implicated in the Catholic rebellion.[36] He had been ordered to leave the country. On January 19 he crossed into Guatemala,[37] and within a few days was en route to the United States via Havana. On February 1 he disembarked in New York, where he was greeted at the pier by some sixty persons, led by Monsignor Thomas Carroll, representing the Archdiocese of New York, and went immediately to St. Francis Xavier College, where he took up temporary residence.[38]

Díaz's arrival in the United States put into motion a tangle of events that in a few chaotic weeks fundamentally altered the course of the Catholic resistance movement in Mexico. Accusations and countercharges would fly for years, as the principals involved and their partisans told their versions of what had happened. All the accounts were to a degree plausible, and none was entirely objective.

Nearly two years later, Capistrán Garza addressed a long state-

[34] Capistrán Garza to Directive Committee, February 9, 1927, LA-1.

[35] *Excélsior*, January 11, 1927.

[36] *New York Times*, January 11, 1927.

[37] *Excélsior*, January 20, 1927.

[38] *New York Times*, February 2, 1927; Alberto María Carreño, *El arzobispo de México, excmo. Sr. Dr. D. Pascual Díaz y el conflicto religioso*, pp. 263–264.

ment to the Mexican bishops.[39] He had had three roles in the United States, he said: (a) head of the liberation movement, (b) representative of the LNDLR and (c) representative of the Mexican hierarchy to the U.S. hierarchy. The first was conferred on him after the Episcopal Committee, through Díaz, had approved the lawfulness of the movement, the program, and himself as chief. Regarding his position as representative of the Mexican episcopate, he said the credential from Mora y del Río and the letter from that prelate to the Knights of Columbus had surprised him—he had expected only a letter of introduction.

When Díaz arrived in New York, Capistrán Garza stated, he sent Núñez to greet him and offered to see the bishop in person, but Díaz preferred to communicate through an intermediary. Shortly afterward, Capistrán Garza went on, rumors began to reach him that Díaz was saying, among other things, that Mexico needed a coalition government led by distinguished liberals. Núñez reported, however, that Díaz was determined to support Capistrán Garza against any "dissident" Catholic elements, such as the El Paso *junta*. Capistrán Garza sent Manuel de la Peza to New York to counter any attempt by the "dissidents" to influence Díaz. Early in March, Díaz, although appearing to be neutral, asked de la Peza at least to listen to two of these, Juan Lainé, once an aide to René but now disaffected, and a Jesuit priest, Father Ricardo Alvarez, of the El Paso group, who were proposing that Lainé be named financial agent for the movement in the United States.

Late in 1926, Capistrán Garza continued, he had opened talks with William F. Buckley, a U.S. Catholic prominent in petroleum circles, through whom he hoped to get financial aid. The prospective donor was Buckley's friend Nicholas Brady, a multimillionaire and prominent Catholic layman. It was hoped that Brady would provide $500,000 with which to finance initial armed operations. Buckley had interested him in the Mexican situation, helped by a Dr. Malone, another New York Catholic who several years

[39] "Informe del Sr. Don René Capistrán Garza a los Ilustrísimos y Reverendísimos señores Arzobispos y Obispos Mexicanos, reunidos en San Antonio, Texas," November 14, 1928, LA-1.

earlier had given signal help to de Valera and the Irish independence cause. Malone had important connections in United States financial circles and was also Governor Alfred E. Smith's personal physician. In late February, said Capistrán Garza, Buckley thought the groundwork was well enough prepared to put the matter formally before Brady. The latter asked how much was needed; Buckley told him $350,000 to $500,000 and said that he (Buckley) would provide half the total sum. Capistrán Garza left San Antonio March 1 and reached New York two days later. On the eighth he learned from Buckley's secretary that the oilman was just leaving San Antonio and would reach New York on the tenth. The proposal was already in the hands of Dr. Malone. March tenth passed with no word from Buckley. On the eleventh Capistrán Garza, growing suspicious, told Ramón Ruiz Rueda to get him an interview with Pascual Díaz. The bishop did not answer the request, although the nun who had received the note at the college said it had been given to Díaz. Also on the eleventh, de la Peza, who was working closely with Capistrán Garza, visited Father Wilfred Parsons, S.J., editor of the Jesuit weekly, *America*, who was a friend of Díaz and known to be one of the "dissidents." Parsons told de la Peza that Buckley had reached New York the tenth and the next day had called on him to ask if it were true that Díaz was in total disagreement with Capistrán Garza. Parsons had said it was true; at Buckley's request he had set up a meeting between Buckley and Díaz for the fourteenth (Díaz was out of the city and would return by that date).

Capistrán Garza now ordered Ruiz Rueda to get him an appointment with Díaz at any cost. Late on March 13, after he and de la Peza had waited at Díaz's residence for hours, the bishop arrived, surprised to see them, and said he had received no word that they wanted to talk with him. The three conferred for an hour and a half. Díaz said that any opinions he had expressed were purely his own and were not given in the name of the Mexican episcopate. Capistrán Garza pointed out that anything Díaz said would naturally carry enormous weight; he further asserted that he had been given his post by the LNDLR in agreement with the bishops and deserved to be supported, not destroyed. Díaz agreed and promised to tell Buckley that there was no dissension, that the Episcopal Committee approved of the LNDLR, Capistrán Garza, the movement, and the program.

Díaz and Buckley met. Two days later Buckley came to Capistrán Garza's room at the Hotel Pennsylvania. He said that, while he was en route from Texas, Malone had contacted him, asking to see him as soon as he arrived in New York. There Malone had told him that he (Buckley) had been deceived, that Capistrán Garza was an imposter. This, Malone said, had been told him by Father Parsons, who said he could prove it by testimony from Díaz. Malone had told all this to Brady, who on the spot had dropped all further connection with the matter. Buckley went to Parsons, who repeated the story, told him to be careful, and said that, if he really wanted to help Mexico, he should see Díaz. At his meeting with Díaz, Buckley went on, the bishop told him that he had been "deeply hurt" that Capistrán Garza had not come to see him when he arrived in New York. He also told Buckley that Capistrán Garza represented the LNDLR but not the episcopate—that Mora y del Río's letter was only an introduction, not a credential, and that Capistrán Garza by using it as a credential was committing an imposture. Díaz added that the hierarchy and people of Mexico wanted a coalition government led by fair-minded liberals, not Catholics, and mentioned as possible leaders Félix Díaz (a nephew of Porfirio and a ringleader in the 1913 coup against Madero) and Nemesio García Naranjo (a journalist-litterateur exiled by the revolutionary regimes).[40] Buckley told Capistrán Garza that personally he had no doubts concerning the latter's credentials or honor, but that the attitude of Díaz and Parsons had collapsed the whole project and had put him (Buckley) in an embarrassing position with his friends. At this point, Capistrán Garza called in de la Peza, who related to Buckley the substance of their talk with Díaz on March 13. Buckley was stupefied.

[40] García Naranjo was also a long-time friend of Buckley and occasionally represented him in international oil deals. See Nemesio García Naranjo, *Memorias de García Naranjo*, IX, 167–193, 238–251.

A few days later, Capistrán Garza continued, de la Peza visited Díaz at the Jesuit novitiate at Woodstock, Maryland, and told him that it would be necessary to inform the Catholic leadership in Mexico City of all that had happened. Díaz became angry and said that if this were done he would accuse de la Peza and Capistrán Garza before the Holy See of disobedience and rebellion to ecclesiastical authority.

Efforts were made, Capistrán Garza concluded his report, to revive the negotiations, but to no avail. Father Parsons now approached García Naranjo and asked him to use his influence to interest Brady in helping the "dissidents." García Naranjo refused. Later, Father Carlos María de Heredia, S.J., got García Naranjo and Díaz together. Díaz told García Naranjo that he had $350,000 at his disposal and offered it to him if he would accept leadership of the movement. García Naranjo finally agreed but reminded Díaz that he was a liberal and that his only point of contact with Catholics was his desire to rid Mexico of Calles. No money changed hands, however.

Pascual Díaz's side of the story was provided in an *informe* which he addressed to his fellow bishops in 1928 and which included a copy of a letter he had written shortly before to Capistrán Garza;[41] this was supplemented a few years later in a book published by Díaz's alter ego and longtime personal friend and secretary, Alberto María Carreño.[42] As for Capistrán Garza's status in the United States, Díaz said that Mora y del Río (who died shortly before the *informe* appeared) had not indicated in signing his missive to Capistrán Garza that he was doing so as president of the Episcopal Committee; the "we" in the document was the standard pronoun used by a bishop in formal discourse, and he was convinced that the archbishop intended only to make Capistrán Garza his personal representative. As for the accusation that he

---

[41] Pascual Díaz y Barreto, *Informe que rinde al V. Episcopado Mexicano el Obispo de Tabasco Pascual Díaz en relación con las actividades de la Liga Nacional Defensora de la Libertad Religiosa en los Estados Unidos de América*, n.p.

[42] Carreño, *El arzobispo de México*.

had sought to wreck the financial transaction, Díaz said, addressing Capistrán Garza: "You probably thought that I had interposed
myself between you and Messrs. Buckley and Brady, whereas in
reality I was completely unaware that you, through Mr. Buckley,
were trying to obtain funds from Mr. Brady."[43]

Brady had indeed offered money to Díaz, through a Mr. John
Stuart, an employee of Father Parsons, who had talked with Brady
and interested him in the cause. (Díaz later told González Valencia, archbishop of Durango, that Brady offered $200,000 for the
armed defense if Díaz approved.)[44] Díaz said that he hurried to
inform de la Peza of the offer and asked to be put in touch with
Capistrán Garza but received no reply.[45] Díaz denied offering the
leadership of the movement to García Naranjo, although he said
he did telephone him to tell him of Brady's offer and advised him
to come to an agreement with Núñez, after which the two of them
should talk with de la Peza. The situation, Carreño later insisted,
was this: Brady wished to make funds available, but only under
certain conditions; Díaz told the bishops that "a certain sum would
be given to help the Catholics, provided they enlisted individuals
who would not arouse opposition in this country—the United
States—in view of the campaign being directed in the United
States against Catholics by various Protestant groups." Díaz had
hurried to ask de la Peza to have Capistrán Garza contact him so
that the offer might be taken advantage of, but nothing happened.
Díaz's approach to García Naranjo was a move to help satisfy
the donor. But, said Carreño, days passed with no word from de la
Peza, and finally Díaz learned that Brady had been advised by
someone whom he held in high esteem not to give a single cent.[46]

Díaz told Capistrán Garza that when he spoke with Buckley he
said nothing against René or the LNDLR, but he admitted having

[43] Díaz, *Informe*.

[44] Sworn statement of González Valencia, appended to a statement signed by
Palomar y Vizcarra January 25, 1943, LA-1.

[45] Carreño, *El arzobispo de México*, pp. 257–260.

[46] Ibid., pp. 237, 243–245; Díaz, *Informe*.

said that if insurmountable difficulties prevented the establishment of an exclusively Catholic government, then other men of integrity who were well disposed toward the Church could be acceptable in forming a coalition government.[47] He could not, he went on, disagree with what everyone in the United States was thinking and saying, but this did not mean that Capistrán Garza would be excluded from his post or that he or the league would be opposed.[48] As for the dispute with de la Peza at Woodstock, Díaz said it resulted from his (Díaz's) insistence that de la Peza tell Capistrán Garza "all that was being said, so that you [Capistrán Garza] might study the orientation that it seemed indispensable to give to your labors, and the complete refusal of Mr. Peza to do this." It was his duty, he went on, to point out to Capistrán Garza and his group that the road they had chosen could lead them to failure. De la Peza had been disrespectful, he said, but he denied threatening to accuse him of disobedience. "What I did tell him was that I was prepared, if you were following a mistaken path, to indicate publicly my disapproval of your labors, since only this would reveal that you had not understood the mission the League had entrusted to you." He had reproached de la Peza, he said, for being unwilling to take steps to avoid disaster.[49]

Obviously no important differences exist in the accounts of the protagonists, so far as salient facts go. Both sides agree that Capistrán Garza was in touch with Buckley and Brady regarding funds; that at what appeared to be the crucial point, the prospective donors, or at least one of them, switched and adopted Díaz as the channel for aid; and that Díaz assented to the idea of broadening the base of the anti-Calles movement to include non-Catholics and even liberals—in fact, that he believed this to be the only sensible course. The difference in the accounts comes over motives: Capistrán Garza was convinced that Díaz worked calculatedly and with deceit to push him and the league aside and raise to at least equal

[47] Díaz, *Informe*.
[48] Ibid.
[49] Carreño, *El arzobispo de México*, pp. 294–296.

command another element, whereas Díaz maintained that he was working to help the cause and that he did not know that Capistrán Garza was already negotiating on funds.

Díaz had entered the picture at a time when two factions were contending for authority and money, and he listened sympathetically to the group Capistrán Garza labeled the "dissidents." That group, not completely identifiable as regards either personnel or outlook, was unified in its opposition to René Capistrán Garza. The Supreme Chief had accumulated more than a few enemies well before Díaz reached U.S. soil.

One of Capistrán Garza's adversaries, Father Wilfrid Parsons, seems to have had good reasons for his jaded opinion of the young chief. He had met Capistrán Garza in August, 1926, and the two had developed a close and even affectionate relationship. Parsons gave him a letter of introduction to the apostolic delegate in Washington and obtained financial donations and letters of introduction from Cardinal Hayes and some other American bishops.[50] Parsons later said that René had assured him the funds would be used for civic action, not rebellion. In October, Parsons heard that the LNDLR had decided to resort to arms. He immediately asked Capistrán Garza, then in Houston, if this was true and told him that, if it was, he must send back the letters that had been obtained from the hierarchy because they had been given with the understanding that only peaceful means were involved. René wired Parsons on October 25, denying the report, and Parsons accepted his word. When it became obvious in December that a revolt was indeed in the offing, Parsons still maintained contact and in fact gave tacit approval to the rebellion; he approved the pact with Gándara and, when dissension developed, insisted that Capistrán Garza honor the agreement. He wanted to do all possible to unite the two factions, he said, and at the same time he steadfastly refused to help anyone except Capistrán Garza with money or influence.[51]

But by the time the Buckley-Brady matter came up, Parsons

---

[50] Parsons to Díaz, February 1, 1928 [1929?], cited in ibid., pp. 266–267, 280.
[51] Carreño, *El arzobispo de México*, pp. 280–289.

was totally disenchanted: "I had gradually become convinced, in spite of myself, that the League had made a mistake in naming René to the post it had given him." Capistrán Garza, he said, had surrounded himself with men of mediocre ability who flattered him; also, he had a great facility for making agreements he could not keep. "I spoke of all this to my friend Dr. Malone, who is one of the few men really sincere and enthusiastic about helping Mexico. . . . We both judged that no money should be given as long as dissensions existed." One day, he said, Dr. Malone called him to his office to meet Mr. Buckley and asked him to tell Buckley what they had discussed. Parsons—unaware, he maintained, of the relationship between Buckley and René—did so, saying that he did not think René was the right person for the leadership position and that he was not the accredited representative of the Mexican hierarchy. He did not, he insisted, use the word "imposter"—he thought René had also been deceived in the matter.[52]

Yet Parsons always denied that he was an enemy of René or a member of the "dissident" camp. When John Stuart brought word to him that Brady was offering money, Father Parsons sent him to Díaz—for the purpose, he said, of having Díaz inform Capistrán Garza via de la Peza. (Why he did not send Stuart directly to Capistrán Garza he did not say.) René, said Parsons, was completely misinformed by the men surrounding him and probably misinterpreted his (Father Parsons's) relations with the "dissidents"—whose anger, Parsons insisted, he had himself drawn more than once—"just as he misinterpreted his own relations with the American hierarchy, with Buckley, and with Brady . . ."[53]

But Pascual Díaz, not Parsons, was Capistrán Garza's chief nemesis. Díaz, until January, shared the LNDLR's confidence that it could overthrow the government. But after the January risings he concluded that Catholics could not do it alone; moreover, if the movement retained an exclusively Catholic character, the United

---

[52] Ibid., pp. 289–292. Parsons said that before relations were broken off Buckley gave René "several thousand" dollars (ibid., p. 292).

[53] Ibid., pp. 269–270.

States would oppose it, and no group aspiring to power in Mexico, he believed, could succeed without American support.[54] When it became clear that the league would not relinquish sole direction of the rebellion, Díaz withdrew his support. He always denied that he told Buckley not to help the league, that the Mexican bishops and people wanted an interim government led by liberals, or that he was promoting Félix Díaz or García Naranjo,[55] but his activities in the United States caused an irreparable break between him and Catholic militants.

After the spring of 1927 Pascual Díaz was to the leaders of the Cristero rebellion a Judas Iscariot. Carreño's later defense of the bishop—that he had only wanted to correct what had gone off the track, "in order to help the work of the League, but in the best, most appropriate way,"[56] would be for them the epitome of cynical dishonesty.

By the middle of March, Capistrán Garza had his back to the wall. Undercut (as he saw it, with some reason) by influential Mexican Catholics in the United States, out of favor with important U.S. Catholics, both lay and clerical, his financial plans a shambles, he nevertheless struggled on. The Directive Committee in Mexico City still pledged him unwavering support. So did Archbishop Mora y del Río: the directors wrote Capistrán Garza on March 23 that the primate was entirely opposed to a change in leadership and that he regretted sincerely that his October letter to Capistrán Garza had not been heeded as its obvious meaning indicated it should be; he was not sending another, he said, because that could be taken to mean that the first lacked force, but he was prepared to answer categorically any interpellation on the matter from those who recognized his authority as president of the Episcopal Committee and head of Catholic Action in Mexico.[57]

The battle spread to Rome, where the LNDLR and Capistrán Garza had a momentary advantage. The previous autumn, the

[54] Ibid., pp. 187–188.
[55] Ibid., p. 314.
[56] Ibid., p. 184.
[57] José Luis Orozco to Capistrán Garza, March 23, 1927, LA-1.

Episcopal Committee had sent three of their number as a commission to represent them at the Vatican—González Valencia of Durango, Emeterio Valverde y Téllez of León, and Jenaro Méndez del Río of Tehuantepec, all of them unswerving friends of the league and of the militant position. Since their arrival they had labored mightily to get their views an ample hearing. Late in March Capistrán Garza sent de la Peza to Rome to present his case and try to obtain direct intervention by the Holy See. De la Peza told the three bishops Capistrán Garza's version of the whole affair. He said that when he (de la Peza) first met Díaz in New York, the latter flatly advised him to write the league directors to tell them that it was necessary to find another man to head the movement, which should not continue to appear to be directed by the league; that for it to appear to be a holy war would impede U.S. recognition and aid. De la Peza said he had disagreed with Díaz; the purpose of the movement was not exclusively religious, Capistrán Garza had met no such opposition from Americans, and to take away the cry of "*¡Viva Cristo Rey!*" would dissipate popular enthusiasm. He did say that, when he saw Díaz at Woodstock, Díaz offered to make a statement of support. This came in the form of a letter to Buckley, to be shown to Brady, and said that Capistrán Garza had been delegated by the league, which the episcopate had blessed and approved in all its works thus far, and that he wished him success. But, said de la Peza, much damage had been done. Capistrán Garza had sent him to ask the Commission of Bishops in Rome to use its influence to obtain three things from the Holy See: some indication to Brady to help financially, a general statement of support for the movement, and an order to members of the clergy to stop making war on the league and its cause.[58]

On April 6 de la Peza was received in private audience by Pius XI, to whom he presented a memorandum together with a statement from the three bishops endorsing his mission and the

---

[58] "Informe que presenta Manuel de la Peza a la Comisión de Prelados Residentes en Roma que Representa al Episcopado Mexicano ante la Santa Sede," April 5, 1927, LA-1.

league.[59] The pope told him that the matter should have been taken up with Archbishop Pietro Fumasoni-Biondi, apostolic delegate to the United States, who was now also in charge of Mexican affairs. De la Peza explained that this had not been done because Díaz had already seen the delegate, and the league representatives would have been at a great disadvantage trying to counter his influence. The pope told him to see Gasparri and explain the whole matter, both orally and in writing. This de la Peza did three days later. He told his story again and expressed his opinion that a coalition government for Mexico would be dangerous because it would risk leaving Catholics in limbo, as they were in the days of Porfirio Díaz. Catholics, he insisted, were capable of governing the nation. Many of them, for example Rafael Ceniceros y Villarreal, had experience in high government positions, and the public would give them strong support. As for the United States, the league had reason to believe there was no opposition, that in fact Washington realized that a Catholic triumph would serve American interests.[60]

Most of Rome's information and advice at this juncture came from the three prelates on the Bishops' Commission, and it was having its effect. The league had grounds for believing it had Vatican support. On January 3 the pope praised a group of young Mexicans who were in Rome for the commemoration of the birth of Saint Luis Gonzaga, calling them "sons of a people who are offering their blood for the faith, for the honor of the Lord Jesus Christ, Jesus Christ the King, and for the honor of the Church, our common mother." He extended greetings to all Mexican Catholics, especially the young: "Tell them that We know all they are doing, that We know they are fighting, and how they are fighting in that great war that can be called the battle of Christ . . ."[61] How much, if anything, the pontiff knew at that time of the rebellion is not

[59] "Memorial que el Comisionado Especial de la Liga Nacional Defensora de la Libertad Religiosa de México presenta a Su Santidad Pío XI," April 6, 1927, LA-1.

[60] De la Peza to Gasparri, April 9, 1927, LA-1.

[61] Quoted in Antonio J. López Ortega, *Las naciones extranjeras y la persecución religiosa*, pp. 62–63.

certain and the words may have been spoken in a spirit of imagery, but Mexicans who wished to could take them as indication of strong approval.

Throughout January the Vatican intensified its diplomatic efforts on behalf of Mexico's Catholics. On the tenth the Holy See, through the apostolic delegate in Washington, called the attention of the U.S. government to the "barbarous religious persecution" in Mexico, where "ordinary acts of religious worship, even in private homes, are prohibited and punished as crimes," and asked the United States to make any remonstrance it deemed opportune.[62] A few days later the Vatican urged all nations maintaining diplomatic relations with the Holy See to take action on behalf of Catholics in Mexico.[63]

While Rome sought support from official sources, the Bishops' Commission labored in the unofficial sector. When Bishop Francis Kelley of Oklahoma, a veteran champion of the Church cause in Mexico, was in Rome in January, the prelates gave him a detailed report on the Mexican situation and lauded the LNDLR.[64] Armed intervention by the United States, they assured Kelley, was not desired. What was critically needed from Americans, especially American Catholics, was financial help for the freedom fighters. Once liberty was won, they said, the future would be bright. Mexican Catholics had always been known for their enterprising and progressive spirit; commercial relations with the United States would flourish, and the active and secure flow of capital would be facilitated.[65]

González Valencia went the furthest in giving open and public support to the rebellion. In a pastoral letter to his archdiocese in

[62] Fumasoni Biondi to Kellogg, January 10, 1927, NA, RG 59, 812.404/737.

[63] Ambassador Henry P. Fletcher, Rome, to SecState, January 29, 1927, NA, RG 59, 812.404/749.

[64] On the activities of Kelley and other American Catholics in connection with the religious imbroglio of the teens, see Justin L. Kestenbaum, "The Question of Intervention in Mexico, 1913–1917."

[65] "Memorándum que la Comisión de Obispos Mexicanos ante la Santa Sede presentó a Mons. Kelly [sic]," January 17, 1927, LA-1.

February, he said he had consulted the best theologians in Rome about the matter and that Catholics who had taken up arms should be tranquil in conscience.[66]

The Vatican did not respond immediately to de la Peza's pleas, but the three bishops wrote to both Buckley and Brady endorsing the league's efforts and asking them to lend all possible assistance through the league's authorized representatives in the United States.[67]

But the views of the combative bishops and of Capistrán Garza did not go unchallenged for long in Rome. On April 11, Pascual Díaz arrived for the first of several visits to the Eternal City.[68] He would help persuade the Vatican that the league and its rebellion could not succeed. And the news from Mexico as the months passed seemed to confirm his advice.

[66] Copy in LA-1. The league reproduced the pastoral and distributed it widely in Mexico. The document has been erroneously cited by Walter Lippmann and others, who have claimed that it reported Pius XI approving and blessing the rebellion. It does not; González Valencia's reference to the pope said that the pontiff hoped the people would persevere in their trials; reference to the armed action, which does include González Valencia's own approval of it, comes later in the letter, where the pope is not mentioned. See Walter Lippmann, "The Church and State in Mexico: American Mediation," *Foreign Affairs* 8 (January 1930): 186–207.

[67] González Valencia, Valverde y Téllez, and Méndez del Río to Nicholas Brady, April 15, 1927; idem to William Buckley, April 15, 1927; both cited in Andrés Barquín y Ruiz [pseud. Joaquín Blanco Gil], *El clamor de la sangre,* pp. 143–145.

[68] Ríus Facius, *Méjico cristero,* p. 208.

6. Stalemate

AT THE BEGINNING OF 1927 a student of warfare, in assessing the likelihood of success of the Cristero rebellion, might well have given a pessimistic response. The disadvantages of the Catholic rebels were numerous. The several thousand men who had answered the call to battle were numerically far inferior to the Mexican army, which was, moreover, well provisioned, disciplined, and capably led. The rebels were disorganized, often isolated, and led by untrained and inexperienced men. Supply problems bedeviled the Cristeros. The cities, where war materials might have been obtained, stayed in government hands, and the urban populace's reluctance to involve itself in the rebellion was heightened by the government's tough stand, which could make itself felt more in towns than in the countryside. As a result, arms and ammunition came to the rebels only in trickles and at great danger to the persons who procured them. The rebels thrived only where they had strong public backing, and that meant in the main Jalisco, Colima, Michoacán, and parts of a handful of other states. Within weeks the rebellion had restricted itself geographically and settled into a pattern of rural guerrilla warfare from which it never emerged.

Nevertheless, observers of the Catholic resistance in its broader aspects could have been less pessimistic. If the rebellion sustained itself, as it seemed to be doing; if it could secure foreign support; if the bishops and the pope gave the movement a full and public endorsement; and if then a few spectacular victories in the field destroyed confidence in the Calles regime, the tide might turn.

During 1927 the Cristeros, despite a mixture of successes and reverses, became an effective fighting machine. Correspondingly, however, the possibilities of political breakthroughs that might have insured victory faded one by one.

After the January risings the rebellion slackened but was by no means suffocated. In Jalisco, where government attempts were particularly determined, Cristero leaders adopted the tactic of fragmenting many of their units into small squads—often no more than four or five men—which could evade pursuit and still do occasional damage. At the same time, a number of larger contingents were kept intact.[1] The U.S. military attaché reported late in February that rebel bands had decreased in size and number but continued to show "remarkable tenacity"; he added that according to reliable information there were around a hundred skirmishes between January 23 and February 20.[2] On March 10 the army launched a fresh offensive in Los Altos, with Gen. Joaquín Amaro, the secretary of war and marine, in personal command. The campaign was spirited, and a number of rebel-held towns were quickly retaken,[3] but there was no appreciable effect either on the number of Cristeros in the field or on the sympathy of the rural populace for them.[4] Meanwhile, Cristeros in adjacent states were creat-

[1] G-2 report, no. 1394, Lt. Col. Edward Davis, U.S. military attaché, February 18, 1927, NA, RG 165.

[2] G-2 report, no. 1404, Davis, February 25, 1927, NA, RG 165.

[3] *El Universal*, March 11, 1927; March 12, 1927; *New York Times*, March 12, 1927.

[4] See G-2 report, no. 1450, Davis, March 22, 1927, NA, RG 165.

ing turmoil. In southern Zacatecas, the "Libres de Jalpa," after lying low during February, resumed operations. On March 5 they swooped down on Tlaltenango, northwest of Jalpa, and abandoned the attack only when a federal column of six hundred men came up to drive them off.[5] To the east, in Aguascalientes and Guanajuato, the Cristeros were growing in numbers by the first of April, when they assaulted San Miguel Allende. One estimate placed their strength in the two states at between fifteen hundred and two thousand men, and there was general agreement that they were better mounted than the federals.[6] Also in April, Jalpa, Zacatecas, was in Cristero hands, and Fresnillo was captured and sacked.[7] There was organized rebel activity in Guerrero, Michoacán, Morelos, Puebla, San Luis Potosí—and, most notably, Colima.[8]

Government efforts to suppress the rebellion in Colima had failed utterly. Cristeros struck numerous towns and even raided into the outskirts of the capital, where state officials were sleeping in the government palace for protection. U.S. Consul Earl Eaton reported that brutality was common on both sides. On one incursion into the city of Colima, Cristeros hanged progovernment peons from trees on a main boulevard, and at Suchitlán, to the north, they killed the twelve men of the home guard to shouts of "¡Viva Cristo Rey!" General Ferreira, in a new attempt to dislodge the Cristeros from their enclaves around the volcano, achieved nothing more spectacular, said Eaton, than the shooting of civilians and the burning of some small ranches. In March Gen. Manuel Avila Camacho arrived from Jalisco to direct another drive in the same area but

[5] Rafael Ceniceros y Villarreal, "Historia de la L.N.D.R."

[6] G-2 report, no. 1483, Maj. Harold Thompson, acting military attaché, April 19, 1927, NA, RG 165.

[7] Ibid.

[8] Ibid.; Heriberto Navarrete, "Por Dios y Por la Patria": Memorias de mi participación en la defensa de la libertad de conciencia y culto durante la persecución religiosa en México de 1926 a 1929, pp. 130–131. The government publicly admitted the existence of "relatively large" rebel forces in Jalisco, Colima, Guanajuato, and Guerrero (El Universal, April 4, 1927).

had no success. By late April government forces had abandoned the countryside and fortified themselves in a few urban centers.[9]

The main problem for the Cristeros, in Colima as elsewhere, was lack of ammunition. Arms, while never in excess, were seldom a major concern. Years of strife in Mexico had left quantities of weapons in public and private hands; and, from the first, large numbers of them flowed to the rebels. When Heriberto Navarrete visited Luis Ibarra and his force in southern Jalisco early in February, he found that they had taken all the guns they needed from the enemy; their desperate need was for cartridges.[10]

Leaders in Guadalajara were devoting most of their attention to the supply problem. In March, González Flores sent Navarrete to Mexico City to demand more help from the LNDLR. In the capital, Navarrete found a well functioning underground traffic in war materials, and within a few weeks he succeeded in dispatching thirty thousand rounds of ammunition to Jalisco. The clandestine network involved an array of people and transport routes. A worker in a cement factory would slip a package of shells into a bag of cement destined for Guadalajara; the owner of a vegetable stand would hide two or three thousand cartridges in crates of cabbages, which would then sail peacefully down the Xochimilco canal to a freight depot, where a railway agent awaiting their arrival would see them safely aboard a train; a vendor peddling *rebozos* a block from the National Palace would sell a certain person one of his creations with a packet of bullets carefully wrapped inside. Most of the supplies went west by regular freight train, often completing the last few kilometers of their journey on the backs of burros.[11] The system was ingenious and efficient, but at best it was woefully inadequate to sustain military operations on the scale the leadership knew was necessary.

Although the rebellion produced new leaders in 1927, it also took a toll of veterans that left permanent voids. The movement

[9] Earl Eaton, Manzanillo, to Consul General, April 25, 1927, NA, RG 59, 812.00/28385.

[10] Navarrete, *Por Dios*, p. 127.

[11] Ibid., pp. 128–130.

gained its first eminent martyr the first day of April. Anacleto
González Flores early in 1927 was the personification of Catholic
militancy in western Mexico. He was the head of the LNDLR in Jalisco, president of the Unión Popular, and a leader of a secret organization called the "U."[12] He was also chief of military operations,
commissioning Cristero officers and laboring to coordinate strategy. Orders for his apprehension had been out since late December, and, as it became evident that he was the kingpin of the rebellion in the west, the government intensified efforts to find him.
In March, agents picked up the trail in León, Guanajuato, where a
young ACJM member inadvertently provided a clue that led to
his capture.[13] At midnight on March 31, combined units of secret
police from Mexico City and city agents from Guadalajara raided
four homes in the Jalisco capital belonging to persons known to
be involved in rebel activity. In one of them, that belonging to Dr.
Antonio Vargas, they found the Maestro. They also arrested the
two Vargas sons, Jorge and Ramón, and Luis Padilla, a close associate of the leader. All four were taken to the Colorado Barracks.
González Flores and two of the others were interrogated under torture throughout the night and early morning. Suspended by their
thumbs and alternately whipped and lacerated with bayonet
points, they gave no information—the Maestro encouraged the
others to remain silent through the ordeal. At noon on April 1, all
four were executed. González Flores's last words were, "I die, but
God does not die. *¡Viva Cristo Rey!*"[14]

[12] Little is known of the "U" except that it was a fiercely Catholic clandestine
group that always refused to sacrifice its independence to other jurisdictions. Its
origins are obscure, but it may have started in Michoacán in the early 1920's.
Throughout the conflict it crossed swords with the LNDLR, despite the fact that
a number of influential leaders, including González Flores and Degollado, belonged to both organizations. The league archive contains many references to the
"U", most of them complaints from the directors that it was undercutting their
authority.
[13] Navarrete, *Por Dios*, pp. 132–133.
[14] Ibid., pp. 133–134; Antonio Gómez Robledo, *Anacleto González Flores: El
Maestro*, pp. 188–189; Andrés Barquín y Ruiz [pseud. Joaquín Blanco Gil], *El
clamor de la sangre*, p. 128. General Ferreira's private secretary said later that
the executions were carried out on Calles's express orders. See José Pérez, "La

The growing list of the rebellion's victims included clergymen as well as laymen. More than a few of the priests who lost their lives were with the rebels, fighting with or without permission of their superiors as combat soldiers or serving as chaplains. Data gathered by the U.S. military attaché placed this number at between sixteen and twenty-one for 1927 alone.[15] But nearly as many more who perished were noncombatants, executed often for little or no reason by local military or civil authorities. Such apparently was the case with Father José Genaro Sánchez of Tecolotlán, Jalisco, who was hanged in January 1927 for refusing to tell where the pastor of the parish was hiding,[16] and Father David Uribe, pastor of Iguala, Guerrero, shot in April allegedly for exercising the ministry without registering as a priest.[17] Another was Father Mateo Correa Magallanes, sixty-two–year–old priest of Valparaíso, Zacatecas, executed in February because, it was said, he would not tell government officers what several Cristeros had told him in confession.[18] Sadly indicative of the ferocious passions the conflict provoked is the fact that such executions were frequently accompanied by torture and mutilation of the victims. Father Sabás Reyes, a Jalisco priest who refused to reveal the whereabouts of another clergyman sought by the military, was suspended for three days from

---

muerte del Gral. Ferreira: Quién era este jefe fallecido," *Hoy*, February 19, 1928, p. 30. See also Andrés Barquín y Ruiz, *Los mártires de Cristo Rey*, I, 248–249.

[15] G-2 report, no. 2077, Col. Alexander Macnab, Jr., May 22, 1928, NA, RG 165. Jean A. Meyer, in "La Christiade: Société et idéologie dans le Mexique contemporain," II, 542, calculates that between 1926 and 1929 fifteen priests were chaplains, and twenty-five more were otherwise involved, five of whom actually took up arms. He estimates that a total of ninety were executed during the rebellion (II, 553).

[16] See Barquín y Ruiz [pseud. Blanco Gil], *El clamor de la sangre*, p. 51. The source is admittedly biased in the extreme, and particular incidents he relates must be taken as suggestive rather than accurate in all details. But that atrocities occurred there can be no doubt. Some local commanders proceeded on the assumption that all clerics were preforce rebels.

[17] Ibid., pp. 137–138.

[18] Ibid., pp. 68–69.

a portico of his church and jabbed with bayonets by soldiers, who finally cut off the soles of his feet and then forced him to walk to the cemetery, where they shot him.[19] In all, some eighteen non-combatant priests were executed during 1927, eight of them in Jalisco.[20] The number grew as the rebellion dragged on.

The priests' superiors, the bishops, escaped such dire fates, but most of them were as effectively removed from the scene in 1927. It happened in the wake of violence.

The afternoon train for Mexico City left Guadalajara on schedule Tuesday, April 19. Like most trains in recent months, it carried a military escort. Around 8:30 P.M., at a point just north of La Barca, Jalisco, it derailed when it struck a section of roadbed where the track had been torn up. It was immediately attacked by a large force of Cristero guerrillas. The troops on the train returned the fire, and there ensued a general action which ended when the defenders were overwhelmed. The Cristeros then collected over 100,-000 pesos being shipped to Mexico City in the baggage car, set fire to the train, and departed.[21] In all, some 150 passengers and soldiers perished.[22]

The incident roused a tempest of charges and countercharges. An official of the Ministry of War and Marine claimed that priests had led the attack and that the assailants, after killing the escort, had butchered some of the passengers and left the wounded in the coaches to be burned alive.[23] A Calles aide said that the barbarous behavior of "this clerical gang" was typical of methods the Catholic church had employed since the Inquisition. He added that the

[19] Ibid., pp. 138–141.

[20] G-2 report, no. 2077, Col. Alexander Macnab, Jr., May 22, 1928, NA, RG 165. The U.S. military attaché reported that a total of between thirty-five and forty priests, combatant and noncombatant, were killed during 1927.

[21] Antonio Ríus Facius, *Méjico cristero: Historia de la ACJM, 1925 a 1931*, pp. 214–215; *New York Times*, April 22, 1927; *El Universal*, April 21, 1927.

[22] *New York Times*, April 22, 1927. The *Times*'s Mexico City correspondent reported deaths of 100 passengers and 48 soldiers.

[23] *El Universal*, April 21, 1927. Ríus Facius (*Méjico cristero*, p. 214) says Father José Reyes Vega commanded the operation.

priests involved "receive instructions from the Episcopate in this capital."[24] The LNDLR, in a hand-distributed bulletin, insisted that the troop escort had used the passengers as shields and that after the battle the attackers had treated the noncombatants correctly. However, the statement continued, even if the Cristeros had been guilty of excesses, it ill behove a government that had perpetrated horrible crimes for years, of which the brutal death of González Flores was a recent example, to be scandalized at atrocities. The clergy, it added, was with few exceptions not involved in the armed struggle, and none received orders from the bishops.[25] Ruiz y Flores, speaking for the Episcopal Committee, denied episcopal responsibility for the assault and said the bishops had organized no rebellion; the alleged cruelties, if true, were deplorable, but the guilt belonged to "those who have provoked this situation."[26]

While argument raged, the government took extraordinary measures. On the afternoon of April 21, police arrested Ruiz y Flores, Mora y del Río, and four other prelates.[27] At the Ministry of Gobernación they were confronted by Adalberto Tejeda, who accused them of being responsible for crime and bloodshed and of fomenting and directing the rebellion. Mora y del Río was defiant. He rejected the charges, but said that the armed movement was justified; the bishops were not directing the Catholics in arms, "but we approve of them and bless them." Tejeda ended the interview

[24] *El Universal*, April 21, 1927.

[25] League Bulletin No. 28, April 30, 1927, enclosed in Sheffield to SecState, May 10, 1927, NA, RG 59, 812.404/791. The *New York Times* reports tended to support the league version; they quoted passengers as saying that the high loss of life was due to the escort's entering the passenger cars and fighting from there. The survivors did say that, although the assailants ordered the passengers out of the cars before setting them afire, some of the wounded were unable to crawl to safety and perished inside. The *Times* also reported that the Cristeros robbed the passengers as well as the baggage car (April 21, 1927; April 22, 1927).

[26] Sheffield to SecState, April 26, 1927, NA, RG 59, 812.404/780. Sheffield enclosed a copy of the statement, which he said was not printed in the press because of censorship.

[27] Sheffield to SecState, April 23, 1927, NA, RG 59, 812.404/799. The four bishops were Valdespino of Aguascalientes, Echavarría of Saltillo, Anaya of Chiapas, and Uranga of Cuernavaca.

by telling the six that the government was expelling them from Mexico.[28]

At 9:00 P.M., guarded by federal agents, the prelates boarded a train leaving Mexico City.[29] Gobernación issued a statement saying that the bishops, confronted with evidence of their guilt, had chosen to leave the country rather than stand trial.[30] At Nuevo Laredo, U.S. Consul Harry Walsh met the exiles and accompanied them across the international boundary. They told U.S. newsmen that they had not left Mexico voluntarily and that they had been given no choice.[31]

But the departure of the six was only the beginning. The next day Archbishop Pedro Vera y Zuria of Puebla and the government's long-time bane, Manríquez y Zárate of Huejutla, also arrived at the border under police escort.[32] During the next few weeks the expulsions continued until, by the end of May, only a handful of bishops remained in Mexico—in hiding, either in their own dioceses, like Orozco y Jiménez and Amador Velasco of Colima, or in private homes in Mexico City. The Episcopal Committee henceforth convened in San Antonio, Texas.[33]

The expulsion of Mexico's spiritual leaders was the government's doing. The Catholic insurgents themselves removed their

[28] The conversation was quoted in League Bulletin No. 28 of April 30, 1927 (LA-1), which claimed to have an eye-witness account of the interview.

[29] Sheffield to SecState, April 23, 1927, NA, RG 59, 812.404/779.

[30] *Excélsior*, April 23, 1927.

[31] *New York Times*, April 24, 1927.

[32] Walsh to SecState, April 24, 1927, NA, RG 59, 812.404/776; Walsh to Sheffield, April 26, 1927, NA, RG 59, 812.404/795.

[33] Walsh to SecState, May 11, 1927, NA, RG 59, 812.404/786; May 13, 1927, NA, RG 59, 812.404/790; May 24, 1927, NA, RG 59, 812.404/794; *New York Times*, May 14, 1927. The expulsions were only one of a number of steps that added up to a general toughening of the government's stance after the train incident. Many Catholics, lay and clerical, were arrested in late April and early May, and in border towns Mexican officials put a stop to Mexicans' crossing the border to attend Sunday Mass in the United States—the government said these persons had been receiving seditious propaganda across the boundary. See, for example, Sheffield to SecState, May 3, 1927, NA, RG 59, 812.404/782; Vice Consul Oscar C. Harper, Piedras Negras, to SecState, June 2, 1927, NA, RG 59, 812.404/803.

own chief, René Capistrán Garza. By April there was widespread dissatisfaction with him. There were whispers that he was getting rich in the United States. Some complained that he had surrounded himself with impulsive and erratic advisers. The LNDLR directors tried to counter the criticism, but their own confidence in the Supreme Chief had worn thin, and at length they decided something must be done. Luis G. Bustos, first vice-president of the Directive Committee, agreed to go to the United States to assess the situation.[34] He carried with him full authority to act for the league, as well as pointed instructions for Capistrán Garza: René must enter Mexico; further delay would weaken his prestige and demoralize the cause; he must not wait until he secured funds; a second major offensive was in the offing, and Capistrán Garza must be personally part of it.[35]

Bustos left Mexico City in disguise and crossed the border without incident; and on May 21 the directors received his first report. It was not encouraging. Bustos told his colleagues that René had alienated persons who sincerely wanted to help him, while others who were uncommitted had tried to get interviews with him but had not even received replies. Bustos said some of the Mexican bishops were listening to René's enemies.[36] On the twenty-first Bustos wrote from New York, where he had met with Capistrán Garza. The failure to move, he said, was partly the fault of René and his group, partly not—he did comment that their vision was a bit limited.[37] But by now the league directors were entirely out of patience. They replied on June 1 that they deduced from Bustos's reports that Capistrán Garza and his associates were still working exclusively on financial matters and that in this they had failed; they would not even be surprised if René went off to Europe in search of money, leaving the beleaguered fighters in Mexico to perish.[38]

[34] Ceniceros y Villarreal, "Historia."
[35] Directive Committee to Luis G. Bustos, May 3, 1927, with memorandum appended, LA-1.
[36] Ceniceros y Villarreal, "Historia."
[37] Bustos to Directive Committee, May 21, 1927, LA-1.
[38] Directive Committee to Bustos, June 1, 1927, LA-1.

Matters now came rapidly to a head. Capistrán Garza received a report that Emmanuel Amor, his agent in Washington, had approached the Mexican Embassy to ask aid in opening access to the U.S. government. He asked Bustos to repudiate Amor publicly. Instead, Bustos wired Amor, saying he refused to believe the report and asking for details. Capistrán Garza was irked at Bustos' refusal to follow his advice and said so. Bustos told him to calm down, that he would handle the matter, whereupon Capistrán Garza submitted his resignation—which Bustos refused to accept.[39] At this point Dr. José Mesa Gutiérrez, a league official whom the directors had sent from Mexico City to assist Bustos, and Father Rafael Martínez del Campo, a long-time league adviser, invited René to San Antonio for a talk. By the time he reached Texas, his spirits had revived. He brought news that the Brady matter once again looked promising: the Bishops' Commission in Rome had just informed him that Monsignor Bernardini, an official at the Apostolic Delegation in Washington and a nephew of Cardinal Gasparri, was intervening to urge Brady to support the cause. De la Peza had written to Brady enclosing a copy of the bishops' letter and asking for an interview.[40] Capistrán Garza now said he was willing to continue as head of the movement inside Mexico; he would cross the border soon. This, however, was not agreeable to Bustos, who had joined the group in San Antonio. After protracted discussion, he and Capistrán Garza sent a joint memorandum to the Directive Committee. Bustos proposed that Capistrán Garza continue at the head of the movement but that his actions be subject to Bustos's approval. Capistrán Garza said that he could not agree to this. He admitted that he had not been taken seriously in the United States (Bustos, he added, had been well received there) but insisted he was entirely capable of carrying out his duties as head of the revolt

[39] "Informe del Dr. Mesa Gutiérrez al Comité Directivo de la Liga, en la sesión plenaria del 3 de julio de 1927," cited in Ríus Facius, *Méjico cristero*, pp. 208–209.

[40] Ríus Facius, *Méjico cristero*, pp. 209, 210 n. Presumably Bernardini was acting on instructions from higher authority, but from whom is not clear, nor is there any record available of exactly what he told Brady.

in Mexico.[41] But the closing days of June saw the collapse of Capistrán Garza's motives for optimism. After meeting with de la
Peza, Brady wrote that he had decided definitely not to proceed
with the matter.[42]

Mesa Gutiérrez returned to Mexico City on July 3 and went immediately into conference with the Directive Committee and several advisers. The session was a frank review of the entire situation,
both foreign and domestic, and the tone was generally doleful: the
league's diplomatic and financial gestures in the United States had
come to nought. The military effort, lacking money, organization,
and adequate planning, had been essentially a failure to date.
There were a few heartening items: both the pope and Gasparri
seemed wholly sympathetic to the league, and there were reports
that Pascual Díaz had not been well received in Rome. Bustos had
persuaded the El Paso junta to adhere to the league and to place
its funds at the league's disposal. Finally the discussion turned to
Capistrán Garza, of whom Mesa Gutiérrez was sharply critical.
After much debate it was decided to accept his resignation from the
leadership both in the United States and in Mexico.[43]

It was the end of the young leader's short revolutionary career,
although he continued to profess loyalty to the cause and even performed a few minor tasks in its behalf. Palomar y Vizcarra wrote
to González Valencia that René's separation was due to his impetu-
ous character, a certain deficiency of temperament, and his failure to enter Mexico when battle was raging; he also blamed Capistrán Garza's adviser, Amor, for misleading him regarding the
views of the American government.[44]

In the eyes of the directors and others, Capistrán Garza's exclusive preoccupation with finance had been a mistake, but they realized that failure to get money could be fatal to the effort. The

[41] Bustos and Capistrán Garza to Directive Committee, June 29, 1927, LA-1.

[42] Brady to de la Peza, June 27, 1927, cited in Alberto María Carreño, *El
arzobispo de México, excmo. Sr. Dr. D. Pascual Díaz y el conflicto religioso*, p.
286.

[43] "Resumen de lo que se dijo en la junta del 3 de julio de 1927," LA-1.

[44] Palomar y Vizcarra to González Valencia, September 22, 1927, LA-1.

league had made imaginative attempts. Early in 1927 it initiated a campaign to raise funds by selling bonds. In March, league personnel were circulating them in Mexico, and by May they were trying to sell them in Europe.[45] These efforts apparently failed to produce significant results. There was, however, a source of cash that league leaders had been eyeing for some time: the bishops. Early in June, in one of his frequent letters to Archbishop González Valencia, Palomar y Vizcarra said that the pope should order the Mexican bishops to give all they had or controlled to the cause; if they did so, Church dignitaries in other countries would also give. The league, he said, knew that several Mexican dioceses had large sums deposited in U.S. banks.[46]

After the Brady negotiation collapsed in June, the spotlight turned directly and glaringly to the bishops. On June 30 Luis Bustos addressed a long letter to the Episcopal Committee. The essential ingredient needed to propel the movement forward, he said, was money; without it the movement would die, and if that happened, religion would be dead in Mexico for many years and perhaps forever. The league had done everything possible to secure funds, but at the moment its efforts must be counted a failure. In Mexico money was scarce, he stated, and the wealthy were selfish. Potential donors were understandably afraid of persecution. Private individuals and groups in the United States, including the oilmen, had made it clear they would not contribute without some indication of approval from the State Department. A benevolent attitude did exist in Washington, Bustos insisted, but it would not show itself until the movement inside Mexico gave substantial signs of success. The only hope left, Bustos concluded, was the Mexican episcopate. Since the prelates had suspended public worship and acquiesced in the resort to arms, they surely understood the necessity of seeing matters through to the end; furthermore, "it

[45] See, for example, Juan Farías, Monterrey, to Directive Committee, March 21, 1927; Directive Committee to Luz Goríbar de Philippe, May 30, 1927; Palomar y Vizcarra to Father David G. Ramírez, June 2, 1927; LA-1.

[46] Palomar y Vizcarra to González Valencia, June 6, 1927, LA-1.

is known to be the desire of the Holy Father that the episcopate actively help the League." It was also known, Bustos went on, that the Mexican bishops had money in Mexico, the United States, and Canada. Now was the time to use it. It was time also to sell the sacred vessels—eminent theologians in Rome had already been consulted on this and had acquiesced. As for the need of the bishops to stay out of partisan politics, he asserted, the league did not see this as a serious obstacle; the movement was a heroic act of popular resistance, not the action of a political party. The entire matter, he assured the prelates, would be kept secret. Specifically, the league needed $500,000—$200,000 within two weeks, the rest within a month.[47]

The bishops replied four days later. They told Bustos that they could dispose of ecclesiastical funds and property only if ordered or authorized by the Holy See.[48] Bustos answered immediately, asking the Episcopal Committee to apply for the necessary permission and adding that the league would also work to obtain the mandate needed from the pope.[49]

On July 10 Mora y del Río wrote to Valverde y Téllez in Rome that the bishops were meeting the next day to act on the league's request that they approach the Holy See. The primate was obviously uneasy; the league seemed to believe, he said, that the Church in Mexico had preserved great wealth, while the fact was that, after being plundered for eighty years, it had very little left; and to comply with the league's plea for financial help would be to endanger even that. If all available resources were turned over to the league, would they really and effectively serve to help? And when it all became known, as was bound to happen, what then would be the episcopate's predicament?[50]

There followed some diligent episcopal side-stepping. In a re-

[47] Bustos to Episcopal Committee, June 30, 1927, LA-1.
[48] Gerardo Anaya to Bustos, July 4, 1927, LA-1. Anaya, bishop of Chiapas, was serving as secretary to the Episcopal Committee.
[49] Bustos to Anaya, July 10, 1927, LA-1.
[50] Mora y del Río to Valverde y Téllez, July 10, 1927, LA-1.

port to the apostolic delegate, Mora y del Río said that the bishops would do as Rome might direct in the matter, but he wished to point out a number of considerations. The few holdings left to the Church were in general either subject to the will of the donors or earmarked for the maintenance of diocesan offices, seminaries, and charitable institutions. It was not true that there existed vessels and other religious treasures worth millions of pesos; what there were, if worth 100.000 pesos, would bring only a fraction of that if mortgaged or sold. Chalices, vestments, ornaments, images, and the like were either in the hands of village Indians, who would never part with them, or were hidden in private homes, where attempts to get them could seriously endanger those who had undertaken to hide them—and, even if this were attempted, it would take months to complete such an operation. As for the bishops making themselves collectively responsible for a loan—another move the league was suggesting—this would require express approval of the Holy See and the acquiescence of each bishop. The amount so raised would surely fall short of the league's needs, which were very large indeed. And finally, he argued, for the bishops to contribute financially would hurt the movement because it would heighten its religious complexion and thereby weaken chances of attracting official U.S. support. He said that he and fifteen other bishops, two of whom dissented somewhat from the view of the rest, opposed meeting the league's request for money.[51]

On July 11 Bustos wrote to González Valencia urging his help in getting Vatican permission for the bishops to act,[52] González Valencia, ever the staunch supporter of the league, replied at once, congratulating Bustos on his efforts and urging him to hold firm.[53]

What happened to the various communications in Rome is not known, but evidently the Holy See gave no formal instructions in the matter. Ruiz y Flores later said that the bishops were amazed when Bustos told them the pope wanted them to help financially.

[51] Cited in Carreño, El arzobispo de México, pp. 100–105.
[52] Ibid., pp. 106–107.
[53] Ibid., p. 107.

They learned later, he said, that one of the Mexican bishops in Rome had written the league that some cardinal or theologian had said the bishops should contribute, and that the league interpreted this as a papal order.[54] Ceniceros y Villarreal said that when the Bishops' Commission in Rome received Bustos' request for assistance, Valverde y Téllez and Méndez del Río talked with Cardinal Buenaventura Cerretti, who told them that Gasparri said yes to the whole matter, provided the funds in question were not already designated for another purpose, such as trust funds for Masses; that moreover the secretary of state had said that if he were a Mexican bishop he would sell all his personal effects to back the effort.[55] It was a consoling comment, if true, but not an order.

The money matter showed the degree to which the LNDLR and the episcopate had drawn apart. To smile on the probable success of an armed movement in November was one thing, but to invest in "the League's armed movement" (as Mora y del Río now called it) in June when it looked far less likely to succeed was something else. The bishops still hoped fervently that Calles would fall. Some of them, individually, continued to help the league and the Cristeros. But, if the revolt were quashed, they were determined collectively not to be drawn under with the wreckage. The Church's material interests were at stake, but so also was the entire ecclesiastical structure in Mexico. They were, if somewhat belatedly, moving to regain autonomy of action.

The league, in turn, in its search for support, was being made more aware of the basic problem of its nature. It was by its own definition a civic association, but it was also essentially Catholic. Victory would perhaps make it unnecessary to face the implications of this duality, but adversity magnified them. As a Catholic body it had appealed to the episcopate for aid; but because it was pursuing a politico-military program whose failure would redound on the bishops if they were too closely identified with the effort, aid had been refused. The failure to attract American support, on the

[54] Leopoldo Ruiz y Flores, *Recuerdo de recuerdos*, p. 88.
[55] Ceniceros y Villarreal, "Historia."

other hand, had stemmed in large part, so many believed, from the movement's appearing to be exclusively Catholic. Beginning in the summer of 1927, important league leaders groped for a solution. Bustos and others decided that, if the price of U.S. recognition and support was a change in the movement's image, they would pay it.

In July plans to effect the transformation began to take shape. José Luis Orozco, secretary to the Directive Committee, wrote to Miguel Gómez Loza (who had replaced González Flores as the league's chief agent in the west) that it was possible and even probable that, "without changing fundamentals, there will be some variations in our program, with the exclusive object of securing the favor and good will of the U.S."[56] On July 31 Bustos met in New York with Alberto María Carreño, whom the directors had dispatched to the United States in June, and José Ortiz Monasterio, a league military adviser.[57] The three approved a manifesto drafted by Carreño which outlined the formation of a new political party for Mexico, to be called the National Union (Unión Nacional). A tentative party program included in the document proclaimed the reinstitution of the Constitution of 1857, minus provisions that conflicted with the bishops' September, 1926, memorial to Congress. It affirmed the need to improve the lot of the industrial worker and the *campesino*, without injury to the legitimate interests of capital or of rural property; it guaranteed freedom of conscience, education, and the press, and promised free elections and the enforcement of the no-re-election principle. Finally, it pledged that the party would seek an agreement with the U.S. government which would in no way prejudice national dignity and independence.[58]

Five days later the trio informed Pascual Díaz of their work.

[56] Orozco to Gómez Loza, July 23, 1927, LA-1.

[57] Ortiz Monasterio was a federal general uunder Porfirio Díaz. Carreño, a professor, had previously expressed reservations concerning league policy and later became a bitter opponent of the militant position.

[58] Memorandum dated July 31, 1927, LA-1; Ríus Facius, *Méjico cristero*, p. 221.

Díaz was delighted: the project harmonized with views he had held for months. He agreed to communicate it to the other bishops.[59] The three also asked him to help them get the plan before the U.S. government. Díaz conferred with the apostolic delegate, who was also impressed with the plan and immediately designated "certain persons" to communicate the matter to the State Department and ascertain whether the U.S. government would thwart the work of such a movement. The intermediaries reported that the department found the proposal extremely interesting and that, of the many plans it had seen to reorganize Mexico, no other was as complete and well thought out.[60] Perhaps, at last, the right formula had been found.

Ceniceros y Villarreal and Palomar y Vizcarra accepted the program unenthusiastically. They feared it would demoralize Catholics and jeopardize the league's control of the "armed defense." Palomar y Vizcarra in particular cringed at the idea of resurrecting the 1857 constitution.[61] Bustos, however, was complacent. To him the creation of the Unión Nacional was a ploy and nothing more. He explained to González Valencia, with amazing candor, that the league would continue to function as usual in Mexico, while in the United States the movement would appear to be a true national coalition. In that way, "without crippling in the least, without silencing the cry of *Viva Cristo Rey*, we will throw dust in the eyes of Washington and of the Mexican public . . ."[62]

By October, preparations for initiating the new party were well advanced. On the eleventh Bustos forwarded to the directors various documents and memoranda relative to the planning that had been done. He had also sent details to the Episcopal Committee and

[59] Statement signed August 5, 1927, by Bustos, Carreño, and Ortiz Monasterio, LA-1.

[60] "Memorándum cronológico para el Sr. Alfredo Méndez," June 19, 1928, signed by Carreño, LA-1; Carreño, *El arzobispo de México*, pp. 342–343. Díaz said the intermediaries (unidentified) had dealt with the under secretary of state (Díaz to de la Mora, May 30, 1928, LA-1).

[61] Palomar y Vizcarra to González Valencia, September 22, 1927, LA-1.

[62] Bustos to González Valencia, July 22, 1927. Copy in possession of Antonio Ríus Facius.

to the Bishops' Commission in Rome.[63] With the groundwork laid, he hurried to Mexico to help inaugurate the new body.

The Unión Nacional was formally launched at a meeting in Mexico City on November 11, chaired by Bustos. The party's platform was largely a restatement of principles advocated by the National Catholic party of the previous decade. The program called for enactment of advanced social legislation—laws to protect organized labor and insure decent working conditions, to protect women in industry, to provide pensions for the elderly, and to provide industrial accident insurance. It advocated the division of large landholdings (with just compensation for owners and respect for the rights of private property). The party pledged to uphold "mutual and effective" independence of Church and State and guaranteed the right of all religious denominations to own and administer property. It affirmed its devotion to the principles of effective suffrage and no re-election and promised to defend all national interests, with due respect for the principles of international law. The Constitution of 1857 was declared re-established, with the proviso that it would be amended to guarantee freedom of conscience and association, incorporating the principles contained in the September, 1926, petitions to Congress.[64] The November 11 gathering constituted itself the "National Assembly of the Unión Nacional" and nominated a triumvirate to head a provisional government to serve in the interim after Calles's overthrow. Chosen were José Ortiz Monasterio, representing the *porfirista* persuasion; Emilio Madero, a younger brother of Francisco, representing the revolution; and Bartolomé Ontiveros, the league's military chairman, to represent the "civic-religious rebirth." Since none of the three was present, the assembly made provision to inform them and obtain their acceptance. At the end of the evening the assembly voted itself out of existence and disbanded.[65] Bustos

[63] Bustos to Directive Committee, October 11, 1927; "Memorándum cronológico."

[64] Minutes of the meeting of the National Assembly, November 11, 1927; draft project for the Unión Nacional; LA-1.

[65] Ortiz Monasterio evidently agreed to join the triumvirate, but sources are silent on the other two. See Palomar y Vizcarra to Bustos, October 3, 1927, LA-1.

returned immediately to the United States, where he hoped to make rapid and effective use of the new tool in both official and private circles.[66]

While the LNDLR maneuvered to gain American support, the Cristeros held on grimly in the face of mounting government attacks. Immediately after the train incident in April, the army sharply intensified efforts to stamp out the rebellion. In Jalisco the first step was a drastic one: planes dropped leaflets over rural areas of Los Altos announcing orders for a "reconcentration" of the civilian populace; inhabitants of areas affected by rebel activity were directed to abandon the countryside by May 3 and move into fifteen designated towns.[67] Four thousand additional cavalry moved into the state,[68] and an offensive was launched the first week of May. On May 11 the general staff announced that the rebels had suffered heavy casualties the past week and that most of the important "episcopal bands" were in full flight.[69] The same source said on May 23 that the insurgents in Los Altos had been scattered and that many had surrendered.[70] Secretary of War Amaro, who was on the scene supervising the drive, announced the last week of May that the campaign was nearly over.[71] U.S. Consul Dudley G. Dwyre in Guadalajara was more cautious in his estimate of things, saying that news from the combat areas was conflicting, although the government appeared to be making headway. The campaign, he said, had been merciless and had wrought heavy destruction; many or most of the crops were ruined, and suffering was widespread. He noted that four priests had been executed in the past few days and that there were rumors of many more.[72]

In Colima the federal onslaught drove the rebellion to the brink of dissolution. The Cristeros abandoned Caucentla in a retreat that

[66] "Memorándum cronológico."

[67] Rafael Martínez Camarena, "Rectificando al Mayor Heriberto Navarrete," David 5, no. 120 (July 22, 1962): 388–391; New York Times, April 25, 1927.

[68] New York Times, April 28, 1927.

[69] El Universal, May 12, 1927.

[70] Ibid., May 24, 1927.

[71] New York Times, May 27, 1927.

[72] Dwyre, Guadalajara, to SecState, May 26, 1927, NA, RG 59, 812.404/799.

turned into a rout as hundreds of terrified women, children, and old men who had taken refuge in the encampment tried to flee with the rebels. The survivors regrouped at Zapotitlán, across the Jalisco border. Their ammunition nearly exhausted, under constant attack through May, they scattered in tiny handfuls to conceal themselves in the mountainous terrain. In June, Amaro transferred cavalry units to the region for what he hoped was a final mopping up. Cristero chief Dionisio Eduardo Ochoa, however, managed to forestall total collapse, and slowly the hungry and demoralized remnants of his command reassembled on the volcano's slopes.[73]

By early summer the rebellion had suffered signal reverses almost everywhere, but stubborn cores of resistance were still intact, even in areas where government pressure had been heaviest. There were clashes between federals and rebels throughout the summer in Jalisco. El Catorce, with around three hundred men, ranged through Los Altos and periodically punished pursuing federals. Many Jalisco Cristeros moved to Nayarit, hitherto little affected by the rebellion, where they bedeviled mining camps and interrupted rail transportation. Cristeros were active in the states of México and Morelos. The Durango Cristeros continued to be moderately active, and in northwestern Michoacán there were sizable engagements in August, when rebels attacked Coalcomán and Zitácuaro.[74]

The death of Anacleto González Flores led to a shakeup in both the civil and military commands in the west. On April 26 the LNDLR Directive Committee appointed Miguel Gómez Loza provisional governor of Jalisco and Antonio Ruiz Rueda special representative of the War Committee.[75] The league also named Jesús Degollado Guízar chief of operations in southern Jalisco with jurisdiction in Nayarit and western Michoacán. Degollado, a fervent Catholic, was born in Michoacán in 1892. He settled in Atotonilco

[73] Enrique de Jesús Ochoa [pseud. Spectator], *Los cristeros del Volcán de Colima*, I, 224–301; G-2 report, no. 1604, Thompson, July 19, 1927, NA, RG 165.

[74] G-2 report, no. 1710, Thompson, September 9, 1927, NA, RG 165.

[75] Gómez Loza to Directive Committee, July 13, 1927; González Pacheco to Gómez Loza, July 23, 1927; LA-1.

el Alto, Jalisco, and became a successful pharmaceutical dealer. He was an early member of the ACJM and active in Catholic lay organizational work. In 1923 he backed Adolfo de la Huerta in the hope that Catholics might gain surcease under a government headed by Obregón's one-time comrade. Degollado accepted his new commission reluctantly, but his performance lacked nothing in vigor and effectiveness.[76]

A major concern of the new commander was discipline. Cristero units that had withstood the spring offensive were disorganized and disheartened, and some of them had taken to victimizing noncombatants. Degollado implemented a tighter command system, then issued a warning that any individual found guilty of marauding would be shot. In practice he employed less dramatic devices, as in the case of Esteban Caro, a sector chief whose depredations had alienated local civilian supporters. Degollado exacted a pledge of good conduct and assigned a priest to counsel Caro's unruly troops.[77] There was no further trouble, and Caro later died honorably in combat.

Late in the summer Heriberto Navarrete joined the Cristeros in the hills of Los Altos, and later he recorded his impressions of the crusaders. The outfit he enlisted in was led by "Chema" Huerta, a Unión Popular leader, and numbered some 150 men. Initially, Navarrete was disillusioned: "Poorly clad, filthy, their hair matted with sweat and dirt, the horses' equipment and their cartridge belts dirty, they spent most of the day stretched out under the trees. . ." Their chief was no more prepossessing, in his torn shirt and khaki trousers, a .38 revolver hanging from his cartridge belt, and religious medals ("like sordid badges of misery") hanging from his neck. Food, Navarrete found, was adequate but not choice. Like most of the other rebels, Huerta's men lived mainly on the charity of sympathetic inhabitants of the region. The staple, of which there

---

[76] José Gutiérrez Gutiérrez, "El General Degollado Guízar: Breves apuntes histórico-biográficos sobre la noble figura," *David* 3, no. 63 (October 22, 1957): 235–240.

[77] Jesús Degollado Guízar, *Memorias de Jesús Degollado Guízar, último general en jefe del ejército cristero*, pp. 113–116.

was usually enough, was beef, which the men dried until it had the appearance and texture of leather. This was supplemented sporadically by tortillas, beans, biscuits, and now and then some milk or cheese. Navarrete was bothered by the neglect of such routine military procedures as scouting and posting sentinels, but he soon came to admire the band's ability to operate in tight situations. The leadership, Navarrete finally decided, was in general mature, in many ways competent, and above all full of faith in final victory. The ranks were simple and honest men not given to sophisticated analysis: "They were soldiers of a new army and their enemies were allies of the devil, persecutors of religion, and Masons. That was enough. They would fight as hard as necessary. Just give them something to fight with."[78]

As rebellion settled over western Mexico early in 1927, former President Alvaro Obregón, already an undeclared candidate to succeed Calles for a second term in 1928, decided to try personal mediation to end the Church-State conflict.[79] His efforts failed, but they brought forth a clearer definition of positions.

Obregón arrived in Mexico City on February 25 aboard the presidential train. Calles and top government officials met him at the station and accompanied him to Chapultepec Castle. There began a round of banquets in honor of the revolutionary hero. Three weeks later, in the midst of his busy schedule, Obregón moved quietly into the religious controversy. On March 16, working through Eduardo Mestre, who had arranged the August meeting between Calles and the bishops, he contacted the Episcopal Committee and asked it to send a representative to meet with him.[80] The conference took place several days later, with Ruiz y Flores and Ignacio Valdespino of Aguascalientes representing the hierarchy. Obregón asked the bishops for a written statement of their terms for a settlement. When they handed one to him (its contents are not known), Obregón characterized it as "intransigent" and

[78] Navarrete, *Por Dios*, pp. 141–149.

[79] On January 22 Calles promulgated a constitutional amendment that allowed a former president to serve again after an intervening term.

[80] Ríus Facius, *Méjico cristero*, pp. 213–214.

said he would not even show it to the president. The next day he asked to meet with some bishop who had not participated in the 1926 talks with Calles. The prelates detailed Manuel Fulcheri of Zamora, who conferred with Obregón early on the morning of March 23 on the terrace at Chapultepec. Obregón proposed that public worship resume at once and that the episcopate trust the government to pursue a reasonable course in religious matters. Fulcheri refused to agree, and the meeting ended. Calles wired the state governors that Obregón's negotiations had failed because of the obstinacy of the bishops, "who are asking a return to the situation they were in before the Laws of Reform."[81]

The LNDLR was upset when it learned of the interviews. The Directive Committee suspected that the bishops might conclude some arrangement that would betray the Catholic resistance movement. Palomar y Vizcarra wrote to González Valencia that the negotiations had caused confusion and bitterness in the ranks of dedicated Catholics.[82] Ruiz y Flores, however, put the matter quite differently in a letter to Pascual Díaz: The league, he said, seemed to believe that the bishops were obliged to consult it before making any move, and had even threatened to place full blame on the episcopate if the armed movement should fail.[83] The bishops ignored the impertinence; even as Ruiz y Flores wrote, they were once more entertaining peace proposals.

On June 25 Obregón made his long-expected announcement that he would run for president in 1928. His statement, in essence his campaign platform, included lengthy references to the Catholic opposition to the revolution. The religious conflict, he said, had been provoked the previous year by the clergy, who thought that Calles would not dare to face up to them. They had supposed that the revolution could be intimidated by its adversaries, whose headquarters were in Rome and Wall Street. The clergy, he charged,

---

[81] Ibid., p. 214; Carreño, *El arzobispo de México*, pp. 159–163.

[82] Palomar y Vizcarra to González Valencia, March 28, 1927, LA-1.

[83] Ruiz y Flores to Díaz, July 26, 1927, cited in Carreño, *El arzobispo de México*, p. 160.

had fomented rebellion.[84] In other speeches during the summer Obregón hammered at the same theme. Then, late in August, his remarks took on an even harsher tone. Unscrupulous agitators, he told a meeting in Ciudad General Terán, Nuevo León, had encouraged fanaticism, "because they know that fanaticism is the best anesthetic for atrophying the spirits of those who suffer, offering them in the next life the well-being they do not have the character to give them in this life. Fanaticism . . . allows them to deny liberty and well-being: it is the anesthetic capital uses, and we still remember the rural priest on the hacienda whose duty it was to tell the peons: 'Work without rest, work diligently, work, and suffer hunger, cold, and sun, for after your share of earthly afflictions you will enjoy the glory of eternal life.' "[85]

The shift in tone from sternness to asperity was doubtless a reaction to events that had transpired a few weeks before. Early in August rumors were circulating that Obregón was again trying to end the religious war. *Excélsior* for August 7 said that Aarón Sáenz, governor-elect of Nuevo León and an Obregón intimate, had visited the bishops in Texas. Both Sáenz and Archbishop Mora y del Río, the report added, had refused comment.[86] On the eighth Calles told newsmen that the laws on religion would not be changed, that he had authorized no move to invite the bishops back, and that he did not believe Sáenz had extended any such invitation; the bishops could return only when they agreed to observe the law and obey the authorities. Obregón indignantly denied that he was involved in any intrigues with the episcopate.[87]

But talks had taken place. Late in July, with Eduardo Mestre again acting as go-between, Sáenz—with Calles's "tacit approval" —had conferred secretly with the bishops in San Antonio. After the meeting Mestre drew up a statement of positions, which Calles

[84] Statement of June 25, 1927, in Aarón Sáenz, Fernando Torreblanca, and Joaquín Amaro, eds., *Discursos del General Alvaro Obregón*, II, 80.

[85] Speech in Ciudad General Terán, August 27, 1928, in Sáenz, Torreblanca, and Amaro, eds., *Discursos*, pp. 248–249.

[86] *Excélsior*, August 7, 1927.

[87] Ibid., August 9, 1927.

approved. It said simply that the registration of priests was a formality, that the government would not interfere in religious matters, and that the bishops would not hinder the civil authorities in their task of governing Mexico. Mestre told the bishops that the settlement would be a gentleman's agreement, without formal documentation. The bishops were receptive, but they wanted to alter the draft slightly before referring it to Rome. Obregón objected to changes, and, while Mestre was trying to obtain agreement, news reports began to appear and contacts were broken off.[88]

Although the feelers died aborning, word of them prompted the Holy See to indicate its position at that point in the conflict. Upon receipt of a letter from Mora y del Río reporting the overture, the Bishop's Commission met with the pope and Gasparri. The pope laid down guidelines: if emissaries asked to see the bishops, they should be received and listened to noncommittally; if their proposals showed no indications of containing anything different from previous ones, the contact should be ended; if they were worthy of consideration, then the emissaries should be requested to produce credentials; if these were valid, the bishops should then ask for the proposals in writing; if provided, these should then be passed on to each bishop and to the LNDLR for their written opinions; both the proposals and the opinions were then to be forwarded to Rome for a final decision.[89]

The Vatican, then, hoped to get more favorable terms than those offered by Obregón in March. To leave the objectionable statutes on the books, with the Church relying on the good will of the government, was unacceptable. The Holy See wanted a de jure, not merely a de facto, settlement. The directive also showed Rome's determination to see to it that any solution was supported as nearly

[88] Memorandum of conference between General Aarón Sáenz and Ambassador Morrow and Colonel Macnab, enclosure no. 3, in Morrow to SecState, July 31, 1928, NA, RG 59, 812.404/902; outline of statement of Lic. Mestre made in conversation with Ambassador Morrow on October 8, 1928, Dwight Morrow Papers.

[89] Tritschler, González Valencia, and Méndez del Río to Mora y del Río, August 15, 1927; González Valencia to Manríquez y Zárate, August 30, 1927, LA-1.

unanimously as possible by all Mexican Catholics, clerical and lay, and to keep a final decision firmly in its own hands in all details.

The papal ruling also recognized the LNDLR as a component in the conflict. González Valencia commented enthusiastically on this point in a letter to Manríquez y Zárate, adding that "the two or three of us radicals left" must hold unflinchingly to the line so that the Catholic warriors would not believe that the episcopate had abandoned them. He saw the pope's directions as a strong endorsement for the firm viewpoint.[90]

As Obregón's peace maneuvers sank into oblivion, the Cristero military effort rebounded. There was heavy fighting in Jalisco the last week of August, with action spreading over into Nayarit.[91] In southern Jalisco, Degollado completed his reorganization and moved to the attack. On September 9 he took Juchitlán, and two days later Cocula fell to him. On October 8 he won a bloody engagement at Unión de Tula, then crowned the campaign on October 20 with a victory at El Chante, one of the largest battles of the rebellion. His fame skyrocketed; most of Jalisco between Guadalajara and the Pacific coast was under Cristero control.[92] In Zacatecas, Pedro Quintanar reappeared in late summer with a force that grew to five hundred by the end of the year. Quintanar reported that he fought eighteen battles "of some importance" during the period, estimating that he had inflicted between four and five hundred casualties on the enemy.[93] The Colima Cristeros reoccupied their Caucentla bastion in August and began a new offensive that culminated in their young leader's death. Ochoa, following Degollado's example, streamlined his command, and by late September some one thousand Cristeros were under arms in the state. On September 12, rebels stormed and took the well defended town of Suchitlán. Arms and ammunition were in better supply than ever, and success followed success. At the end of

[90] González Valencia to Manríquez y Zárate, August 30, 1927, LA-1.

[91] *New York Times*, August 28, 1927.

[92] Gutiérrez Gutiérrez, "El General Degollado Guízar," pp. 237–238.

[93] "Boletín de las operaciones del grupo libertador de Huejuquilla el Alto al mando del Sr. General D. Pedro Quintanar," December 31, 1927, LA-1.

October, Ochoa led his troops in a massive celebration of the feast of Christ the King; eleven days later he was killed when a store of explosives at the encampment blew up. Ochoa's death was a serious loss but not fatal to his movement, which went forward under his lieutenant, Miguel Anguiano Márquez.[94]

The increased flow of war material that aided the Colima rebels as well as Cristeros elsewhere was largely the work of an organization called the Feminine Brigades, founded in June by a group of young Jalisco women with headquarters in Guadalajara. Operating in "squadrons," the ladies obtained ammunition in various ways, including manufacturing it themselves, and distributed it through a complex network of supply routes.[95] Although they operated too independently and secretly for the LNDLR's taste—in the same manner as the "U," from which the brigades apparently sprang—commanders in the field then and later gave them major credit for the rebellion's success in sustaining itself.[96]

Michoacán was the scene of one of the most spectacular Cristero efforts of 1927. Luis Navarro Origel, who had fled from the Bajío after his incipient movement collapsed, placed himself at the league's orders, adopted the pseudonym of Fermín Gutiérrez, and in April commenced operations in the foothills near the Jalisco border. First securing the town of Coalcomán as a base, he directed a campaign that by the end of the year had removed much of the western part of the state and most of the coast from government control. As elsewhere, most of the battles were small, but a three-day engagement in June involved nearly a thousand men. Navarro suffered reverses in the summer, as did other Cristero chieftains—in part because of the general federal offensive and in part for other reasons; the temporary loss of Coalcomán in June, Navarro reported to the league, was due to the fact that most of his men had

---

[94] Ochoa [pseud. Spectator], *Los cristeros del Volcán de Colima*, I, 331–342, 359–370.

[95] Ibid., pp. 327–328, 333–335, 360–361, Ríus Facius, *Méjico cristero*, p. 225.

[96] See Degollado, *Memorias*, p. 163; Directive Committee to Enrique Gorostieta, December 3, 1928, and Gorostieta to Directive Committee, December 28, 1928, LA-1.

gone home to tend to their crops—"No human force could hold them once the rains began." But by autumn his columns were victorious everywhere. Early in October he besieged seven hundred government troops at Cañada de Ticuilucan, northeast of Coalcomán. The federal general Tranquilino Mendoza finally managed to break out, but lost two hundred dead and, according to Cristero reports, abandoned his troops in his flight.[97]

While the Cristeros gained in strength and fighting effectiveness, the government late in 1927 turned back a challenge from within its own revolutionary ranks that was a greater immediate danger to its existence. Obregón's determination to reoccupy the presidency, with Calles's support, had stirred up opposition in various quarters, and his formal declaration of candidacy brought the more hardy of his enemies into the open. Anti-Obregón sentiment congealed around two generals, Arnulfo R. Gómez, federal chief of operations in Veracruz, and Francisco R. Serrano, governor of the Federal District, who soon combined forces to wrest national leadership from the Calles-Obregón axis. It was all quite clearly a struggle for power, devoid of ideological content (both generals of course waved the "no re-election" banner, rather unconvincingly). Although they began on a note of high principle, with decorous appeals for support at the polls, they had no real hope of winning an election and by midsummer were preparing to use more direct methods. Gómez, speaking in Puebla on July 17, told supporters that he had in mind two locales for Obregón and his cronies: either the Islas Marías prison colony or plots two meters below ground.[98]

The LNDLR watched the development of the Gómez-Serrano drive with apprehension. The directors feared both that it might siphon off Catholic support and that a *coup* might succeed and

[97] Alfonso Trueba [pseud. Martín Chowell], *Luis Navarro Origel: El primer cristero*, pp. 92–115; report of the Ejército Libertador Nacional, Michoacán, Brigada Anacleto González Flores, October 25, 1927, LA-1.

[98] Juan Gualberto Amaya, *Los gobiernos de Obregón, Calles y regímenes "peleles" derivados del callismo: Tercera etapa, 1920 a 1935*, p. 41. John W. F. Dulles, in *Yesterday in Mexico: A Chronicle of the Revolution, 1919–1936*, pp. 332–354, has a good general account of the Gómez-Serrano affair.

thereby complicate the league's own plans for Mexico's future. When Serrano approached the league to offer some kind of alliance, the Directive Committee feigned mild interest while holding him at arm's length. They were relieved when the problem solved itself.[99]

Gómez and Serrano made their move on October 2. Some units of the federal army joined the revolt, but not enough of them, and after a few tense hours the outcome was certain. Serrano and thirteen associates were captured in Morelos the next day and hastily shot.[100] Gómez, after failing to get the upper hand in Veracruz, was hunted down and on November 5 also executed.[101] The government devoted all of October to mopping up pockets of resistance and dealing ruthlessly with those who had gambled their support on the losers. In Torreón, where the Sixteenth Federal Battalion had revolted, every officer in the unit died before a firing squad.[102]

Some Catholic militants, too, saw Obregón as the prime obstacle to the fulfillment of their desires. A few weeks after Gómez and Serrano failed in their bid to unhorse the revolutionary leader, a handful of league members tried to assassinate him.

The attempt came on Sunday, November 13. Obregón arrived in Mexico City that morning and went at once to his home on Jalisco Street. Scheduled to attend the bullfight that afternoon, he left the house with a few companions shortly after 3:00 P.M. for a drive in Chapultepec Park en route to the plaza. A second car carrying more friends followed. As Obregón's Cadillac neared a bridge over a small lake in the park, an Essex sedan with four men in it pulled alongside. Its occupants threw several bombs at the leader's car, and at least one of them fired pistol shots at it. Neither the intended victim nor his associates were seriously injured. The Cadillac was damaged but drivable. Obregón's friends in the other car darted after the Essex, and there ensued a wild shooting chase

---

[99] See LNDLR memorandum, September 1, 1927, and Directive Committee to Bustos, May 3, 1927, LA-1.

[100] *El Universal*, October 4, 1927.

[101] Amaya, *Los gobiernos*, p. 150; *El Universal*, November 6, 1927.

[102] Amaya, *Los gobiernos*, p. 152.

along the avenues leading toward the center of the city; it ended on Insurgentes Avenue at Niza and Liverpool Streets when the Essex collided with another car. The pursuers grabbed two of the men, Juan Tirado and Nahúm Lamberto Ruiz— the latter critically wounded with a bullet in the head. The other two fled on foot. Obregón returned to his home for a brief treatment of scratches on his hand and cheek, then proceeded to the bullfight.[103]

One of the two who escaped was Luis Segura Vilchis, a twenty-four-year-old engineer who had succeeded Bartolomé Ontiveros as chief of the league's Special War Committee. Segura Vilchis had decided at least a year before to kill Obregón. He was convinced that the persecution of the Church in Mexico was primarily the work of a handful of evil men, of whom Obregón was the most powerful, and that unless the persecution were checked it would destroy both Catholicism and the Mexican nation. Under these circumstances, he believed, assassination was an act of justice. He had strengthened his convictions by reading theological treatises on the subject of tyrannicide. He first attempted to carry out his aim in April, 1927, when he and a few close associates arranged to dynamite the general's private train as it neared Mexico City; they abandoned their scheme at the last moment when they learned that Obregón was traveling in a private car attached to a regular passenger train.[104]

The November plot was more flexible. Segura Vilchis planned either to blow up the train, providing Obregón used a private one (he did not) or to kill the general outright after he reached the capital. The Essex belonged to the LNDLR. José González (who drove it in the attempt and was the other who escaped) borrowed it several days before the attempt, on instructions from Segura Vilchis, from the league's regional delegate in Mexico City, Humberto Pro Juárez. Neither González nor the other accomplices knew

[103] "Acta de policía levantada con motivo del atentado dinamitero en contra del Gral. Alvaro Obregón, efectuado el 13 de noviembre de 1927 en el Bosque de Chapultepec," November 19, 1927, LA-1; El Universal, November 14, 1927; November 15, 1927.

[104] Andrés Barquín y Ruiz, Luis Segura Vilchis, pp. 154, 164–166.

of the plan until shortly before it was put into operation, although they were acquainted with Segura Vilchis and were, like him, active ACJM members. The engineer made the bombs at a house he had rented on Alzate Street the week before. On the morning of the thirteenth the four were at the Colonia Station when Obregón arrived. They followed him to his home, parked nearby, and waited until he emerged for his ride in the park.[105]

Segura Vilchis eluded his pursuers by boarding a streetcar on Insurgentes, then paid a short visit to the residence of one Roberto Núñez in the suburb of Tacubaya. The house was the hiding place of the Directive Committee of the LNDLR. The directors had discussed sometime before the possibility of killing Obregón but had finally voted not to approve such a step. Palomar y Vizcarra, however, had proceeded on his own responsibility. The leaders were finishing dinner when a servant announced that a young man was at the door asking to see Palomar y Vizcarra. The league vice-president received his visitor in an adjoining room. Segura Vilchis told him what had happened but added that the attempt had failed. Palomar y Vizcarra, badly shaken, returned to the dining room to tell his colleagues of the report. Segura Vilchis left at once for the bull ring, where he managed to get close enough to Obregón to shake his hand and congratulate him on his escape.[106]

Four days later police arrested the engineer at the electric power company where he worked and took him to headquarters for ques-

[105] "Acta de policía"; Barquín y Ruiz, Segura Vilchis, pp. 211–213.

[106] Interview with Antonio Ríus Facius, July, 1968. Ríus Facius was given this information by Palomar y Vizcarra before the latter's death. See also Ríus Facius, Méjico cristero, pp. 270–274. Barquín y Ruiz (Segura Vilchis, pp. 193–194) says the Directive Committee had decided Obregón must die and had left the details to Segura Vilchis; Ríus Facius (Méjico cristero, pp. 271–272) says the directors at first vetoed the idea but later approved it. But, if the full committee had been involved, Segura Vilchis would presumably have reported to it as a body, or to the president, Ceniceros y Villarreal. Barquín y Ruiz also says that the engineer thought the attempt had been successful and went to the bull-fight to verify it (p. 215). This is unlikely—news of the outcome would have been public knowledge within hours. More probably, Segura Vilchis was trying to establish an alibi.

tioning.[107] He denied any part in the assassination attempt, and his partial alibi—he produced the stub of the ticket that had admitted him to the bullfight—was substantiated by Obregón himself, who remembered seeing him at the plaza. Obregón told the investigators he doubted Segura Vilchis was involved.[108] The police were about to release him when the situation suddenly changed. Early the next morning officers raided a house on Londres Street, where they found Humberto Pro Juárez and his brothers Roberto and Miguel, the latter a Catholic priest. The three were taken into custody and charged with complicity in the crime.[109]

Father Miguel Pro Juárez, S.J., had entered the Society of Jesus in 1911. After several years of work and study with the order in the United States, Nicaragua, Spain, and Belgium, he was ordained a priest in 1925 and returned to Mexico the following year.[110] There his brothers told him of their work with the LNDLR. Soon Father Pro was also involved; for a time in 1926 he headed a sort of speakers' bureau that provided programs to explain the league's aims and activities.[111] For several months before his arrest, he carried on his priestly functions underground in Mexico City, becoming famous among Catholics for his piety and charitable work. Among his activities, he was in charge of work financed by the league to care for the widows and orphans of Cristeros who died

[107] Chief of Police Roberto Cruz told the press that Lamberto Ruiz gave them Segura Vilchis's name; he later said that the prisoner, wounded and blind, was tricked into talking by a police agent posing as a relative (*El Universal*, November 22, 1927; Julio Scherer García, "Roberto Cruz en la Epoca de la Violencia," *Excélsior*, October 7, 1961 [the latter is an article in a series based on personal interviews with Cruz]). Barquín y Ruiz, in *Segura Vilchis*, pp. 226–228, says the police got their information from Lamberto Ruiz's wife.

[108] Barquín y Ruiz, *Segura Vilchis*, pp. 230–231, 234.

[109] *El Universal*, November 22, 1927; Barquín y Ruiz, *Segura Vilchis*, pp. 232–233. As in the case of Segura Vilchis, the police story was that Lamberto Ruiz had told his supposed kin to get word to the Pro brothers that they should hide. See Scherer García, "Roberto Cruz." Barquín y Ruiz (p. 228) says that a turncoat named José Montes de Oca revealed the whereabouts of the Pros.

[110] Thomas Ryan, S.J., *Murdered in Mexico: Father Michael Anthony Pro, S.J.*

[111] Barquín y Ruiz, *Segura Vilchis*, pp. 138–139.

in combat. He also gave spiritual and material help to ACJM and league members who were smuggling supplies to the rebels.[112]

Both Father Pro and Humberto denied having anything to do with the assassination attempt. (Roberto did also and was released.) Humberto said he had owned the Essex but had sold it shortly before to a friend—like Segura Vilchis, he was anxious to conceal the league connection. He said he and his brothers had gone into hiding because when they read of the attack they knew the car would probably be traced.[113]

When Segura Vilchis learned that the Pros were under arrest and probably in serious danger—the police had been looking for the priest for months, and they might have little difficulty connecting Humberto with the league—he decided to change his story. After exacting a pledge from Police Chief Roberto Cruz that if he told the truth no innocent person would suffer, he confessed everything, omitting only his relationship to the league. Cruz retorted that the engineer was obviously altering his statement in order to save the Pro brothers. He had the engineer's story investigated, however, and decided that he was indeed involved; but he refused to release the priest and Humberto.[114] On November 22 the papers carried a statement by Cruz saying there was absolute proof of the guilt of all three men and that they had confessed. (Juan Tirado's involvement had never been in doubt, and Lamberto Ruiz had died of his injuries two days before.) Cruz added that all were known to be prominent LNDLR members.[115]

The police chief had given Calles daily personal reports on the course of the investigation, and on the morning of November 22 he

112 Ibid., p. 198; Directive Committee to José González Pacheco, May 23, 1928, LA-1.

113 "Acta de policía."

114 Ibid.; Barquín y Ruiz, *Segura Vilchis,* pp. 234–239.

115 *El Universal,* November 22, 1927. In his 1961 interviews given to Scherer García, however, Cruz said that Father Pro maintained his innocence to the end. Cruz said that, when police went to the house on Alzate Street, they found a valise belonging to the priest that contained holy oils, hosts, and other ecclesiastical items, and that the priest could not explain how it got there. See Scherer García, "Roberto Cruz."

delivered a dossier on the case to the president. Later, Cruz could not remember exactly what the file contained, but he never forgot Calles's words after reading it: "So there is proof of the guilt of these individuals, and of the priest, who was the mastermind behind it. Here, it was General Obregón. Tomorrow it will be me. And then you. Give the necessary orders and have them all shot." Calles refused to consider Cruz's suggestion that the four stand trial.[116]

The next morning, November 23, passers-by noticed an unusual amount of activity around police headquarters, including the stationing of mounted gendarmes in the street outside. Some surmised the reason, and within an hour several Catholic attorneys were making frantic efforts to obtain a writ of *amparo*.[117] But there was not enough time. Shortly before noon Father Pro, Segura Vilchis, Humberto Pro, and Juan Tirado died before a firing squad in the courtyard of the headquarters.[118]

The attack on Obregón and the ten days of public excitement that culminated in the executions carried the religious conflict to new levels of bitterness. Fear, hatred, and cold determination gripped persons on both sides of the struggle. Four days later Obregón told an audience in Toluca:

We know what to do when an ant bites us: we don't look for the ant . . . we get a pan of boiling water and throw it on the ant hill. When a scorpion bites us we get a lantern and look for it; and if we find another scorpion, we don't let it live just because it hasn't bitten us; we kill it because it can poison us with its venom, too; and it is necessary that the reaction abandon the idea of conquering us . . . It is necessary

[116] Scherer García, "Roberto Cruz." Scherer García pressed Cruz to explain what proofs Calles was referring to. Cruz answered that he could not recall, but that he did know they were there—a surprising statement, since Cruz deeply resented having been stigmatized for more than thirty years as a barbarian and priest killer.

[117] An order issued by a federal court to block action by some public authority.

[118] *El Sol*, November 23, 1927; *El Universal*, November 24, 1927; *El Universal Gráfico*, November 23, 1927. The press carried lurid and detailed pictures of the executions, which reporters and cameramen were allowed to cover.

that the reaction know that if it carries dynamite in its criminal hands, we will carry dynamite in our souls in order to overcome it.[119]

Father Pro's funeral on November 24 was marked by public demonstrations of devotion that amounted to a popular canonization of the young Jesuit.[120] Stories about him multiplied overnight. According to one, in Nayarit the evening before the executions a large luminous dove surrounded by three smaller doves had appeared in the sky. Miraculous cures were said to have taken place when sick persons touched handkerchiefs that had been dipped in the priest's blood and commended themselves to his intercession.[121]

Segura Vilchis, too, became a hero to Catholic zealots. Manríquez y Zárate referred to him as an "athlete of Christ" whose virtues and sense of duty placed him in the company of the Church's greatest saints.[122]

The Catholic insurgents venerated the memory of Father Pro and Segura Vilchis long after the rebellion ended. So would they remember another man, who emerged in 1927 to become the most eminent and also the most enigmatic of all Cristero chiefs.

Enrique Gorostieta y Velarde, a thirty-seven–year–old native of Monterrey, had been a cadet at the Colegio Militar de Chapultepec when the Madero revolt began in 1910. As a young career officer in 1913 and 1914, he remained loyal to the regime of Victoriano Huerta. After the Constitutionalist triumph he went to the United States and then to Cuba. Returning to Mexico in 1919, he settled down in Monterrey to the life of a successful businessman.[123] Although he hated the revolution, he took no side in the religious con-

[119] Speech in Toluca, November 27, 1927, in Sáenz, Torreblanca, and Amaro, eds., *Discursos*, II, 308.

[120] Palomar y Vizcarra to Bustos, November 28, 1927, LA-1.

[121] *Peoresnada*, February 1, 1928, no. 28. One of a number of crudely printed Cristero periodicals. Copy in LA-1.

[122] José de Jesús Manríquez y Zárate, *¡Viva Cristo Rey! en la hora de suprema angustia*.

[123] Miguel Palomar y Vizcarra, "Gorostieta," *David* 2, no. 39 (October 22, 1955): 233–240; Alicia Olivera Sedano, *Aspectos del conflicto religioso de 1926 a 1929: Sus antecedentes y consecuencias*, p. 195.

flict until after armed hostilities began. When the LNDLR, trying to enlist professional military talent, approached him, he was at first reluctant. His decision to accept a command was, he later recounted, the result of a personal experience. His wife had given birth to a son, and he went in search of a priest to baptize the child. He found one only with considerable difficulty—most were in hiding—but in his wanderings through Monterrey he was struck by the spectacle of open prostitution. Gorostieta was not a practicing Catholic, but he concluded that the government's oppression of clergymen, coupled with toleration of public licentiousness, meant that the survival of the Mexican nation was in jeopardy. He decided to accept the league's offer.[124]

In July, 1927, Gorostieta left Monterrey to assume the post of chief of operations in Jalisco. A careful inspection of rebel-held areas in Los Altos convinced him that much of the movement's orientation had been faulty. He gave priority to strengthening relations between the Cristeros and the civilian populace, not only to assure maximum support for the fighting men, but also to give the movement an air of permanence that would hasten reconstruction after the military victory. Concurrently, he believed that Cristeros should establish as stable a control as possible over a maximum amount of territory rather than dissipate their efforts in mere raids. After carefully reconnoitering his sector, he led his first offensive. On September 15 he engaged a federal force at Jalpa, across the Zacatecas border, and defeated it so soundly that the chief of operations in that state sent a desperate plea for help to avoid a complete disaster. (Gorostieta intercepted the message.)[125]

There was about the new leader a good measure of the inscrutable and even the mysterious. He was nominally a Catholic but did not frequent the sacraments, and his dedication to the Cristero

[124] René Velázquez López, "El problema religioso en México, 1917–1929," pp. 179–180.

[125] Gorostieta to Directive Committee, LA-1 (undated but written probably early in March, 1928); Olivera Sedano, *Aspectos del conflicto religioso*, pp. 196–197.

cause sprang from motives that differed from those of most of his associates. His strong sense of decency and justice was grounded in natural philosophy; he was in fact close to the liberal secular persuasion but respected practicing Catholics (he later became fervently religious).[126] He was always a puzzle to others in the Catholic resistance movement, and his reluctance to reveal himself to others helped nourish a variety of stories about him. Some said he was secretly a Mason; others whispered that he believed himself to be a reincarnation of Miguel Miramón, Maximilian's general.[127] The league directors were aware that Gorostieta did not in all respects conform to their predilections in matters philosophical, but they were convinced of his deep dedication to the cause of ridding the country of Calles and the revolutionary regime, and of his military capabilities.[128] Their relations with him would be sometimes cool, occasionally stormy; but their respect for him would never diminish.

As autumn gave way to winter, some league leaders found reason for optimism. Miguel Palomar y Vizcarra reported to Luis Bustos in October that the military situation was "very satisfactory." He said there were over four thousand men under arms in Jalisco alone, and these, added to the forces in Colima, Michoacán, and Zacatecas, meant that the total might be as high as ten thousand.[129]

Don Miguel might take justifiable satisfaction in the Cristeros' ability to survive and in a few cases thrive, but in fact the religious conflict was stalemated as 1927 drew to an end. The Cristeros were

[126] Navarrete, *Por Dios*, pp. 171–172; Olivera Sedano, *Aspectos del conflicto religioso*, pp. 195–196. Navarrete was a member of Gorostieta's staff and a constant companion.

[127] Olivera Sedano, *Aspectos del conflicto religioso*, p. 196.

[128] See Palomar y Vizcarra to González Valencia, December 26, 1927, LA-1.

[129] Palomar y Vizcarra to Bustos, October 3, 1927, LA-1. Government estimates were lower: an army general staff report in October (obtained confidentially by the U.S. military attaché) placed rebel strength in the states most affected by Cristero activity—Jalisco, Colima, Aguascalientes, Querétaro, Guanajuato, Michoacán, Nayarit, and Zacatecas—at 4,500, about a third of them in Jalisco (G-2 report, no. 1765, Thompson, October 14, 1927, NA, RG 165).

not defeated, but they were far from their goal of destroying the Calles regime. The Church hierarchy and the Mexican government had abandoned attempts to resolve their differences by negotiation. An end to the struggle was more remote than ever. But an American ambassador and an American priest would try to find an answer.

7. The Ambassador and the Priest

JAMES R. SHEFFIELD SUBMITTED his resignation as ambassador to Mexico on July 18, 1927. He had never enjoyed his post. He shared the American business community's aversion to the Mexican Revolution, and he was frustrated by the Coolidge administration's determination to avoid a clash with Mexico. U.S.-Mexican relations deteriorated steadily during his four years at the embassy. The efforts of various joint commissions to settle claims of American citizens for damages and losses suffered during the revolution had come to nought. Calles's hard line on the matter of foreign oil holdings had renewed a controversy that was thought to have been settled during Obregón's administration.[1] As the problems mounted, Sheffield became increasingly exasperated over what he considered to be the unjust and erratic posture of the revolutionary regime, and his inability to mediate matters to the satisfaction of American interests only made it harder for him to work in the tense diplo-

[1] The Bucareli Accords of 1923 calmed American fears that Mexico might seize foreign oil holdings wholesale; Obregón agreed tacitly not to apply provisions of the 1917 constitution retroactively to corporations that could show by "positive acts" that they were seriously engaged in petroleum exploitation.

matic climate. The religious conflict had added to his distress; Calles's stance on the Church question strengthened the ambassador's conviction that the man was incapable of behaving reasonably or honorably. Sheffield had had more than enough of the whole business.[2]

On September 20 Coolidge announced his choice of Sheffield's replacement. The new ambassador was Dwight Whitney Morrow, a partner in the firm of J. P. Morgan and Company and a close personal friend of the president since their student days together at Amherst. Morrow was no stranger to Mexican affairs. For more than six years he had been continually involved in financial matters relating to Mexico, both as representative of the Morgan interests in claims cases and as chairman of the International Committee of Bankers on Mexico. He was on intimate terms with Agustín Legorreta, head of the Bank of Mexico, and his financier brother Luis, and had visited Mexico in 1921.[3] Coolidge had often sought his advice on monetary matters and foreign policy.[4] Mexican reaction to the appointment was at first cautious, but by the time the new envoy arrived the press at any rate was willing to give him a chance.[5]

Morrow reached Mexico City on October 23, accompanied by his wife and his daughter Constance. On the twenty-ninth, amidst the usual elegant protocol surrounding such occasions, he presented

[2] Historians are almost unanimously critical of Sheffield, the exception being partisans of the LNDLR and the Cristeros.

[3] See Morrow to Legorreta, January 14, 1927, Dwight Morrow Papers; also *New York Times*, September 21, 1927.

[4] *New York Times*, September 21, 1927.

[5] The Mexico City dailies reported Morrow's appointment on September 21, with the news that the Mexican government had advised Washington of its approval. *Excélsior* said editorially on September 23 that Morrow was a man of well-defined character and situation and that it was assumed that he would act accordingly; as for the J. P. Morgan link, it commented only that he would probably share the views of the U.S. banking community. The press was more amiable by the time the ambassador arrived: *El Universal*, for example, said in an editorial welcoming him (October 24) that his appointment was after all a frank recognition that the problems between the two countries were mainly financial.

his credentials to Calles at the National Palace. His formal address struck a harmonious note: "It is my earnest hope that we shall not fail to adjust outstanding questions with that dignity and mutual respect which should mark the international relations of two sovereign and independent states."[6]

Calles decided it might be worthwhile to learn more about the new ambassador. Four days later he invited him to breakfast at his Santa Bárbara ranch east of Mexico City. Morrow accepted, and said he would be perfectly willing to let the president's own interpreter handle the conversation—a reference perhaps to Mr. James Smithers, an American resident of Mexico who was a Calles intimate and who was often present at interviews with U.S. visitors. Smithers had not been welcome at the embassy when Sheffield was there. In his talk with the president, Morrow did not bring up oil or reparations; he chose instead to discuss irrigation, which he knew was a pet Calles concern. Within a week there was a second early-morning meeting. This time their chat touched on oil, but they exchanged further observations on irrigation, too.[7]

Morrow had given first priority to establishing a friendly and relaxed official relationship, and his natural talent for charming people quickly made itself felt in nonofficial circles as well. His very appearance aided him: small in stature, not very fastidious about his dress, he looked anything but formidable. His relish for ambling through market places, where he would carefully and with seeming expertise inspect a piece of pottery before buying it and then warmly congratulate the artisan on his skill, was widely commented upon. He was even studying Spanish.[8]

Morrow was aware before his appointment of the seriousness of the religious situation in Mexico. In a letter to Agustín Legorretta in January, 1927, he commented that it was causing strife and

[6] *New York Times*, October 24, 1927, and November 3, 1927; *El Universal*, October 30, 1927; Harold Nicolson, *Dwight Morrow*, p. 316.

[7] Nicolson, *Dwight Morrow*, pp. 316–317; *El Universal*, November 4, 1927. The news accounts said the breakfast menus included hotcakes, ham, and eggs, thus originating the tale of Morrow's "ham-and-eggs diplomacy." Nicolson says, however (p. 318), that Calles ate popcorn lightly powdered with chocolate.

[8] Nicolson, *Dwight Morrow*, p. 310; *New York Times*, October 26, 1927.

ruin, and that, although Americans had no right to take sides in the conflict, it was a stumbling block to good relations between the two countries; it impinged on such legitimate concerns as the oil matter, because it added to the unfavorable opinion many Americans had of Calles. There were, he noted, eighteen million Catholics, "strong and aggressive," in the United States, and they could not be expected to ignore what they considered to be an attack on their coreligionists. It ought to be possible, he told Legorretta, to find some way to resolve the issue, as well as others that troubled relations between the two nations.[9]

By the time he left the United States in October, he had been formally inducted into the controversy. At the request of Patrick Cardinal Hayes, archbishop of New York, and Judge Morgan O'Brien of New York City, a prominent Catholic layman, he met with Father John Burke for a talk on the subject.[10] Father Burke, who two years before had lent sympathetic support to the newly founded LNDLR, had lost none of his concern for the plight of the Church in Mexico. But, like other U.S. Church leaders, he had refused to condone a Catholic rebellion. Unlike most of the others, however, he began actively to search for another solution. Burke's new involvement in the matter, like his earlier one, stemmed from his leadership of the NCWC. As he later explained, "an opportunity had been offered" to the Administrative Committee of Bishops of the NCWC to see if something might be done to make it possible for the Mexican bishops to return to their dioceses and for public worship to be restored. The Administrative Committee referred the question to Archbishop Pietro Fumasoni-Biondi, the apostolic delegate to the United States, who was also in charge of Mexican ecclesiastical affairs. Fumasoni-Biondi subsequently named Father Burke his agent in matters relating to the Mexican religious conflict.[11]

[9] Morrow to Legorretta, January 14, 1927, Dwight Morrow Papers.

[10] Morrow to Kellogg, July 23, 1928, NA, RG 59, 812.404/895 2/9.

[11] Excerpt from Father Burke's diary, in Under Secretary of State Robert Olds to Morrow, April 18, 1928, Dwight Morrow Papers. Burke did not say who approached the NCWC.

Father Burke asked Morrow if it might be possible for the ambassador to discuss with Calles the matter of finding some basis for a settlement.[12] Although Morrow was noncommittal, he was in fact highly receptive to the idea. For years his favorite pastime had been the study of Church-State relations—the works of Stubbs, Creighton, Lord Acton, and Maitland were his favorites. As his biographer later said, "the temptation to regard the Mexican controversy as a problem in applied history was almost irresistible."[13] Morrow was not a Catholic, but he believed the practice of religion was good and necessary in any society. Moreover, he believed that no Mexican government could have order at home or respect abroad until the corrosive hostility of religious strife was ended. All this, added to his knack for solving complex problems, made it almost inevitable that he would tackle the issue.[14]

Morrow spent his first weeks in Mexico in the hate-filled atmosphere engendered by the attempt on Obregón's life and the subsequent executions. He knew it was an inauspicious time to move on the religious problem, but at least he would do nothing to lessen his chances for accomplishing something later, when a better opportunity might present itself.[15] He was familiar with the State Department's low opinion of Calles and had no intention of helping make it worse. When a league member handed an embassy official a memorandum pointing out the illegality of the government's procedure in summarily executing Father Pro and the others, Morrow forwarded it to Washington without comment;[16] Sheffield would have added expressions of shock and indignation. At the same time, although few Catholics knew it, Morrow showed his distaste for the government's tactics by quietly using his influ-

[12] Nicolson, *Dwight Morrow*, p. 342.

[13] Ibid., p. 339.

[14] Ibid., pp. 339–340.

[15] Morrow to Olds, November 30, 1927, NA, RG 59, 812.6363/2446½.

[16] See memorandum from Lane to Kellogg and Olds, December 13, 1927, NA, RG 59, 812.404/845; also Palomar y Vizcarra to Bustos, November 28, 1927, LA-1. Arthur Bliss Lane, formerly first secretary at the Mexico City embassy, had just become chief of the State Department's Mexican Division.

ence to obtain the release of several persons being held by the police during the investigation of the assassination attempt.[17]

But Morrow was determined at all costs to maintain good relations with Calles, even at the risk of drawing criticism from other
quarters. A few days after the November executions he accepted
an invitation to accompany the president on a trip through northern Mexico to inspect irrigation projects, although he realized
that some Catholics would interpret this as condoning Calles's actions.[18] But he knew that without the president's good will there
would be no chance of resolving any matter of concern in the
peaceful way in which he intended to operate. The Church question
was on his agenda from the start. He wrote Under Secretary of
State Robert Olds on December 9 that, if his relations with Calles
remained cordial, "it is possible that later I may be of some small
assistance in helping to compose this trouble."[19]

The advent of Dwight Morrow led to a decisive American involvement in the religious conflict. The ambassador's decision to
work for a settlement translated itself into a U.S. commitment,
which would be technically unofficial but very potent. And his
decision would rest on premises that dashed any remaining hope
of Mexican Catholics for American aid or even American neutrality. Morrow from the first proceeded on the basis that the Calles
regime was a viable government, recognized as such by the United
States. He would seek an agreement that preserved that government's integrity, in a manner that did not arouse Calles's antipathy.[20]

[17] Statement of Víctor Velázquez, May 29, 1931; copy in possession of Antonio Ríus Facius. Velázquez was a Mexico City attorney acquainted with various members of the embassy staff during both Sheffield's and Morrow's tenures.

[18] Morrow to Olds, December 17, 1927, Dwight Morrow Papers; Lane to
Kellogg and Olds, December 13, 1927, NA, RG 59, 812.404/845¾.

[19] Morrow to Olds, December 9, 1927, Dwight Morrow Papers.

[20] For a good overview of Morrow's three years in Mexico, see Stanley R.
Ross, "Dwight Morrow and the Mexican Revolution," *Hispanic American Historical Review* 38 (November 1958): 506–528, and the same author's "Dwight
W. Morrow, Ambassador to Mexico," *The Americas* 14 (January 1958): 373–
389.

Morrow's appearance on the scene was one of several events which, coming within a few weeks of each other, marked a turning point in the conflict. The new American posture did not become apparent at once, but the other developments had an immediate impact on the LNDLR and the armed movement it directed.

Despite the papal instructions given in August, which recognized the league as a component in the Church-State conflict, the league was nervous about its standing with Rome. Palomar y Vizcarra wrote to González Valencia in September that matters were going well militarily and that the only fear was that the Holy See might change its attitude toward the Catholic resistance. He urged the archbishop to exert even greater efforts to prevent such a thing.[21]

González Valencia was doing his level best, but he realized that the militant viewpoint might be in trouble: "You cannot imagine how much damage [Pascual Díaz] has done," he wrote to Palomar y Vizcarra, adding that he and his two colleagues on the Bishops' Commission had managed to counter the bishop of Tabasco at least in part. He said that the pope himself had read sections of some of Palomar y Vizcarra's letters.[22] In November the archbishop's secretary, Father David G. Ramírez, told the Directive Committee not to worry; the pope was on the side of the league. Díaz, he assured the directors, had been snubbed during a recent visit. He did say that unfortunately some of the exiled bishops had begun to think Díaz was the "fair-haired boy" and were identifying with him.[23]

But the tide had turned, and turned strongly. The reasons are far from clear and must remain so at least until the Vatican archives can be studied. Probably the influence of Pascual Díaz was important—his detractors then and later were certain of it, and his defenders never denied it. Still more likely, the Vatican by late

21 Palomar y Vizcarra to González Valencia, September 22, 1927, cited in Andrés Barquín y Ruiz [pseud. Joaquín Blanco Gil], El clamor de la sangre, p. 306.

22 González Valencia to Palomar y Vizcarra, September [?], 1927, LA-1.

23 David G. Ramírez to Palomar y Vizcarra, November 6, 1927, LA-1.

1927 was receptive to advice that armed force could not succeed in redressing Catholic grievances and, moreover, that for the Church to be any longer identified with it would undermine whatever chance Catholicism had to survive in Mexico in any organized way.

Whatever the motivation for the shift, its consummation followed closely on Díaz's November, 1927, trip to Rome. Shortly after he arrived, Gasparri summoned the Bishops' Commission and read it a statement that amounted to an accusation that it had been misinforming the Holy See. Two weeks later he told the bishops that the Holy See felt it advisable that the commission be disbanded. Díaz left for New York two days later.[24] On December 12 Fumasoni-Biondi informed Díaz that, by authority from Rome, he was naming him his official intermediary with the Mexican episcopate, "so that in these difficult and sorrowful moments through which the Church in Mexico is passing, the Bishops will be sure of knowing with certainty what the Holy See communicates through the Apostolic Delegation." The bishops, the letter said, were to take as the word of the Holy See only what Díaz told them by order of the delegate.[25]

Díaz notified the bishops of his appointment in a circular letter dated December 19. In the same letter, by direction of Fumasoni-Biondi, he also transmitted instructions from the pope on two subjects. Regarding a settlement of the religious question, the pope said that the prelates must return to their dioceses as a matter of divine right, but only when they could do so peacefully and with dignity. The government, the pope said, was laying down unacceptable conditions, such as refusing to correct the situation which had obliged the clergy and the Holy See to suspend public worship in the first place. The pope reiterated that any proposals from the government must come from someone officially author-

[24] See Antonio Ríus Facius, *Méjico cristero: Historia de la ACJM, 1925 a 1931*, p. 222. The source cited is a statement signed by González Valencia in 1928, copy in possession of Antonio Ríus Facius.

[25] Circular letter from Díaz to members of the hierarchy. Copy in Díaz to Morrow, July 24, 1928, enclosed in Lane to Morrow, July 25, 1928, NA, RG 59, 812.404/896.

ized to make them and that Rome reserved to itself the final decision on a settlement.[26]

The second matter concerned the LNDLR and the bishops' relations with it. The pope, the instruction said, reaffirmed all he had stated in his apostolic letter of February 2, 1926 (which prohibited the clergy and Catholic organizations from participating in political affairs). The bishops therefore must not support armed action and must also remain aloof from any political party. They must not take part in the league's military or political activities. If the league intended to devote itself to "action purely and simply Catholic," the bishops should direct that action; however, since the league had been involved in bellicose pursuits, it would be impossible for it to reorient itself under the same name and the same leaders—who were considered to be revolutionaries—without arousing suspicions as to its intentions. Díaz added that Fumasoni-Biondi wanted the bishops to know the pope's position regarding the league so that they might remain strictly united in their relations with it. He said he was also communicating the pontiff's instructions to the league leaders, "so that they may freely choose the kind of action to which they wish to devote themselves and so that as they have thus far done with such great abnegation and unequaled heroism, they may continue working for the good of the Church in Mexico." The delegate, he concluded, advised the bishops to keep the papal injunctions confidential.[27]

Rome had spoken, and in a manner that left little room for interpretation. It had moved decisively to separate the official Church from any connection with the armed movement or with partisan politics in Mexico. It did not—and never would—condemn the rebellion, nor did it prohibit Catholics (other than bishops) from participating in it; but Mexicans who did were acting henceforth as individuals, not as "the Church." The league was not proscribed, but it was forbidden to continue as an agent of Catholic action unless it changed its program, name, and leadership.

Díaz gave the league the word in a letter to Luis Bustos on Jan-

26 Ibid.
27 Ibid.

uary 7, 1928. He made it as gentle as possible. The pope, he told
Bustos, wanted the league to know how much consolation he had
received from the firmness and constancy it had shown the whole
world, and from the conduct of its members, "complete Christians
and obedient sons of the Holy See." The pontiff, he went on, in no
way intended to deprive them of their right to involve themselves
for the welfare of their nation, but he also desired that the exercise
of those rights not serve as a pretext for unjust attacks on the
Church, the bishops, or Mexican Catholics who were not league
members. In order to avoid that danger and to prevent mistakes,
Díaz continued, the pope had named him intermediary between
the apostolic delegate and the bishops and had also ordered him to
make known to the league the manner in which distinctions were
to be made between religious and social activities, on the one hand,
and, on the other, those that were political and, even more importantly, of an armed nature. He said that for the present the league
should accept as the views of the Holy See only what he relayed
to it from the apostolic delegate and that likewise the pope wished
him to be the official channel between the Episcopal Committee
and the league. Finally, Díaz wanted the directors to know that
he stood ready to assist them in any way he could.[28]

The news stunned the Directive Committee. "I felt ill," Palomar
y Vizcarra wrote to González Valencia (who must have felt little
better), "and the heroic old man [Ceniceros y Villarreal], nearly
in tears, said to me: 'Now they have really made certain that I
shall not be able to sleep—nothing like this has ever happened to
me . . .' " Palomar y Vizcarra went on to say that personally he
had strongly considered abandoning the cause that, he said, was
what he believed Díaz had wanted them all to do for nearly two
years—however, he would not do so; the league was having its
Good Friday, but its Easter Sunday would come. The most pain
was caused, he asserted, by the comment in the instruction that
the leaders were considered to be revolutionists—this had cut them
to the quick. The committee, he said, was preparing a defense.[29]

[28] Díaz to Bustos, January 7, 1928, LA-1.
[29] Palomar y Vizcarra to González Valencia, February 15, 1928, LA-1.

The drafting of the refutation took more than a month. The directors had been separated since the death of Roberto Núñez, in whose home they had been living, and communication was difficult. Also, they wanted the advice of a number of individuals, including several of the bishops still in Mexico City.[30] The finished statement, sent to Bustos on March 5 with instructions that he forward it to Díaz, was a long, carefully constructed exposition of the league's position. It was a determined attempt to reconcile what Rome had decided was irreconcilable.

The league, it said, had always been "by specific tendency" a civic organization, whose mission was to defend such essential rights as life, freedom, and the bases of human society: religion, family, and property. It had not intended to operate in the political field. It had decided to lead the armed movement in conformity with its civic duty and to defend the Church from grave danger. No other organization was available for the task, and the league had accepted it, with the approval of the bishops. The armed defense, the letter continued, had not failed; it was growing in strength daily. For several months, since it had become clear that the armed movement's exclusively Catholic complexion was impeding American support, the league had been working to transfer the political and bellicose duties it had temporarily assumed to the Unión Nacional, but this must be done in a careful and orderly manner and would require time. For the league to change its program and leadership at once and to abandon its civic duties and its defense of the Church would plunge the armed defense into anarchy. Catholics would despair, and the persecution would continue. The league saw only two courses open to it: destroy the government or at least oblige it to come to terms, or abandon the field and allow the tyranny to work its will. The league chose the first. It found in the papal instruction no categorical order suppressing it, and it desired to lay its case before the pope "with absolute submission but at the same time with filial confidence." It would

[30] "Nota sobre la carta dirigida al Sr. Luis G. Bustos por el Comité Directivo de la L.N.D.L.R. en fecha de 5 de marzo de 1928," annotation written by Palomar y Vizcarra January 27, 1941, LA-1.

strive to relinquish its political and military concerns to the Unión Nacional as soon as possible and in the meantime would be careful not to pursue these in the name of the Church. It asked that, if the Holy See entered into negotiations with the Mexican government, it hear the league's opinion regarding the advisability of its intervening to specify political guarantees to assure the rights of the Church and to protect Catholics who had taken up arms. Such was the league's position; if it could not continue its work as a civic association while preparing the Unión Nacional, it would sacrifice its essential character and concentrate exclusively on political and military affairs, because without success in those fields purely Catholic action would be impossible in Mexico now or in the future. But if the organization was to die as the LNDLR, the directors asked for a decisive order to that effect and hoped that in that case the Holy See would solicit the views of all the bishops on the question. The directors noted that Díaz had been named their channel of communication; they extended their respects to him and prayed that God would give him the judgment and strength to work for the good of Mexico and the Church.[31]

The league had important and sympathetic partisans in its ordeal. Miguel de la Mora told the Directive Committee on March 2 that he was certain, and that Ruiz y Flores had told him the same thing in a letter, that the league had been left full freedom to continue its current activities, provided they did not provide grounds for unjust attacks on the Church.[32] The directors sent copies of their statement to other bishops. Mora y del Río wrote from Havana that he was entirely satisfied with their reply.[33] Lara y Torres of Tacambaro also expressed approval.[34] The directors never received a reply to their letter from the Holy See.[35]

[31] Directive Committee to Bustos, March 5, 1928, LA-1.

[32] De la Mora to Directive Committee, March 2, 1928, LA-1.

[33] Mora y del Río to Ceniceros y Villarreal, March 18, 1928, LA-1.

[34] Lara y Torres to Directive Committee, March 12, 1928, LA-1.

[35] Palomar y Vizcarra said later that Díaz did not forward it, his excuse being that it had not been sent to him with a copy ("Nota sobre la carta dirigida al Sr. Luis G. Bustos"). Mora y del Río, however, transmitted a copy to Rome. See Mora y del Río to Ceniceros y Villarreal, March 18, 1928. LA-1.

The bishops' reaction to the pope's bringing them to heel was mixed. Some of them—González Valencia, Manríquez y Zárate, Lara y Torres, even Mora y del Río—would disobey it as individuals. González Valencia, writing to the league directors from Germany, where he had gone after the Bishops' Commission was dissolved, lauded their defense and said that, as always, he was with the league and was doing everything he could "in word and deed" to get financial aid to it. He said he was sure that "we are supported by [the pope's] affection and blessings."[36] Manríquez y Zárate wrote that they must not end the struggle until the Church had triumphed and national freedom had been won.[37]

At about the time the bishops were being ordered not to support the rebellion, they received from the league a report on the military situation. It said that in the entire country there were over twenty thousand men under arms in organized units, plus another ten thousand less well provisioned and only partially under league control.[38] Despite supply shortages and lack of career military men, morale was magnificent. Some units had chaplains, and it was not unusual for six hundred or seven hundred soldiers at a time to receive Communion at field Masses.[39]

The report was probably a reasonably accurate appraisal of the

---

[36] González Valencia to Palomar y Vizcarra, May 18, 1928, LA-1.

[37] Manríquez y Zárate to Orozco, January 24, 1928, LA-1.

[38] "Situación militar de la Defensa Armada a fines del año de 1927," in Jesús Degollado Guízar, *Memorias de Jesús Degollado Guízar, último general en jefe del ejército cristero*, pp. 259–264. The report said the forces were distributed as follows:

Colima, Jalisco, Nayarit and part of Zacatecas:	10,000
Coastal region of Michoacán:	7,000
Interior of Michoacán:	1,000
State of México:	1,500
Guanajuato:	800
Northern Zacatecas:	500
Aguascalientes:	500

The balance was in Durango, Tlaxcala, Oaxaca, San Luis Potosí, Puebla, Morelos, Veracruz, Sinaloa, Hidalgo, and Guerrero. The report did not make clear whether the breakdown by states included only organized units or irregulars as well.

[39] Ibid.

Cristeros' numerical strength. Certainly the insurgent ranks had grown markedly since October. The U.S. military attaché in Mexico City, who had access to confidential Mexican army reports, estimated total rebel numbers in January at 23,400 and in February at 24,650. He did not stipulate that all of these were Cristeros, but he excluded mere brigands and Yaqui Indians, and since no other rebel movement of consequence was afoot, most of them undoubtedly were.[40]

The league's supreme command unit, its Special War Committee, labored under severe handicaps to coordinate and expand rebel operations. Its four members met only irregularly because of police vigilance. Poor communications bedeviled their attempts to direct strategy; orders and reports were lost or arrived weeks late, contributing to confusion and rifts in the higher command echelons. The rebel military control in Guadalajara (composed of Unión Popular adherents) was technically subordinate to the league but often acted independently. The Special War Committee had some success in attempts to broaden the rebellion's geographic base. It managed to mount a spirited effort in Oaxaca and stimulate action in Querétaro and Guanajuato by early 1928, but wrestled dispiritedly with the problem of identifying bands of marauders who appeared continuously in the countryside, some of whom were willing to join the cause, while others were patently bandits. The committee was sometimes disheartened by results of its efforts in most states, but Michoacán, Colima, and Jalisco remained bulwarks of the cause.[41]

The good tidings from Jalisco were due to the accomplishments of Enrique Gorostieta. He had imposed a modern command system in Los Altos, dividing the Cristeros there into regiments that formed one brigade (later commanded by Father Aristeo Pedroza as brigadier general). He was winning military victories, at the same

[40] See G-2 report, no. 2109, June 11, 1928, Col. Alexander J. Macnab, Jr., to War Department, NA, RG 165.

[41] Rafael Ceniceros y Villarreal, "Historia de la L.N.D.R."; José Rebollo to Ceniceros y Villarreal, March 7 and March 25, 1928, LA-1. Rebollo was chairman of the Special War Committee after November, 1927. His code name, fittingly, was Santiago Guerrero.

time establishing local civilian governments in regions he controlled. By the spring of 1928 he was urging the league to move beyond guerrilla warfare in its thinking; with a master plan and sufficient ammunition (which he said should be given only to chiefs who would undertake major campaigns) he could mount an offensive to seize the Bajío.[42]

Gorostieta's work in Jalisco had provoked a corresponding increase in the government's brutal attempts to crush the rebellion in the state. By February some 76,000 civilians had been herded into reconcentration towns—Tepatitlán, with a normal population of 10,000, received 40,000 of them. Smallpox and typhoid fever reached epidemic levels. Over a million and a half hectares of rich agricultural land were left uncultivated. Around the towns, zones were designated as crop and cattle lands to provision the refugees and deny the Cristeros access to food supplies, but rebels raided them at night to commandeer livestock and other foodstuffs.[43] In April the government announced an end to the reconcentration, asserting that the rebellion in the state was nearly over.[44] But in fact this move was a recognition that reconcentration had failed. Army sources admitted privately that more than 300 federals were killed in some sixty engagements in March alone in Jalisco.[45] Action diminished somewhat by April,[46] but even the Mexico City press carried almost daily stories of clashes between rebel and government forces. In May, fighting slackened in most states affected

[42] Gorostieta to Directive Committee, LA-1. The letter is undated but was written after February 28, 1928. See also Heriberto Navarrete, *"Por Dios y Por la Patria": Memorias de mi participación en la defensa de la libertad de conciencia y culto durante la persecución religiosa en México de 1926 a 1929*, pp. 176–181.

[43] *El Universal*, February 19, 1928. The "reconcentration" was not limited to Jalisco. On January 19, 1928, the inhabitants of San Diego de Alejandría and neighboring villages in Guanajuato were given forty-eight hours to remove themselves to León, under threat of bombardment (Barquín y Ruiz [pseud. Blanco Gil], *El clamor de la sangre*, p. 52).

[44] *El Universal*, April 3, 1928.

[45] G-2 report, no. 2028, April 17, 1928, Macnab to War Department, NA, RG 165.

[46] Ibid.

by the rebellion, but in Jalisco it intensified. So did it in Colima, where official sources recorded 100 federal combat deaths and claimed to have killed 144 rebels in combat. The same source said that an additional 300 Cristeros were executed.[47]

While the fighting raged, some men searched for a peaceful resolution. The Sixth Pan American Conference convened in Havana on January 16, 1928. Like most such gatherings, it was longer on camaraderie and protestations of hemispheric solidarity than on items of dramatic import. Attempts to bring the Mexican religious issue before the conference failed. Vatican diplomats in Latin America raised the possibility informally with governments to which they were accredited and tried indirectly to interest the U.S. State Department in the idea, but the matter never reached the agenda, in part because of objections expressed by Calles.[48]

Although the subject was not formally pursued, it generated considerable activity at Havana nevertheless. Father Burke was in the Cuban capital and conferred with several persons, beginning with Dwight Morrow. For some weeks Morrow had been considering the possibility that the priest might serve as a mediator in the religious conflict. He wrote to Robert Olds early in December that "a *modus vivendi* could be worked out without loss of dignity to either side if there were any method by which a liberal Catholic of the type of Father Burke, who talked with us in Washington, were dealing directly with President Calles."[49] In Havana the ambassador and the priest discussed the idea. Burke told Morrow he was willing to request an interview with Calles, through the ambassador, if there were a reasonable likelihood that the reply would be affirmative.[50]

---

[47] G-2 report, no. 2109, June 11, 1928, Macnab to War Department, NA, RG 165.

[48] The papal nuncio in Buenos Aires communicated the suggestion to the U.S. Embassy through the Brazilian ambassador to Argentina. The U.S. ambassador reported to Washington that Brazil's envoy in Mexico City had talked to Calles on the matter and that the president opposed the idea (Ambassador Robert Woods Bliss to SecState, January 14, 1928, NA, RG 59, 812.404/845).

[49] Morrow to Olds, December 9, 1927, Dwight Morrow Papers.

[50] Morrow to Olds, February 21, 1928, Dwight Morrow Papers. The docu-

Burke also called on Mora y del Río and Archbishop Martín Tritschler of Yucatán, both of whom were residing temporarily in Havana, to ascertain their views about a possible visit by him to Mexico. Tritschler expressed the opinion that Calles was determined to crush the church in Mexico, but he assented to the priest's going; with the intercession of the U.S. Embassy, he might obtain useful results.[51] The next day, Burke met Mora y del Río. The aged and ailing primate, who may have sensed that his long life was nearly over, told the American priest that his sole desire was to return to Mexico. When Father Burke asked how he might work to that end, the archbishop told him that the key to a solution was in the hands of the American government. If the United States told Calles to amend the laws, stop the killing of Catholics, and restore the churches, the persecution would be over. Calles, he said, was not his own master; he was the slave of a group that guided him and kept him in power. He said further that, if the United States lifted the embargo and allowed the Cristeros to obtain military supplies, Calles would fall within a month. Burke reminded the archbishop of the limitations under which the U.S. government had to operate; if it demanded that Calles change the laws and Calles refused (experience, he noted, showed that Calles would resent such an attempt at interference), what could the United States do then except intervene militarily? Mora y del Río replied that he did not want armed intervention, but that, if Washington would allow Mexican Catholics to get arms, they would deal with Calles themselves. Father Burke asked whether negotiation might work. The answer was perhaps, but there could be no settlement unless the laws were changed—and the United States had induced the revolutionary regime to change other regulations it found distasteful. He

---

mentation does not indicate whether Burke or Morrow first raised the possibility of Burke's going to Mexico. Both, however, were obviously enthusiastic about the idea.

[51] "Interview with His Grace, Martin Tritschler, Archbishop of Yucatan, at Havana, Cuba, January 18, 1928," Philip McDevitt Papers. McDevitt, bishop of Pittsburgh, was one of the five members of the NCWC Administrative Board. William F. Montavon, who wrote the memorandum cited, accompanied Burke and served as interpreter.

added that economic pressure might be applied, that with the cooperation of U.S. bankers an emissary like Father Burke could probably succeed.[52]

When Morrow returned to Mexico City he had a frank talk with
Calles about the religious problem. Domestic peace, he told the
president, was essential to Mexican progress, and any issue one
tackled led sooner or later to the Church-State quagmire. He then
broached the question of a visit by Father Burke. Calles replied
that he was willing, as always, to talk with anyone who was open-
minded on the subject and that he would be happy to receive the
American priest.[53]

Morrow sent the news to Burke immediately,[54] and the priest
prepared to leave for Mexico. Then suddenly the project fell
through. A report of the planned meeting appeared in the *New
York Herald Tribune*, whereupon Calles canceled the interview
and denied the story publicly.[55] Privately, he speculated that the
leak was the work of Mexican Catholics who opposed the conference. Burke later agreed that this was probably the case.[56]

Morrow and Olds were getting a clearer picture of the rebellion's
relationship to Church officialdom. In March the ambassador reported that he had learned from a Mexican source that the Episcopal Committee had given tacit prior approval to the resort to

[52] "Interview with His Grace the Most Reverend Jose Mora y del Rio, Archbishop of Mexico City, at Havana, Cuba, January 19, 1928," Philip McDevitt
Papers.
[53] Morrow to Olds, February 21, 1928, Dwight Morrow Papers.
[54] Ibid.
[55] *El Universal*, February 12, 1928.
[56] Burke thought the leak had come about in this way: he had believed it
his duty to tell Mora y del Río of the projected visit. On February 6, just before
his planned departure, three men connected with the LNDLR had called on him
in New York and told him they objected to his going to Mexico. They opposed
any settlement that left Calles in power. Burke said he told them he deplored
their attitude, that they were not good Catholics. At the meeting, the three gave
him a memorandum outlining the program of the Unión Nacional and asked
the help of the NCWC in getting U.S. acceptance of the plan. Burke was sure
they had tipped off the *Tribune*. Burke did not identify the visitors, but probably Luis Bustos was one of them. See Olds to Morrow, March 23, 1928, and Morrow to Olds, May 22, 1928, Dwight Morrow Papers.

arms.[57] Olds, after a long talk with Burke a few days later, confirmed that this was almost certainly true, that the league and the hierarchy were "tied up together in this business." Burke had told him that the league's attitude was a serious impediment to a settlement; the league insisted on Calles's overthrow, and he feared that the rebellion would continue even if an agreement were reached. He assured Olds, however, that the Holy See's attitude toward the league had been strictly correct.[58]

Morrow was not discouraged by the failure to bring Burke and Calles together. If the door had been opened once, it could be opened again. As to what course negotiations would take, the ambassador had come to certain conclusions: "No one but a madman would endeavor to settle the question of principle between the Church and Mexico," he wrote Olds on February 21.[59] The only productive approach, he was convinced, was to tackle the issue on practical grounds. Olds agreed: the whole matter, he told Morrow, should be handled on a basis of practical adjustments; a continuing battle over abstract absolutes could lead only to the ruin of one of the adversaries.[60]

March presented another opportunity. The oil controversy had been substantially settled to the satisfaction of both governments,[61] and Calles's opinion of Morrow was high indeed. He told a group of visiting U.S. newsmen and economists that Mexican-American relations were increasingly cordial and that this was due mainly to Ambassador Morrow's work.[62] On March 13 Morrow once more turned to the religious issue. In a telegram to the State Department he enclosed a letter he had drafted; if someone with proper au-

[57] Morrow to Olds, March 9, 1928, Dwight Morrow Papers.

[58] Olds to Morrow, March 23, 1928, Dwight Morrow Papers.

[59] Morrow to Olds, February 21, 1928, Dwight Morrow Papers.

[60] Olds to Morrow, March 9, 1928, Dwight Morrow Papers.

[61] In sum, the United States recognized Mexico's sovereignty over its own subsoil and its right to legislate on all matters concerning it, while the Mexicans agreed that in the case of oil lands being worked, regulations would not be retroactive and there would be no time limit on the holding of such concessions. See New York Times, March 28, 1928.

[62] Excélsior, March 10, 1928.

thority—Father Burke, for example—could write him a personal and confidential letter incorporating its essentials, he thought he could get a favorable response from Calles. The draft said that the signer had learned reliably that the president had stated that he had never sought "to destroy the identity of the Church nor to interfere with its spiritual function"; that the purpose of the constitution and laws and of their enforcement "has been and will be to keep ecclesiastics from being implicated in political struggles while at the same time leaving them free to dedicate themselves to the welfare of souls." The Mexican bishops, the letter continued, had felt that the laws, "if enforced in a spirit of antagonism," threatened the identity of the Church by giving the state control over its spiritual offices. The hierarchy desired to resume public worship if it could be assured of "a tolerance within the law" permitting the Church freedom to live and to exercise its spiritual offices. If President Calles could make a statement to the effect that the Church's identity was not being attacked and that, to avoid "unreasonable application of the laws," the government would agree to discuss matters of mutual concern from time to time with the head of the Church in Mexico, the clergy would resume their spiritual duties. The bishops or their representative, the letter concluded, would be glad to communicate with Calles in this sense if Calles would entertain such an approach and would give the assurances suggested.[63]

Morrow noted that in preparing the draft he had studied Cardinal Gasparri's letter to Aarón Sáenz of September 5, 1924,[64] and the statement made to Calles by Ruiz y Flores and Díaz in August, 1926. He had also read an editorial in *Commonweal* for January 4, 1928, which Father Burke had shown him in Havana. The editorial, he recalled, had stressed the point that the "identity of the Church" must be preserved and that, to assure this in practice, it would be important to establish conferences between the head of the Church and government officials, rather than having the government deal with individual clergymen. Morrow pointed out that

[63] Morrow to SecState, March 13, 1928, NA, RG 59, 812.404/872.
[64] See chapter 2.

this was included in his proposed draft. He also noted that, as regards the clergy participating in politics, he had followed in part Gasparri's own wording—that in fact he had where possible used phraseology already employed by Church officials. He further stressed that the letter contained an implication that, once peace and good will were restored, it might be possible to obtain changes in the laws, although this could not be definitely promised. Calles, he said, did not believe that most of the bishops wanted a settlement. It was also doubtful whether Calles would deal directly with the Vatican at present, although later it might be possible to return to the Gasparri-Sáenz agreement. Therefore, the best approach might be for someone to send a personal letter to the ambassador, with the idea that another, similar one might later be addressed to Calles by the bishops.[65]

There was no immediate reply from Father Burke. Both he and Fumasoni-Biondi were reluctant to sign such a letter without Rome's approval. The delegate, who was aware that parleys might be in the offing, had anticipated that Burke and Calles would first meet informally and that afterwards someone from the apostolic delegation would report to the Holy See.[66] Morrow provided an opening for this approach in a second draft letter he sent March 27. It was nearly identical to the first but contained no absolute commitment that a statement signed by the bishops would be forthcoming. If Father Burke could agree to this form, he said, he thought it possible to get permission for the priest to make the trip; he would approach Calles if he received an affirmative reply. He urged speed.[67]

Matters now moved quickly. Burke and the apostolic delegate approved the second draft. On the morning of March 29, Morrow showed Calles a copy of the letter Burke would present at the meeting and read to Calles a suggested response the president might make to Burke. Calles expressed satisfaction and agreed to see the

65 Morrow to SecState, March 13, 1928, NA, RG 59, 812.404/872.

66 Olds to Morrow, March 20, 1928, Dwight Morrow Papers.

67 Morrow to SecState, March 27, 1928, NA, RG 59, 812.404/874.

priest. A few hours later, in Washington, Burke signed the letter, which Olds immediately dispatched to Mexico City by diplomatic pouch.[68] The priest left Washington at once, accompanied by William Montavon. It was arranged that A. F. Smithers, James Smithers's brother, who was also a Calles confidant, would meet them at Laredo.[69]

The conference took place on April 4 at the old castle fortress of San Juan de Ulúa in the harbor at Veracruz. Both parties had insisted that Morrow be present at the talks, and he joined Burke and Montavon in Mexico City for the trip to the coast.[70] The interview lasted five hours and was cordial beyond expectations. Burke wrote in his diary:

The Apostolic Delegate had asked me to represent him and to come in his name, with no power to promise, with no formal authority, and with no power to accept anything. But to come to the President, to make clear the mind of the Holy Father and to see if recognition could not be given to the Church and to its own organized life; if the laws referring to registration and the limitation of the clergy could not be interpreted in a way that the Church might, with preservation of her own organization and dignity, accept, and provision made whereby, after public worship were resumed, opportunity be given for changes in the laws and constitution that would give the Church fuller freedom. I had come with that authority. I had come for that purpose.[71]

In a short opening statement, the priest told the president he should

[68] Olds to Morrow, March 29, 1928, NA, RG 59, 812.404/872; 872b; Morrow, memorandum, March 30, 1928, Dwight Morrow Papers; Burke to Morrow, May 0, 1928, Dwight Morrow Papers

[69] Memorandum to Lane, March 31, 1928.

[70] Consul John Q. Wood, Veracruz, to SecState, April 4, 1928, NA, RG 59, 812.404/876. Morrow reported that he said very little at the meeting, "beyond asking an occasional question when the discussion seemed to be drifting into dangerous ground." See Morrow to Olds, April 10, 1928, cited in Rublee Memorandum, Dwight Morrow Papers. George Rublee, an American lawyer privately employed by Morrow as an adviser in Mexico City, wrote this lengthy account of the religious controversy at its conclusion. He drew upon Department of State correspondence and other sources which Morrow made available to him.

[71] Excerpts from Father Burke's diary, in Olds to Morrow, April 18, 1928, Dwight Morrow Papers.

not judge the attitude of the Church and of the Holy See by the actions of some of the Mexican bishops.[72] Calles told Burke that he had had no intention of taking action on the religious question until the Mora y del Río interview of February, 1926, and later events had shown him that the bishops were trying to debilitate and overthrow the government. He alluded to the boycott and the suspension of worship. He noted that the bishops called his government Bolshevist; it was not, Calles insisted: it emanated from the movement initiated by Francisco Madero, which preceded the Bolshevist Revolution. He said the bishops were intriguing with foreign powers in order to gain their ends. The Church, he asserted, could not win; in fact, it had already lost. He said that he had worked for the poor and that the bishops had fought him every step of the way. The bishops were ignoring Mexico's social and moral evils. They were trying to work through the peons who obeyed them. He added that reports indicated the pope was supporting the bishops in all this. He had never tried to destroy the Church; he had insisted only on "fidelity to the institutions and laws of Mexico." Father Burke ignored Calles's version of the origin of the conflict, but he contradicted him by saying that the pope fully supported efforts to better the condition of the Mexican people; the pope supported the bishops in spiritual matters but was not behind any moves to destroy the government.[73]

The letters were exchanged, as planned.[74] Burke's was a verbatim copy of Morrow's draft. Calles's differed only in minor and insubstantial detail from the suggested form the ambassador had given him. It said that the president, by Burke's letter and as a result of the interview, was advised of the bishops' desire to resume public worship. The president said he wished to specify, as he had on other occasions, that "it is not the purpose of the Constitution

[72] Morrow to Olds, April 10, 1928, Dwight Morrow Papers.

[73] Excerpts from Burke's diary.

[74] Morrow to SecState, April 6, 1928, NA, RG 59, 812.404/877. Copies of the letters actually exchanged, as well as the draft Morrow gave Calles, are included in a memorandum written by Morrow, March 30, 1928, Dwight Morrow Papers. See also Morrow to Under Secretary of State J. Ruben Clark, October 19, 1928, NA, RG 59, 812.404/931½2.

nor of the laws, nor my own purpose, to destroy the identity of any church, nor to interfere, in any way, with its spiritual functions." His purpose, he said, was to comply with his oath of office to observe and enforce the constitution and laws "and to see that the law be applied in a spirit of reasonableness and without any prejudice, being myself as well as my collaborators, always disposed to hear from any person, be he a dignitary of some church or merely a private individual, the complaints they [sic] may have regarding injustices that may be committed through excess of application of the laws."

Calles asked what the next step would be. Burke said he would make a report to the apostolic delegate, who would then refer the matter to Rome. In response to a query from Burke regarding the presence of an apostolic delegate in Mexico, Calles said that, although he could not give diplomatic recognition to one, the Church was free to send such a person, and that the government would be willing to talk with him unofficially.[75] At the end of the meeting Calles thanked Father Burke for coming and for explaining the position of the Holy See; and he added—"to my utter amazement," Burke recalled—"I hope your visit means a new era for the life and people of Mexico."[76]

There was no publicity leak. The Mexico City press on April 6 reported routinely that Ambassador Morrow had visited the president, who was in Veracruz.[77]

In the days that followed there were signs that Mexican officialdom was extending an olive branch, however gingerly. Speaking at Celaya on April 15, with both Calles and Obregón present, Education Minister J. M. Puig Casauranc invited all good revolutionaries to demonstrate that those who fought to better the lot of the people could not commit the error of persecuting a religious conviction. "We are respectful of religious beliefs," he insisted. "In all Mexicans we find equality, whether in their hearts there is lodged a Masonic belief or whether they have an altar of the Lady of

[75] Excerpts from Burke's diary.
[76] Ibid.
[77] See *El Universal*, April 6, 1928.

Guadalupe, the blessed virgin who signifies comfort and a feeling of love for the Mexican people."[78] *El Universal* on April 29 reported that rumors were circulating in the United States of a possible early settlement and that the optimism was based in part on the Puig Casauranc speech.[79]

Back in Washingon, Burke reported in detail to Fumasoni-Biondi. The delegate delayed communicating with Rome, however, so that some of the Mexican bishops, about to gather in San Antonio, could be sounded out on the subject of a settlement.[80]

On April 22 the man who had held the primacy of the Mexican Church during the most difficult years of its turbulent history died in Texas. José Mora y del Río ended his days in exile, and even in death his wish to return home was not immediately fulfilled; he was given a temporary resting place in the cemetery of the San Fernando Cathedral in San Antonio. He was followed in death three weeks later by Ignacio Valdespino, bishop of Aguascalientes, who was buried beside him. The two events evoked notes that were not in harmony with the relaxation of tensions that had begun to appear. Archbishop Arthur Drossaerts of San Antonio preached the sermons at both funerals. They included bitter attacks on the Calles regime and on U.S. policy in Mexico. The archbishop likened Mora y del Río's death to the sacrifice of Calvary, with Calles in the role of Pontius Pilate.[81] At the requiem Mass for Valdespino he said that liberty was being crucified on the United States's doorstep while this country contemplated the act with complete indifference and even courted the friendship of men whose hands "are dripping with the blood of their countless innocent victims."[82]

The second oration, widely reported in the U.S. press, drew a sharp retort from the Mexican consul general in Washington, who challenged Drossaerts to show his courage, if he dared, by going

---

[78] Ibid., April 16, 1928. Morrow reported to the State Department that some well-informed people believed the speech had the prior authorization of Calles and Obregón (Morrow to SecState, April 16, 1928, NA, RG 59, 812.404/878).

[79] *El Universal*, April 29, 1928.

[80] Nicolson, *Dwight Morrow*, p. 342.

[81] *New York Times*, April 25, 1928.

[82] Ibid., May 16, 1928.

into Mexico and converting "his filibustering words into filibustering deeds."[83]

Of more importance to the conflict and its eventual solution, the death of Mora y del Río led to a new ordering of rank within the Mexican episcopate. The vacant See of Mexico could not be filled for over a year, but the role of senior prelate was now taken by Leopoldo Ruiz y Flores, whom the bishops elected president of the Episcopal Committee when it convened on April 25.[84]

Ruiz y Flores, who had been living at Father Burke's home in Washington, was the only Mexican churchman who knew of the Burke-Calles meeting. Fumasoni-Biondi and Burke now entrusted him with the task of persuading his fellow bishops—without telling them of the Veracruz meeting—that the Cristeros could not succeed and that it was idle to hold out for a change in the constitution or laws. The delegate instructed Ruiz y Flores to obtain from the bishops a commitment endorsing the principles contained in the Burke letter to Calles of March 29;[85] he knew that unity among the members of the episcopate was almost essential if Rome were to agree to terms which were a departure from those formerly demanded.

Ruiz y Flores was less than successful. In San Antonio he read to the Episcopal Committee a communication from the delegate, asking the bishops for a general statement for use by the Holy See when the time came to move for a possible understanding with the government. Ruiz y Flores then asked for discussion on the question of whether the committee favored an absolutely uncompromising position. After deliberation, the prelates approved a resolution saying that those present (ten bishops attended) were determined to obey the pope in any decision he reached, and that in that sense they were not uncompromising. But, they added, the way the problem was finally solved would critically affect all civilized nations, and they wished to suggest several considerations: if

[83] *El Universal* of May 18, 1928, must have mystified its readers by reporting the consul general's blast but not Drossaerts's sermon.

[84] Ríus Facius, *Méjico cristero*, p. 339.

[85] Rice, *Diplomatic Relations*, p. 129.

the persecutory laws were not revoked, the Church would remain in chains, with its clergy worse off than before; the sacrifices and wishes of the LNDLR ought to be taken into account; the longing of the Mexican people, who had given martyrs to the cause, must be kept in mind. The bishops also proposed some specific points: for example, any settlement should contain assurances that properties formerly used for religious purposes would be restored. Also, the government should grant an amnesty to Catholics engaged in the armed movement.[86]

It was all a rather serious hitch in the peace drive, but Fumasoni-Biondi and Burke decided to try to bridge the gap. On May 9 the priest sent Morrow a letter for transmission to Calles. In it he told the president that he had been working to follow up their talk and that Calles would be pleased to know that he had met with evidences of a sincere desire for peace. He would, however, appreciate receiving some clarification: "We take it that the present laws do not destroy [the] identity of any church—for example, priests would be removed from a post when so moved by church order, and duly authorized church authorities would be permitted to see that sufficient priests are secured and authorized" and also that religious instruction in primary education would not be prohibited outside the regular curriculum and regular school hours. Might it also be assumed that consideration would be given to the question of bishops' being able to reoccupy their residences?[87] The tone was tactful and cordial. (Burke's first draft raised the question of a general amnesty, but Fumasoni-Biondi, although sympathetic, deleted it, saying that it did not directly concern the religious question.)[88] Secretary of State Kellogg, in an accompanying note to Morrow, said that Father Burke hoped Calles would answer to the effect that the assumptions mentioned correctly interpreted the president's thinking. If Calles could acquiesce here, he added,

---

[86] A copy of the statement is in a circular letter from the Episcopal Committee to other members of the hierarchy, dated July 2, 1928, in LA-1.

[87] Burke to Calles, May 9, 1928, in Olds to Morrow, same date, Dwight Morrow Papers.

[88] Burke to Morrow, May 9, 1928, Dwight Morrow Papers.

there need be no fear of any new demands or requests for assurances.[89]

Morrow replied that it would be almost hopeless to get anything more, especially by letter. There might be a chance, however, if Burke and Ruiz y Flores came to Mexico. Burke and the archbishop speedily agreed, and Morrow approached Calles. The president at first strongly opposed Ruiz y Flores's presence in Mexico, which, he said, would incite bad publicity and agitate Mexican Catholics. But Burke insisted that Ruiz y Flores be included, and at length Calles grudgingly agreed to receive them both.[90]

Traveling incognito and unrecognized, the priest, the archbishop, and Montavon reached Mexico City early on the morning of May 17. They got off the train in the suburb of Tacuba, where they were met by Capt. Lewis B. McBride, the naval attaché at the U.S. Embassy. McBride took them to his home, where they remained during their two days in the capital, leaving only once— to see Calles. Morrow was with them all day on the seventeenth until 4:00 P.M.; an hour later they were in conference with the president.[91]

Burke told Calles that, although Ruiz y Flores had accompanied him, he alone was representing the Holy See, and that he considered the meeting to be a continuation of the Veracruz talks.[92] Burke reviewed the stipulations suggested by the bishops in San Antonio. Calles said he could not accept them. After some discussion, Ruiz y Flores offered to write a letter to the president substantially like Burke's of March 29 but including a refernce to Puig Casauranc's Celaya address. On that basis, agreement was reached. As soon as higher ecclesiastical authority approved the letter, Calles would write Ruiz a reply in the same form he had used in his letter to Burke but indicating his approval of Puig Casauranc's re-

[89] Kellogg to Morrow, May 9, 1928, NA, RG 59, 812.404/882b.

[90] Rublee Memorandum, Dwight Morrow Papers.

[91] Morrow to SecState, May 17, 1928, NA, RG 59, 812.404/884; Rice, *Diplomatic Relations*, p. 130.

[92] Burke to Clark, June 28, 1932, cited in Rice, *Diplomatic Relations*, pp. 130–131.

marks. When the churchmen received final approval of the entire
negotiation, the exchange would be published, concluding the settlement.[93]

Burke immediately wired Fumasoni-Biondi, the message traveling from the embassy to the State Department in U.S. diplomatic code and thence in plain text to the Apostolic Delegation.
Burke told the delegate that the meeting had been satisfactory,
that all agreed it was futile to try to get further concessions, and
that it was "advisable to rely upon the broad assurance . . . that
the government would enforce the laws reasonably and without
prejudice." The government would guarantee to receive any complaints of injustices from a Church official, and, therefore, in the
spirit of good will that all hoped would prevail, it would be possible
to negotiate regarding unreasonable application of the laws. Burke
said Ruiz y Flores requested authority to (a) write a letter to
Calles similar to the one of March 29 and including a statement to
the effect that he understood Calles endorsed the Puig Casauranc
speech and (b) release this together with Calles's reply, as well as
a statement saying that in light of the exchange the Holy See
authorized resumption of worship. Burke said they would wait for
an answer, adding that Ruiz y Flores was anxious to receive the
authority requested as soon as possible so that the clergy could officiate in the churches on May 27, the feast of Pentecost.[94]

Morrow expected an affirmative reply within hours. At his request Olds stayed at the State Department the night of May 17 in
order to insure fast communication between Burke and the Apostolic Delegation. But no answer came that night, nor the next day.
On the afternoon of the nineteenth a telegram arrived from Monsignor James H. Ryan of the NCWC. It said that Fumasoni-Biondi
wanted Burke and Ruiz y Flores to return to Washington immediately and that they would then proceed to Rome: "This is [the]
quickest and only sure way to achieve purposes."[95] There was to
be no cutting corners.

[93] Rublee Memorandum, Dwight Morrow Papers.
[94] Ibid.
[95] Ibid.

When the two clerics reached Washington there was another disquieting turn of events; Fumasoni-Biondi announced that only Ruiz y Flores would make the trip to Rome. Before he left, the archbishop gave Burke the letter he had planned to give to Calles, with instructions that it be given to Morrow to hold; Morrow would present it to Calles when and if Vatican approval was obtained.[96]

Ruiz y Flores hastened to Rome by the fastest means available, traveling day and night. Within hours after he arrived he was closeted with Gasparri, who had already learned of his mission. Ruiz y Flores had apparently lost some of his enthusiasm for a settlement along the lines he had supported in Mexico City. When the cardinal asked his opinion, he said he thought Calles was offering very little.[97] He saw Pius XI on June 7. The pontiff did not commit himself, although he was inclined toward compromise. He was anxious that the bishops be of one mind and accept any solution willingly.[98]

Two weeks after the conference in Mexico City, Morrow returned to the United States for consultation and a vacation. In Washington he and Olds talked several times with Father Burke, and twice all three conferred with Fumasoni-Biondi at the Apostolic Delegation. The delegate told them that the matter had been referred to the Congregation on Extraordinary Ecclesiastical Affairs and that no decision had been reached.[99]

Morrow searched for a way to stimulate action in Rome. He enlisted the aid of an old friend, John J. Raskob, president of General Motors and a prominent Catholic who was also a close friend of Papal Under Secretary of State Giuseppe Pizzardo. Raskob, after conferring with Burke, agreed to intercede.[100] In cablegrams to Pizzardo on June 19 and 25, he urged that the proposed settlement be accepted and also that Father Burke be called to Rome to help

[96] Ibid.

[97] Leopoldo Ruiz y Flores, *Recuerdo de recuerdos*, p. 90.

[98] Ibid.

[99] Morrow to Kellogg, July 23, 1928, NA, RG 59, 812.404/895⅔, cited in Rice, *Diplomatic Relations*, pp. 134–135.

[100] Raskob to Morrow, n.d., 1928, Dwight Morrow Papers.

explain the situation to Vatican officials.[101] Pizzardo replied that
he would appreciate having Raskob's views in more detail.[102] Raskob obliged. He wrote at length on July 3, strongly endorsing Morrow's efforts. He said the ambassador feared that exiled Mexican
bishops might be giving Rome an inaccurate picture because of
their unfamiliarity with the situation. He felt confident that the
Mexican government would live up to the proposed agreement; if
it did not, it would lose the respect and confidence of the American
government. Moreover, Morrow's presence in Mexico, he asserted,
would practically guarantee against unfairness.[103] Raskob enclosed
a letter he had received from Morrow, reviewing the steps taken
since March to end the conflict. Morrow said that, while some
changes in the Calles letter might be obtained, he doubted that it
would be possible now or in the near future to get the government
to agree to modify any particular laws as a condition for resuming
public worship; but he felt that in the amicable atmosphere that
should follow the return of the clergy to the churches, "changes
in the laws might later be made by which the church would be
in a better legal position in Mexico than it has been for many
years." He emphasized to Raskob that Calles was not asking the
priests to come back; Calles, he said, had agreed to receive Father
Burke "only after great reluctance," and it was only because of
the priest's favorable impression on the president that he later assented to Ruiz y Flores's going with Burke for the second interview. Morrow lavished praise on the American priest.[104]

Both Morrow and the State Department were cautiously optimistic that a settlement was near, but a shadow crossed the horizon
on July 12. Burke and Montavon called on Lane concerning an

[101] Raskob to Pizzardo, June 19, 1928; June 25, 1928; copies to Morrow and
Fumasoni-Biondi, Dwight Morrow Papers.

[102] Pizzardo to Raskob, June 21, 1928, Dwight Morrow Papers.

[103] Raskob to Pizzardo, July 3, 1928, Dwight Morrow Papers.

[104] Morrow to Raskob, June 28, 1928, Dwight Morrow Papers. Both the pope
and Gasparri read the two letters. See Pizzardo to Raskob, July 26, 1928, Dwight
Morrow Papers. There is a discrepancy between Morrow's comment to Raskob
that Calles was reluctant to see Burke in April and his earlier report to Olds
that Calles would be happy to meet with the priest.

article that had appeared two days before in the *New York World*. It said that a group of Mexican Catholics was urging the pope not to agree to a truce except on the firm terms he had always insisted upon. The message to the pope, the story reported, was sponsored by the LNDLR, which was urging Rome to stand by its refusal to let priests register without authorization of Church authorities. The league also demanded freedom of operation for Catholic educational and charitable establishments. Burke told Lane he was not worried by the article. He said the league had little or no influence with Rome because it was waging armed revolt in Mexico. He added that he believed Morrow knew that the Holy See had repudiated the league for that reason and had directed that even if it should end its revolutionary work it must change its name before Rome would recognize it. The priest said he did not know whether the Vatican's position on this had been made public—the Holy See was reluctant to reprimand Catholics who in good faith were fighting and dying for the Church, however mistaken and even harmful to the Church's real interests their actions might be.[105]

The league had indeed moved to counter the work of Morrow, Burke, and the other mediators. Apparently as much in the dark as everyone else about the Veracruz meeting in April, the Directive Committee did learn of the May conference in Mexico City. On May 31, spokesmen of a number of Catholic groups, headed by the league, dispatched a memorial to Rome. The signers stated their opposition to any "provisional settlement."[106] In a telegram to Gasparri, Ceniceros y Villarreal said that the league wished to inform His Eminence that the election of Ruiz y Flores to the presidency of the Episcopal Committee, as well as the resolution voted by the bishops in San Antonio regarding a possible accord, had been decided without the participation of the eleven bishops still in Mexico. He asked that this latter group, which had been constituted a subcommittee of the Episcopal Committee, be consulted, since its members knew best the prevailing situation within the country,

[105] Lane to Morrow, July 13, 1928, NA, RG 59, 812.404/894a.
[106] Memorial to Pius XI, May 31, 1928, LA-1.

"unlike Ruiz and Díaz, whose judgment appears [to the] Catholic people to be too conciliatory."[107]

Back at his post in Mexico City early in July, Morrow waited. He had every reason to believe his course was the correct one. He had reached definite conclusions regarding the nature of the conflict. If those conclusioins were correct—and Morrow was convinced they were—then the strategy for achieving a solution suggested itself, and success depended only on tact, patience, and a modicum of benevolence on all sides. His reasoning seemed to him sound: because of a legal dispute with the government, the Church had suspended public worship in Mexico. This was the crux of the conflict. If the laws ceased to be a threat, either by being changed or by being applied in a manner the Church could accept, the priests would return. That might not solve all difficulties, but there was good likelihood that remaining differences could then be handled. Morrow was sure that responsible people could be persuaded of this. Some already were, and the rest could be worked with or, if necessary, bypassed.

The protagonists, Morrow took for granted, were Calles and the Vatican—and to a secondary degree the bishops. He knew less about the other components of the Catholic opposition to Calles and had quickly concluded that they were irrelevant to the central issue, although they might by their mindless tactics complicate the road to peace. The Cristeros, he believed, were misguided rebels scarcely distinguishable from other brigands who had plagued Mexico in the past; the very notion that the United States might support such men was to him simply absurd. The Calles government was lawful authority and, despite its shortcomings, was at heart sincere. This Morrow never doubted. Morrow rejected the proposition that the revolutionary regime was incompatible with Catholicism. Mexico needed both its government and its Church. Morrow was not anti-Catholic. He believed in the need for the Church to play a role in the lives of Mexicans. In this, he was surely more broadminded than millions of other Americans in that

[107] Ceniceros y Villarreal to Gasparri, LA-1. The copy of the telegram is undated but evidently was sent at about the same time as the memorial.

heyday of the Ku Klux Klan and the viciousness aroused by Al Smith's campaign for the presidency. And, finally, Morrow believed he was in tune with the opinion of responsible American Catholic leaders regarding the Mexican situation. The cardinal archbishop of New York had introduced him to Father Burke, who, as executive secretary of the NCWC, could be deemed a spokesman of the American episcopate—an estimate that was further confirmed when he learned that Burke was acting as the personal representative of the apostolic delegate. Moreover, prominent U.S. Catholic laymen, whose standing both as Catholics and as Americans was beyond reproach, were applauding and assisting his work.

Morrow's conscience was clear. With no cause to doubt the rectitude of his position, he was patiently determined to hold his course.

8. The Ways of Frustration

HOPE THAT AMERICAN HELP might come died hard in the breasts of the Catholic insurgents, and disputes over what should or should not be done to win that support plagued the leadership long after the question had become moot. Contention reached its climax over the issue of broadening the movement's base through the medium of the Unión Nacional.

Bustos was angry as he sat out the gray winter days of early 1928 in a New York hotel. After the Unión Nacional's paper birth he had returned to the United States, confident that at last he had the tool he needed to attract U.S. aid. But weeks passed with no sign that the Directive Committee was close to completing even the minimum organization in Mexico that would give the *unión* a believable existence. The committee, he knew, was not enthusiastic about the plan, and he became increasingly certain that the directors meant to leave his cherished cure-all to die.[1]

On February 16 he poured out his feelings in a letter to the directors. He and they were on divergent paths, he told them. They

[1] The LNDLR leaders had promised to provide Bustos with documentation giving organizational details and names of adherents to the new party, but by

obviously believed that the league by itself could overpower the revolution and create a de facto situation that the United States would have to accept. They were mistaken, he warned: Victoriano Huerta had produced a de facto regime, supported in Mexico and recognized in Europe; Adolfo de la Huerta had accumulated quantities of men and material as well as a large popular backing. Had the U.S. government recognized those de facto situations? No. Only a party that the United States accepted could win. If the rebellion continued to appear to be the work of "white radicals," the cause was doomed, "because this government [the United States] *is determined to support the red radicals more strongly, and never White Radicals.*" The league must decide which way it would go. It was strong and capable; if it could not hold its own in a coalition like the Unión Nacional, how could its ideals survive later in an organism as complex as a nation? As for Pascual Díaz, Bustos told the directors that they had misjudged the bishop. Díaz had done everything he could to help. He had established important contacts and lent support in other ways. Father Parsons had been a friend too. As for the league's favorite, González Valencia, Bustos said that, although he liked and respected the archbishop of Durango, he believed his ignorance of conditions in the United States had misled him completely.[2]

Bustos's impatience with the directors was reciprocated. They decided that his carping was an excuse for his own lack of success, and they refused to be intimidated. Palomar y Vizcarra told Ceniceros y Villarreal early in April that he believed Bustos's mission had failed, that he had taken too long and got no results.[3]

---

the end of January Bustos had received only a few pieces of data ("Memorándum cronológico," June 19, 1928, LA-1).

[2] Bustos to Directive Committee, February 16, 1928, LA-1. Italics in original. The directors' failure to act with more dispatch was not due only to a lack of enthusiasm. As Miguel de la Mora pointed out in a letter to Pascual Díaz, they were hampered by government vigilance and an understandable reluctance on the part of many persons to affix their names to documents having to do with the new organization (de la Mora to Díaz, June 22, 1928, LA-1).

[3] Palomar y Vizcarra to Ceniceros y Villarreal, April 8, 1928, LA-1.

The directors also had to contend with grumbling from some of their lieutenants in Mexico. In May local LNDLR leaders in the Federal District posed to the Directive Committee a wide-ranging list of questions and offered some advice.[4] The people, they said, were questioning the leaders' conduct of affairs and were saying that the armed struggle was a stalemate. The chiefs felt frankly that, when right-minded Mexicans stopped thinking about U.S. assistance and put their confidence completely in God, they would be closer to total victory. The directors replied in detail,[5] reviewing their efforts patiently and concluding on a note of near desperation. The support of the United States, they said, would doubtless be the most effective arm the movement could acquire, but, if efforts to obtain it failed, then God would see to it that other means sufficed. He would in fact be obliged to do so, "because we have done all that right reason counseled should be done, because we are defending the cause that is for Him the most beloved, the liberty of His Church, and because we have trusted in Him with the greatest and firmest confidence."

But the sharpest barb came from the purist flank. The directors received a communication from San Antonio signed by a group of ACJM veterans, among them Capistrán Garza, Luis and Ramón Ruiz Rueda, Carlos Blanco, and Salvador and Luis Chávez Hayhoe.[6] The letter attacked the Unión Nacional plan and expressed holy horror that the league could lend itself to such a sellout of principle. The signers found it incredible that the Mexican Catholic majority should make common cause with its enemies, who had scourged the Church for a century. To restore the Constitution of 1857, they said, was simple madness. The league had begun the current struggle under a different banner, for which men had died; Anacleto González Flores and other martyrs had not sacrificed their lives for the Constitution of 1857, and to bring it forth now would profane their blood. Moreover, the notion that such a ploy

[4] José González Pacheco to Directive Committee, May 10, 1928, LA-1.

[5] Directive Committee to González Pacheco, May 23, 1928, LA-1.

[6] Memorandum to the Directive Committee and to Luis G. Bustos, March 29, 1928, LA-1.

would gain American aid was a deplorable illusion. The letter's signers said they could "not permit to be done without our disagreement and protest that which honor and conscience will not allow us to accept when it is completed."

The missive struck nerves. The directors delivered a rebuttal, the tone of which grew in rage with every line:[7] the Unión Nacional plan had been adopted to save the movement; it was done on excellent advice from well informed sources; the directors too had a strong aversion to the Constitution of 1857 and had made this a matter of record, but they saw no danger to Catholic interests. The party would welcome honorable men, not enemies of freedom. The Holy See had been informed of the plan and, no objection having been received, its approval was assumed. The martyrs would not blame the Directive Committee, but they might well rise to deplore disunity and cry alarm at "satanic attempts" to make vain their martyrdom. The directors made their plea particular and personal: "We are living a life that is being poured out drop by drop in the unceasing struggle, and when we have one foot in the grave, there come to the sad enclosure of our seclusion none other than those whom we love most, to drench our hearts with bitterness and haughtily, almost aggressively, accuse us of the crime that is to us the most abominable of all: treachery." They urged those who had affixed their names to the letter to search their consciences, and they begged for unity.

The directors were cornered. They had no intention of breathing life into the Unión Nacional, at least for the time being. But to repudiate it openly might destroy the shaky image of propriety they had tried to project to the Holy See and possibly draw an outright papal condemnation. They were playing for time, hoping that something would turn up to extricate them from the dilemma.

Matters indeed untangled, if not in the happiest way. By late spring it was obvious even to the most naïve that American aid, official or unofficial, would not be forthcoming. Early in May, Bustos and his associates learned that the State Department had ceased

[7] Miguel de Loaiza (temporary secretary to the Directive Committee) to Messrs. Pedro González et al., June 1, 1928, LA-1.

to show any interest in the Unión Nacional. Díaz wrote to one of
his fellow bishops that the division among Catholics and the practical abandonment of the plan in Mexico City were probably fac-
tors. He went on to say that, to complete the debacle, when the
U.S. government first approached Calles regarding a possible settlement of the religious question and an intermediary went to New
York to consult with Bustos, Ortiz Monasterio, and Carreño, the
first two were so obdurate that the intermediary was openly displeased. The official door had been closed, and with it all the others, at least for some time, Díaz reported.[8]

Bustos was all but through. There was a showdown meeting in
New York on May 30, attended by Bustos, Carreño, Díaz, and
Mariano Ramírez, the latter sent from Mexico City by the Directive Committee to investigate the situation in the United States.
Díaz explained that failure to implement the Unión Nacional project had caused the State Department to lose interest in it, that
United States policy was to back Calles, and that this would make
it impossible to obtain funds.[9] Díaz said that in order not to hurt
the cause, and in view of the constant attacks being made on him,
he had decided to separate himself from everything relating to the
"present sorrowful conflict," as, he said, he had in fact been doing
since Mora y del Río's death and the election of Ruiz y Flores as
president of the Episcopal Committee. He spoke highly of the archbishop of Morelia. Ramírez denied that the LNDLR or its supporters had deprecated Díaz, a statement which Carreño contradicted.
Pressed by Carreño, Ramírez said that, although the Directive
Committee believed U.S. policy would be decisive, the armed action must continue with or without American support. Carreño
countered that since the directors had in their hands the fate of

8 Díaz to [de la Mora?], May 30, 1928, LA-1. The intermediary was almost
certainly Father Burke, who met with three Mexicans in New York on February 6. See above, chapter 7. Burke may also have been the intermediary that
Fumasoni-Biondi procured the previous summer to help get the Unión Nacional
plan before the State Department. See above, chapter 6.

9 "Memorándum de la conversación habida entre los Sres. Lic. M[ariano]
R[amírez], L[uis] G. B[ustos] y P[ascual] D[íaz]," New York, May 30, 1928,
sworn statement signed by Ramírez June 2, 1930, LA-1.

those fighting, and were convinced that if the United States reached an agreement with Calles or his successors there was no hope of victory, he wanted to know what the league would do if the United States in fact supported the present government of Mexico. "We will fight until we are all dead," Ramírez replied. Carreño reacted heatedly. The league leaders, he retorted, could squander their own lives if they chose, but they had no right to sacrifice the lives of others and devastate the nation in an endless and hopeless guerrilla war. Ramírez said the truth would be told to those fighting, and they could decide whether to continue. Díaz again insisted that the United States was determined to support Calles fully.[10]

There was a final get-together two days later. Díaz again spoke of the desire of the U.S. government to bring the religious conflict to an end. Bustos praised the bishop; then he told Ramírez to inform the league directors that he was resigning both as league representative in the United States and as second vice-president of the Directive Committee. Carreño told Ramírez that he was cutting all ties with the work he had been doing in conjunction with Bustos and Ortiz Monasterio because he disagreed absolutely with the league's procedures. Ortiz Monasterio, who was also present at the meeting, said that he, too, considered his mission terminated.[11]

With Bustos's resignation, the Unión Nacional scheme was quietly abandoned, together with any hope of official American aid or benevolence. The league directors (Mariano Ramírez replaced Bustos on the committee) were unperturbed. Indeed, Ceniceros y Villarreal professed relief: "For my part, I can tell you that the news of the failure of the Unión Nacional took a big weight off my shoulders," he wrote to Manríquez y Zárate. "Now I believe it will be easier, or less difficult, to achieve a union with the League of all elements of good will."[12] Manríquez y Zárate also faced the future serenely: "It seems to me that we are strong-

[10] Díaz to [de la Mora?], May 30, 1928, with postscript June 1, 1928, LA-1.
[11] Ibid.
[12] Ceniceros y Villarreal to Manríquez y Zárate, June 29, 1928, cited in Antonio Ríus Facius, *Méjico cristero: Historia de la ACJM, 1925 a 1931*, p. 224.

er, and that we will soon win; that Providence was only waiting for this act of faith and confidence in the God of our fathers in order to give us the triumph."[13]

Ceniceros y Villarreal's prediction of unity was partially fulfilled. The warring Mexican Catholic factions in the United States finally made peace—after their feuding had already ruined the movement's image among potential American supporters. The ACJM contingent in Texas had joined with other bodies in the spring to form a Federation of Catholic Societies with headquarters in San Antonio; this in turn affiliated with the Beneficent Society Pro-Mexico, based in Chicago and with chapters in Detroit, in Gary, Indiana, and in Melrose Park, Aurora, and Joliet, Illinois.[14] In June, unity efforts were pressed, and a harmony meeting was finally held in El Paso the last week of July. It was presided over by Luis Chávez Hayhoe, an ACJM dissident whom the LNDLR, in a conciliatory move, had recently designated its agent in California.[15] Out of it came an organization that would remain the league's arm in the United States, the Unión Nacionalista Mexicana, which expressly recognized the league as the sole leader of the Catholic liberation movement.[16] Elected president was Fernando Díez de Urdanivia, managing editor of the Jesuit *Diario de El Paso*, who was acceptable to all sides.[17] Absent from the El Paso gathering was René Capistrán Garza, who wrote to one of the participants that the tendency toward coalition with non-Catholic elements, which he still saw as a dominant trend, made it impossible for him to participate; he would save his support for whatever group would clearly repudiate both the revolution and Mexican liberals of whatever stripe.[18]

For the league, giving up hope of succor from the U.S. govern-

[13] Manríquez y Zárate to Palomar y Vizcarra, July 15, 1928, LA-1.

[14] Carlos Fernández to NCWC, May 7, 1928, LA-1. Fernández was head of the Beneficent Society.

[15] Directive Committee to Chávez Hayhoe, July 14, 1928; statement signed by Chávez Hayhoe, August 29, 1942; LA-1.

[16] Statement signed by Chávez Hayhoe, August 29, 1942, LA-1.

[17] Urdanivia to Fernández, July 27, 1928, LA-1.

[18] Capistrán Garza to Fernández, June 29, 1928, LA-1.

ment did not mean abandoning attempts to procure it from private sources. The securing of money and military stores from abroad, including the United States, remained a prime concern. In the United States, Manríquez y Zárate and González Valencia, the latter now residing in Texas after returning from Europe, were enthusiastic collaborators. Both worked feverishly to collect and channel funds to the Cristeros.[19] González Valencia provided Beneficent Society President Carlos Fernández with credentials endorsing his work.[20] Manríquez y Zárate agonized over the munitions problem: "I have learned from various sources that the liberators are very short of ammunition," he wrote to Palomar y Vizcarra in August. "I implore you to help those poor men as much as possible. I have resolved to send them each month at least a few thousand cartridges."[21]

Repeated attempts to get aid in South America and Europe failed. A carefully planned effort by league representatives in Argentina to raise money fell through when the archdiocese of Buenos Aires became uneasy over press reports that the funds would be devoted to military purposes and cancelled permission to carry out a collection among the city's Catholics.[22] In Europe the league was represented by the Unión Internacional de Todos los Amigos de la Liga Nacional Defensora de la Libertad Religiosa de México, commonly called V.I.T.A.-MEXICO, with main offices in Louvain and Rome and branches in other major European cities.[23] Its work

[19] See, for example, Manríquez y Zárate to Palomar y Vizcarra, May 17 and June 17, 1928, LA-1.

[20] See credential signed by González Valencia August 24, 1928, LA-1.

[21] Manríquez y Zárate to Palomar y Vizcarra, August 3, 1928, LA-1.

[22] Manríquez y Zárate to Palomar y Vizcarra, December 10, 1928; January 10, 1929; "Instrucciones para la comisión," July 3, 1928; LA-1.

[23] Antonio J. López Ortega, "A propósito del archivo de la 'V.I.T.A.-MEXICO' en Roma, Italia," David 6, no. 129, (April 22, 1963): 132; Bishops' Commission, Rome, to Mons. Louis Picard, February 20, 1927, in David 8, no. 175 (February 22, 1967): 101–104; Directive Committee report to League Convention, August, 1929, LA-2. The genesis of the organization was the result of a tour by Father Mariano Cuevas, S.J., made at the direction of the Episcopal Committee late in 1926. His exact mission is not known, but in Rome he proposed to the Bishops' Commission the establishment of "Committees Pro-Mexico" in all for-

was devoted mainly to propaganda; apparently no financial aid
ever reached Mexico.

The LNDLR also tried, without success, to interest the League
of Nations in its struggle. In a letter in June, 1928, the Directive
Committee asked the assistance of that body in breaking the "conspiracy of silence" regarding Mexico's plight. It also asked the
League of Nations to urge its members to withdraw diplomatic
recognition from the Calles government and to help influence the
United States to stop abetting the Calles oppression.[24]

Failure in LNDLR attempts to obtain aid abroad was soon overshadowed by dark drama in Mexico. The presidential election of
July 1, 1928, was only a formality; Alvaro Obregón received the
news of his victory at his home in Sonora and left soon afterward
on an unhurried trip to Mexico City. He reached the capital on
Sunday, July 15. The next day Aarón Sáenz, the president-elect's
closest advisor, informed Dwight Morrow that Obregón wanted an
interview with the ambassador. An appointment was arranged
for the following day at 5:00 P.M. In the morning Sáenz visited
the embassy for a preconference talk. He and Morrow ranged over
a number of topics, including the Church question. Sáenz said that
Calles had consulted with Obregón about the proposed settlement;
Obregón hoped it might be concluded as soon as possible and fore-
saw that a later adjustment of the religious laws might be made
in the peaceful atmosphere which he hoped would characterize his
administration.[25] Sáenz left the embassy to join Obregón at a luncheon honoring the leader.

The luncheon was at a restaurant called La Bombilla in the

---

eign countries whose duty would be to disseminate information supporting the
Catholic cause and to encourage pressure on the United States in favor of Mexico's Catholics. The Bishops' Commission was enthusiastic and also lent its support to a project for a world-wide collection of funds. The Belgian Catholic youth
movement took the initiative, establishing a Union Mondiale, headed by Monsignor Louis Picard and Giovanni Hoyois and which was the parent organization of V.I.T.A.-MEXICO.

[24] Directive Committee to League of Nations, June 4, 1928, LA-1.

[25] Morrow to SecState, July 23, 1928, NA, RG 59, 812.404/895 2/9.

San Angel quarter of the capital. While the gala affair was in progress, a young man who had been making caricature drawings of the guests moved toward Obregón, who turned smilingly to view the sketches. The artist raised a revolver and fired several shots, aiming the first in the president-elect's face. Obregón died instantly. In the ensuing pandemonium the assassin was grabbed and disarmed. He had expected to be killed on the spot; instead he was hurried off to a car and taken to police headquarters.[26]

The assailant was José de León Toral, a twenty-seven-year-old native of Matehuala, San Luis Potosí. He was intensely Catholic, fervent to a point that approached mysticism—or, as many insisted after Obregón's murder, fanaticism. He had not been involved in the attempt on Obregón's life the previous autumn; in fact the act had repelled him. But the execution of Humberto Pro, who was one of his few friends and whom he replaced as LNDLR agent in the Colonia de Santa María in Mexico City, had moved him deeply. His religious fervor increased, and he dedicated nearly all his available time to arranging spiritual ministrations for the poor and organizing holy hours. Toral had known Segura Vilchis only slightly, but he knew him to be a good Catholic, a man not given to excesses, and he began to ponder the justice of his deed. The spreading persecution, the growing tendency of the people to accept it, the danger that the faith might die in Mexico—all this led him gradually to a conclusion: the Cristeros in the field were dying in a stalemated struggle; if Mexicans did not help them, they would perish. He, Toral, could help them. He would kill the tyrant Obregón.[27]

At police headquarters Toral's interrogation began immediately, accompanied by such motivational devices as suspending him by

[26] *El jurado de Toral y la Madre Conchita (lo que se dijo y lo que no se dijo en el sensacional juicio): Versión taquigráfica textual*, n.d., I, 24–26. The book is a transcript of the trial. Also see *El Universal*, July 18, 1928.

[27] *El jurado de Toral*, I, 7, 9, 10; María Elena Sodi de Pallares, *Los cristeros y José de León Toral*, pp. 33–34, 39. The author of the latter was the daughter of Demetrio Sodi, who defended Toral at the trial. She based her account on her father's papers and on personal recollections.

one thumb and one toe for prolonged periods and burning him with matches on the face and hands.[28] The rest of the day and throughout the night the police made no headway. Toral refused to reveal even his name and would say only that he had acted alone and for personal reasons. The next morning he gave his identity but still insisted no one else was involved. Officers quickly arrested his wife and parents. All three denied any knowledge of the crime, but the police were far from satisfied that others were not also responsible. Later in the day, after further questioning, Toral said he wanted to talk that evening with a certain person, after which he would be able to tell the police more. An agent agreed to escort him to see the individual. The destination, a house on Zaragoza Street, was the current quarters of the convent and religious center directed by Sister Concepción Acevedo de la Llata —Madre Conchita.[29] As police swarmed over the premises, Toral told the nun, "I'm here to see if they will believe you. I'm here to see if you want to die with me." She answered, "Yes, gladly."[30] Toral later explained that he had been at wits' end to try to convince the police that he had acted alone; the arrest of his family had caused him acute anxiety, and he felt sure that Madre Conchita, who had known him for several months, would believe him and persuade the police of his sincerity. The authorities, however, saw it differently. They arrested the nun and charged her as an accomplice in the assassination—specifically, with having cunningly implanted the idea in the mind of the impressionable Toral.[31]

Stunned friends of the dead Obregón, however, had another theory about the genesis of the crime. It was an undeniable fact that Obregón's removal benefited a number of individuals, not least among them the incumbent president of the republic. With Obre-

---

[28] Sodi de Pallares, *Los cristeros y José de León Toral,* pp. 108–109; *El jurado de Toral,* I, 59.

[29] *El jurado de Toral,* II, 56–57.

[30] Ibid., I, 166.

[31] Ibid., I, 121–138.

gón gone, Calles would no longer have to share the revolutionary pinnacle with his one-time mentor.

The next few days were the most dangerous ever faced by the regime of Plutarco Elías Calles. When the president arrived at Obregón's residence shortly after the assassination, a surly mob in front of the house met him with shouts of "We want justice!" Later he made a brief visit to police headquarters, where Toral refused to say anything more to him than he had to the interrogators. But Ricardo Topete, a federal deputy from Sonora and a close friend of Obregón, handed Calles the murder weapon and blurted out insolently, "Here is the pistol, with which you are familiar."[32] Emilio Portes Gil, the governor of Tamaulipas, later recalled that, when he went to the Obregón home the afternoon of the assassination, he found the yard filled with a frenzied throng of generals and politicians, all of them protégés of the deceased and most of them convinced that the crime was the work of Calles and his labor allies. Some of the military among them announced that they were leaving at once for their home bases to commence armed operations against the president. A few Obregón partisans, however, urged calm until there was a chance to establish the facts.[33]

Obregón's murder had in a trice awakened old animosities within the revolutionary camp, most notably between Obregón followers and the *laborista* group led by Luis Morones, which had been particularly influential in the Calles administration. On the evening of July 20 the fire-eating Antonio Díaz Soto y Gama, once an intimate of Emiliano Zapata, told a large public meeting that Calles should be supported, but that he must eliminate the labor leaders from their positions of power.[34] Emilio Portes Gil, Arturo Orci, and others pressed Calles to act fast. Specifically, they urged the immediate removal of Roberto Cruz, who as chief of police would

[32] John W. F. Dulles, *Yesterday in Mexico: A Chronicle of the Revolution, 1919–1936*, pp. 370–371; *El jurado de Toral*, I, 55–56.

[33] Emilio Portes Gil, *Autobiografía de la Revolución Mexicana*, p. 408.

[34] *El Universal*, July 21, 1928.

head the investigation of the crime and who had not been on friendly terms with the dead leader. Calles readily agreed.[35] Morones too
was speedily sacrificed; his resignation from the cabinet was announced the twenty-second.[36]

That the assassination had been provoked by religious motives
rather than political ones was a point Calles was anxious to have
immediately and clearly understood, particularly by the army,
where Obregón had been immensely popular. On July 23 Calles
sent a circular telegram to chiefs of military operations throughout
the country expressing gratitude for the army's revolutionary dedication "in these moments when the criminal hand armed by the
Catholic clergy has plunged the entire nation into mourning."[37]
Several days later, with the crisis abating, Calles modified his indictment, telling a reporter that, although certain Catholics had
probably influenced Toral, he could not say that the assassin was a
tool of the Church.[38] He added that he did not wish to continue
in office beyond the end of his term in December.[39]

Dwight Morrow knew that Obregón's death had damaged efforts to settle the religious conflict, but he refused to see the incident as a permanent blight. His first move to salvage matters was
to urge both Calles and the Catholic side represented by Father
Burke to show restraint in their words and actions.[40] With Calles
he was not entirely successful. The president had the urgent problem of saving his government. His broadside inculpation of the
clergy was made despite Morrow's plea, and it caused Father
Burke to react bitterly. Only by strenuous efforts were State Department officials able to dissuade the priest from making a public
reply in kind.[41]

Morrow reviewed the situation in a letter to Kellogg on July 23.

[35] Portes Gil, *Autobiografía*, pp. 410–411.

[36] *El Universal*, July 22, 1928.

[37] Ibid., July 25, 1928.

[38] *Excélsior*, August 1, 1928.

[39] Ibid., August 3, 1928.

[40] Memorandum of telephone conversation with Ambassador Morrow (written by Lane), July 19, 1928, NA, RG 59, 812.404/895½.

[41] Lane to Morrow, July 25, 1928, NA, RG 59, 812.404/895a.

He was discouraged that Rome had delayed action on the proposed settlement. Father Burke, he said, had succeeded in persuading Calles to deal with Rome because the Holy See would be more reasonable than the Mexican episcopate, but now no one seemed able to find out whether Rome really wanted an agreement of the kind Calles would make. Morrow said he had already pressured Calles considerably, and he could do nothing more unless it was leading to an end that Church authorities could accept. Obregón's death had stalled things, he concluded, but a settlement was still possible.[42]

During the next few days Morrow received new information regarding the ecclesiastical chain of command, plus some one-sided advice on the LNDLR's status in the religious tangle. In his letter to Kellogg he had enclosed a translation of a league bulletin, which he described as a publication of an irresponsible group distinct from the "Federation for the Defense of Religious Liberty" referred to in terms of approbation in the papal encyclical of November 18, 1926. He said confusion over the identity of the two groups added to government distrust of Catholic intentions.[43]

Arthur Bliss Lane clarified the matter for the ambassador two days later. He told him that the two organizations were identical and that the confusion was due to a loose translation of the encyclical.[44] Lane also forwarded a memorandum from William Montavon which purported to explain the pope's opinion of the league. Montavon said the league had fallen from favor after it turned to "political and physical action," and that "the Holy Father repudiated that action." The pope, Montavon insisted, was opposed to politics and violence.[45]

But who, then, spoke for the Church? Morrow asked Father Burke to explain this to him. The answer, relayed by the State Department, came from Pascual Díaz, who said the priest had forwarded Morrow's query to him. Díaz enclosed copies of Fumasoni-Biondi's letter to him of the previous December and of his own let-

[42] Morrow to SecState, July 23, 1928, NA, RG 59, 812.404/895⅔.
[43] Ibid.
[44] Lane to Morrow, July 25, 1928, NA, RG 59, 812.404/896.
[45] Memorandum from Montavon, July 25, 1928, Dwight Morrow Papers.

ter to the bishops.[46] He pointed out that he was himself the liaison
between the apostolic delegate and the bishops, and that Father
Burke was the delegate's agent. As for the league, Díaz said, in
1926 Pius XI had approved it when it sought to work by legal
means alone to win religious freedom in Mexico. Later, however,
the league, "on its own responsibility," decided to take up arms to
win liberty. When matters reached the stage at which the pope
and bishops were being blamed for the armed action, the pope
gave instructions, "in which, leaving Catholics as individuals entirely free, he instructed the bishops to have no part, physical or
moral, direct or indirect, in any armed action by Catholics under
the direction of the League." Díaz offered to provide any further
information on the subject that the ambassador might desire.[47]
He added that the information was not confidential and that the
ambassador could use it as he pleased.[48]

If Morrow had read the correspondence with his usual thoroughness, he might have wondered at the disparity between Montavon's insistence that the pope had repudiated the league's actions
and Díaz's explanation that the pontiff had only forbidden the
bishops to associate themselves with it. Díaz's instruction to Bustos
of January 7, 1928, which Montavon enclosed, in fact contradicted
Montavon's memorandum. Indeed, fuller reflection might have
suggested to Morrow that one reason Rome was in no hurry to
settle with Calles was that it had not abandoned hope of forcing
better terms—something the rebellion might yet accomplish.

But Morrow evidently was satisfied: the league and the Cristeros
were as much outlaws in the eyes of the Church as they were in
the eyes of the government. The pope and the bishops were the
people to deal with.

On August 9 Morrow had a long breakfast meeting with Calles.
The president, Morrow reported, had talked mainly about nonreligious problems. He believed that Rome had repudiated Father

[46] See above, chapter 7.
[47] Díaz to Morrow, July 24, 1928, NA, RG 59, 812.404/896, with enclosures.
[48] See Morrow to Díaz, August 3, 1928, Dwight Morrow Papers.

Burke and that the matter was closed; unless the clergy wanted to return in the spirit shown by Father Burke, they would not be welcome. Morrow added that Calles believed fanatical Catholics operating with LNDLR funds were responsible for Obregón's murder. But Morrow was determined not to give up. "Don't get discouraged," he told Lane, "In another week or two we may be able to go on."[49] After another meeting five days later, Morrow told Lane that the president now had about the same opinion of the Vatican that he had of William Randolph Hearst. Morrow, too, was exasperated; someone in Rome, he said, must have gone out of his mind. He referred to violently anti-Calles editorials that had been appearing in *Osservatore Romano*. The rebel problem, he added, seemed to be under control—Calles had told him the rebellion had all but collapsed.[50]

Calles delivered his annual message to Congress on September 1. One topic overshadowed all others: the presidential succession. His reported statement the month before that he did not wish to continue in office had not been definitive. Many believed that the president, now undisputed master of the revolutionary coterie, would stake out an indefinite hold on the highest office. But his opening words indicated they were wrong. He categorically ruled out any prolongation of his mandate after December 1 and declared that he would never again aspire to the presidency.[51] There were

[49] Memorandum of telephone conversation with Ambassador Morrow, August 9, 1928, NA, RG 59, 812.404/895½; Morrow to Kellogg, August 14, 1928, NA, RG 59, 812.404/894 8/9.

[50] Memorandum of telephone conversation wih Ambassador Morrow, August 14, 1928, NA, RG 59, 812.404/903 3/5.

[51] Eduardo Iglesias, S.J., and Rafael Martínez del Campo, S.J. [Pseud. Aquiles P. Moctezuma], *El conflicto religioso de 1926: sus orígenes, su desarrollo, su solución*, II, 481. The constitution had been amended during Calles's administration to lengthen the presidential term to six years, beginning in 1928. By law, new elections had to be held to replace Obregón (technically, to complete the term to which he had been elected). Congress would choose a provisional president to serve during the interim from December 1 to the accession of a new president. In September, Congress set November 20, 1929, for the election, the winner to take office February 5, 1930.

other surprises. He appealed for a political system based in fact
as well as theory on genuine political democracy. Free elections, he
said, even if they should result in giving national representation
to such groups as the "clerical reaction," should not alarm true
revolutionaries.[52] The speech amounted to a display of statesman-
ship that none of Calles's enemies and perhaps few of his friends
had thought him capable of.

Even Catholics were impressed. There seemed to be hope that
things were changing. In the weeks that followed Congress received
a number of petitions. The first, which was probably in preparation before the presidential address was delivered, arrived September 3, signed by a distinguished group that included Toribio Esqui-
vel Obregón, Miguel Alessio Robles, and Eduardo J. Correa. It
asked for the reform of the constitutional articles on religion. Three
things were essential, it said: (a) recognition of the existence and
personality of churches, (b) recognition of the separation and independence between the State and all churches and therefore ab-
stention by the State from legislating on religious questions, and
(c) recognition that such separation must entail friendly cooperation for the common good rather than hostility. Specific and detailed amendments to each relevant constitutional article were also
proposed.[53] El Universal devoted an editorial to the memorial and
the religious problem generally, something rarely seen in the Mexican press since 1926. While neither supporting nor opposing the
memorial, the editors called for mature consideration of it and
spoke of the need for just laws appropriate to national needs.[54] Another petition, essentially a restatement of the first and bearing
additional names, was submitted on September 16.[55] A third, early

[52] Ibid., p. 484.

[53] El Universal, September 4, 1928; Iglesias and Martínez del Campo [pseud.
Moctezuma], El conflicto religioso, II, 485–488; Ríus Facius, Méjico cristero, p.
343. Excélsior for August 29 carried a report that the Mexican bishops would
soon petition Congress again for a change in the laws, but I have found no evidence linking the prelates to the memorials of September and October.

[54] El Universal, September 6, 1928.

[55] Ibid., September 20, 1928.

in October, contained a detailed comparison of Mexico's religious laws with those of a number of other nations, the theme being that legislation hostile to religion was inadmissible in civilized societies and that harmonious separation of the spiritual and temporal spheres was a hallmark of national modernity.[56] Other petitions in like vein arrived during September and October from various parts of the country.[57]

The petition drive failed to confirm the existence of a thaw. Congress did not even acknowledge receipt of the communications. Some deputies were quoted as saying that they would not recognize them unless Catholics specifically repudiated the rebellion.[58] Yet there was during autumn a perceptible lessening in the intensity of the government's handling of individual infractions of the religious laws, a shift to a more matter-of-fact approach as opposed to the coarse overreaction of the previous three years.[59] Part of the reason may have been the changes in Calles's cabinet that followed Obregón's death.

Emilio Portes Gil replaced Adalberto Tejeda as secretary of *gobernación* on August 16. Portes Gil would later claim credit for relaxing religious tensions during his three months at Gobernación. Unquestionably he was more moderate on the subject than Tejeda; at the same time, he acted with Calles's approval.[60] Portes Gil had not been a Calles intimate. He was generally thought of as leaning

[56] Ibid., October 5, 1928. Iglesias and Martínez del Campo [pseud. Moctezuma], *El conflicto religioso*, II, 493–495.

[57] Iglesias and Martínez del Campo [pseud. Moctezuma], *El conflicto religioso*, II, 495–496. Copies of petitions submitted to Congress in September and October are in LA-1.

[58] Iglesias and Martínez del Campo [pseud. Moctezuma], *El conflicto religioso*, II, 498–499.

[59] Ibid., p. 484.

[60] Portes Gil (*Autobiografía*, p. 554) says that, upon taking over his cabinet post, he acted to persuade Calles that it was necessary to end the violence being perpetrated by government officials in connection with the enforcement of the religious laws and that Calles gave him a free hand so long as the laws were not compromised; he then moved to instruct officials at all levels to put an end to unjust and arbitrary actions.

toward the Obregón faction. At first, his appointment to the number two position in the government was seen as a further step to pacify the Obregónists, but after Calles's September message to Congress it took on a new light. Many suspected that the young Tamaulipas politician might be in the line of succession. He was, after all, a plausible choice—acceptable to Calles's opponents, but without a national following that could make it possible for him to challenge Calles for control of the revolutionary coalition. On September 19 Congress chose him to succeed Calles as interim president on December 1.

While the government moved toward harmony within its own ranks and a slightly milder line on religious matters, Rome remained silent. Father Burke hopefully told U.S. Under Secretary of State J. Ruben Clark in September that he understood the Holy See wanted to keep the door open,[61] but Robert Olds, who was in Europe for a visit and offered to probe matters personally at the Vatican, learned through intermediaries that a visit might be of little use unless he was bringing new facts or proposals. Morrow advised against pursuing the matter.[62] The next move, he believed, must come from Rome, and he did not understand what the essential difficulty was.[63]

Rome finally made its position known in November, through Ruiz y Flores. While still at sea on his return trip to the United States the archbishop addressed a letter to Miguel de la Mora, living in seclusion in Mexico City. He said that the pope wanted all the bishops to know that the Holy See was prepared to enter into talks with the Mexican government, to be held preferably in Rome, provided the purpose of such talks was to discuss reform of the constitution and laws. The pope was prepared to authorize a return of the bishops and the resumption of public worship even before the termination of an agreement, as soon as he had adequate guaran-

---

[61] See Clark to Morrow, September 6, 1928, NA, RG 59, 812.404/908a.

[62] Norman Armour, Paris, to SecState, September 13, 1928; September 17, 1928; NA, RG 59, 812.404/913 and 812.404/915; Morrow to SecState, September 19, 1928, NA, RG 59, 812.404/916.

[63] See Morrow to Clark, October 5, 1928, NA, RG 59, 812.404/931²⁄₁₂.

tees regarding freedom of the Church. The pontiff, Ruiz y Flores added, wanted the bishops to be of one mind with him on the matter.[64]

Immediately upon reaching Washington, Ruiz y Flores set to work to obtain the unity Rome wanted. He wired the Episcopal Committee, then meeting in San Antonio, stressing the need for them to remain strictly united with the Holy See and the importance of doing nothing to damage the good will that the Mexican and American governments had evinced. The day after he sent the message, he received instructions from Rome to go at once to Texas to meet with the Episcopal Committee, then to proceed to California to confer with several prelates who were not attending the San Antonio meeting.[65]

The State Department learned of the Vatican's position on November 16, when Montavon brought the news to Clark. Morrow, informed the same day,[66] said it might be worthwhile for Ruiz y Flores to see Calles again to explain the pope's stand.[67] Calles had told him two weeks before that he would discuss the religious question only with Father Burke or someone introduced by him.[68] Fumasoni-Biondi, however, vetoed the suggestion. On the twenty-first he told Burke (who had promoted the idea) that the Holy See was not disposed to allow the resumption of worship "unless and until the Mexican Government offers more favorable conditions than those expressed in the letter of President Calles to Dr. Burke." The fact that the government might allow an apostolic delegate to function in Mexico (Burke had stressed this in a memorandum to the delegate on November 8) represented nothing new; that had been

[64] Circular letter [from de la Mora?] to the bishops in Mexico, undated, transmitting letter from Ruiz y Flores of November 5, 1928, LA-1. Ruiz y Flores seems to have eclipsed Díaz as the Vatican's spokesman among the bishops after November. I have found no explanation of this, but, in view of the fact that Díaz emerged as a key figure again a few months later, it was evidently not due to any displeasure with him.

[65] Kellogg to Morrow, November 19, 1928, NA, RG 59, 812.404/936b.

[66] Clark to Morrow, November 16, 1928, NA, RG 59, 812.404/936a.

[67] Rublee Memorandum, Dwight Morrow Papers.

[68] Morrow to SecState, November 8, 1928, NA, RG 59, 812.404/931.

granted in the Veracruz interview.[69] Fumasoni-Biondi noted that Montavon had reported on the eighteenth[70] that Calles, after the return of the bishops, would be willing to undertake amiable discussions looking toward either an acceptable interpretation of the laws or their amendment. This, the delegate said, was interesting, but any promises of a change in position should be submitted over the signature of an official of the Mexican government.[71]

But Calles had decided against further talks. The day before Morrow received a copy of Fumasoni-Biondi's letter to Burke, he had broached to the president the idea of a visit by Burke or someone else. Calles had said no; he had only a few days left in office and could give no further assurances on the religious question. He added that, in view of the agitated state of public opinion, it would be difficult for Portes Gil to move on the matter at the start of his term. Morrow did not try to force the issue. He proceeded with plans to depart for a visit to the United States, telling Kellogg that he expected to be in Washington on December 9.[72]

Calles did not exaggerate the unsettled public mood of November. *Excélsior* correctly labeled the trial of José de León Toral and Madre Conchita, which began November 2, the most sensational legal proceeding in Mexico since the one that had convicted Maximilian of Habsburg in 1867.[73] The courtroom periodically dissolved into chaos. At one session a band of federal deputies invaded the chamber waving pistols and threatening to lynch the young assassin. Demetrio Sodi, the distinguished jurist who headed the defense, had to defend his client by main force until order was restored.[74] Some members of the jury wore sidearms after receiving

[69] Fumasoni-Biondi to Burke, November 21, 1928, in Clark to Morrow, November 23, 1928, NA, RG 59, 812.404/938a.

[70] Montavon was relaying a message from the State Department. See Rublee Memorandum.

[71] Fumasoni-Biondi to Burke, November 21, 1928, in Clark to Morrow, November 23, 1928, NA, RG 59, 812.404/938a.

[72] Morrow to SecState, November 23, 1928, NA, RG 59, 812.404/939; Rublee Memorandum.

[73] *Excélsior*, November 2, 1928.

[74] Sodi de Pallares, *Los cristeros y José de León Toral*, p. 113.

threats that they would be killed if they acquitted Toral.[75] In the streets outside, mounted troops battled rioting demonstrators—it was not quite clear which were for Toral and which against him— and many persons were injured.[76] Inside the courtroom every session was marked by high drama. There was a renewal of innuendos that influential men not connected with the religious question had been involved in the murder.[77] The testimony was laced with lurid details. It was revealed that some of the young militants who frequented religious devotions at Madre Conchita's convent had been manufacturing bombs, one of which had exploded in the Chamber of Deputies early in the summer. Several devotees had hatched a plan to poison both Obregón and Calles at a dance in Celaya the previous spring—and the poison had changed hands in the convent.[78] The nun denied that she had induced Toral to kill the president-elect or that she had any knowledge of her young friends' doings. On the witness stand she performed so brilliantly that the team for the prosecution, led by the attorney general, appeared at times to be the defendants.

The outcome of the week-long proceeding caused no surprise, however. Toral was condemned to death. Madre Conchita was sentenced to twenty years in prison[79] and a few weeks later was interned in the Islas Marías penal colony off the Nayarit coast.

The trial deterred Morrow's and Burke's efforts, but Ruiz y Flores went ahead with his mission to rally the bishops. He pronounced himself satisfied after his meeting with the Episcopal Committee in San Antonio. The prelates agreed to the request for

[75] *New York Times*, November 8, 1928.

[76] Portes Gil, *Autobiografía*, p. 555.

[77] *El jurado de Toral*, I, 101, 104–106. The defense limited itself to oblique hints at this during the trial, but Sodi claimed that the bullet holes in the corpse were of three different calibers. One physician, he said, fled into hiding to avoid having to sign the falsified official autopsy report (Sodi de Pallares, *Los cristeros y José de León Toral*, pp. 125–126).

[78] *El jurado de Toral*, I, 168–170; II, 80–84. The Celaya poison plot was referred to in a published report of the investigation in August, but the trial produced new details. See *Excélsior*, August 22, 1928.

[79] *Excélsior*, November 9, 1928. Mexican Law forbade the execution of women.

unity and pledged their obedience to the pope, but they retained a workable reserve of self-assertiveness.[80] On November 21 they issued a collective pastoral letter. It was in part conciliatory, going so far as to praise Calles's September 1 speech, which it termed a call to true patriotism that, if followed, would lead to brighter days. Mexico, said the bishops, because of its large Catholic majority, might aspire to be ruled by a Catholic government. This, however, was not being sought, but only a "friendly separation" of Church and State. Catholic governments, said the pastoral, must be "not a product of politics or laws, much less of violent and aggressive action . . . but rather the spontaneous fruit of the unity of faith that comes to reign in all social life by means of ordered, peaceful, Catholic action which does not perturb the social order." Then, however, the bishops heaped plaudits on groups that were indeed perturbing the social order, by including both the LNDLR and the ACJM in a list of Catholic organizations praiseworthy for their "constancy and heroism."[81]

But it was faint encouragement indeed alongside that being given by the prelate who stood sternly at the extreme end of the intransigency spectrum. In the summer of 1928 the *Revista Católica* press in El Paso published Bishop Manríquez y Zárate's strongest defense of the rebellion, filled with slashing attacks on Calles ("the most abominable, hypocritical, and vile man to appear in the history of America") and encomiums for the Cristeros ("glorious soldiers of freedom . . . champions of Christian right in this century of apostasy and cowardice").[82] The LNDLR directors urged the bishop to join the men in the field. He replied that he would do so in an instant if he could be sure it would not provoke the pope's public disapproval and thereby cripple the movement—González

[80] Clark to Morrow, November 28, 1928, NA, RG 59, 812.404/942a.

[81] Carta Pastoral Colectiva, November 21, 1928, LA-1.

[82] José de Jesús Manríquez y Zárate, *¡Viva Cristo Rey! en la hora de suprema angustia*, pp. 18, 76–77. In sending a copy to Palomar y Vizcarra, he said he hoped it would encourage them all. He added that the LNDLR had exclusive publishing rights in Mexico and that any earnings were to be applied exclusively to the "armed defense" (Manríquez y Zárate to Palomar y Vizcarra, June 17, 1928, LA-3).

Valencia, he added, was restraining him for that reason.[83] His ab-
horrence of the United States was becoming apocalyptic: Herbert
Hoover's victory over Al Smith, he wrote, showed that God desired
the complete and final defeat of the "children of darkness," which
would ensure the resurgence of the Hispanic race and of Mexico.[84]

While the LNDLR groped for support, the insurrection waxed
and waned. As in the previous year, the late spring of 1928 saw
a decline in rebel activity, due to a drop in the number of men
under arms. Attaché Harold Thompson estimated the Cristero total at five thousand in June.[85] The decline was attributed to more
efficient federal military leadership and to rebel ammunition shortages,[86] but these were probably not the most important reasons.
Nearly all the Cristeros were farmers, and to neglect the crops in
early summer was to confront their families with starvation.

Still, the decline in hostilities was not as marked as it had been
the year before, and May brought an impressive indication that
the rebellion was very much alive. After weeks of preparation
Jesús Degollado Guízar attacked the Pacific coast port of Manzanillo with 1,600 men. The town fell after a stiff resistance in which
the government defenders were aided by a barrage from a federal
gunboat in the harbor. But the victory was brief. Cristero units
which had been ordered to pin down government forces in the city
of Colima did not attack the capital until midafternoon, by which
time most of the federals had evaded them and were rushing toward Manzanillo. Failure to destroy a railroad bridge on the main
line to the coast made it easy for the relief column to reach the
town, where it appeared in such strength that Degollado withdrew
hastily in order to avoid being trapped. He saved most of his command, but 45 men were cut off and died fighting.[87] Nevertheless,

[83] Manríquez y Zárate to Palomar y Vizcarra, 1928, LA-3.

[84] Ibid.

[85] G-2 report, no. 2288, September 24, 1928, Maj. Harold Thompson to War
Department, NA, RG 165. Yaquis and bandits are not included in the total.

[86] G-2 report, no. 2109, June 11, 1928, Col. Alexander Macnab to War Department, NA, RG 165.

[87] Jesús Degollado Guízar, *Memorias de Jesús Degollado Guízar, último general en jefe del ejército cristero*, pp. 136–150. The U.S. military attaché report,

it had been a major engagement, total casualties for both sides running into the hundreds.[88]

In Michoacán, Luis Navarro Origel was well on top of events as 1928 opened. A league official who visited his headquarters was received with full military honors and reviewed 5,000 troops, nearly all of whom, he reported, had new arms captured from government units. He praised the strict discipline and strong religious spirit.[89] On January 14, federal general Juan Domínguez occupied Coalcomán without opposition—to find himself in a well prepared ambush. His command was besieged for over two weeks and escaped annihilation only by the last-minute arrival of a relief force.[90] Navarro reported that he was in action during all of January and that the enemy had suffered losses every day of the month.[91] On March 23, near Zamora, his men cut to pieces the federal Thirty-fourth Battalion and killed 229 men.[92] He was at the pinnacle of his fame; the LNDLR was at the point of naming him supreme civil head of the movement.[93] Then, in the space of a few days, Navarro's career collapsed.

Navarro's followers and most of the other Cristeros were probably not markedly different in their behavior from men who had

---

based on official Mexican sources, put the total Cristero force involved in the day's action at 800. A Mexican War Department official told Attaché Macnab that the Cristero attack had been made for the purpose of clearing the port to receive a ship due to arrive from California with contraband arms. See G-2 report, no. 2109, June 11, 1928, Macnab to War Department, NA, RG 165. This is plausible; Degollado would hardly have undertaken such a complex and dangerous operation without a tangible reason. Moreover, he well knew that even under ideal conditions he could not have held Manzanillo for long.

[88] Rafael Ceniceros y Villarreal, in "Historia de la L.N.D.R.," said the government admitted to 350 casualties. The June 11 G-2 report cited above says 125 federal troops were killed, plus 16 civilians and local police, and that the Cristeros lost 184 men.

[89] Palomar y Vizcarra to González Valencia, December 16, 1927, LA-1.

[90] *El Universal,* January 15, 1928; Alfonso Trueba [pseud. Martín Chowell], *Luis Navarro Origel: El primer cristero,* pp. 132–133.

[91] Trueba [pseud. Chowell], *Navarro Origel,* p. 133.

[92] G-2 report, no. 2028, April 17, 1928, Macnab to War Department, NA, RG 165.

[93] Directive Committee report to League Convention, August, 1929, LA-2.

fought in Mexico's other civil upheavals. Heriberto Navarrete commented, on the basis of his experience in Jalisco, that "they were no better or worse, as a general rule, than they were when they lived as simple *rancheros* before the persecution."[94] Overall, they may have been a cut above the usual guerrilla types—more than a few of them led exemplary lives in the field—but they were by no means all saints. Navarro, however, was determined that his men would be in every sense "Christian soldiers." The Michoacán Cristeros had tasted severe discipline more than once, and resentment had grown. A clash came when some of Navarro's officers decided to sack and destroy a village whose inhabitants had been notoriously unsympathetic to the Cristeros. Unable to prevent the assault, Navarro bent slightly; he managed to dissuade them from burning the town and obtained a pledge that all goods and money collected would be placed at the disposal of the command. After the attack, however, no money was turned in. Navarro thereupon ordered a personal search of the troops, which produced over a hundred pesos and infuriated many of the men. To give matters a chance to cool, Navarro ordered that each man be given a furlough and supplied with food, clothing, or money for his family. The order was not obeyed. Instead, several officers managed with little difficulty to organize a mutiny. Navarro was seized and was at the point of being shot when the parish priest of Coalcomán arrived and persuaded the troops to spare the leader's life. In June, Navarro left Michoacán with a portion of his brigade that chose to follow him. He joined Carlos Bouquet's forces in southern Jalisco, where he was killed in action two months later.[95]

The summer was by no means quiet in the rebel areas. Father Aristeo Pedroza and Father José Reyes Vega led 350 Cristeros against government forces in Los Altos on June 20.[96] Command problems were less serious. Degollado reported that he was no

---

[94] Heriberto Navarrete, *"Por Dios y Por la Patria": Memorias de mi participación en la defensa de la libertad de conciencia y culto durante la persecución religiosa en México de 1926 a 1929*, p. 187.

[95] Trueba [pseud. Chowell], *Navarro Origel*, pp. 137–141.

[96] *Excélsior*, June 22, 1928.

longer plagued by disharmony among his chiefs, that the troops were having success in most of their engagements, and that even the supply problem was not as critical as it had been.[97]

The LNDLR was often inept in its choice of leaders, but its most crucial selection was brilliant. In August the Directive Committee appointed Enrique Gorostieta y Velarde commander-in-chief of the "National Liberation Army."[98] The decision required some soul-searching. Ever since Gorostieta had joined the movement, there had been murmurings that worried the directors. His subordinates were uneasy over his lack of piety. It was said, for example, that he made slighting remarks about bishops.[99] In April the directors told Gorostieta that they were entirely satisfied with his efforts but wanted to pass along to him reports, perhaps exaggerated, that they had received. These were to the effect that the general had said things that offended the beliefs of his soldiers and even that he had made fun of their religious practices. The directors went on to say—somewhat tongue in cheek—that they did not believe the reports but that as jealous defenders of the general they wanted him to be aware of such rumors, which could be divisive.[100]

Gorostieta assumed formal command in October with the issuance of a "Manifesto to the Nation." The document, drafted by Palomar y Vizcarra and approved by the Directive Committee, provided for a reorganization of the "liberation movement." The forces in the field were to be known henceforth as the National Guard (Guardia Nacional). As military chief, Gorostieta had "all necessary authority" in matters of war and finance. It was projected that a supreme civil head of the movement would be chosen by the Directive Committee in consultation with the Guardia Nacional.[101]

The manifesto also included another attempt to broaden the

[97] Degollado, *Memorias*, p. 163.
[98] Chief, Special Committee, to Ceniceros y Villarreal, August 30, 1928, LA-1.
[99] Palomar y Vizcarra to González Valencia, December 26, 1927, LA-1.
[100] Directive Committee to Gorostieta, April 6, 1928, LA-1.
[101] "Manifiesto a la Nación," October 28, 1928, printed handbill, LA-1; James W. Wilkie and Edna Monzón de Wilkie, *México visto en el siglo XX*, p. 458.

movement's appeal. The Constitution of 1857, "although not in fact expressing the real and tangible sentiments of the Mexican people," was declared re-established, minus the Laws of Reform but incorporating the principles of the "national plebiscite in 1926 [the petition bearing some two million signatures], supporting the petition formulated by the Most Reverend Mexican Prelates on September 6 of that year," plus the amplifications contained in the memorial to Congress of September 3, 1928. The manifesto pledged the new government to recognize as valid and to enforce fairly all just measures currently in force "designed to recognize the right of laboring men to unionize, protect and defend their rights, and better their condition." The national government eventually to be formed was committed to the establishment of commissions to work out agreements between landowners and *ejidatarios* (inhabitants of communal farms) and to adopt procedures to assure just and effective compensation for the former. Where necessary for the common good, redistribution of rural lands would continue, "but in a just and equitable way and with prior indemnification." It was specified that the manifesto could be altered only by mutual consent of the Directive Committee and the supreme military chief.[102]

None of the participants has related how details of the manifesto were agreed upon, but undoubtedly it entailed some considerable giving-in on the part of the directors. The document was pre-eminontly a war measure; evidently the committee decided that giving the military arm equal standing and accepting the 1857 constitution were prices it had to pay. It was a recognition that dramatic measures were necessary and that Gorostieta was indispensable.

Harmony was, as always, a paramount concern. One of Gorostieta's first problems on that score concerned the Feminine Brigades. The organization had grown in numbers and efficiency and by the middle of 1928 was an important cog in the Cristero effort. The brigades had, however, guarded their autonomy to such an extent

102 "Manifiesto a la Nación."

as to constitute a self-governing military organization, obeying the LNDLR only when they chose to. The league, ever jealous of its prerogatives, forced the issue, and by autumn there was open dissension. Gorostieta attempted mediation. He suggested that the brigades be placed under his direct authority, which, he pointed out to Ceniceros y Villarreal, would make them in fact subject to the league.[103] The directors vetoed the idea, and the scrap went on. By December, Gorostieta was irked. He told the committee that the friction had resulted in a serious decrease in the flow of ammunition, and even though the directors were now assuring him that acceptable harmony had been re-established, the forces in the field were getting almost nothing. At the height of the dispute, he said, the Guardia Nacional would have succumbed had he not been able to rely on other sources he had established.[104] Apparently the situation improved, and the directors and the ladies resumed a cold but correct relationship, while Gorostieta struggled gamely to broaden sources of supply.

The main source of ammunition used by the Cristeros, whether supplied by the Feminine Brigades or someone else, was the government itself. Cartridges were regularly purchased from dishonest federal officials. In the spring of 1928 Felipe Brondo Alvarez and some companions were obtaining sizable amounts in this way in San Luis Potosí, at 6½ or 7 centavos a shell—a relatively low price in such transactions. When they had the money, Brondo's group would buy as many as ten cases at a time, dealing through army officers who were in partnership with a chief at the munitions depot. The next most usual means of procurement was capture, both in raids and on the battlefield. Relatively little ever came from outside Mexico.[105]

As before, there was a resurgence of military activity in late

103 Gorostieta to Ceniceros y Villarreal, November 21, 1928, LA-1.

104 Directive Committee to Gorostieta, December 3, 1928; Gorostieta to Directive Committee, December 28, 1928; LA-1.

105 Felipe Brondo Alvarez, Memoirs; interview with Felipe Brondo Alvarez, June, 1968.

summer and autumn.[106] By November much of Jalisco was again aflame, and in Colima, where Cristeros nearly demolished a large government force near Comala, businesses and government offices in the state capital closed in fear of a general attack.[107] December saw increased action in Michoacán and Guanajuato, with activity on a smaller scale reported in Zacatecas, Aguascalientes, Chihuahua, Hidalgo, Tamaulipas, Veracruz, Guerrero, Durango, and the state of Mexico.[108] Much of Nayarit was in rebel hands, and in January the government acknowledged that rebels were causing serious disruption in Oaxaca.[109] In January and February the government again resorted to "reconcentration" of civilians in Jalisco, Querétaro, and Guanajuato,[110] and launched a no-quarter offensive bolstered by air squadrons and fresh army units transferred from Chiapas and Tabasco.[111] Armed agrarians, formally organized into local defense units as a paramilitary army reserve, also joined the all-out effort.[112]

[106] See G-2 report, no. 2288, September 24, 1928, Thompson to War Department, NA, RG 165. The attaché's estimate put total Cristero strength at 5,750 for August. He said that during the month 375 rebels and 254 federals and agrarians had died in combat.

[107] Enrique de Jesús Ochoa [pseud. Spectator], *Los cristeros del Volcán de Colima*, II, 128–130.

[108] "Noticias captadas del 1º al 31 de diciembre [1928]," LA-1; *Excélsior*, December 3, 1928; *El Universal*, December 11, 1928; December 18, 1928.

[109] *El Universal*, January 15, 1929; January 30, 1929.

[110] *El Universal*, January 12, 1929; Chief of La Cruz Brigade, Querétaro, to Chief of Special Committee, February 16, 1929, in *David* 5, no. 120 (July 22, 1962): 385–386.

[111] *El Universal*, January 24, 1929; February 1, 1929; February 25, 1929. The air-force contingent included twenty-one pilots, flying Bristol and Borhaund aircraft.

[112] *El Universal*, December 29, 1928. The mustering of agrarians no doubt had another objective as well. At the time of the Gómez-Serrano revolt in 1927, the government had distributed arms to agrarian groups, whom it detailed to patrol areas from which regular troops had to be temporarily withdrawn. This greatly increased the number of agrarians under arms. Many had already been serving as auxiliaries to government forces fighting the Cristeros, and it soon became obvious that they were often as much a threat to public tranquility, especially when left to their own devices, as were declared rebels. Once the 1927 revolt was over, the government took steps to disarm them, but large numbers

As the new year of 1929 began, chances for peace seemed remote. The rebellion, it appeared, might continue for years, now ebbing, now flowing, neither succeeding nor failing in its objectives. And an end to the religious conflict that had triggered it seemed almost equally unattainable. On January 5 Morrow, in Washington, discussed matters with Burke, Clark, and Lane at the State Department. Morrow observed that there was little point in Father Burke's going to Mexico for more talks only to find that an agreement reached would not get Rome's approval. He said the new administration in Mexico City would be busy with financial matters, and it might be as long as a year before progress could be made toward a settlement of the religious issue. He said he did not plan to do anything further unless Father Burke requested it—although he would of course be glad to be of service.[113] Father Burke sailed the last week of February for a two-month visit to Europe and the Holy Land. Morrow returned to his post in Mexico City on February 3. If he was discouraged, he did not show it. In fact, he immediately began probing for a new way to unlock the Church-State puzzle—although he knew that for the moment the time was not propitious.

Once again, events within Mexico hindered the search for peace. Emilio Portes Gil's attempts to relax religious tensions, begun while he was secretary of *gobernación*, had borne no fruit. Soon after taking the presidential oath on December 1, he offered amnesties and land to Cristeros who laid down their arms.[114] But this did nothing to slow the rebel drive, and a few weeks later he faced a situation that further tried his equanimity.

On February 6 the Mexican Supreme Court refused to set aside the death sentence imposed on José de León Toral, and the next day Portes Gil rejected a plea for commutation, on the ground that due process had been adhered to throughout the case.[115] He received the clemency plea while on a trip through the northeast, along with

---

of weapons were never recovered. The December, 1928, order was an attempt both to supplement regular military units and to control the unruly irregulars.

113 Memorandum of conversation, January 5, 1929, NA, RG 59, 812.404/949⅔.

114 See *El Universal*, January 3, 1929.

115 *El Universal*, February 7, 1929; February 8, 1929.

a police report that LNDLR members had threatened to assassinate him and his family if Toral was executed.[116] Portes Gil ignored the report, and apparently no special precautions were taken. Toral died before a firing squad in the Mexico City penitentiary on Saturday, February 9. Around 6:30 the next morning, near Comonfort, Guanajuato, Portes Gil's train was wrecked by an exploding dynamite charge hidden in the roadbed. The president and his party escaped injury, but a brakeman was killed and the locomotive and two pullman cars demolished. Greater damage was averted because some of the dynamite failed to ignite.[117]

In Mexico City, later the same day, Toral's funeral procession was the occasion of massive demonstrations that at times reached uncontrollable proportions. Mobs threw flowers at the casket and rocks at police and firemen. Many arrests were made.[118] The next day Portes Gil issued a strongly worded statement deploring the riot. The restrictive measures it had been necessary to impose at the start of the religious conflict in 1926, he said, had been in the process of being gradually relaxed, but the government's moderation had not been reciprocated. The real villains, he asserted, were agitators who were not sincere Catholics, but rather "wealthy bourgeois" who had abetted the rebel fanatics to protect their own privileges. He vowed stern measures, including confiscation of property belonging to those found responsible.[119] The next day he stated that the train attack had not been politically motivated; all evidence indicated that it had been the work of individuals obeying "impassioned Catholic fanatics."[120]

The promised official response was nevertheless restrained and showed that the president had not abandoned hope of pacifying Catholics. Secretary of Gobernación Felipe Canales directed that, in the interest of public security and in view of the "subversive

[116] Portes Gil, *Autobiografía*, p. 555. The league archives are silent on the matter of league involvement. Portes Gil said the police's information came from a "lady of the old aristocracy."

[117] Portes Gil, *Autobiografía*, p. 558; *El Universal*, February 11, 1929.

[118] *El Universal*, February 11, 1929.

[119] Ibid., February 12, 1929.

[120] Ibid., February 13, 1929.

conduct" of a portion of the higher clergy, all Catholic priests in the country must notify the government of their places of residence within two weeks; failure to do so would be considered prima facie evidence of involvement with the Catholic rebellion. He stipulated, however, that there was no intention to jail or persecute priests, "who, in the opinion of the Government, are also victims of the material interests which have been placed in combat in connection with the religious question"; nor was it the intention of the government to act against families who had charitably opened their homes to clergymen. The order added that there would be no interference with religious practices either in churches or in private homes.[121]

Nevertheless, some clergymen balked at the order to register. When the directive was extended the next day to include the few bishops still in Mexico,[122] Miguel de la Mora, secretary of the Episcopal Subcommittee, took immediate exception. He told the press that, although priests could register their addresses without violating canon law, the directive was unconstitutional, unjustified, and humiliating. He denied that clergy were involved in the recent incidents and reminded the government that it could bring peace by "satisfying the just desires of the people and reforming the laws."[123] A government spokesman replied that de la Mora's words were seditious and that he was probably one of the leaders of the armed fanatics in Jalisco. The same official added that newspapers which had printed the bishop's statement (El Universal, Excélsior, and La Prensa) had thereby made themselves accessories to sedition and warned that "those responsible for any publication that

---

121 Ibid., February 12, 1929; February 13, 1929. Almost certainly the registration order had no ulterior intent. Two days earlier the government had confidentially instructed state governors that any priest apprehended and accused of violating the law in matters of religion was to be sent immediately to Mexico City and turned over to Gobernación. See Francisco M. Delgado, Chief of Department, Ministry of Gobernación, to governors, circular no. 86, February 1, 1929, legajo 15, expediente 2/11, State of Coahuila Archives, 1929. The object was probably to stop atrocities perpetrated against clergymen by local authorities.
122 El Universal, February 14, 1929.
123 Ibid., February 19, 1929.

incites or tends to incite to altercation of public order and rebellion will be energetically punished . . . "[124]

De la Mora did not reveal his whereabouts, but other bishops did. Antonio Guízar Valencia of Chihuahua registered his residence (in Mexico City) and congratulated Portes Gil on escaping assassination.[125] Nicolás Corona of Papantla informed Gobernación of his address and condemned the attempt on the president's life, adding that all "nonfanatical" Catholics did likewise. Francisco Banegas Galván of Querétaro, who also deplored the attack, and Manuel Fulcheri of Zamora complied with the order before the deadline.[126] Not surprisingly, no communication arrived from Francisco Orozco y Jiménez, somewhere in Jalisco.

The LNDLR may or may not have been involved in the train assault and the funeral riot, but it was devoting attention to a matter of wider possible import. Beginning with Enrique Estrada's abortive attempt to invade Mexico in 1926, the league had flirted with individuals and movements that were also anxious to overthrow the regime, and the directors had periodically debated both the practical and the ideological questions involved in cooperating with one or another of these. Early in 1929 the league threw both principle and caution to the wind and formally allied itself with a cabal that looked more potent than the others had. The directors recognized the realities of their situation. The armed movement was in no immediate danger of collapse, but victory was at best a remote prospect. Perhaps the best to be hoped for was to help another movement oust Calles and gain some limited concessions in return.

Calles's decision to retire from office and his proclaimed prefor ence for a government of institutions rather than *caudillos* had not convinced influential followers of the dead Obregón that the day of open political processes had dawned. They surmised, correctly,

124 Ibid., February 20, 1929.

125 Ibid., February 16, 1929; February 20, 1929.

126 Ibid., February 27, 1929; Morrow to Clark, May 8, 1929, NA, RG 59, 812.404/974³⁄₁₇. *Excélsior* reported on March 21 that 1,662 clergymen, including five bishops, had registered.

that Calles intended to perpetuate his control by ruling through handpicked figureheads. Even the establishment of an official revolutionary political party coincident with Calles's departure from the presidency was, they suspected, a device to institutionalize Calles rather than the revolution.[127]

The disgruntled opposition solidified in December and January, a conglomerate of generals and politicians united mainly by their determination to seize power for themselves. The top personalities in the conspiracy were the federal chiefs of military operations in several states—José Gonzalo Escobar in Coahuila (who was chosen supreme leader), Francisco R. Manzo in Sonora, Francisco Urbalejo in Durango, and Jesús M. Aguirre in Veracruz—and the governors of Sonora, Durango, and Chihuahua. Other men who had once held high office but were now in eclipse—Roberto Cruz, Gilberto Valenzuela, Antonio I. Villarreal—also joined.

Their chances looked reasonably good, certainly better than those of the rather amateurish Gómez-Serrano plunge of 1927. This the LNDLR was well aware of, and in February representatives of both the Directive Committee and Gorostieta concluded a pact with Escobar. By its terms the "Renovators," in exchange for Catholic support, promised that when they took power they would provide ample guarantees of religious freedom based on the bishops' 1926 memorial and that they would incorporate the Guardia Nacional into the national army.[128] The agreement was silent concerning other matters that had been of crucial interest to the Catholic opposition. As for the 1917 constitution, it was clear that the Escobaristas did not intend to scrap it, and the league had to settle for unspecified guarantees that the charter would be modified.

The revolt broke in the early morning hours of March 3, joined by a sizeable minority of the federal army. Escobar occupied Monterrey the same day, while Manzo and other chieftains quickly

---

[127] See Juan Gualberto Amaya, *Los gobiernos de Obregón, Calles y regímenes "peleles" derivados del callismo: Tercera etapa, 1920 a 1935*, pp. 219–292.

[128] Lorenzo García, Pedro Ponce, and Luis G. Palacios to Ceniceros y Villarreal, March 19, 1929, LA-1. It is not known whether the "Renovators" or the LNDLR made the first approach.

seized control of most of Sonora, Chihuahua, and Durango. Aguirre withdrew the main garrisons in Veracruz from federal control.[129] The government acted with formidable speed and efficiency. Within hours Calles entered the cabinet as secretary of war and marine. Loyal troops were rushed into action. On March 6 Escobar withdrew from Monterrey toward Saltillo, pursued by Gen. Eulogio Ortiz. By the eighth Lázaro Cárdenas was assembling a massive force at Irapuato for a thrust northward, and Calles, having stabilized things in Veracruz, was hurrying there to assume personal command. The border town of Naco fell to federal forces on the twelfth, Durango on the fourteenth.[130] The rebel plan called for Manzo to advance swiftly down the west coast through Sinaloa and Nayarit into Jalisco, something the government was determined to stop at any cost. Portes Gil nervously wired Calles on the twenty-fifth that if Manzo reached Guadalajara the outlook would be desperate.[131] Manzo got only as far as Sinaloa.

The Cristeros seized their momentary advantage. They occupied considerable territory in Jalisco, including most of the important towns except Guadalajara, as federal troops vacated them to confront Escobar in the north. But the alliance, never amicable to begin with, languished in mutual distrust and contempt. Escobar's "Plan of Hermosillo," the revolt's formal justification, failed to mention religion.[132] On March 4 Escobar decreed an end to the "Calles Law" of 1926 but specified that Article 130 of the constitution would remain in force.[133] Gorostieta informed the "Renovators" that with adequate ammunition he would invade the Bajío, occupy Guadalajara, and interrupt communications throughout the west, but that he would move only if he first received explicit guarantees regarding freedom, religious freedom in particular.[134]

[129] *Excélsior*, March 4, 1929.

[130] Ibid., also March 7, 9, 13, 16, and 19, 1929.

[131] Amaya, *Los gobiernos de Obregón, Calles*, pp. 245, 271.

[132] A copy of the plan was forwarded to the State Department on March 3 by an Escobar spokesman (NA, RG 59, 812.00 Sonora/478).

[133] Escobar decree of March 4, 1929, enclosed in Vice-Consul James C. Powell, Jr., Torreón, report of March 12, 1929, NA, RG 59, 812.00 Sonora/485.

[134] Gorostieta to Luis Alcorta, March 20, 1929, LA-1.

Gorostieta received no pledges, but he decided to launch a maximum effort nonetheless. If Escobar should fail, he told subordinates, then "the Turk" (Calles), flushed with victory and commanding newly increased manpower, would turn on the Cristeros with heightened fury.[135]

The "Renovators" withheld ammunition as well as guarantees from their Catholic allies. Chávez Hayhoe, the league's emissary to Escobar, spent late March and early April negotiating in California, Arizona, and Sonora for cartridges, which the Escobaristas promised to pay for.[136] But, as the rebellion lost momentum, Escobar reneged. He told Chávez Hayhoe that, with as many Catholics as there were in Mexico, the Cristeros should pay for their own ammunition, and he warned that they must cooperate strongly if they expected later the liberties they were asking for.[137]

By now the revolt was collapsing. A four-day battle around La Reforma, Sonora, ending April 3, had turned the tide. Federal forces took Ciudad Juárez a few days later, and on the twelfth Manzo fled across the border with a large share of the funds, reportedly to escape his colleagues' wrath over his failures in the field.[138] During the next three weeks the rebellion disintegrated. Nogales fell on April 30, Agua Prieta the following day. On May 4 it was revealed that Escobar had escaped by plane to safety in the United States.[139]

Gorostieta's apprehensions were justified. He was mistaken only

[135] Gorostieta to Cols. Vicente Viramontes and Aurelio R. Acevedo, March 31, 1929, in *David* 2, no. 47 (June 22, 1956): 362.

[136] Chávez Hayhoe to Directive Committee, April 5 and April 9, 1929, LA-1. Chávez Hayhoe's appointment as LNDLR representative was apparently a ratification of an existing situation. Manríquez y Zárate wrote to Palomar y Vizcarra from Los Angeles on April 1 that "we" (meaning the Unión Nacionalista Mexicana) had sent Chávez Hayhoe to Nogales in mid-March to deal with the Escobar people and hoped the league would approve. Manríquez y Zárate said the contact promised great things (Manríquez y Zárate to Palomar y Vizcarra, April 1, 1929, LA-3).

[137] Chávez Hayhoe to Directive Committee, April 13, 1929; April 16, 1929; LA-1.

[138] Ibid., April 16, 1921, LA-1; *El Universal*, April 13, 1929.

[139] *El Universal*, April 28, 1929; May 2, 1929; May 4, 1929.

in believing that the government would wait until Escobar was finished before directing its aroused wrath at the Cristeros. On March 27 the president's office announced that Calles was outfitting a division, to be commanded by Gen. Saturnino Cedillo, for action in Jalisco and Guanajuato against "the fanatics known as Cristeros."[140]

Washington's refusal to support Mexican rebels—a policy from which, despite some trying times, it had not deviated since recognizing Venustiano Carranza's provisional government in 1915— definitely included the "Renovators." In March, President Hoover, during his first week in office, announced that the United States would continue to issue licenses for arms shipments to the Mexican government and, moreover, that it would allow the Portes Gil regime to buy directly from U.S. army arsenals.[141] The next day the United States arranged to deliver ten thousand Enfield rifles and ten million rounds of ammunition to the Mexican army and was reported prepared to send machine guns, bombs, and ammunition for use by military aircraft.[142] A sale of planes to the Mexican air force was announced on March 30.[143]

In a telegram to Morrow late in April, Clark summarized the official U.S. attitude regarding Mexican insurgents of whatever breed. They had no legal status in international law, he said, and from any standpoint of legal principle they must be classified as common outlaws.

The ambassador could not have agreed more.[144]

[140] *Excélsior*, March 28, 1929. This seems to be the first time the term "Cristero" was used in an official pronouncement.

[141] *New York Times*, March 9, 1929; Clark to U.S. Consul, Nogales, March 8, 1929, NA, RG 59, 812.113/10455a.

[142] *New York Times*, March 10, 1929. The supplies were sold on short-term credit. See *Times*, March 13, 1929.

[143] *Excélsior*, March 30, 1929.

[144] Clark to Morrow, April 25, 1929, NA, RG 59, 812.00 Sonora/833.

9. An Arrangement of Sorts

When Morrow returned to Mexico City in February, he renewed his efforts to end the Church-State conflict. His strategy remained unchanged: to persuade Church authority that it was useless to insist on a change in the laws, to secure from the government sufficient guarantees to allay Catholic fears, and to convince each side that the other intended to behave reasonably in the future. The Catholic rebels interested him only to the extent that their activities could complicate arbitration. An end to the religious strife must come through a political adjustment, he believed, and his work during the next four months proved his premise.

Portes Gil, with whom Morrow had cultivated friendly relations, was willing to let the ambassador proceed. As early as mid-February the provisional president agreed to receive Father Burke. The priest, though, decided against a visit, explaining to Morrow that to delay his planned trip to Rome might hurt the cause rather than help it.[1] Morrow kept probing. The outbreak of the Esco-

[1] Rublee Memorandum, Dwight Morrow Papers.

bar rebellion retarded matters, but by the middle of March the immediate danger to the government had passed, and on the nineteenth, after a conference with Portes Gil, Morrow dictated a memorandum to William Montavon. He said the president would discuss an adjustment on the basis of Calles's April 4, 1928, letter to Burke. Perhaps, if Burke presented the case in Rome, Gasparri might be willing to conclude that Calles's 1928 letter to the priest, which was still unanswered, was sufficient to justify the cardinal's communicating directly with the Mexican minister of foreign relations. Gasparri might suggest that a Mexican envoy be sent to Rome, or that a Vatican representative go to Mexico; or the cardinal could propose by letter terms for a settlement which, if satisfactory, would end the conflict then and there. Morrow thought, however, that the government would accept only the last plan. If Gasparri wanted previous assurance of a positive reply, he would try to get one from Portes Gil. He reminded Montavon that there was a possibility that the constitution and laws might be changed later. Morrow said he stood ready to make a "real effort" to help bring peace and that he would draw on whatever reserves of good will he had built up with Mexican officialdom. But he did not wish to reopen the issue unless Church authorities were ready to negotiate "along the lines already discussed." He said the coming weeks would be a favorable time; to wait longer might risk entangling the problem with the fall elections. If Burke wanted to communicate with him directly, he had arranged for the British minister to the Holy See to relay messages via the British Embassy in Mexico City.[2] As Morrow obviously intended, his memorandum was not read only in Washington. Clark informed him on March 28 that Montavon was forwarding it to Father Burke in Rome "by our pouch today."[3]

For a month nothing happened. Then on April 20 Morrow heard from Father Burke by way of Montavon. The priest said he be-

[2] Morrow, memorandum of conversation with Portes Gil and Memorandum for Mr. William F. Montavon, in Morrow to Clark, March 19, 1929, Dwight Morrow Papers; Rublee Memorandum.
[3] Clark to Morrow, March 28, 1929, NA, RG 59, 812.404/949⅜.

lieved there was an atmosphere of sincerity and good will in Rome regarding negotiations. He added that it would be necessary for an officially authorized representative of the Mexican government to come to Rome—this could be done in complete secrecy. He asked Morrow to lay the proposal before Portes Gil.[4] Morrow replied that there was also a conciliatory spirit in Mexico City, but that he believed it would be futile to approach Portes Gil unless there were assurances that negotiations would proceed on the basis of the Burke–Calles–Ruiz y Flores talks of the previous year. He would like to know if this were the case. If so, he would ask Portes Gil to send an envoy. But, if the Vatican wished to start anew, he thought it would be better if persons other than himself or Father Burke acted as intermediaries, since both would be at a disadvantage if they had to abandon the original bases without offering an explanation. In any event he would be glad to help, since his object was to see the problem resolved to the satisfaction of all concerned.[5]

With indications growing that negotiations might resume, Morrow and the State Department turned their attention to the Cristeros. They were annoyed and baffled by the rebellion, which could obviously complicate efforts to resolve the religious question in the manner they were pursuing. If the Church disapproved of the Catholic insurgents, as they had been led to believe was the case, why did the pope and the bishops not say so?

Lane and Montavon discussed the rebellion at the State Department on April 27. Both were anxious to have Church officialdom publicly repudiate the Cristeros, but neither knew how this might be brought about. Montavon said that Ruiz y Flores had told him that he doubted whether the bishops had authority to order a stop to the fighting and that they would also be reluctant to advise moderates that their preference for a compromise solution had Church approval. Lane said it seemed to him that the bishops, by refusing to dissuade Catholics from armed action, were in conflict with the pope's wishes. Montavon said he agreed—then he further added to Lane's bewilderment by saying that Ruiz y Flores had told him

[4] Clark to Morrow, April 20, 1929, NA, RG 59, 812.404/965a.
[5] Morrow to Montavon, May 1, 1929, NA, RG 59, 812.404/974½₇.

the Holy See opposed making public Díaz's letter of January 7, 1928, to the LNDLR. Lane said that, if the Vatican in fact disapproved of the rebellion, it would be a sign of strength to speak out.[6] Montavon, who could surely have explained that the Vatican's position was more complex than Lane realized, chose not to go into the matter further.

The Mexican government was not waiting for diplomacy to end the rebellion. In the first week of April, Cedillo's division of six thousand men, made up of both regulars and agrarians, which had been concentrated in Torreón for possible use against Escobar, began moving to the west and south. All military commanders in central and western Mexico were directed to cooperate in the all-out drive.[7] By April 8, Cedillo was in Jalisco. He reported that he was pressing the offensive and that several important towns were already in his hands.[8]

The government assault struck just as Gorostieta was putting his own maximum plan into operation. In the closing days of March the Brigade of Los Altos was advancing on Guadalajara in two columns, one by way of Puente Grande, the other farther south, along the rail line through Poncitlán. The strategy called for the northern column to pin down the federal units screening Guadalajara while the other attacked the city from the southeast. Aristeo Pedroza, who was with the latter force, decided on a bold stroke: he would capture the Mexico City–Guadalajara train near Poncitlán, put a special task force aboard it, and make a lightning dash into the Jalisco capital, where he would surprise and destroy the depleted federal garrison and open the way for entry of the main Cristero units.

It might have worked. The federals were at minimum strength, and a sizable portion of the civilian populace could be counted on for support. But a combination of bad intelligence and worse luck

[6] Lane, Memorandum of Conversation with Mr. William F. Montavon, April 27, 1929, NA, RG 59, 812.404/949⅜; idem, Memorandum for the Under Secretary, April 27, NA, RG 59, 812.404/949⅞.

[7] *El Universal*, April 4, 1929; April 5, 1929.

[8] Ibid., April 10, 1929.

doomed the plan. As the train neared the ambush point, when it was too late to call off the attack, the Cristeros discovered that it was not the regular passenger express but a troop convoy, followed closely by a second military train. They carried a part of Lázaro Cárdenas's division, en route to Sonora via Guadalajara and the west-coast Southern Pacific line. To make matters worse, the lead train managed to stop before being derailed, and within moments the Cristeros found themselves in combat with hundreds of regulars, who, although momentarily withered by heavy fire, quickly formed into battle lines. Both sides held their ground, but by nightfall the Cristeros were down to less than twenty cartridges per man and had to retreat. The northern column had also fared badly; it ran into stronger opposition than expected and had to withdraw eastward. By the second week of April the brigade was back in Los Altos, where it faced the rolling wave of Cedillo's advancing army.[9]

The federal invasion of Jalisco suffered a temporary reverse the third week of April in the most widely publicized battle of the rebellion. Cedillo's division was moving across the state in three columns. The center one, spearheaded by agrarians and numbering some 2,500 men, had cleared Jalostitlán in the middle of April and was advancing toward Tepatitlán. The Cristero leadership decided to engage it there with a strong concentration commanded by Father José Reyes Vega.[10] The priest-colonel devised a ruse. Leaving around 70 of his troops inside the town, positioned atop churches and other tall buildings, he withdrew the rest, between 500 and 600 men, and concealed them several kilometers to the north and west.[11] The federals entered Tepatitlán shortly after dawn on April 19 and within minutes were under fire from Vega's snipers, whom they set to work to dislodge. Then around 7:00 A.M. a part of the Cristero force outside the town appeared. The federal commander, instantly aware that he was in a trap, ordered a fast

[9] Heriberto Navarrete, "Por Dios y Por la Patria": Memorias de mi participación en la defensa de la libertad de conciencia y culto durante la persecución religiosa en México de 1926 a 1929, pp. 213–218.

[10] Ibid., pp. 221–223.

[11] Agustín Ramírez, "El combate de Tepatitlán: Rectificación a Juan Rizo," David 7, no. 178 (May 22, 1967): 163.

withdrawal. As the federals moved back along the Jalostitlán road, Cristero cavalry struck from both sides, and by 11:00 scattered knots of panic-stricken agrarians and regulars were in disorganized flight. The pursuit had to be abandoned when Cristero ammunition gave out.[12] Rebel reports said 225 of the enemy were killed;[13]

Cristero jubilation was clouded by a serious loss. More than a hundred government troops, cut off in the retreat, had barricaded themselves on a small ranch at the edge of town. While reconnoitering the situation, Father Vega was shot. He died a few hours later, after making a general confession to the parish priest. The movement had lost a remarkable leader, a priest turned soldier whom veterans of the struggle later likened to Hidalgo and Morelos. Heriberto Navarrete wrote years later of Vega that he possessed a great spirit of faith and a strong love of God: "No matter how great his faults, it is certain that no one can doubt the rectitude of his intentions in the undertakings he carried out."[14]

Tepatitlán, like so many others, was a Cristero victory that did not long remain a victory. Three days later Cedillo attacked the town, rescuing his cut-off troops. The Cristeros, out of ammunition and without Father Vega's leadership, fled.[15]

Cedillo's campaign was of a type the Cristeros had never experienced. The general took great pains to assure both the armed enemy and the civilian populace that he bore no animosity and that he believed in the possibility of a peaceful settlement of the religious question.[16] He ended "reconcentration," sternly restrained his troops from molesting noncombatants, stopped the execution of captured Cristeros,[17] and offered generous amnesties.[18]

---

[12] Ibid., Navarrete, *Por Dios*, p. 227.

[13] Ramírez, "El combate de Tepatitlán," p. 163.

[14] Navarrete, *Por Dios*, pp. 229–230; *El Universal*, April 27, 1929.

[15] *El Universal*, April 27, 1929. The federal command said it lost 37 dead and 40 wounded in the three days of fighting and that the Cristero force numbered at least 1,500, comprising the entire rebel army in the state. Actually, Pedroza and most of the brigade were not even in the region.

[16] Navarrete, *Por Dios*, p. 234.

[17] Ibid., p. 236; *El Universal*, April 16, 1929.

[18] *El Universal*, April 24, 1929; April 26, 1929.

Cedillo's field tactics were designed to counter the Cristero stratagem of atomizing into small bands when outnumbered. He divided his troops into units of a hundred men or less and moved them out simultaneously, in constant communication with each other, to comb a sector ranch by ranch. When one unit made contact with Cristeros, reinforcements could be on the scene in a matter of minutes. The federals were everywhere, not only in populated areas, but also in remote regions the Cristeros had held for nearly three years. Gorostieta ordered much of his command to disperse, but to be ready to reassemble when the pressure slackened. He directed that, if worse came to worst, arms were to be buried and the horses released into the hills. Navarrete recalled that it was the hardest time the Cristeros ever faced, but that they never doubted they could ride out the storm; the government could not sustain the effort indefinitely, costly as it was in men and money.[19] For the time being, though, the pressure was maintained and even increased. On May 2, with Escobar totally crushed, Calles announced that he was mobilizing fifteen thousand more troops to add to Cedillo's already formidable force.[20]

Despite the onslaught, the Cristeros held their own. General Amaro late in April told a visitor in Guadalajara that fifty rebels had just destroyed an entire regiment and that rebel resistance was growing; he said it was urgent that Portes Gil work out some kind of settlement.[21]

Gorostieta told the LNDLR late in May that the Guardia Nacional had twenty thousand men under arms. They were, he said, limited to guerrilla operations because of lack of ammunition. He described his soldiers as "men of order, of a morality such as has not existed nor will . . . in Mexico; [troops] which I doubt can be bettered in any other country." He reported that there were over two thousand civil officials functioning in areas controlled by the Guardia Nacional, and more than three hundred schools. The

[19] Navarrete, *Por Dios*, pp. 236–237.

[20] *El Universal*, May 4, 1929.

[21] René Velázquez López, "El problema religioso en México, 1917–1929," pp. 197–198.

tyranny, he believed, even with continuing U.S. aid, would not last more than a year or two.[22]

Gorostieta's opinion that peace was in sight soon proved well founded, although not for the reasons he thought. On May 1 Portes Gil answered a question put to him by a foreign correspondent in Mexico City. It concerned his views on the relationship of the religious conflict to the Escobar rebellion. The president said he did not think the Catholic church as an institution had been involved in the Escobar matter. He went on to say that in certain parts of Jalisco, Michoacán, and Guanajuato there were Catholics under arms who, "forgetting their Christian morality, dedicate themselves to acts of absolute banditry on the pretext of defending the doctrine of their Church," but that "in contrast with that attitude there are other worthy representatives of Catholicism who counsel respect for law and authority." He said the government's position on the religious question would not change: "No religion will be persecuted nor is the government guilty of persecuting any sect. Liberty of conscience will be respected, as heretofore. The Catholic Clergy, when they wish, may renew the exercise of their rites with only one obligation, that they respect the laws of the land."[23]

In Washington the next day, a few hours after news of Portes Gil's press conference appeared in U.S. papers, Ruiz y Flores issued a statement answering the Mexican president. Although newsmen did not know it, he spoke for the Apostolic Delegation.[24] The tone was highly conciliatory:

The religious conflict in Mexico arises from no cause which cannot be corrected by men of sincere good will. As an evidence of good will, the

[22] Miguel Palomar y Vizcarra, "Gorostieta," *David* 2, no. 39 (October 22, 1955): 236–237. The U.S. military attaché estimated early in May that there were 8,000 to 8,200 armed Cristeros in Jalisco, Michoacán, Colima, and Guanajuato. He gave no figures for Zacatecas, Durango, Nayarit, and other areas of rebel activity, but described bands there as "numerous." See G-2 reports, nos. 2380 (May 3, 1929) and 2387 (May 10, 1929), Lt. Col. Gordon Johnston to War Department, NA, RG 165.

[23] *New York Times*, May 2, 1929. The president's remarks were not reported in the Mexican press until May 3, and then under a New York May 2 dateline. See *Excélsior*, May 3, 1929.

[24] Leopoldo Ruiz y Flores, *Recuerdo de recuerdos*, p. 93.

words of President Portes Gil are most important. The Church and her ministers are prepared to cooperate with him in every just and moral effort made for the betterment of the people.

Not able in conscience to accept laws that are enforced in my country, the Catholic Church in Mexico, not willfully, but as a solemn duty, has found it necessary to completely suspend all acts of public worship.

With sincere respect, I ask the Government of my country to reconsider existing legislation in a spirit of sincere patriotism and good will, to the end that steps be taken to remove the confusion between religion and politics and prepare the way for an era of true peace and tranquility.[25]

The archbishop went on to say that "should there arise any seemingly insurmountable difficulty to prevent this action, the logical solution would be found in the submission of disputed points to specially authorized representatives of the Church and of the Government." The Church, he added, asked no special privileges, but only that, on a basis of "friendly separation" from the State, she be allowed the freedom that was indispensable for the welfare and happiness of the nation. He prayed that God might speed the day when Mexicans would work as one to make effective the three guarantees of unity, religion, and patriotism. Catholics, he said, would accept sincerely whatever arrangement might be reached between the Church and the government.[26]

The exchange amounted to a decisive breakthrough. Portes Gil's words, it was true, held out no promise of a change in the laws, but his absolving of the Church from any blame for the Escobar revolt and his praise of the moderate Catholic position was a gesture of good will that invited a response. Ruiz y Flores's reply was not only a quick acknowledgement of the peace signal but also a careful statement of a fundamental change in policy. It did not demand the removal or reform of the objectionable laws; suspension of worship, Ruiz y Flores said, had been decreed because of "laws that are enforced"; he asked the government to "reconsider existing legislation in a spirit of sincere patriotism"—which could refer to ap-

[25] *New York Times*, May 3, 1929.

[26] Ibid. The text appeared in the Mexico City press simultaneously with the report of Portes Gil's statement.

plication of the laws, not necessarily to their repeal; and any "seemingly insurmountable difficulties to prevent this action" (i.e., the reconsideration of the laws and the putting an end to "confusion between religion and politics") could be worked out by negotiation—in effect it was an offer to talk without specific preconditions. The two statements were, in sum, a reiteration of the spirit and even much of the detail of the position reached by Calles and Burke more than a year before.

There is no direct evidence that Dwight Morrow arranged the exchange, but circumstances strongly suggest it. Two weeks earlier, when an official of the archdiocese of Oaxaca had publicly urged Catholics to respect constituted authority. Morrow had suggested to Portes Gil that a reply through the press commenting favorably on the cleric's words "might be very useful" and had asked the president to receive an Associated Press correspondent for that purpose. Portes Gil had agreed, and Morrow had provided him with a memorandum outlining some appropriate remarks. In the interview on April 20, Portes Gil had followed the ambassador's cue. He had said the Church was not supporting Escobar or the Catholic insurgents; any Catholics involved were individual fanatics.[27] There had been, however, no official Catholic response to the president, and the May 1 interview may have been a second try. Ruiz y Flores later said he suspected Morrow had suggested Portes Gil's statement,[28] but the archbishop said nothing about how his reply originated. Doubtless it had been prepared before Portes Gil's remarks were publicized; so important a pronouncement could not have been drafted and approved on a few hours' notice. Fumasoni-Biondi was away from Washington, and the chargé d'affaires, Morela, would not have assumed such authority himself. Montavon apparently knew something about the matter, but as usual he told the State Department no more than he wished it to know; on May 9, in response to a question from Clark, he said only that Ruiz y Flores's statement had been authorized

[27] Captain Lewis B. McBride (U.S. naval attaché), memorandum, May 18, 1929, Dwight Morrow Papers.
[28] Ruiz y Flores, *Recuerdo*, p. 93.

by the Apostolic Delegation and thus could be considered official.[29]

Whatever the origins of the exchange, Morrow acted speedily to exploit it. He suggested to Portes Gil that he indicate his satisfaction with the archbishop's statement and his willingness to discuss peace with the Church. He gave the president a draft he might wish to consider using for the purpose. The presidential reply, which appeared on May 7, was almost identical to the statement Morrow provided,[30] and it made headlines in the Mexican press. Portes Gil said he had read the archbishop's May 2 press release with interest and that he was pleased at the comments that men of good will could solve the religious problem and that the Church and clergy were prepared to cooperate with the government for the well-being of the Mexican people. Such cooperation, he said, was exactly what the government had always wanted. Newsmen asked the president to comment on Ruiz y Flores's observation that difficulties might be submitted to authorized representatives of the Church and government. Portes Gil said that, although Mexico did not have diplomatic relations with the Vatican, this did not prevent the government from "exchanging impressions with ministers of the Catholic Church or in a personal way holding talks with dignitaries of the Church concerning the scope and interpretation of laws applicable to the clergy." He recalled that Ruiz y Flores had had an interview with President Calles nearly three years before (the August, 1926, meeting) which unfortunately, and through no fault of Calles, had proved fruitless. If the archbishop now wanted to discuss ways of cooperating to help the Mexican people, he would have no objection to dealing with him on the matter.[31]

Three new faces had joined the peace party in Mexico City. On April 23 Morrow was visited by Manuel Echevarría, a Mexican banker who was acquainted with the Legorreta brothers. Echeva-

[29] Clark, Memorandum of Conversation with Mr. William F. Montavon, May 9, 1929, NA, RG 59, 812.404/974⅚₇.

[30] Rublee Memorandum.

[31] *El Universal*, May 8, 1929.

rría said he agreed with the ambassador's approach to settling the religious controversy and that he too had been trying to bridge the gap between the president and the bishops.[32] The other two peacemakers, whom Morrow had met in Washington the previous year, reached Mexico City together the first week of May. They were Manuel Cruchaga Tocornal, former Chilean ambassador to the United States, who had served on claims commissions charged with adjusting differences between Mexico and various European countries, and Father Edmund A. Walsh, S.J., vice-president of Georgetown University and director of its School of Foreign Service. Father Walsh had fulfilled several delicate missions for the Vatican, including supervision of relief work in Russia at the time of the Bolshevik Revolution. Cruchaga called on Morrow on May 3. He said he had talked at length with Pope Pius XI about the Mexican problem and had persuaded the pontiff to send Father Walsh to survey the situation.[33] Walsh came to the embassy the following day. He told Morrow that the Holy See very much wanted to settle the conflict but was confused regarding the facts of the situation. He said his mission was not known to Father Burke and that he had no authority to negotiate a settlement, but expected to stay perhaps a month and then make a full report to Rome. He added that he would be in touch with some of the more uncompromising bishops residing in Mexico.[34]

On May 8, the day after Portes Gil's second statement appeared, Father Walsh dined with Morrow. He said the bishops were very pleased with what the president had said; he reported that de la Mora, who had been in the intransigent camp, was coming around. He also told Morrow that both he and Echevarría had cabled Rome, calling favorable attention to Portes Gil's statement.[35] Cruchaga

[32] Rublee Memorandum. Echevarría knew Portes Gil and was also on close terms with Church leaders.

[33] Morrow, memorandum, May 6, 1929, Dwight Morrow Papers; Morrow to Clark, May 6, 1929, NA, RG 59, 812.404/974⁸/17; *Excélsior*, June 22, 1929.

[34] Morrow, memorandum to Clark, May 6, 1929, NA, RG 59, 812.404/974⁸/17.

[35] Memorandum to Montavon, in Morrow to Clark, May 10, 1929, NA, RG 59, 812.404/974⁸/17.

also had cabled, telling the Vatican that as a result of the president's gestures the moment was auspicious for an adjustment.[36]

Montavon, whom Clark had kept informed, said the next move should be to get permission from Portes Gil for Ruiz y Flores to go to Mexico. He said that the Apostolic Delegation had mailed to Rome a report of Portes Gil's May 7 remarks. It had not been cabled because the delegation did not have sufficient funds. Clark said that as soon as the text of the statement arrived from Morrow he would be willing to have it cabled to the U.S. Embassy in Rome for transmission there to whomever Montavon designated; he added that Montavon should have Morela send a short telegram to Rome urging immediate action. Time was crucial, he said, because the government offensive being waged against the rebels was costing lives.[37] The text arrived from Mexico City a few hours later, and the next day Clark informed Morrow that he had relayed it to Rome.[38]

Agustín Legorreta, after consulting with Morrow, added his voice to those urging Rome to move. He wired Gasparri on May 9 that the Portes Gil–Ruiz y Flores exchange meant that peace was in sight if prompt and decisive steps were taken. He said it would be impossible to persuade the Mexican government to send an official representative to Rome; the best approach would be to arrange an exchange of letters between the president and the archbishop.[39]

[36] Morrow, memorandum, May 9, 1929, Dwight Morrow Papers.

[37] Ibid.

[38] Clark to Morrow, May 10, 1929, NA, RG 59, 812.404/973. Ruiz y Flores says in his memoirs (*Recuerdo*, p. 93) that when he heard that Portes Gil was willing to receive him, he wrote the president that he had no authority to deal; such a matter required papal intervention. He adds that when the pope learned of Portes Gil's words he asked that the texts of the statements made by both the president and the archbishop be cabled to the Holy See. This would mean that the Vatican was in the dark on what had transpired before. It is possible that Ruiz y Flores did not know exactly who authorized the statement he issued on May 2. Not explained is the chargé's reluctance to cable the texts, although possibly Rome's request did not arrive until after May 9. It should be noted that Ruiz y Flores wrote his recollections long after the events of 1929 and that they contain several factual inaccuracies.

[39] Rublee Memorandum.

Morrow was uneasy over the possibility of a delay—or worse—
in Rome. On May 11 he wired Ruiz y Flores (via the State Department), proposing two possible responses to Portes Gil: the
archbishop could accept the president's statement as an invitation
to come to Mexico, or he could start negotiations by writing directly
to the chief magistrate. He thought the second course might be best,
and he enclosed a draft letter that Ruiz y Flores might consider
appropriate. He had read it to Portes Gil, who had expressed satisfaction with it. Calles, to whom he had outlined its contents orally, also approved. The draft courteously acknowledged the president's words, reaffirmed the desire of the bishops to work for the
good of the nation, and asked that the Church be assured of freedom
"within the law" to carry out its spiritual mission. Such an assurance would be deemed to have been given if the president could
state:

1. That it is not the purpose of the Government to destroy the identity of the Church;
2. That the provision which requires the registration of priests does
   not contemplate that the Government would register a priest who
   has not been named by the Bishop of his Diocese;
3. That the laws, while requiring secular instruction in the schools,
   do not prohibit the giving of purely religious instruction in a suitable part of any church;
4. That in order to avoid unreasonable application of the laws, the
   Government would be willing to confer from time to time with
   the authorized head of the Church in Mexico;
5. That nothing in the Constitution or laws and no policy of the
   Government denies to the clergy the right to apply to appropriate
   constitutional authorities for modification of the laws and that in
   your [Portes Gil's] opinion such application on their part should
   receive such impartial consideration as the reasons offered in
   support might deserve.

The letter concluded by saying that, if Portes Gil could make such
a declaration, Ruiz y Flores was authorized to state that the clergy
could at once resume their functions. Morrow went on to note that

the second point was more specifically put than it had been in previous exchanges and that the third and fifth points should please the more intransigent-minded. He said that, if he could be sure Ruiz y Flores had Rome's approval to submit the letter, he would find out in advance whether Portes Gil would accept it.[40]

Agustín Legorretta seconded Morrow the same day, urging Ruiz y Flores to contact Rome. Two days later he learned from his brother in New York that Ruiz y Flores had agreed. Legorretta cabled Rome on May 14, supporting the plan and offering his full cooperation. Gasparri meanwhile answered the banker's May 9 message, via the Vatican's diplomatic mission in Paris: "Bishop [who has] confidence of the Holy See has received necessary instructions. Please tell Father Walsh to cooperate [with] Msgr. Ruiz and support whatever action eventually taken [by the] Holy See."[41]

The conciliators among the bishops spoke out during the second week of May. On the eighth, Francisco Banegas Galván of Querétaro addressed a pastoral letter to his diocese. He asked his flock to remain in "peace, tranquility, and order" during the current solemn moments in the country's life and to implore God to "calm passions, illuminate understanding, and move wills in order that the peace we so much long for may reign in our nation."[42] Morrow forwarded a copy of the letter to Washington. He reported that Echevarría had told him that Gerardo Anaya of Chiapas and Maximiliano Ruiz, auxiliary bishop of the archdiocese of Mexico, were known to be opposed to the LNDLR's activities.[43] A pastoral letter from Archbishop Vera y Zuria of Puebla, in exile in the United States, was also in circulation; it expressed hope for a rapid solution of the religious conflict and advised the faithful to use peaceful means as the best way of arriving at an accord between the Church and the government.[44] The pacific-minded were also represented in

[40] Suggested Draft Letter from Archbishop Ruiz to President Portes Gil, May 10, 1929, Dwight Morrow Papers; Rublee Memorandum.

[41] Rublee Memorandum; copy of Gasparri's message to Walsh in Dwight Morrow Papers.

[42] *El Universal*, May 12, 1929.

[43] Morrow to Clark, May 8, 1929, NA, RG 59, 812.404/974¾₁₇.

[44] *La Prensa*, May 14, 1929.

Rome; Guízar Valencia of Chihuahua arrived May 11. Echevarría had paid his expenses for the trip, hoping that the prelate's conciliatory views would help strengthen the compromise viewpoint there.[45]

Reports of the steps toward negotiations aroused fear and anger among Catholics committed to resolving the struggle by force. From the beginning the LNDLR had insisted on having a voice in any settlement, and Enrique Gorostieta now asserted the claim more strongly than the Directive Committee had ever done.

He sent a message to the directors on May 16 with a request that they transmit it to the Episcopal Committee and if possible to even higher Church authority. Its tone was measured but menacing. Since the start of the struggle, he said, reports that certain bishops were trying to negotiate with the government had periodically undermined the morale of the fighting men. Now, with Escobar vanquished, at a time of uncertainty and fear, there were rumors of possible talks between Archbishop Ruiz y Flores and Portes Gil, based on the latter's "ambiguous, hypocritical, and stupid statements." For the bishops to attempt to make peace independently of the Guardia Nacional, he said, would be unworthy and treacherous, and he would personally levy charges to that effect. At stake were not only the rights of religion, but also broad issues of national freedom. Even if the conflict were viewed as essentially religious, the Guardia Nacional and the Mexican people it represented were part of the Catholic church in Mexico and had a right to be heard. The Guardia Nacional was compelling the government to seek a solution, and the Guardia Nacional, not the bishops, must resolve the conflict. If the bishops from the first had counseled a stand worthy of Christians, if they had declared the armed defense to be lawful and obligatory, perhaps by now Mexicans would have freed themselves from their oppressors. There was still time for the hierarchy to rise to its obligations. The men in arms, however, demanded that the solution be left in their hands. The Guardia Nacional

[45] *El Universal*, May 17, 1929; Morrow, Confidential Memorandum of Conversation, April 23, 1929, Dwight Morrow Papers.

would do its duty in the trying months ahead, he concluded, "but I ask that no one demand of it that it go beyond duty."[46]

The military situation had no doubt heightened Gorostieta's bitterness. The government offensive struck the Colima Cristeros in May. By the middle of the month five thousand federal troops had poured into the state capital by train, and military aircraft were arriving at the city airfield. Commanded by Eulogio Ortiz, magnificently armed and mounted, the soldiers were veterans fresh from the Escobar campaign.[47] Ortiz let it be known that he would tolerate no nonsense. He began by calling a meeting, attendance required, of the state's leading *hacendados*, cattlemen, merchants, and industrialists. He addressed the gathering with brutal directness, his remarks peppered with barracks prose not meant to soothe the ear. He blamed his listeners for the chaotic situation in Colima; if the Cristeros had thrived and multiplied, it was their fault because they were abetting the rebels; he would level the very hills it necessary to put an end to it all, and if the rebels rose again he would return and liquidate not only the rebels but also the *hacendados*, cattlemen, merchants, and industrialists.[48]

Ortiz tried briefly to persuade the Cristeros to lay down their arms, sending a captured priest to describe the military might about to be hurled against them, but the try failed, and Ortiz attacked rebel positions in the Cerro Grande on May 28. Cristero resistance was determined, but by the thirtieth organized defense had become futile, and the leaders ordered the units to abandon the encampments and move toward Coquimatlán. The federals had won ground, at a high price in lives, but had not destroyed the rebel potential.[49]

Ortiz next turned to the Volcano of Colima, where hymn-singing Cristeros fought him to a standstill in a bloody clash at the encamp-

[46] Gorostieta to Directive Committee, May 16, 1929, LA-1.

[47] Enrique de Jesús Ochoa [pseud. Spectator], *Los cristeros del Volcán de Colima*, II, 189–190.

[48] Ibid., p. 191.

[49] Ibid., pp. 191, 199–200. The priest-emissary wrote a vivid account of his adventure, including his impressions of the Colima Cristeros. See J. Andrés Lara, S.J., *Prisionero de callistas y cristeros*.

ment called El Borbollón on June 4 and 5 and forced the federals
to retreat to San José del Carmen across the Jalisco border. Nine
days later a government counterthrust overran the headquarters
camp, but the Cristeros withdrew in good order toward Tonila and
San Jerónimo.[50] By the middle of June, Ortiz's offensive had caused
havoc in the ranks of the Cristeros, who had been forced out of long-
held positions and had suffered severely, but it had failed almost
completely to destroy or capture rebels or to weaken their will to
fight. Government units had taken heavy punishment, and for the
time being Ortiz was in no mood to keep up the drive.[51]

Fighting in all rebel areas in western Mexico was intense
throughout May. Official government sources recorded twenty-two
major engagements, half of them initiated by Cristeros. Battle
deaths climbed sharply. Federal officers in Jalisco alone admitted
losing nearly 400 men in major clashes, not counting dozens of
smaller ones. Cedillo lost over 50 killed in a complete rout at La-
guna de los Cocos on May 28. Total Cristero losses were not tal-
lied, but an informant trusted by the U.S. military attaché believed deaths for both sides in all states affected by the rebellion
were around 1,250 for the month.[52]

In Jalisco, as May drew to a close, the dispersal and in some cases
the temporary disbanding of Cristero units was well advanced.
Gorostieta believed the Guardia Nacional would survive the storm.
What concerned him were the reports that the episcopate might
make its own peace with the government. The strong Catholicism
of his men and of the supporting civilian populace entailed a deep
spirit of respect for and obedience to the clergy. If ecclesiastical authority should announce that the religious conflict was over, would
they continue the struggle? Gorostieta was determined to fight on,
he said, even if public worship was resumed. But he repeated this
so often and so vehemently that his staff began to suspect that the
general was trying to convince himself and that he was uncertain

[50] Ochoa [pseud. Spectator], *Los cristeros*, II, 200–208.

[51] Ibid., pp. 209–210.

[52] G-2 report, no. 2467, June 28, 1929, Col. Gordon Johnston to War Department, NA, RG 165.

how many of his followers shared his determination. The *generalissimo* also stated his conviction that, if the Cristeros laid down their arms, few if any of their leaders would escape death afterward.[53]

In any event, there was little he could do in Jalisco for the time being. The diffusion of command had left local chiefs in nearly autonomous control. He decided to go to Michoacán to attend personally to organizational matters there. On June 1 he was riding eastward toward Atotonilco, accompanied by his staff, the chief of operations for Michoacán, the civil chief for Los Altos, and a few soldiers—seventeen men in all. The journey was both unpleasant and hazardous. Government patrols were everywhere. It had rained almost without letup for days—a cold, driving rain—and the mud of the plain of La Barca clung to the horses' hooves in large clods. The party was dull with cold and fatigue as it approached a friendly hacienda where it planned to spend the night. But federal troops were spotted, and the little band had to move on, stopping in a small woods around 2:00 A.M. for a few hours of sleep. At dawn they pressed forward and shortly before 10:00 arrived at El Valle Hacienda, where it was thought safe to halt for a few hours to eat and to rest the horses. After a breakfast of eggs, toast, and milk, Gorostieta lay down for a while. He suffered from conjunctivitis, and his eyes pained him more than usual.

Suddenly a sentry on the roof shouted that federal cavalry were coming. Heriberto Navarrete was a witness to what happened next:[54] instantly, Gorostieta was on his feet calling for his horse. Members of the staff were doing the same and grabbing their weapons, while confusion reigned over whether to fight or flee. In the patio some of the horses were already saddled, and Gorostieta was hurrying to mount when the first federals burst through the gate. The general opened fire with his revolver, while Navarrete and another officer galloped toward him to help. He waved them off, tell-

[53] Navarrete, *Por Dios*, pp. 238–240.

[54] Ibid., pp. 242–254. See also Pedroza to Directive Committee, June 6, 1929, LA-1.

ing them to get to safety and cover him as best they could—he would be right behind them. When Navarrete reined up some distance away, he turned to see the house surrounded by troops. Gorostieta lay on the ground, one leg pinned under his dead horse. He seemed to be trying to get up. At that moment a group of soldiers wheeled and headed after Navarrete and the officer with him. They managed to escape; they were the only ones who did. Gorostieta, they later learned, had succeeded in reaching the house, but rather than surrender he tried to shoot his way out through the enemy, alone. He was shot down in seconds. The rest were captured, except for one man who had been killed by the first federals on the scene.

Cedillo telegraphed word of Gorostieta's death to War Minister Amaro the next day. He said the body of the "so-called supreme chief of the fanatical rebellion" had been embalmed and was in Atotonilco. It might be advisable, he suggested, to send the corpse to Mexico City for delivery to relatives so that the "so-called League for the Defense of Religious Liberty" would know that its general-in-chief was dead. Amaro replied immediately; he extended congratulations from Portes Gil and directed that the body be shipped to Mexico City.[55]

The loss of Gorostieta was a body blow to the LNDLR directors. In a letter to the archbishop of Yucatán in Havana they asked that prelate's prayers for the soul of the fallen leader, whom they praised unstintingly: "The hero conducted himself with a selflessness and a valor that will forever do honor to his memory. He was one of the few career military men who had the courage to place himself at the side of the liberators; he organized and unified them. A great loss has been sustained"[56]

Other Catholics were less grief-stricken. On June 3 the U.S. Embassy wired news of Gorostieta's death to the State Department. Lane phoned the NCWC to tell Montavon and noted the latter's

[55] *Excélsior*, June 4, 1929.

[56] Directive Committee to Tritschler, LA-1. The date on the file copy is May 30; the section concerning Gorostieta is a postscript added after news of his death was received.

reaction in a memorandum: "Mr. Montavon said that it was probably just as well to have this matter disposed of before the meeting between President Portes Gil and Archbishop Ruiz."[57]

There had been dramatic developments in Washington. Fumasoni-Biondi returned from Europe on May 13, and the next day Ruiz y Flores sent identical telegrams to all members of the episcopate: "[Acting on] higher orders I request you telegraph me whether in principle you vote acceptance [of] conferences [regarding a] settlement."[58] Apparently all the responses were positive,[59] although a few were qualified. González Valencia said he was in favor provided that the talks were official, that they were aimed at securing effective reform of the laws, and that the Holy See would have the last word.[60]

On May 22 Father Burke, also back in Washington, phoned the State Department to say that Archbishop Leopoldo Ruiz y Flores had just been named apostolic delegate to Mexico. He said that the news was still confidential but that he thought Morrow should know. Clark informed the ambassador at once.[61] Morrow was just leaving Mexico City for the United States to attend the wedding of his daughter Anne to Col. Charles A. Lindbergh.

Ruiz y Flores's appointment had been made *ad referendum*, that is, for the purpose of dealing with a matter at hand. Ruiz y Flores understood this to be a clear indication that the pope had decided to move for a solution. He immediately informed Mexican Ambassador Manuel C. Téllez of his appointment and asked him to tell Portes Gil. He proposed that the talks take place in Washington,

---

[57] S. W. Morgan to SecState, June 3, 1929, NA, RG 59, 812.404/988; Lane, memorandum, June 4, 1929, NA, RG 59, 812.404/992⅛.

[58] "Declaraciones del Excmo. y Revmo. Sr. Dr. y Maestro D. Manuel Aspetia y Palomar, Obispo de Tepic," May 26, 1929, LA-1.

[59] *El Universal* reported on May 19, quoting a Washington dispatch, that the replies had been 100 percent favorable and that Ruiz y Flores had so informed Rome and had requested instructions.

[60] Andrés Barquín y Ruiz, *José María González Valencia: Arzobispo de Durango*, pp. 91–92. Orozco y Jiménez replied, "Absolutely" (Francisco Orozco y Jiménez, "Memorándum del Excmo. Sr. Francisco Orozco y Jiménez, Arzobispo de Guadalajara, México," *David* 7, no. 155 [June 1965]: 169.)

[61] Clark to Morrow, May 22, 1929, NA, RG 59, 812.404/980a.

conducted by him and the ambassador, in order to avoid notoriety in Mexico. But Portes Gil replied that he preferred Mexico City,[62] and Ruiz y Flores did not argue the point. He now addressed himself to the matter of whom to take with him to Mexico. He ruled out Father Burke on grounds that he did not want to take a foreigner.[63] After approaching two Mexican priests living in the United States, both of whom advanced reasons why they might not be suitable, he turned to Pascual Díaz, who was in Louisiana, preaching missions and supervising spiritual exercises. Díaz accepted.[64]

But a final meeting of minds remained problematical. Ruiz y Flores told Morrow on May 28 during a chat at Father Burke's Washington residence that the pope was anxious to see the laws amended and that he believed Pius XI still considered that to be the main issue. Morrow replied that, if legal changes were to be insisted upon, he saw no point in continuing his role as arbiter.[65] The next day Morrow commented to Téllez at the Mexican Embassy that it would be best if Montavon or Burke accompanied Ruiz y Flores to Mexico.[66] But the Americans were not invited, and Morrow made no further issue of it. Besides, he would be in Mexico City himself. He had originally planned to spend at least a month in the United States, but at Portes Gil's request he agreed to return early in order to be there for the negotiations.[67]

The new apostolic delegate was keeping his own counsel, but he confided some of his thoughts in a letter to a militant functionary of VITA-MEXICO in Rome. He said that the continued use of force was not the way to accomplish what they all desired. The

[62] Ruiz y Flores, *Recuerdo*, p. 94.

[63] Memorandum of Conversation with Mr. William F. Montavon, May 23, 1929, NA, RG 59, 812.404/974$\frac{12}{17}$.

[64] Ruiz y Flores, *Recuerdo*, p. 94.

[65] Memorandum of Conversation between Ambassador Morrow and Archbishop Ruiz held at Fr. Burke's residence, May 28, 1929, NA, RG 59, 812.404/974$\frac{14}{17}$.

[66] Memorandum of Conversation between Ambassador Morrow and Ambassador Téllez held at the Mexican Embassy, May 29, 1929, NA, RG 59, 812.404/974$\frac{15}{17}$.

[67] Rublee Memorandum.

"armed defense" had failed to overthrow the government, which had full U.S. physical and moral support. "Moral hostility" was likewise useless because it only exacerbated passions on both sides. The Church must abstain from both armed action and partisan politics, "seeking independently of everything her freedom and her rights." The pope wanted an honorable settlement and desired the help of everyone—bishops, priests, and faithful—to achieve it, at the same time "leaving to the citizens in arms the use of their rights." He told his correspondent that "if this flexibility on the part of the Pope produces the evils which you deplore, I believe that the evils which the Pope sees in the uncompromising stance are greater." The "armed defense," the efforts in Europe and South America, the passive resistance of priests and laity—all this, he believed, had not been in vain, because it was compelling the government to seek a solution and would be a warning for the future.[68]

The Directive Committee watched with growing despair while the peace shoot sprouted. It strongly suspected that the LNDLR would be ignored in the negotiations but tried nevertheless to get a place at the conference table. Ceniceros y Villarreal cabled Pius XI on May 14: "We humbly request in the name of our brothers committed to the struggle that they be heard and heeded in negotiating a settlement."[69] The directors were trimming their sails now. On May 30 they wrote Archbishop Tritschler that communication difficulties had resulted in the league's real designs not being well understood, that some believed the directors thought victory could be won only by overthrowing the government. That would certainly be desirable, they said, but they understood the realities of the situation; powerful foreign interests, bigoted Protestants, who wished to destroy Mexico by first destroying her vital nerve, Catholicism, were protecting the tyranny and would apparently continue to do so. But even if the government could not be overthrown, it still could be forced to change "through the hero-

---

[68] Ruiz y Flores to Antonio J. López Ortega, June 2, 1929, LA-1.
[69] Ceniceros y Villarreal to Pius XI, May 14, 1929, LA-1.

ic effort being made by the heroes who are fighting to the cry of
¡Viva Cristo Rey! . . . we are not opposed to settlements and deal-
ings; the only thing we want is 'to sell high, in cash, and make the
buyer realize the great value of our merchandise.' " They agreed
that further bloodshed should be avoided but added that the struggle had not been fruitless. In the natural order it had shown that
Mexico's Catholics were capable of sacrificing everything to save
their faith and their traditions. In the supernatural order, "we well
understand that the noble blood that has been shed cannot but be
acceptable to God." They asked the archbishop to communicate
their views to his confreres if possible, "because we are most anxious to have it known that we are not motivated by a radicalism
that would be prejudicial to the cause of the freedom of the
Church."[70]

Gorostieta's body arrived in Mexico City on June 5 and was
claimed by his sister, at whose home the vigil was kept.[71] Burial
was two days later in the suburb of Atzcapotzalco. Mourners
prayed the rosary aloud during the procession to the cemetery and
sang the national hymn as the casket, covered with a Mexican flag
on which was lettered VIVA CRISTO REY, was lowered into the
grave.[72] A poem written for the occasion was read by its author,
Francisco de P. Morales:

In our sky, clouded and sad
With your death there has bloomed in the distance
A rainbow of light and hope.
If peace, by your death, is finally won,
    Then like the Cid Campeador, dying you have conquered.[73]

Ruiz y Flores and Díaz left Washington for St. Louis by train
on the evening of June 4, on the first stage of their trip to Mexico

---

[70] Directive Committee to Tritschler, May 30, 1929, LA-1. Tritschler, once a
hard-line intransigent, now wanted a negotiated peace. See Tritschler to Directive Committee, May 20, 1929, LA-1.

[71] Excélsior, June 6, 1929.

[72] Ceniceros y Villarreal to Pedroza, June 12, 1929, LA-1.

[73] "A la muerte del Señor General D. Enrique Gorostieta y Velarde," LA-1.

City. Montavon had phoned the State Department that morning
with a message from Father Burke, saying that Ruiz y Flores would
not demand a change in the laws—that, in other words, the archbishop would proceed on the basis of the Veracruz negotiations.[74]
Dwight Morrow was also en route back to Mexico. Reaching St.
Louis at the same time as Ruiz y Flores and Díaz, he had his private coach switched to their train. Soon after leaving the station,
he sent his secretary to invite the two prelates to his car for the
first of several conversations during the next twenty-four hours.
Morrow asked the bishops what terms they would propose to Portes
Gil. Their answer confirmed that Rome was indeed at last ready
for compromise. They told him that their great wish was to see the
antireligious laws repealed and that, if the government wanted
some kind of settlement before this was done, the pope would agree,
on condition that the Church's right to live and function be recognized, that there be specific recognition of the hierarchy and the
freedom to possess rectories, episcopal residences, seminaries, and
other religious facilities, and that freedom of education be guaranteed.[75] Morrow reported later that the prelates' attitude was flexible and conciliatory and that they were not disposed to make unreasonable demands.[76]

In San Antonio, Morrow's car was uncoupled, and he remained
behind while the two bishops proceeded toward the border. At Nuevo Laredo, Mexican officials quickly passed them through immigration and customs without requiring the usual formalities.[77] Inside Mexico they traveled south in a Pullman car. Railway employees respected Ruiz y Flores's orders that the doors and windows
be kept closed.[78] Ruiz y Flores had arranged for Luis Legorretta to
have quarters ready for them in Mexico City and to meet them at
the Tacuba station. Just out of Querétaro, however, a message from

[74] Memorandum of Conversation with Mr. William F. Montavon, June 4,
1929, NA, RG 59, 812.404/992⅛.
[75] Rublee Memorandum; Ruiz y Flores, *Recuerdo*, p. 94.
[76] Rublee Memorandum.
[77] Ruiz y Flores, *Recuerdo*, p. 95.
[78] *Excélsior*, June 9, 1929.

Cruchaga was passed in, advising the prelates not to get off at Tacuba, as news of their arrival was out and a crowd would probably
be on hand. Cruchaga said he would meet them at Lechería.[79] At
5:30 P.M. they descended at the small wayside station. To a few
reporters who somehow had learned of the change in plans, Ruiz y
Flores said only that he was happy to be in Mexico again and that
the government had been helpful in facilitating their journey. He
said he would have no statement until after he saw the president.
Then he and Díaz entered a waiting Lincoln for the drive into
Mexico City.[80]

On June 8 the LNDLR Directive Committee wrote de la Mora
that they understood that Ruiz y Flores was coming and that the
episcopate and the pope were thus assuming responsibility for efforts to achieve religious peace. The league was therefore suspending all civic activity, including propaganda work, in order not to
be responsible for hampering the effort. The armed action, though,
would continue. The directors urged that in the talks special consideration be given the men in arms. They reminded de la Mora
that he and other bishops still in Mexico had assured them that this
concern would not be separated from others.[81]

Later the same day the directors sent to de la Mora Gorostieta's
letter of May 16, which they said Jesús Degollado Guízar had relayed to them with the notation that he endorsed it completely.[82]
Two days later they wrote again to say that they did not endorse
the ideas expressed by Gorostieta and had had no hand in drafting
the missive.[83]

The Guardia Nacional continued its struggle under a new chief.

[79] Ruiz y Flores, *Recuerdo*, p. 95.

[80] *Excélsior*, June 9, 1929.

[81] Directive Committee to de la Mora, June 8, 1929, LA-1. The order to
league officials to suspend activities was made public June 12. See "Instrucciones que el Comité Directivo de la Liga da a sus Delegados Regionales, jefes
locales, a sus agentes y socios de toda la República," June 12, 1929, printed handbill, LA-1.

[82] Directive Committee to de la Mora, June 8, 1929, LA-1. It is not known
when the committee received the missive, but apparently it was after Gorostieta's death.

[83] Directive Committee to de la Mora, June 10, 1929, LA-1.

On June 4 the Directive Committee appointed Degollado to the supreme command. Gorostieta would have approved. Before his death he had named Degollado his second in command and alternate.[84] The new leader accepted his promotion reluctantly. In a circular message to Guardia Nacional officers, he said he had agreed to the appointment with the understanding that it would be temporary, because the post was beyond his capabilities.[85] Moreover, it was a personal sacrifice. The police in Guadalajara had arrested his wife, and he told the directors he was afraid she would be the first casualty of his new command.[86]

Degollado was under no illusions regarding the military situation. The Cristeros were in the most difficult position they had ever known. At the same time, their situation was not hopeless. U.S. Attaché Gordon Johnston told the War Department the first week of June that there were an estimated ten to twelve thousand rebels in arms despite the aggressive campaign against them in Jalisco, Michoacán, Colima, Guanajuato, Durango, Zacatecas, and Aguascalientes.[87] Even news bulletins released by government sources gave a mixed impression. On one hand, official statements spoke almost daily of rebels surrendering in growing numbers, of demoralization in their ranks, and of disintegrating resistance.[88] On the other hand, such optimistic reports were hedged and even contradicted by others equally authoritative. After troops of Lázaro Cárdenas's command captured the Michoacán Cristero base of Coalcomán in the second week of June, military spokesmen told the press that the campaign in that state and in Jalisco was considered to be at an end; but two days later there appeared a report that Cárdenas had organized two columns for a general offensive along

---

[84] Directive Committee report to League Convention, August, 1929, LA-2; Ceniceros y Villarreal to Pedroza, June 12, 1929, LA-1; Directive Committee to Degollado, June 4, 1929, LA-1.

[85] Degollado to Guardia Nacional officers, June 5, 1929, LA-1.

[86] Ceniceros y Villarreal to Degollado, June 3, 1929; Degollado to Directive Committee, June 7, 1929; LA-1.

[87] G-2 report, no. 2428, June 7, 1929, Johnston to War Department, NA, RG 165.

[88] See, for example, Excélsior, June 7, 1929; June 8, 1929.

the Jalisco-Michoacán border to deal with rebels who had moved from the former state to the latter to continue operations. Cárdenas said he was certain that the band would be completely destroyed within ten days at the most.[89] The next day the papers said Cedillo had informed Portes Gil and Amaro that the spring offensive had shattered the rebels, and that his task in the past week had been to prevent the splinters from reassembling; he was confident that by keeping up the pressure and denying the rebels provisions, his forces could completely pacify Los Altos and northern Guanajuato —within two months.[90] On June 17 it was reported that the agrarians who had accompanied Cedillo from San Luis Potosí were being returned to their homes because their services were no longer needed in Los Altos; but the announcement added that regular troops from Sonora and Sinaloa would replace them.[91] Col. Gordon Johnston reported on June 18 that, although the government was claiming publicly to have subdued the Cristeros completely in Jalisco, Colima, and Michoacán, it admitted privately that only around four hundred rebels had surrendered, no important leaders among them.[92]

Remote from the agony of physical combat, the political decision makers convened in Mexico City. Dwight Morrow arrived on Sunday, June 9, and the stage for the negotiations was set. Ruiz y Flores and Díaz had taken up residence in downtown Mexico City. Walsh and Cruchaga were staying at the home of the secretary of the Chilean Embassy, where they had access to cable and code facilities and would be Ruiz y Flores's channel of communication with the Holy See.[93]

Father Walsh called on the ambassador the evening of June 10. He said Ruiz y Flores and Díaz had no definite course in mind for the coming talks. He then proceeded to deliver an intricate discourse on Mexican laws relating to religion, with ideas for modify-

[89] Ibid., June 16, 1929.

[90] Ibid., June 17, 1929.

[91] Ibid., June 18, 1929.

[92] G-2 report, no. 2441, June 18, 1929, Johnston to War Department, NA, RG 165.

[93] Excélsior, June 11, 1929; Rublee Memorandum.

ing them. Morrow said that it would be useless to approach Portes Gil from such an angle and that to do so might jeopardize the entire effort. The next day Walsh told him that the bishops would not enter the negotiations with specific demands.[94]

At noon on June 12 Ruiz y Flores and Díaz met Portes Gil at Chapultepec Castle. The three conferred in the formal atmosphere of the Salón de Acuerdos, but the mood was friendly and relaxed. Portes Gil said he was ready to renew the guarantees Calles had given Father Burke, and the bishops agreed to proceed on that basis.[95] It was decided that each party would prepare a statement. If they were mutually acceptable and were approved by the Holy See, they would be released to the press. The president and the bishops agreed to meet the next day. Morrow was not present at the interview, but he reported to Washington that he was keeping close track of things and that chances for agreement were good.[96]

The second meeting, however, was less auspicious. Portes Gil produced a statement almost identical to Calles's 1928 letter to Burke, but the bishops did not present one. The conversation drifted instead to a discussion of the anticlerical laws. Afterward, Walsh reported to Morrow that the prelates were discouraged; they had found Portes Gil's statement and even his attitude to be brusque and unbending.[97]

Morrow moved quickly to prevent a backslide. He decided that the best tactic would be to have each party read and approve the other's statement before meeting again. He composed drafts for both sides and delivered them personally. The texts contained the five points covered in his May 11 memorandum to Ruiz y Flores.[98]

Before seeing Portes Gil, Morrow called on Plutarco Elías Calles. Without the ex-president's approval, he knew, nothing could be accomplished; besides, Portes Gil would not oppose the strong man's wishes. He showed Calles the statement he had prepared for

[94] Rublee Memorandum.

[95] Ibid.; *Excélsior*, June 13, 1929.

[96] Morrow to SecState, June 13, 1929, NA, RG 59, 812.404/997.

[97] Rublee Memorandum.

[98] Morrow to SecState, June 15, 1929, NA, RG 59, 812.404/1001; Rublee Memorandum.

Portes Gil. Calles said it was acceptable; it conceded no more than he had granted to Father Burke at Veracruz. Morrow showed Portes Gil both statements and told him Calles had approved the presidential one. The president said he would have them translated into Spanish and give his opinion later.[99]

The bishops, Morrow reported to Washington, were satisfied with the statements, were communicating with Rome, and hoped for quick approval.[100] In the evening Ruiz y Flores, Walsh, and Cruchaga cabled the Vatican, giving the gist of the proposals and advising acceptance.[101] Morrow was puzzled at the need to submit the matter to the Holy See. He believed Ruiz y Flores already had ample authority, although he admitted he might not understand precisely what the archbishop's instructions were.[102]

With negotiations in mid-course and with the press speculating daily that a settlement was imminent, criticism from unyielding factions on both sides of the conflict intensified. Portes Gil was growing nervous at the reaction of the extreme anticlericals, and Calles's private support gave him little comfort; he, not the former president, would bear the brunt of any adverse reaction. On June 14 he told reporters that his position on the religious question was one of strict compliance with the duties of his office and that "the resumption of worship in the Republic may be achieved whenever it is desired, provided the dignitaries of the Catholic church first submit to the mandates of the Constitution and the other existing laws."[103] He was under severe pressure. The American Embassy forwarded to Washington the text of a telegram received by *Excélsior*, containing a message reportedly sent to the president on June 14 by Adalberto Tejeda, former secretary of *gobernación* and now governor of Veracruz. *Excélsior*, understandably, did not print it, but a member of the paper's staff passed it to an

---

[99] Rublee Memorandum. Rublee noted that "during the final negotiations [Calles] was always in touch with President Portes Gil and the Ambassador and he approved each step as it was taken."

[100] Morrow to SecState, June 15, 1929, NA, RG 59, 812.404/1001.

[101] Walsh to Morrow, June 18, 1929, Dwight Morrow Papers.

[102] Rublee Memorandum.

[103] *Excélsior*, June 15, 1929.

embassy official. In it, Tejeda deplored reports of the imminent return of the "dismal Catholic clergy," who "continue to darken the future of the nation." They had led a "criminal rebellion" and now wanted to return to the school, the pulpit, and the confessional to deform the popular conscience. The people, said Tejeda, did not need them; during their absence the country had acquired "that high knowledge of the truth which the revolution has given." He urged Portes Gil not to betray his revolutionary trust and to preserve the constitution and Laws of Reform inviolate.[104] The embassy also reported that various labor unions and Masonic lodges were sending energetic messages urging Portes Gil not to surrender to the clergy.[105]

On June 12 the Directive Committee sent Ruiz y Flores a copy of its instruction ordering LNDLR members to abstain from any action that might interfere with the talks. The archbishop, in reply, expressed gratitude at the league's demonstration of respect and obedience; it was, he said, worthy of "an institution that has worked so zealously to defend the rights of the Church." He observed, however, that he could not endorse the items in the statement that called for a continuation of the armed action. He said the Holy See's instructions regarding the relations of the episcopate with the league, "instructions of which you are aware and the exact observance of which the Holy See has recommended to me," prevented him even from giving his views on the subject.[106]

Other Catholic militants appealed desperately to higher authority. Around the middle of June—the exact date is not known—a messenger was sent to Texas with telegrams to be dispatched to Rome. They were signed by leaders of the LNDLR, the Guardia Nacional, the ACJM, and other activist organizations. They asked the pope not to compromise with the government and to hear the views of those whose representatives had signed the messages. The

104 S. W. Morgan to Clark, June 18, 1929, NA, RG 59, 812.404/992⅝.

105 Ibid. The government denied that any such protests had been received (*Excélsior*, June 20, 1929).

106 Ruiz y Flores to Ceniceros y Villarreal, June 13, 1929, LA-1.

telegrams never reached their destination; somehow, they ended up in government hands.[107]

A plea for patience and submission to ecclesiastical authority came from Archbishop Francisco Orozco y Jiménez. In a pastoral letter to his war-torn archdiocese, issued from his place of hiding on June 12, he told his people they must accept whatever decision the pope made; the Holy Father knew the situation, had received the advice of the hierarchy, and was surrounded by eminent and prudent men.[108]

Morrow wired the State Department on June 17 that he expected to have later that day Portes Gil's reaction to the statements he had prepared for the president and the bishops.[109] In the afternoon he spent more than two hours with the president. They discussed some changes Portes Gil wanted.[110] Morrow also conferred again with Calles.[111] The next morning Morrow received word from Clark that, according to Montavon, the Holy See had cabled to Ruiz y Flores and that the statements would no doubt be issued immediately.[112] Morrow wired back, telling Clark to inform Montavon that the archbishop had received no message from Rome. He added that Portes Gil had not given final approval either; some modifications were being worked on, although Morrow thought they would be minor. Rome's immediate go-ahead was vital, he said.[113]

June 19 was a day of anxiety. In the morning Morrow wired Clark the final texts, which both parties had now accepted. He had seen the bishops the evening before, and they were "very much pleased." But he did not think Rome's endorsement had arrived. He said the delay was serious because the president was being

[107] Oscar Vargas, "Algunos rasgos del Lic. Ceniceros y Villarreal," *David 2*, no. 36 (July 22, 1955): 183–184.

[108] *Excélsior*, June 20, 1929.

[109] Morrow to SecState, June 17, 1929, NA, RG 59, 812.404/1002.

[110] Rublee Memorandum.

[111] Ibid.

[112] Clark to Morrow, June 18, 1929, NA, RG 59, 812.404/1002.

[113] Morrow to Clark, June 18, 1929, NA, RG 59, 812.404/1003.

harassed by opponents of a settlement.[114] Searching for a way to stimulate action, he wired again shortly after noon. It should be noted, he said, that Portes Gil's statement included all the five points in the May 11 draft; only the format was different, because Portes Gil wanted to adhere wherever possible to the wording of Calles's April, 1928, letter to Burke. He added that he had understood Ruiz y Flores to say, when he saw him the day before, that he believed he could settle if the five points in question were included. But the archbishop was still waiting to hear from Rome.[115] Clark checked with Montavon and then wired back; Montavon said that on June 15 Legorretta had told him the Holy See had not explicitly said yes to the drafts then submitted but had told Ruiz y Flores that if he approved them there was no objection. Therefore Ruiz y Flores, according to Montavon, apparently had authority to go ahead. He speculated that Ruiz y Flores was being pressed by third parties to wait for further advice from the Vatican—which, if Legorretta was right, might never come. Montavon said that Fumasoni-Biondi was also perplexed over the delay and that he hoped the delegate would convey this in a telegram to the Holy See that day.[116]

Evening came, and still no message from Rome arrived. Morrow sent a note to Portes Gil saying that the bishops were entirely satisfied with the drafts and expected to receive Vatican approval the next day. He wanted to hedge against a delay or even negative action on the part of the Holy See; if everything collapsed at the last minute, the Vatican, not the principal negotiators, would bear the responsibility.[117]

June 20 saw Morrow briefly at the brink of despair. A cable arrived from Rome, and Walsh carried a summary of it to the ambassador around noon:

1. Holy Father—most anxious for peaceful and laic solution
2. Full amnesty—Bishops, priests and faithful—(religious)

114 Ibid., June 19, 1929, NA, RG 59, 812.404/1003.
115 Ibid., NA, RG 59, 812.404/1005.
116 Clark to Morrow, June 19, 1929, NA, RG 59, 812.404/1003.
117 Rublee Memorandum.

3. Restoration of property—churches, Bishops' and Priests' houses, and Seminaries
4. Free relations between Vatican and Mexican Church
5. Only on these understandings may you close if you think proper before God.[118]

Morrow told Walsh that this altered matters materially. The second and third points had not been included in the statements. This might end the negotiations. Walsh left; he returned later to report that Ruiz y Flores was not worried. The archbishop interpreted "laic" in the first point to mean that the settlement could be in accordance with Mexican laws. This, Ruiz y Flores said, was the governing phrase of the message. Amnesty meant that bishops and other clergy should be free to return to their ecclesiastical posts. The third point he interpreted to mean that the Church should try to secure the use of Church properties to the extent that it could do so. The last point, which implied residence of an apostolic delegate in Mexico, was already assured. Morrow was relieved, but baffled—both by the Vatican's message as reported by Walsh and by Ruiz y Flores's interpretation of it. But he decided that, as he had suspected, Ruiz y Flores from the first had had adequate authority to agree to the projected settlement.[119]

By the evening of June 20 the settlement was all but complete. Ruiz y Flores requested a slight change of wording; Morrow went to Portes Gil with it, and the president had no objection.[120] The final products were nearly verbatim the drafts Morrow had given to Portes Gil and Ruiz y Flores on June 15.[121]

The statement that was to appear over Portes Gil's signature said that the president had hold talks with Ruiz y Flores and Díaz and that the talks had come about because of public statements made by the archbishop on May 2 and by the president on May 8.

[118] Summary of Fr. Walsh of telegram rec'd by him from Holy See, June 20, 1929, Dwight Morrow Papers.
[119] Rublee Memorandum.
[120] Morrow to Clark, June 21, 1929, NA, RG 59, 812.404/1006.
[121] The texts of the two statements as finally agreed to are in the appendix. The drafts submitted by Morrow on June 15 are in Morrow to Clark, June 17, 1929, NA, RG 59, 812.404/1002.

It noted that the two prelates had told the president that the Mexican episcopate felt that the constitution and laws, especially the provisions requiring registration of clergymen and allowing the states to determine the number of priests that could function, threatened the Church's identity by giving the State control over spiritual matters. Ruiz y Flores and Díaz had assured the president that the bishops were motivated by sincere patriotism and that they wished to resume public worship if the Church could enjoy "freedom, within the law, to live and to exercise its spiritual offices." The president wished to take the opportunity to declare publicly, the statement continued, that "it is not the intention of the Constitution, nor of the laws, nor of the Government of the Republic, to destroy the identity of the Catholic Church or any other, nor to intervene in any way in its spiritual functions"; that in fulfilling his oath of office his purpose had been to "insure that the laws be applied without intolerance and without any bias whatever"; and that his administration was disposed to hear complaints from anyone, whether a Church dignitary or a private individual, regarding unjust application of the laws. With respect to certain legal provisions that had been misunderstood, he wished to state that the requirement for registration of clergymen did not mean that the government would register ministers of religion who had not been designated by ecclesiastical authority; that, although the laws prohibited religious instruction in primary and secondary schools, this did not prevent clergymen from teaching religion within the confines of places of worship; and that the constitution and laws guaranteed to every Mexican, and therefore to members of any church, the right to appeal for changes in the laws of the nation.

Ruiz y Flores's statement was shorter. It said only that he and Díaz had conferred several times with the president, that the talks had been marked by mutual respect and good will, and that the results of the meetings were set forth in the president's statement. As a consequence of that declaration, the Mexican clergy would resume religious services "in accordance with the laws in force." The statement expressed the hope that the renewal of public worship would lead the Mexican people to cooperate in all legitimate efforts tending to the national welfare.

Late the next day, after terms of the agreement had been made public, Jesús Degollado Guízar dispatched a telegram to Pius XI. Its fate is not known, but its content was eloquent and desperate: "Mexican Catholic people launched selves armed defense essential liberties prior permission and assurances moral support Episcopal Committee given in November '26. *Guardia Nacional* formed blessings *Cristo Rey*. 20,000 armed men compelling illegitimate Government to seek settlement. Essential liberties people such as life. property, legitimate right of those engaged this struggle we see have not been considered. Mere announcement incomplete settlement Delegate critically weakening our defensive power. In grief we approach Your Holiness humbly imploring words guide us present situation and not forget faithful sons."[122]

But Pius XI had reached a decision. He explained his rationale publicly three years later: the suspension of public worship, he said, had been an effective protest against the Mexican government's arbitrary actions, but to prolong it could seriously harm both religious and civil life. Deprivation of regular priestly ministrations was wreaking severe spiritual damage and could result in Mexicans' permanently abandoning the practice of their faith. Moreover, the continued absence of the bishops from their dioceses could undermine ecclesiastical discipline. Therefore, the pontiff concluded, when the Mexican president gave public assurances that application of the laws would not destroy the Church's identity or disregard hierarchical authority, "We, considering only the salvation of souls, believed it opportune not to let that occasion pass." Restoring worship, he insisted, entailed neither acceptance of the persecutory laws nor an end to efforts to change them, but rather the abandonment of one means of resistance that could injure the faithful.[123]

---

[122] Degollado to Pius XI, June 21, 1929, LA-1.
[123] From the encyclical letter *Acerba Animi*, September 29, 1932, text in *New York Times*, October 1, 1932.

The institutional Church had withdrawn from the fray, and there remained only the formality of sealing the decision that would leave the Catholic insurgents to their own devices. On Friday, June 21, Ruiz y Flores and Pascual Díaz arrived at the National Palace at 11:00 A.M. and were escorted immediately to the president's office.[124] Ruiz y Flores related to Portes Gil the reservations the pope had specified in his cablegram. Portes Gil called in Canales of Gobernación and told him to order an immediate amnesty for the rebels and to stipulate that Cristero officers could retain their sidearms and horses. He also authorized free rail passes to Cristeros for transportation to their homes or wherever they wished to go. The president said that buildings not being used for other purposes would be restored to Church use at once, and told the bishops, "I believe you can wait a bit for us to return the ones we have already occupied." Portes Gil asked as a favor that Orozco y Jiménez and Manríquez y Zárate reside outside Mexico for a time, as an aid to the prompt pacification of the country. The part both had played in the rebellion, he said, was well known. Ruiz y Flores replied that he could not agree to this as a condition, but that he would ask the two to cooperate for a short time. He assured Portes Gil that Orozco y Jiménez had not been associated with the armed movement; he would call the archbishop for a personal talk with the president. This Portes Gil accepted. The two statements, prepared in duplicate, were then signed and exchanged.[125]

The prelates left the palace and drove directly to the Basilica of Guadalupe, where they knelt at the high altar for a few moments.[126] As they rose, Ruiz y Flores turned to Díaz and announced

[124] *Excélsior*, June 22, 1929.

[125] Ruiz y Flores, *Recuerdo*, pp. 96–97. Portes Gil (*Autobiografía de la Revolución Mexicana*, p. 576) says that Díaz posed the question: "And as for our brothers who have mistakenly taken a violent position and have risen in arms, what steps will the Government take so that they may return to their homes?" Portes Gil said he replied that the government would be indulgent to those who surrendered unconditionally and that Cedillo had instructions to see that the men had land and agricultural implements and that they received full protection.

[126] *Excélsior*, June 22, 1929.

to him his appointment as archbishop of Mexico. Shortly after arriving in Mexico City he had recommended to Rome that the bishop be named to the vacant see, and the pope had confirmed the choice.[127]

The new primate and the apostolic delegate left the basilica through an excited crowd of worshipers, who had become aware of their presence and were pressing forward to kiss their hands and receive their blessings.[128] The Cristero rebellion was over, even though the Cristeros were not yet aware of it.

[127] Ruiz y Flores, *Recuerdo*, pp. 97–98.
[128] *Excélsior*, June 22, 1929.

10. Trial by Peace

MORROW TELEPHONED LANE shortly after 5:00 P.M. to say that the settlement was complete and that the statements were being given to the press at that hour. He asked that Burke and Montavon be informed.[1] The next day, Morrow sent a personal message to Father Burke congratulating the priest on "the happy outcome of the work you started more than a year and a half ago." It could not have come about, he said, without Burke's "courage, patience and faith." He extended regards to Montavon, Fumasoni-Biondi, and Cardinal Hayes.[2] Also on June 22, Secretary of State Henry Stimson sent his congratulations and those of President Hoover to the real architect of the arrangement, Morrow. Stimson heaped praise on the am-

[1] Memorandum from Lane to Stimson, June 21, 1929, NA, RG 59, 812. 404/1012.

[2] Morrow to SecState, June 22, 1929, NA, RG 59, 812.404/1008.

bassador's conduct of affairs in Mexico: "The way in which you have brought to the two governments the present friendly good will from a condition of near hostility, is a high achievement in the history of our diplomacy."[3]

News of the settlement spread quickly through the combat areas in western Mexico, in some cases disseminated by leaflets dropped from government planes,[4] and the impact on the Cristero military effort was devastating. Some rebel chiefs immediately accepted offers of amnesty. Others hesitated but told Degollado that, inasmuch as the priests were returning to the churches, they believed it was no longer lawful to continue fighting. The general learned that some clergymen were counseling an end to the struggle and even saying that it would be a mortal sin now for anyone to help the Cristeros. Within a week the situation was desperate, and Degollado decided to place matters personally before the LNDLR dirrectors.[5]

He traveled to Mexico City by train, disguised as a poor *ranchero*. On his arrival he was escorted to the house where Ceniceros y Villarreal was staying and went at once into conference with the Directive Committee. He reported what was happening in the field, at the same time pledging that he would follow the directors' orders. Ceniceros y Villarreal asked the general for his own opinion. Degollado replied that he thought it was useless to continue military operations. Some bishops and priests were still for the cause, he acknowledged, but many had abandoned it. Surrenders were increasing and there were reports of insubordination in the ranks. He said he thought that, if the struggle went on, the only result would be anarchy and scandal.[6] Hours of anguished discussion followed. At length the committee decided to discharge the Guardia Nacional from further duty, under terms which Degollado

[3] Stimson to Morrow, June 22, 1929, NA, RG 59, 812.404/1012.

[4] *Excélsior*, June 22, 1929.

[5] Jesús Degollado Guízar, *Memorias de Jesús Degollado Guízar, último general en jefe del ejército cristero*, p. 234.

[6] Ibid., pp. 234–237.

would work out with the government. Degollado told the directors that his wife was still a hostage of the government and that he could not in honor deal with her captors. The committee sympathized. It instructed him to demand the lady's freedom as a precondition for negotiating. With this, Degollado agreed to proceed. He named league official Luis Beltrán to act as his intermediary with Portes Gil and told him to get an entree to the president through Ruiz y Flores.[7]

At first Portes Gil balked at the demand for Señora Degollado's release, but Beltrán refused to back down, and the president relented. Then Beltrán presented Degollado's conditions: full guarantees of protection for the lives and property of all officers and men and for civilians who had supported the movement; release of all persons in custody for reasons related to religion and the dropping of legal actions in progress against Catholics stemming from religious questions; repatriation of Mexicans exiled during the conflict; payment of twenty-five pesos per rifle to men who turned in their weapons and permission for those who needed their horses to keep them; permission for officers to retain their sidearms; certificates of safe conduct for officers, plus a cash grant-in-aid (the amount to be determined by federal chiefs of operations). Finally, the mustering out was to take place in the presence of federal chiefs of operations.[8] Portes Gil accepted the terms without discussion and said he would issue orders at once to the military to proceed in accordance with them.[9] He offered to make telegraph facilities available to Degollado so that he could order an immediate suspension of hostilities, but this was declined. Beltrán left the same afternoon for Guadalajara. There he dispatched orders to regimental com-

[7] Ibid., pp. 237–238. It was stipulated that what was being ordered was "discharge" (*licenciamiento*), not surrender.

[8] Ibid., pp. 238–239, 269–270.

[9] Ibid., p. 239. Although the government in June was, as always, playing down the magnitude of the fighting in its public statements, Portes Gil said later that, at the time the rebellion ended, it was costing between eight hundred and one thousand deaths a month. If accurate, this would help account for his eagerness to accept Degollado's terms. See Emilio Portes Gil, *Autobiografía de la Revolución Mexicana*, p. 574.

manders of the Guardia Nacional to present themselves with their men at stipulated places for demobilization.[10]

During the next several weeks all but a handful of the Cristeros laid down their arms—over fourteen thousand of them, according to the government.[11] The order to cease resistance reached the Colima Cristeros on July 4, and Father Ochoa left the volcano for Colima City to arrange details of the capitulation. On the fifteenth Cristero units in the state began surrendering. The last military action occurred on the seventeenth—two small skirmishes in the Cerro Grande.[12] A few bands were still at large early in August, reported U.S. Vice-Consul William P. Blocker from Manzanillo, but it was believed they would give little trouble, "due to the fact that they are not regularly organized and have not the sympathy and backing which was given to the revolutionists by many citizens who were in sympathy with their cause up until the time of the settlement in June."[13] The pattern was nearly identical in other regions where the rebellion had flourished.

In August Degollado addressed a final message to the Guardia Nacional. He praised the bravery and loyalty of the fighting men and told them that the same patriotism and love for the cause they had fought for now obliged them to end their struggle. A decision had been taken to regain rights and liberties by other means, and therefore they were absolved of further responsibility. He did not disguise his grief and bitterness; the men of the Guardia Nacional had not won the victory they sought, he admitted, but as Christians they could savor a more intimate satisfaction; they had offered to Christ and his Church the priceless sacrifice of seeing their ideals shattered in the eyes of the world, convinced that in the end Cristo Rey would reign over souls in Mexico. The Guardia Nacional had not been conquered by its enemies, he said, but rather had

[10] Degollado, *Memorias*, p. 239. The circular order, dated July 1, 1929, is reproduced in *David* 5, no. 115 (February 1962): 301.

[11] Portes Gil, *Autobiografía*, p. 574.

[12] Enrique de Jesús Ochoa [pseud. Spectator], *Los cristeros del Volcán de Colima*, II, 327–329.

[13] Blocker to SecState, August 8, 1929, NA, RG 59, 812.00 Colima/42.

been abandoned by "those who were to have been the first to receive the worthy fruits of its sacrifices and abnegations."[14]

One of the intended beneficiaries, Ruiz y Flores, had spoken out publicly for the first time on June 25. It had been hoped, he told Mexico's Catholics, to solve the religious problem definitively by bringing about a change in the laws. But the strong passions of the moment and other difficulties made it plain that more time would be needed to accomplish this, and therefore it had been decided to conclude an arrangement that allowed Catholics to profess their beliefs and to worship lawfully and that at the same time would remedy the evils attendant upon the suspension of worship. The government had recognized the Church's existence and assured it adequate freedom to function in society, he said; this recognition had been obtained on terms that satisfied principle and therefore permitted the resumption of worship. The pope had approved the settlement, and all should accept his decision. The good will shown by the government, he continued, was the best guarantee that a new era of conciliation was at hand. It was now the duty of both clergy and laity to request reform of the laws. A final solution would come, "but without undue haste, because the evils of a century cannot be cured in a day."[15]

The LNDLR directors were uncertain at first what position to take regarding the June 21 settlement. They suspected that, in addition to the public agreement, there were secret ones in which the government had made substantial concessions.[16] Manríquez y Zárate was inclined to the same opinion, although for the moment, he wrote to Palomar y Vizcarra, he was "overcome by deep depression and a mortal sadness." He recommended that the Cristeros or at least a select number of them regroup in remote areas of the country and remain on standby while the others hid their arms and disbanded; armed action should be suspended, he agreed, to avoid strife among Catholics during the current period of confusion,

[14] Degollado, *Memorias*, pp. 270–273.

[15] "Carta del Excelentísimo Señor Delegado Apostólico al Episcopado, Clero y pueblo católico mexicano," June 25, 1929, in *Excélsior*, June 26, 1929.

[16] Directive Committee to Degollado, June 28, 1929; statement signed by Andrés Barquín y Ruiz, August 8, 1941; LA-1.

but the Directive Committee should continue to function from exile in the United States.[17] His letter reached the directors after they had agreed to end hostilities, but it could scarcely have influenced their decision. The rebellion was over. The committee issued a public statement on July 12. It said that, according to press reports, on June 21 "some kind of arrangement, or rather, armistice," had been concluded between the apostolic delegate and Portes Gil. The manifesto noted that, although freedom of worship was one of the league's principal objectives, its program also included restoration of other liberties. However, because a breach had been opened, according to the apostolic delegate, through which freedom might be won by ordinary means, the league had decided to end the armed resistance.[18]

When the directors reported to the league's national convention early in August—the first such gathering in three years—they did not criticize the June accord but rather claimed major credit for it. The Guardia Nacional, they said, had by force of arms obliged the government to recognize, de facto, the pope's authority and the hierarchy's juridical personality, and to allow Mexican Catholics to seek through legal means the freedoms they had fought for with such heroism.[19]

The paucity of what the government had conceded became evident later, when the league had been reduced to absolute impotence. Its emasculation began the week it met in convention and was heralded by a letter from Ruiz y Flores to the directors. He noted that the league, by participating in "activities that are not directly within its province," had encountered obstacles to its development. Although it was up to the convention to decide whether it should still be called the "league," he did not deem it practical that it retain the same name and leaders. Changing these, he said, would free the "new institution" of many difficulties and prejudices. If it chose to operate only in civic matters, he stood ready to help; if it

[17] Manríquez y Zárate to Palomar y Vizcarra, June 25, 1929, LA-1.

[18] Alberto María Carreño, *El arzobispo de México, excmo. Sr. Dr. D. Pascual Díaz y el conflicto religioso*, pp. 63–65.

[19] Directive Committee's report to LNDLR convention, August, 1929, LA-2.

decided to dedicate itself to social action, it would be under the guidance of Archbishop Pascual Díaz, whom the episcopate had recently elected head of all Catholic social activties in Mexico.[20]

The league withstood the pressure for a time. The convention refused to agree to a change in name and gave the Directive Committee a rousing vote of confidence and loyalty. Ruiz y Flores was unperturbed; ever the conciliator, he invited the directors to dinner a week later—and avoided discussing the subject. But the committee understood the situation. It had been one thing to cross swords in the past with Ruiz y Flores, the archbishop of Michoacán, and Díaz, the bishop of Tabasco, when other equally important prelates were on its side; it was quite another to defy the apostolic delegate and the archbishop primate of Mexico. At any moment, Díaz or Ruiz y Flores could snuff out the organization by simple fiat, and in that event the league could decide between dying in disgrace or lapsing into apostasy. To the directors, either was unthinkable, and they took a minimal placative step, changing the name to "National League for the Defense of Liberty" (Liga Nacional Defensora de la Libertad)—dropping the word "religious."[21] The leadership for the time being remained unchanged, but it became increasingly unimportant who headed what was left of the organization. The league lived on into the 1930's, more and more a name on a letterhead which inspired—or perturbed— increasingly fewer Mexicans.

The ACJM went much the same way. In the late summer of 1929 Pascual Díaz appointed a commission to draft statutes for a single federation of Catholic Action in Mexico. The commission proposed that Catholic youth be grouped in the federation under a new name, which would amount to suppressing the ACJM altogether. The association made a lively defense of its life and work, including the participation of many of its members in the rebellion, but in vain. In December Díaz promulgated general ordinances for Mexican Catholic institutional activity, which among other things

[20] Ruiz y Flores to Directive Committee, August 4, 1929, LA-1.
[21] Antonio Ríus Facius, *Méjico cristero: Historia de la ACJM, 1925 a 1931*, pp. 402–403.

provided for a new official Catholic youth organization. Six days later the ACJM's General Committee declared the association dissolved.[22] There followed a year of wrangling, during which ACJM devotees launched fervent appeals to Ruiz y Flores and to the pope. Finally an agreement was reached; the ACJM reactivated itself, and in November, 1930, Díaz admitted it into the Catholic action family.[23] Thus the association survived, but its substance, like that of the league, was gone. It melded tamely into the chastened stream of Mexican religious life, away from the glare of public attention and the noise of national causes, to become a proponent of spiritual growth for a new generation of young Catholics. Members in later years would be awed by accounts of the heroism of those who had lived the saga of the *cristeriada*, but they would honor the memories, not emulate the deeds.

Other Mexican Catholic organizations whose venturesome members had joined the rebellion either disbanded, disappeared from view, or resumed standings of peaceful respectability. The Knights of Columbus managed with little difficulty to retain an esteemed place in Mexican religious life. The Feminine Brigades evaporated with the 1929 demobilization. The fate of the "U," that shadowy brotherhood of elite extremists, remained a mystery. Although banned by ecclesiastical authority, it apparently continued to perpetuate itself as a small underground movement, without influence and completely innocuous.

For a time it seemed that the champions of conciliation had been right, that a new era had indeed dawned for the Church in Mexico. For the most part, the summer of 1929 was auspicious. Gobernación informed state governors that talks would begin at once between the bishops and government representatives to arrange for churches and annexes to be handed over to priests designated to receive them.[24] On June 25, after conferring with Ruiz y Flores and Díaz, Canales announced that the federal government would overrule any state laws on religion which it deemed unconstitu-

[22] Ibid., pp. 412–421.
[23] Ibid., pp. 424–441.
[24] *Excélsior*, June 22, 1929.

tional.[25] Church services resumed in most parts of the country during the last week of June and early July. Within hours after the June settlement, the government ordered the release of various persons being held for violation of religious laws.[26] After the capitulation of the Guardia Nacional, still more individuals were freed. Most of the Cristeros imprisoned on the Islas Marías were released and left for the mainland the first week of July.[27]

But some skeptical souls found cause to worry. For one thing, the government seemed to be going out of its way to drive home the point that the settlement was actually a surrender by the Church. Replying to reporters' questions on June 22, Portes Gil painstakingly pointed out that the outcome of the negotiations was identical to what was almost achieved in 1928 and that the statement he had signed the day before was in no way different from one Calles had approved a year earlier.[28] Other officials asserted the proposition even more strongly. In a circular telegram to state governors giving instructions for the transfer of churches, Canales began by noting that the clergy had "decided to resume religious services soon, submitting to the laws in force"; he ended by saying that "the application of this Circular will be made without contravening local laws which set the maximum number of clergymen in accordance with regional needs."[29] Some public jabs were hostile and inflammatory. Minister of War Joaquín Amaro, addressing the new Commission on Military History, referred to the "clerical insurrection" just concluded and reminded his listeners that the Catholic clergy had been the sole source of Mexico's troubles since the Spanish conquest.[30]

There were more disheartening developments. Months passed, and large numbers of churches, rectories, seminaries and other buildings were not returned. Ruiz y Flores sent intermediaries to

[25] *New York Times*, June 26, 1929.

[26] *Excélsior*, June 22, 1929.

[27] Felipe Brondo Alvarez, Memoirs.

[28] *Excélsior*, June 23, 1929.

[29] Canales to state governors, circular telegram, June 28, 1929, State of Coahuila Archives, *legajo 15, expediente 2/11*, 1929.

[30] *El Universal*, October 23, 1929.

the Ministry of Gobernación to protest the delay. Canales told them with brutal candor, "It is true that the President offered this—I was present—but he did not know what he was offering, because if those buildings were vacated and returned it would stir up a swarm of enemies." Ruiz y Flores and Díaz tried to see Calles, but the strong man would not receive them. Ruiz y Flores was equally unsuccessful in attempts to get permission for González Valencia, Manríquez y Zárate, and Orozco y Jiménez to return to Mexico.[31] In February, 1930, Pascual Ortiz Rubio, hand-picked by Calles, succeeded Portes Gil as president. Ruiz y Flores conferred with him. Ortiz Rubio reiterated what he had told Father Burke and others in Washington the month before: that his policy would be to relax tensions and avoid conflict and that he would move to reform the laws.[32] Time passed, but there was no indication of action. When Ruiz y Flores urged the president at least to honor the promises made by Portes Gil, Ortiz Rubio replied that Portes Gil denied having promised anything.[33]

Gorostieta's fear that many Cristeros would be in jeopardy if they surrendered proved well founded. When Navarrete presented himself to authorities to receive his amnesty, the chief of operations in Jalisco, Gen. Andrés Figueroa, advised him not to stay in Guadalajara. He said that, although Navarrete and the rest had nothing to fear from the federal military, they might become targets of local anticlericals who harbored a desire for vengeance or of politicians who thought they could court favor with superiors by victimizing ex-Cristeros.[34] Navarrete took the advice and moved to Mexico City. Other men who could not or would not take similar precautions were hunted down and killed.

[31] Leopoldo Ruiz y Flores, *Recuerdo de recuerdos*, p. 100. Shortly after the June settlement, Orozco y Jiménez met with Portes Gil. He denied categorically that he had taken part in the rebellion, but the president was unimpressed. The archbishop left the country.

[32] Burke to McDevitt, January 8, 1930, Philip McDevitt Papers.

[33] Ruiz y Flores, *Recuerdo*, p. 101.

[34] Heriberto Navarrete, *"Por Dios y Por la Patria"*: *Memorias de mi participación en la defensa de la libertad de conciencia y culto durante la persecución religiosa en México de 1926 a 1929*, pp. 269–270.

Responsibility for the annihilation of Catholic militants following the 1929 agreement was never fixed. Government officials showed little or no interest in investigating the problem. But for years the depradations kept old fears and hatreds alive. In November an ex–Guardia Nacional colonel, José María Gutiérrez, was assassinated in Jalpa. Primitivo Jiménez, who had been a Cristero chief in Guanajuato, met a similar fate.[35] Former Guardia Nacional general Vicente Cueva was murdered in Jalisco in March, 1930.[36] Victims were not limited to former officers. On February 14, 1930, at San Martín de Bolaños, Jalisco, there was a mass execution of forty-one ex-Cristeros, all of whom allegedly had laid down their arms after the settlement the previous summer.[37] The number of victims mounted month by month and included persons who had held high posts in the LNDLR. José González Pacheco, a league vice-president, was tortured and killed in Hidalgo in 1932, together with Luis Alcorta, a former Guardia Nacional general.[38] Some former leaders went into hiding. Degollado (who refused to apply for an amnesty) stayed under cover for several years to escape assassination.[39] Reports of violence against men who had taken part in the rebellion cropped up again and again until well into the 1950's. Most of the stories were unverified, but many Mexicans agreed with Leopoldo Lara y Torres that more Cristero chiefs perished after the surrender than died on the field of battle.[40]

For two years after the 1929 *arreglos,* the religious situation was uneven. Despite various indications of government hostility, church services were available in most parts of the country, most clergymen performed their duties unhampered, and religious instruction of the young was being carried on in some areas. Then, in 1931,

---

[35] Jorge Téllez to Palomar y Vizcarra, December 1, 1939, LA-1.

[36] Ríus Facius, *Méjico cristero,* p. 395.

[37] Andrés Barquín y Ruiz [pseud. Joaquín Blanco Gil], *El clamor de la sangre,* p. 76.

[38] Ibid., p. 373.

[39] Degollado, *Memorias,* p. 278.

[40] Leopoldo Lara y Torres, *Documentos para la historia de la persecución religiosa en México,* p. 829.

as Catholics prepared to celebrate the four hundredth anniversary of the apparition of the Virgin of Guadalupe, a plunge downward began. In June the irrepressible Adalberto Tejeda of Veracruz approved a law limiting the number of priests in his state to one per 100,000 inhabitants. In a telegram to Ruiz y Flores, he defended the step by branding the Church "the enemy of all work tending toward human redemption."[41] The bishop of Jalapa suspended public worship in the state.[42] Chiapas and Yucatán followed by drastically reducing the number of priests; in Tabasco no clergymen whatever were officiating.[43] After the Guadalupe celebrations in Mexico City in December, and apparently as a response to them, Congress passed a law restricting to twenty-five the number of priests in the Federal District.[44]

By 1932 all signs were bad. When Abelardo Rodríguez, another Calles man, took office as provisional president, Ruiz y Flores, grasping at a possibility of rekindling a little good will, sent congratulations. The message was not even acknowledged.[45] In September Pius XI spoke out publicly and forcefully on the deteriorating Mexican situation. The understanding reached in 1929, he acknowledged, had not brought peace; the government was ignoring the spirit of the *modus vivendi;* it had deported clergymen and had not returned churches, seminaries, and episcopal residences; vengeance had been visited upon priests and laity who had defended the faith; and attacks in the press on the clergy and on religion itself had increased.[46] When the papal pronouncement was reported in Mexican papers, more trouble erupted. Rodríguez said the pope was trying to foment rebellion—an accusation that Ruiz y Flores immediately denied. On October 3, in a session marked by

[41] *Current History* 35 (October 1931): 113; *New York Times,* June 12, 1931.
[42] Eduardo J. Correa, *Mons. Rafael Guízar Valencia: El obispo santo, 1878–1938,* p. 105.
[43] Earle K. James, "Church and State in Mexico," *Foreign Policy Reports* 11 (July 3, 1935): 110.
[44] Ibid., pp. 110–111.
[45] Ruiz y Flores, *Recuerdo,* p. 101.
[46] The text of the encyclical is in the *New York Times* for October 1, 1932.

impassioned oratory, members of the Chamber of Deputies demanded the apostolic delegate's expulsion from the country. Ruiz y Flores was arrested at dawn the next day and deported to the United States.[47]

The bottom came in 1934 and 1935. The Mexican Church was undergoing the worst ordeal of its history. In many states almost every church had been closed by the government. Priests had all but disappeared from sight; in the country at large only around 10 percent of the clergymen who had functioned in 1925 could officiate legally, and the number who were in fact exercising their ministry was even smaller because of such local stipulations as requirements that the clergy be married.[48] Anti-Catholic excesses reached their zenith in the field of education. In Michoacán, teachers had to affirm that they professed no religion and would combat the Catholic Church and any other.[49] Teachers in Yucatán had to profess atheism and promise to work for the destruction of Catholicism.[50] From his exile in San Antonio, Texas, Ruiz y Flores declared that the Church in Mexico had ceased to function.[51] In 1934, driven by fear and despair, some veterans of the rebellion—Aurelio R. Acevedo, Lauro Rocha, Andrés Salazar, and others—tried to launch another Cristero uprising. But most Mexican Catholics had no wish to throw away their lives in a venture that could have only one outcome. A handful joined the new attempt, but only a few survived the pathetic effort, which flickered to an end in 1936.[52] In Mexico City, Pascual Díaz endured stoically one humiliation after another. Once, early in 1935, he and four other clergymen were arrested and thrown into a tiny jail cell like common criminals; Díaz was charged, among other things, with being suspected

[47] Ruiz y Flores, Recuerdo, p. 102.

[48] Charles C. Cumberland, Mexico: The Struggle for Modernity, p. 283.

[49] Kenneth Grubb, "Political and Religious Situation in Mexico," International Affairs 14 (September 1935): 689.

[50] Lyle C. Brown, "Mexican Church-State Relations, 1933–1940," A Journal of Church and State 6 (Spring 1964): 211.

[51] Wilfrid Parsons, Mexican Martyrdom, p. 268.

[52] Degollado, Memorias, pp. 277–278.

of carrying a machine gun in his car.[53] Later the same year he told a visitor that he was looking for a place to live; the archepiscopal residence was still in government hands, and he had been staying in rented houses, but now no one would accept him as a tenant for fear that the government might confiscate the property. He was considering taking a room in a hotel.[54] Harassed by the authorities, under fire from LNDLR recalcitrants who accused him of having betrayed the Catholic cause, he died on May 19, 1936.

The coming of Lázaro Cárdenas to the presidency in 1934 neither promised nor at first produced any improvement in the situation, but the pointlessness of perpetuating a feud that consumed energies needed in other endeavors was becoming apparent. In 1936, firmly in control of national affairs after besting Calles in a test of strength, Cárdenas took steps to reduce the hostility between the revolutionary regime and the Church.[55] In 1937 public worship resumed in Veracruz, long a hotbed of anticlericalism. Details were worked out with the cooperation of the governor, a young lawyer named Miguel Alemán. Alemán typified a new generation in Mexican politics, men who were products of the revolution, intellectually devoted to its goals, and distrustful of Church and clergy, yet less scarred than their seniors by the rancors accumulated during the years after 1910. By 1938 the official thaw was evident everywhere, and that year the Mexican clergy patriotically supported Cárdenas's expropriation of foreign oil holdings. During the next two years the religious climate improved steadily. On December 1, 1940, Gen. Manuel Avila Camacho, one-time scourge of the Colima Cristeros, became president. His headline-making pronouncement, "I am a believer," was taken as a conclusive sign that the long years of strife were ending. Deeds followed. On his second day in office the new president signed an executive decree freeing Madre Con-

[53] Charles S. Macfarland, *Chaos in Mexico: The Conflict of Church and State*, p. 264; Brown, "Mexican Church-State Relations," p. 211.

[54] Macfarland, *Chaos in Mexico*, p. 156.

[55] On the diminution of anticlericalism in the 1930's, see Brown, "Mexican Church-State Relations."

chita from prison on the Islas Marías. The directive was rushed to the penal colony by special courier on orders from the new secretary of *gobernación*, Miguel Alemán, who six years later succeeded to the presidency.[56]

Many of the pivotal figures in the religious conflict of the twenties did not live to see the advent of the real *modus vivendi*. Dwight Morrow left Mexico in September, 1930, and two months later was elected to the U.S. Senate from New Jersey. He died October 5, 1931. His American partner in designing the June, 1929, settlement, Father Burke, survived him by only five years. Rafael Ceniceros y Villarreal, the LNDLR's "heroic old man," died in 1933, his final years spent in abject poverty. Francisco Orozco y Jiménez obediently accepted exile in 1929. He moved restlessly about Europe and the United States, then returned to Mexico, only to be deported again. Once, while in Rome, he met Father Edmund Walsh. He asked the Jesuit what had been the guarantee that the 1929 agreement would be honored. Walsh replied, "Morrow . . . but Morrow died on us!"[57] In 1935 the archbishop told Father Parsons in New York that he was going home to Mexico. When the priest warned that it might be extremely dangerous, he answered: "I don't care. I can't die in this country." He returned to Guadalajara, where he died peacefully on February 18, 1936.[58] His secretary and constant companion in hiding during the rebellion, José Garibi Rivera, succeeded him as archbishop of Guadalajara and in 1958 became the first Mexican to be elevated to the College of Cardinals.

Leopoldo Ruiz y Flores resigned as apostolic delegate in 1937 while in exile. Soon afterward the government allowed him to return to Morelia to resume direction of his archdiocese, and there he died in 1941.[59] Manríquez y Zárate also received permission to

---

[56] Gabriel Cházaro, "El caso de la Madre Conchita: Texto revisado por ella misma," *David* 5 (September 22, 1961): 221.

[57] Parsons, *Mexican Martyrdom*, pp. 58–59; Ríus Facius, *Méjico cristero*, p. 397.

[58] Parsons, *Mexican Martyrdom*, pp. 58–59.

[59] Brown, "Mexican Church-State Relations," pp. 218–219.

return but did not immediately accept. In 1939 he vacated his see of Huejutla and withdrew from any involvement in ecclesiastical affairs, dying quietly in Mexico City in 1951. José María González Valencia outlived all the other prelates who had figured prominently in the conflict. Returning to Mexico in the late 1930's, he governed his archdiocese of Durango until his death in 1959.

Plutarco Elías Calles directed national affairs from behind the scenes for six years after leaving office. Then, in 1934, he miscalculated by allowing Lázaro Cárdenas to become president. The young general, after carefully constructing his own base of support, challenged the *jefe máximo* for control, and in 1936 Calles went the way of so many of his clerical adversaries: he was unceremoniously dumped across the border to exile in the United States. His power gone, he returned to Mexico in 1941 to play an aloof elder statesman's role until his death four years later.

Emilio Portes Gil became a perennial officeholder in successive administrations, first in cabinet positions and then in lower-level sinecures. He sustained on the side a rather prolific literary career, defending his revolutionary purity and touting his importance as a mover of events. His eagerness to enhance his image for future generations led him to the extreme of denying, thirty-five years after the event, that the Yankee Dwight Morrow had any hand in settling the religious conflict.[60]

A few Catholic lay leaders, too, survived into the second half of the twentieth century to tell their stories of the rebellion to a new generation of Mexicans, many of whom were only dimly aware of what had happened. Miguel Palomar y Vizcarra lived on for forty years, the custodian of both the LNDLR's archive and its con-

---

[60] Said Portes Gil in *Autobiografía de la Revolución Mexicana*, pp. 574–575, "As regards the supposed intervention of the U.S. ambassador, I deny absolutely that there was any. Mr. Morrow, a personal friend of mine, had two interviews with me during those days. At the first, while talking with me about some matter pending at the Ministry of Foreign Relations, he expressed to me his congratulations on the talks I was holding with Archbishop Ruiz y Flores and Bishop Díaz; at the second, he transmitted congratulations from his government on the termination of that bloody conflict, as did all other representatives of friendly nations."

science. A prodigious writer and lecturer, he devoted his energies to defending outspokenly the crusade he had helped lead, increasingly certain that it had been necessary and just and even more sure that its enemies—the revolution, Dwight Morrow, the United States, and Mexican Catholic temporizers—were the epitomes of wickedness and treachery.[61] René Capistrán Garza carried his scars into his advancing years, moving toward an uneasy accommodation with the new Mexico while at the same time employing his journalistic talents in wry and often cynical commentary on nearly everyone and everything associated with change. Jesús Degollado Guízar died in 1957. He devoted his later years to serving as honorary chairman of Cristero veteran groups, a symbol of the struggle lionized by the aging men who had taken part in it.

Most of the Cristero rank and file who survived the rebellion returned to the farms and villages they had come from. Over the years some of them gathered periodically to commemorate their epic and remember their dead companions. A few of them, together with some of the men who had been their leaders, were attracted to the quasi-fascist *sinarquista* movement that arose in the late thirties to propound a kind of mystical Hispanic totalitarianism. But most were content to live out their lives quietly, convinced that they had done what they had to do and had done it well.

Controversy over the rebellion continued beyond the lifetimes of most of the participants. Written accounts poured forth, most of them fervid and biased, penned by men who either ignored facts or explained them in metaphysical rather than historical terms. The mound of contentious literature in turn fueled the "common-wisdom" formulas that many would rely upon to explain the conflict. To the polemicists, it was uncomplicated. Defenders of the revolutionary regime said the Cristero rebellion was a final attempt by reactionary clericalism to turn back the forces of progress and that its defeat meant that an ancient enemy of Mexico's well-being had at last been laid low. Partisans of the militant Catholic

[61] He expressed his views in detail in a series of interviews recorded in 1964 by James Wilkie and Edna Monzón de Wilkie (*México visto en el siglo XX*).

position insisted that the "armed defense" was a holy crusade against God's enemies and a patriotic stand against tyranny; it ended short of its goal because the Almighty in his wisdom had permitted an evil government, abetted by wrong-minded or cowardly Mexicans and imperialistic Americans, to suffocate it.

Scholars have usually avoided such simplicities, but they have often misinterpreted the conflict because they ignored the developments in Mexican Catholicism that preceded it, the nature of the militant leadership that emerged, and especially the rebellion's connection with the official Church.

The confrontation of the 1920's was an episode in the great revolution that broke over Mexico in 1910, but its origins lay far in the past. It climaxed a century-old struggle between Mexican liberalism and Mexican Catholicism for control of the national destiny. At the same time, it differed in important ways from the earlier conflicts. Both forces had altered their positions since the middle of the nineteenth century. The revolutionists, like their predecessors of the days of Juárez, meant to transform Mexico into a modern, democratic nation. But the men who emerged to dominate the revolution after 1913 were committed to a more fundamental reordering of Mexican society than that attempted a half century before, and consequently their assaults on the institutions of the past were more determined. They were as certain as their forebears had been that the Mexican clergy was an impediment to advance. They were comtemptuous of the new orientation in Mexican Catholicism. But, whereas the liberals of the Reform had believed they could render the Church innocuous by separating it from the State and shoaring it of its political and economic prerogatives, the revolutionists were convinced that more strident measures were needed—and Catholic opposition to the revolution hardened that conviction.

Mexican Catholicism too had changed. Influential leaders, both lay and clerical, had espoused enlightened social positions that were a radical departure from the negativism of the nineteenth century. Like the revolutionists, they were committed to securing justice, progress, and dignity for the Mexican masses. They advocated pro-

grams that often were strikingly similar to those of the revolution.
But they were convinced that only a new national order leavened
by the spirit of Christ and rooted in Catholic social principles could
be effective and permanent—and genuinely Mexican.

The vigor of the new Catholicism helped provoke the collision
that came in 1926. It was militant and fiercely patriotic, with a
manly élan that had great appeal. The movement probably had
the potential to become something formidable in Mexican life; the
prohibition in the 1917 constitution against political parties with a
religious designation may have been a recognition of that possibility. The thrust of the Catholic rebirth in the decade before 1913
was affirmative and innovative, but the Constitutionalist assault on
the Church and clergy impelled it to a defensive stance. After the
Querétaro constitution appeared, it was obvious that Catholic activism would have to choose between retreating to the sacristy and
somehow breaching the barriers the revolution had placed in its
way. Attempts at the ballot box failed; efforts to rally effective support through propaganda and assorted Catholic social programs
produced, at best, modest results. Then, in 1925, when actions of
the Calles government seemed to indicate that not only Catholic
civic activity, but also the Church itself, was threatened with extinction, matters moved toward a showdown. Embittered lay leaders organized to force repeal of the anticlerical laws, the government pressed its attacks, and in 1926 the fracas reached a crescendo
when the bishops suspended public worship. That action ignited
armed revolt, and the LNDLR, with a benevolent nod from the episcopate, resolved to overthrow the government.

It is obvious in retrospect that the rebellion had little chance of
succeeding. Governments are overturned in various ways: especially common in Latin America has been the coup d'état, a quick
grab for power in the national capital led by influential public figures and supported by all or most of the armed forces. There was
no chance of this in the case at hand; no Catholic opponents of the
regime had power bases from which to engineer a coup; the army,
a creation of the revolution, could be enticed by some of its leaders

to rise against this or that revolutionary president, as happened in 1920, 1923, 1927, and 1929, but it had no sympathy for the Cristeros. Governments are also ousted by foreign intervention—which in this instance would have meant the United States. This was never a possibility. A third route, the one on which the league at first pinned its hopes, is a nation-wide uprising of such magnitude that a government is overpowered by sheer numbers. This did not materialize. It is possible, of course, that if the rebels had had adequate supplies of ammunition and had won a few spectacular victories, large blocs of the populace and even some of the military might have rallied to them. Or perhaps a sustained war of attrition might eventually have so weakened the government that it could have been toppled. But, as it was, the rebellion lapsed into guerrilla warfare, where it remained until the settlement of June 21, 1929, destroyed its morale and it collapsed.

It is impossible to tell how many Mexicans sympathized with the movement, but it is certain that only a small minority actively backed it. Most Mexican Catholics, whether from indifference, antipathy, or fear, merely watched. In the cities, occasional public demonstrations gave evidence of support for the cause, but involvement was limited to efforts to secure war materials for the rebels. The bulk of the urban working class, many of whose members belonged to government-sponsored labor unions, supported the regime. The rebellion was overwhelmingly rural and was centered in a half-dozen states of the west and south. There the Cristeros had mass popular support that enabled them to gather supplies and recruits with relative ease. The rebels were, in the main, farmers. They were poor, but most apparently were not from the landless bottom of the Mexican social pyramid. They were practicing Catholics, but they understood little of the complexities of the Church-State conflict. Their priests had left the churches, Calles and the government were to blame, and they fought to destroy such wickedness.

The rebellion divided Mexican Catholics and engendered bitterness among them that in some cases persists today. The disuni-

ty was most glaring in the ranks of the clergy. A handful of priests
took the field as military commanders or chaplains, and a somewhat larger number supported the rebels covertly. A few condemned the rebellion. The majority of rural priests fled the countryside to the safer cities where, like the urban clergy, they remained inconspicuous and quiet. All the bishops acquiesced in the
decision to suspend public worship, and probably a majority at first
favored the "armed defense." But, as the chance of success by arms
faded, so did their militancy. A handful of them backed the cause
to the end; some abandoned it; others tried to disassociate themselves from responsibility for it while continuing to give it private
encouragement. Rome finally took direction of Mexican Church
affairs into its own hands and returned it to the hierarchy, in part,
only on the eve of the settlement.

The laymen who led the rebellion at both the political and the
military levels were a homogeneous group. Some of its senior figures had been part of the Catholic social resurgence and participants in the Catholic congresses. Many had been influential in the
National Catholic party during its heyday, and some had held public office under the party's auspices. They had a sophisticated social outlook, and most, although not all, believed in political democracy. They were reactionaries only in the sense that they did
not share the philosophical postulates that motivated the revolutionists. The younger lights were products of the Catholic youth movement, notably the ACJM. Almost without exception the leaders belonged to the small Mexican middle class. They were of comfortable
economic and social circumstances—professionals, businessmen, occasionally small landowners. They were well educated, and several of them qualified to be called intellectuals. Conspicuously
absent from their ranks were wealthy *hacendados* and urban en-
trepreneurs. Toward the old Catholic upper class, in fact, the activist leadership harbored an antipathy that became even more
marked when most of its members refused to support the cause. The
other extreme of Mexican society—the underprivileged mass—produced some field chieftains but never penetrated the movement's
policy-making levels.

The Achilles's heel of the Catholic insurgent movement was the problem of its relation to the Church. Had the rebellion succeeded and its leaders formed a national government, this might have presented few difficulties. But as it prolonged itself, while at the same time claiming a tie with the institutional Church, its leaders found themselves in an increasingly untenable position vis-à-vis both the hierarchy and their potential non-Catholic allies. After the failure of the initial uprisings, the LNDLR went through a torturous series of turns, now playing down the movement's religious mainspring to attract American support, now stressing its Catholic image to enhance Cristero morale, again trying to blend both in order to assuage the pope's growing uneasiness. In the end the league lost on all counts. Americans as well as most Mexicans refused to back the rebels, and Rome disassociated the Church from the armed struggle and absolved Catholics from any obligation to support it.

Among the conflict's components, the Holy See is the most enigmatic. But, if many of its actions and motives remain obscure, certain conclusions are nonetheless warranted. The Holy See saw the Mexican Church-State confrontation in broader perspective than the Mexicans did. By the 1920's Rome had had more than a century of experience with the problems of the Church's existence in secular states. It recognized that a variety of arrangements were possible. In some countries, such as Spain and more than a few in Latin America, a formal partnership between Church and State defined relationships. In others, like Britain and the United States, where Catholics were a minority, the Church was functioning and even thriving without enjoying a privileged status. Even in nominally Catholic countries, like France, where anticlerical governments were entrenched, it had been possible to arrive at understandings that allowed the Church an acceptable degree of freedom; such an arrangement in fact was being worked out with the government of Italy at the very time the Mexican crisis was at its height. In every case, Rome's minimum requirement was that the clergy be free to perform its spiritual duties under a chain of hierarchical command that left the episcopate in control of ecclesiastical discipline. More was desirable, of course—Catholic schools, the right to own property, freedom for Catholic organizations to participate in civic affairs—but these things were negotiable. Thus, in the case of Mexico, although the situation after 1913 was admittedly perplexing, it was instinctive for the Vatican to believe that matters could eventually be arranged. It was a question of finding the right formula.

To Rome, the way a solution was reached was as important as the solution itself. It knew that any settlement the bishops did not accept could be as disastrous for the Church in Mexico as no settlement at all; hence its agonizing concern to bring the hierarchy together on a course of action. The Vatican preferred a settlement based on a change in the laws; but when it became persuaded that this was unobtainable in the immediate future and that to leave public worship suspended any longer was hazardous in the extreme, and when, finally, it was sure that the bishops would agree, however reluctantly in some cases, to a de facto arrangement that covered essentials, it acted to end the stalemate at the politico-ecclesiastical level—even though it thereby deprived the LNDLR and the Cristeros of any lingering hope of victory and in fact smothered the rebellion.

Throughout the crisis Rome admonished Mexican Catholics to refrain from organized political activity, and it was from that principle that the Holy See finally severed any link between the Church and the armed action headed by the LNDLR. Yet it acted so late and so cautiously that until the very end both rebels and conciliators could believe that the pope approved their position. Undoubtedly the Holy See would have liked to see the revolutionary regime replaced by one friendly to the Church, and it was understandably reluctant to prejudice chances that this might happen; significantly, it forbade publication of its directive to the league early in 1928. But in the end Rome neither blessed nor condemned the rebellion. Support for the rebels would have placed the Vatican in an untenable position before world opinion and could have ended for years the possibility of organized Catholic life in Mexico. Overt opposition to the armed movement would have further divided Mexican Catholics and could have invited schism or apostasy.

Ultimately Rome withdrew to narrowly spiritual ground as the only feasible position. It sacrificed everything else.

Catholic apologists have uniformly misconstrued the part played in the conflict by the U.S. government. They have explained it in simplistic terms: Washington backed Calles because it knew that Catholicism was the vital nerve of Mexican nationhood and that by weakening or destroying the Church it would further its aim of subjugating and perhaps ultimately absorbing Mexico. The argument is unconvincing. U.S. policy was determined by self-interest, but the U.S. government perceived that interest differently than its critics imagined. The league and its supporters gambled that Washington would welcome the chance to help extirpate the revolution, which after all had plundered American properties and wounded American pride for fifteen years. But, had they been keener observers of the U.S. stance in the 1920's, they would have known that Washington was moving to end the era of intervention in Latin American affairs that had begun in 1898—a policy not dependent on U.S. approval or disapproval of a particular government. They failed to comprehend that, although Washington had often been vexed at the behavior of the Mexican regimes, it had come to believe that it could probably live with them. The Bucareli agreements of 1923 had indicated that the revolutionary leadership could be reasonable and that diplomacy could defend American interests. Moreover, experience had shown that trouble between the two countries came when central authority was weak in Mexico. As first Obregón and then Calles showed that they were able to weather domestic opposition, the new political order in Mexico looked increasingly stable. Calles's backsliding on the oil question, along with other signs of hostility during his first two years in office, presented a serious problem. But the Coolidge administration decided not to act precipitously, and, after Dwight Morrow succeeded in settling major disputes with Calles, it was clear to all but a few chronic doubters in U.S. official circles that wisdom lay in supporting the government in power in Mexico. Morrow's efforts to end the religious conflict were nurtured by his love of a challenge and by his humanitarian instincts; but they were also in keeping with his determination to remove an obstacle to good relations between the two governments. In terms of U.S. interests, his work was eminently successful.

Next to official American support, the LNDLR coveted most the moral and financial backing of U.S. Catholics, but in the final analysis it got little except expresssions of sympathy. The American bishops deplored the persecution in Mexico and extended hospitality to exiles and refugees; but they drew back in horror from the suggestion that they help bankroll a rebellion. Some, like Archbishop Drossaerts, might lambaste the administration for supporting Calles, but they would never dream of violating the neutrality laws. Knights of Columbus leaders and a few Catholic congressmen protested vigorously and demanded withdrawal of U.S. recognition; but, after their complaints had been duly lodged and reported in the press and after State Department officials had explained to them that it would be unwise to take extreme action, they ceased their badgering. A few prominent laymen like William Buckley and Nicholas Brady toyed with the idea of helping finance the revolt but finally concluded that, without Washington's benevolence and without unity among Mexican Catholic leaders, its chances of success were nil. Buckley had good reason to doubt that his interests or those of other U.S. oilmen would be served by investing in the undertaking, and, after his experience with the Mexican Catholic infighting early in 1927, he could well doubt whether the interests of the Church would be served either. Instead, a conciliatory viewpoint prevailed, represented by Father John J. Burke, William F. Montavon, and Cardinal Hayes. To them a *modus vivendi* seemed feasible. American Catholics had learned that they could live on terms of mutual respect and even affection most of the time with people who feared or misunderstood their church. They had found that they could exist peacefully and securely as Catholics under a government run by non-Catholics. They had discovered, in short, that good will could accomplish wonders. Surely Catholics in Mexico could arrive at some similar arrangement.

The militant leaders seriously misgauged the Mexican milieu.

They failed to perceive that the revolution, despite often-inept leadership, disorganization, unfilled promises, and corruption on the part of some of its chiefs, had struck popular roots by 1926. Millions of Mexicans either supported it or were not unhappy enough to oppose it. Most of those who might have wished it gone were exhausted after a decade and a half of civil strife and had no stomach for another venture into bloodshed. Catholic leaders also misjudged the nature of Mexican loyalty to the Church. There can be little doubt that this loyalty was still very great; few Mexicans had formally abandoned their faith—but they had, like most people in other western nations, compartmentalized their lives. The Mexican social cosmos by the 1920's was essentially secular. Religion was Sunday Mass, baptisms, marriages, the last rites, funerals, fiestas—and, for many, private devotions and a guide for personal conduct; but it was not wages, working conditions, food, housing, and land. And, just as many of the people were puzzled when revolutionary orators told them that the Church was an enemy of their happiness, so were they unconvinced by arguments that only a government inspired by Catholic ideals could give them prosperity and justice.

In the terms on which the religious conflict was joined, the revolution won. The possibility of formal Catholic leadership in Mexico, or even of Catholic institutional participation in Mexican national life, was gone, at least for a long time. The anticlerical laws remained and were in fact made more harsh in the few years following the 1929 truce. Yet religion, as it exists in other twentieth-century nation-states—and as accepted by the proponents of the 1929 settlement—did not lose. Most Mexicans wanted Catholicism to be a part of their private lives, and laws, it turned out, were not an insurmountable obstacle to this. The government, having shattered organized Catholic opposition and humbled the clergy, gradually suspended enforcement of legal strictures that Catholics could deem persecutory. The Church accepted unofficial toleration and resumed its mission, not in ways that the generation of *Rerum Novarum* and the Catholic congresses had projected, but certainly in a manner that satisfied most Mexicans. Possibly, as a handful of skeptics on both sides of the fading issue said forty years later, there would one day be a renewal of the Church-State conflict. But it was certain that Mexico under the revolutionary aegis had achieved a level of material well-being and national pride undreamed of a few decades earlier, while at the same time few denied that Catholic spirituality was more vigorous than it had been since Mexico became a nation. And it was obvious that most Mexicans were more interested in conquering a happy future than in battling over their past.

APPENDIX. The June 21, 1929, Agreement

THE JUNE 21, 1929, AGREEMENT*

Portes Gil's statement:

I have had conversations with Archbishop Ruiz y Flores and Bishop Pascual Díaz. These conversations took place as a result of the public statements made by Archbishop Ruiz y Flores on May 2 and by me on May 8.

Archbishop Ruiz y Flores and Bishop Díaz informed me that the Mexican bishops feel that the Constitution and laws, especially the provisions which require the registration of clergymen and which grant to the States the right to determine the number of priests, threaten the identity of the Church by giving the state control of its spiritual offices.

They assure me that the Mexican bishops are motivated by sincere patriotism and that they wish to resume public worship, if this can be done in accordance with their loyalty to the Mexican Republic and to their consciences. They stated that this could be done if the Church could enjoy freedom, within the law, to live and to exercise its spiritual offices.

I am glad to take this opportunity to state publicly and with all clarity that it is not the intention of the Constitution, nor of the laws, nor of the Government of the Republic, to destroy the identity of the Catholic Church or any other, nor to intervene in any way with its spiritual functions. In compliance with the oath I took when I assumed the Provisional Government of Mexico to observe and enforce the Constitution of the Republic and the laws emanating therefrom, my goal

* The texts of the two statements may be found in Eduardo Iglesias, S.J., and Rafael Martínez del Campo, S.J. [pseud. Aquiles P. Moctezuma], *El conflicto religioso de 1926: Sus orígenes, su desarrollo, su solución*, II, 535–537, and numerous other sources.

has always been to fulfill that oath honestly and to insure that the laws be applied without intolerance and without any bias whatever. My administration is prepared to hear from any person, whether a dignitary of some Church or simply a private individual, any complaints he may have regarding injustices which may be committed by undue application of the laws.

With reference to several articles of the Law which have been misunderstood, I also take this opportunity to state:

1. That the provision of the Law which requires the registration of clergymen does not mean that the Government can register those who have not been named by the hierarchical superior of the religious creed in question, or in accordance with the regulations of that creed.

2. With regard to religious instruction, the Constitution and the laws in force prohibit it absolutely in elementary and higher schools, public or private, but this does not prohibit the ministers of any religion from teaching their doctrines, within church confines, to adults or their children who attend for that purpose.

3. That both the Constitution and the laws of the country guarantee to every inhabitant of the Republic the right of petition, and therefore the members of any Church can appeal to the proper authorities for the reform, derogation, or enactment of any law.

(signed) The President of the Republic
E. Portes Gil

Ruiz y Flores's statement:

Bishop Díaz and I have had several conferences with the President of the Republic, and their results are set forth in the statement he issued today.

I am glad to say that all the conversations have been marked by a spirit of mutual good will and respect. As a consequence of the statement made by the President, the Mexican clergy will resume religious services in accordance with the laws in force.

It is my hope that the resumption of religious services may lead the Mexican people, animated by a spirit of good will, to cooperate in all moral efforts undertaken for the welfare of all the people of the country.

(signed)   *Leopoldo Ruiz*
Archbishop of Morelia and Apostolic Delegate

BIBLIOGRAPHICAL ESSAY

The following essay discusses documents, books, and articles that appear in the footnotes, plus a limited selection of related materials. It includes only a fraction of the literature on Mexico's Church-State conflict, although I hope nothing of prime importance is missing. With a few exceptions, I have omitted general histories, bibliographical guides, and other reference works. These are well known to professionals, and others who are interested can find them listed and competently annotated in a number of books on Mexico published in recent years. An alphabetical list of the sources follows the essay.

Unpublished Primary Sources

The basic manuscript collection used for this study was the archive of the National League for the Defense of Religious Liberty (Liga Nacional Defensora de la Libertad Religiosa). For many years in the possession of Miguel Palomar y Vizcarra, most of it is now available on sixty-three rolls of microfilm in the Departamento de Investigaciones Históricas of the Instituto Nacional de Antropología e Historia in Mexico City. The documents are divided into broad categories, and there is a subject index, but the researcher must scan each roll frame by frame in order not to overlook important items. The archive contains materials from the start of the Catholic social movement at the turn of the century to the end of organized Catholic opposition to the revolution in the 1930's. Especially pertinent to my work were minutes of the meetings of the league's Directive Committee, correspondence of league officials, military reports, and league bulletins. Also of value were copies of letters to and from the Mexican bishops during the rebellion, which fill important gaps resulting from the inaccessibility of the Episcopal Committee's files. The latter are in the archives of the Archdiocese of Mexico, unfortunately still off limits to scholars.

Much unpublished material on the conflict is in private hands in

Mexico. The most formidable cache I know of belongs to Antonio Ríus Facius, who allowed me to see a number of documents, including the fragmentary "Historia de la L.N.D.R.," written by Rafael Ceniceros y Villarreal just after the rebellion ended. Other stores of data in the form of letters and personal reminiscences are scattered about the country, and one comes across them largely by accident. Such was the case with the 160-page memoir of Felipe Brondo Alvarez, which describes the uprisings in Zacatecas and Coahuila and is equally interesting as a sensitive account of one man's motives for joining the Catholic resistance. The Cristero veterans' magazine, *David*, was an invaluable primary source; almost every issue prints personal narratives contributed by former rebels.

The Mexican government's Archivo General de la Nación contains almost nothing on the religious crisis of 1926–1929, although the series "Archivo de los Presidentes, Obregón-Calles" has some items dealing with the Church-government skirmishes between 1920 and 1925. The archive of the State of Coahuila produced copies of official correspondence not available in the federal files—most importantly, circulars sent by the Ministry of Gobernación to state governors during the rebellion. Mexican newspapers cited are in the Hemeroteca Nacional.

The National Archives in Washington was the chief repository of documentation in the United States. The Records of the Department of State Relating to the Internal Affairs of Mexico, 1910–1929, Record Group 59, microcopy 274, had the largest amount of information, mainly in files 812.404 (Religious Affairs) and 812.00 (Political Affairs). The series contains a copy of the memorandum on the religious question written in 1926 by Ernest Lagarde, chargé d'affaires of the French Legation in Mexico City. Lagarde was a trusted confidant of leaders in the Mexican government and in the episcopate, and in preparing the report he drew heavily on information from both, as well as from data supplied him by the French diplomatic mission to the Holy See. Dwight Morrow considered Lagarde to be the best-informed man on the subject in Mexico and obtained a copy of the memorandum in 1927.

The post dispatches of the Mexico City Embassy, Record Group 84, supplied a few useful odds and ends. The files of the Military Intelligence Division of the War Department General Staff, Record Group 165, were helpful for gauging the rebellion's size and scope and for following its ebb and flow. They contain reports from U.S. attachés, who regularly obtained information from the Mexican military and from other contacts both in Mexico City and in the rebel areas.

Dwight Morrow's efforts to resolve the conflict can be reconstructed in the main from the State Department files, but a full appreciation of his herculean labors requires a study of his papers at Amherst College. The collection has letters, both private and public, that are not in Washington, as well as Arthur Rublee's memorandum, which summarizes the ambassador's work and adds tidbits not found elsewhere.

The National Catholic Welfare Conference archive is evidently closed to scholars, but a helpful, if inadequate, substitute was found in the papers of Bishop Philip McDevitt at the University of Notre Dame. McDevitt was a member of the NCWC's administrative board and occasionally received memoranda from Father John J. Burke and William F. Montavon. The Catholic Archives of Texas in Austin preserves diocesan newspapers and other publications useful for sampling American Catholic opinion on the Mexican imbroglio.

Published Primary Sources

These fall into several categories. Most important are memoirs and other eye-witness accounts, all of which must be used with caution. On the Catholic side, Jesús Degollado Guízar's *Memorias de Jesús Degollado Guízar, último general en jefe del ejército cristero* is especially valuable for military details. *Los cristeros del Volcán de Colima* by Enrique de Jesús Ochoa [pseud. Spectator], the chaplain of the Colima Cristeros, is a saga of the uprising in that corner of Mexico that combines luxuriant data on military operations with a hagiographic portrayal of the rebels as modern-day Christian knights. A more matter-of-fact approach, by a participant in the Jalisco rebellion who treats the Cristeros as mortal men, is *"Por Dios y Por la Patria": Memorias de mi participación en la defensa de la libertad de conciencia y culto durante la persecución religiosa en México de 1926 a 1929* by Heriberto Navarrete, S.J. Navarrete also relates in vivid and often humorous style his youthful experiences in the ACJM, whose members played so commanding a role in the insurrection. As colorful as its title suggests is Luis Rivero del Val's *Entre las patas de los caballos: Diario de un cristero*, the recollections of another ACJM veteran, who supplements Navarrete with fascinating anecdotes. *Prisionero de callistas y cristeros*, by J. Andrés Lara, S.J., depicts life in the Cristero enclaves of Colima during the rebellion's final weeks in 1929.

Leopoldo Ruiz y Flores's *Recuerdo de recuerdos* is a short, posthumously published autobiography by the controversial archbishop. Sometimes inaccurate on particulars and silent on many touchy issues, it nevertheless adds to an understanding of the conciliatory position in the hierarchy. Pascual Díaz explained his side of the 1927 dispute with the LNDLR and Capistrán Garza in his *Informe que rinde al V. Episcopado Mexicano el Obispo de Tabasco Pascual Díaz en relación con las actividades de la Liga Nacional Defensora de la Libertad Religiosa*

en los Estados Unidos de América. One of the liberals with whom Díaz
flirted, Nemesio García Naranjo, refers only fleetingly to his contacts
with the Catholic rebel exiles in his *Memorias de García Naranjo* but
amply reveals the qualities that made him and others like him attrac-
tive to Catholics who lost hope in a Cristero victory. Several pamphlet-
size sketches written by Francisco Orozco y Jiménez during the 1910's
and 1920's shed light on that complex churchman's thoughts and deeds.
Pertinent to the rebellion and its antecedents is his *Memorándum.*
Mexican Martyrdom, by Wilfrid Parsons, S.J., is especially informative
on the post-1929 troubles but carefully skirts the Catholic infighting
the author himself was involved in. Miguel Palomar y Vizcarra in
1964 recalled highlights of the conflict and his part in them in interviews recorded by James Wilkie and Edna Monzón de Wilkie in their
México visto en el siglo XX. The league leader displayed some lapses
of memory, but the years had not dimmed his sense of passionate
righteousness.

Emilio Portes Gil has staunchly upheld the government's position in
his *Autobiografía de la Revolución Mexicana,* in which he doctors the
record to enhance (or defend) his part in ending the rebellion. Alvaro
Obregón's *Ocho mil kilómetros en campaña: Relación de las acciones
de armas efectuadas en más de veinte estados de la República durante
un período de cuatro años* includes the leader's version of his early
clashes with clergy and militant lay Catholics that solidified their animosity toward him. *Cristeros contra cristianos* by Cristóbal Rodríguez
is a strong indictment of the Cristeros by a federal general who fought
against them.

An important collection of documents on the conflict is *Documentos
para la historia de la persecución religiosa en México,* compiled by
Leopoldo Lara y Torres. Lara was one of the episcopal intransigents,
and the selections buttress that position. The transcript of the trial of
José de León Toral and Madre Conchita is reproduced in *El jurado de
Toral y la Madre Conchita (lo que se dijo y lo que no se dijo en el sensacional juicio): Versión taquigráfica textual.* Many of the public pro-
nouncements of Obregón and Calles on the religious question may be
found in two collections of their addresses: Esperanza Velázquez Bringas, ed., *Méjico ante el mundo: Ideología del Presidente Plutarco Elías
Calles,* and Aarón Sáenz, Fernando Torreblanca, and Joaquín Amaro,
eds., *Discursos del General Alvaro Obregón.* The official attitude of the
U.S. Catholic episcopate on the struggle can be traced in *Our Bishops
Speak: Statements of the Hierarchy of the United States and of the
Administrative Board of the National Catholic Welfare Conference,
1919-1951.* An excellent source for texts and commentary on the teachings of Pope Leo XIII, which sparked the Mexican Catholic renewal, is

Etienne Gilson's *The Church Speaks to the Modern World: The Social Teachings of Leo XIII.*

To a considerable extent, the Church-State clash revolved around legal questions. The texts of Mexican laws on religion can be found conveniently in J. Pérez Lugo, *La cuestión religiosa en México*; Jesús García Gutiérrez [pseud. Félix Navarrete], *La persecución religiosa en Méjico desde el punto de vista jurídico: Colección de leyes y decretos relativos a la reducción de sacerdotes*; and Felipe Tena Ramírez, *Leyes fundamentales de México, 1808–1964.* A good English translation of the 1917 constitution is in the *Annals of the American Academy of Political and Social Science* for March, 1917. Executive decrees and other federal action on religious matters are printed in the Mexican government's *Diario Oficial* for the period of the conflict.

Secondary Sources

The closest thing to a scholarly history of Mexican Church-State relations can be found in Wilfrid Hardy Calcott's two volumes, *Church and State in Mexico, 1822–1857* and *Liberalism in Mexico, 1857–1929*, which contain considerable data generally interpreted to support the anticlerical position. This work is of limited use for the 1920's because little documentation was available to the author when he wrote. John Lloyd Mecham, in *Church and State in Latin America*, provides a good capsule summary of the Mexican experience as part of a larger survey. All general histories of Mexico discuss religion, with varying degrees of thoroughness and objectivity. Ernest Gruening, in *Mexico and Its Heritage*, has quantities of information on the subject, all of it forged into a slashing indictment of Church and clergy. The old, reliable *A History of Mexico*, by Henry Bamford Parkes, leans toward the liberal position without losing its balance. A more recent attempt to put the Church question in dispassionate perspective is found in Charles C. Cumberland's *Mexico: The Struggle for Modernity.*

Mexican writers on the religious question almost invariably divide into extremes. *Historia de la iglesia en México*, by Mariano Cuevas, S.J., is a bonanza of information, but, except for a brief epilogue on the revolution, he ends his account in 1910. It is a one-sided defense of the Church. Alfonso Toro, in *La iglesia y el estado en México*, and Antonio Uroz, in *La cuestión religiosa en México*, sweep through four hundred years of history in single short volumes. Both insist that the Church's presence has wrought little except corruption and ruin.

The colonial background of the religious conflict has been more objectively studied than postindependence Church-State problems. Robert Ricard's *La "conquête spirituelle" du Mexique*, remains unsurpassed on the formative decades of the sixteenth century. Good summaries of the Church's impact on colonial life are included in Charles Gibson's *Spain in America* and Clarence H. Haring's *The Spanish Empire in America*, both of which draw extensively on primary and secondary materials. Hubert Howe Bancroft's six-volume *History of Mexico* is still a worthwhile source, especially for the colonial Church's relationship to Spanish civil authority.

Anticlericalism disrupted Mexican national life for a century. An excellent introduction to the phenomenon's European origins is found in Crane Brinton's *Ideas and Men: The Story of Western Thought*. The titanic battle between liberals and conservatives in nineteenth-century Mexico can best be studied in the writings of each side's major spokesmen. José María Luis Mora, in *México y sus revoluciones* and *Obras sueltas*, constructed the anticlerical platform with such thoroughness that subsequent proponents have added only minor refinements. Mora's worthy adversary, Lucas Alamán, likewise left little ground unplowed in his defense of Catholicism as the cornerstone of Mexico's nationhood. His *Disertaciones sobre la historia de la república megicana, desde la época de la conquista . . . hasta la independencia* and *Historia de Méjico desde los primeros movimientos que prepararon su independencia en el año de 1808, hasta la época presente* have remained ideological bibles for Mexican defenders of the faith, whether moderate or bellicose in their tactics.

There are several modern analyses of the liberal-conservative controversy, of which the best is Charles A. Hale's *Mexican Liberalism in the Age of Mora, 1821–1853*. Hale shows that anticlericalism, while it was always a component of Mexican liberalism, became virulent when the Church refused to relinquish any part of its privileged economic and civil status. He is ably complemented by Jesús Reyes Heroles, in *El liberalismo mexicano*. An excellent study of the philosophical underpinnings of Mexican anticlericalism is Martín Quirarte's *El problema religioso en México*, which attacks various liberal contentions, including Mora's statistics on the extent of the Church's financial activities. *El conflicto religioso de 1926: Sus orígenes, su desarrollo, su solución*, by Eduardo Iglesias, S.J., and Rafael Martínez del Campo, S.J. [pseud. Aquiles P. Moctezuma], is a major fount of information but often unconvincing in its proclerical and anti-Yankee assertions. Less comprehensive but more persuasive is Jesús García Gutiérrez's *Acción anticatólica en Méjico*, which traces Mexican anticlericalism from its roots in the Enlightenment through the age of Porfirio Díaz and concludes that philosophical motives predominated in the recurrent attacks on the Church establishment.

On the religious climate during the Porfiriato, including the rise of social Catholicism, *Historia moderna de México*, edited by Daniel Cosío

Villegas, especially volume 6, *El porfiriato: La vida social,* by Moisés González Navarro, is unsurpassed. Karl M. Schmitt, in "The Evolution of Mexican Thought on Church-State Relations," argues that Church and State were moving toward a workable arrangement during the Díaz period and that events after 1910 reversed the process.

The religious situation during the decade after 1910 receives space in all histories of the revolution. For a balanced treatment of the complexities, see Charles C. Cumberland's two volumes, *Mexican Revolution: Genesis Under Madero* and *Mexican Revolution: The Constitutionalist Years.* On the much-debated matter of the Church's relations with Victoriano Huerta, see Michael C. Meyer's *Huerta: A Political Portrait.* Meyer concludes that Catholic support for Huerta was largely a reaction to the constitutionalists' anticlerical depredations.

Only three professional historians have produced book-length studies concerned entirely with the conflict of the 1920's. Elizabeth Ann Rice, in *The Diplomatic Relations between the United States and Mexico, as Affected by the Struggle for Religious Liberty in Mexico, 1925–1929,* details with meticulous accuracy the official U.S. involvement and in particular Dwight Morrow's quest for a reconciliation. It is written exclusively from American sources. Alicia Olivera Sedano's *Aspectos del conflicto religioso de 1926 a 1929: Sus antecedentes y consecuencias,* although limited to Mexican sources, approaches the Cristero epoch from a base of careful research rather than emotional guesswork. Olivera Sedano was the first researcher to plumb the LNDLR archives. The third work, unpublished at this writing, is Jean A. Meyer's monumental "La Christiade: Société et idéologie dans le Mexique contemporain, 1926–1929." Meyer studies the Cristeros as Catholic peasants and draws a sharp distinction between them and the rebellion's middle-class leaders, whose world outlook, Meyer insists, was closer to that of the Mexican anticlericals. Robert E. Quirk, in "The Mexican Revolution and the Catholic Church, 1910–1929: An Ideological Study," examines the philosophy and goals of Catholic middle-class spokesmen.

Several articles on the conflict and its aftermath deserve special mention. James W. Wilkie's "The Meaning of the Cristero Religious War against the Mexican Revolution," although not as definitive as its title suggests, broke new ground with new sources. The most thoroughly studied aspect of the problem is Morrow's intercession. Contributions include two offerings by Stanley R. Ross, "Dwight W. Morrow, Ambassador to Mexico" and "Dwight Morrow and the Mexican Revolution"; "The Unofficial Intervention of the United States in Mexico's Religious Crisis, 1926–1930," by Edward J. Berbusse, S.J.; L. Ethan Ellis's "Dwight Morrow and the Church-State Controversy"; and Walter Lippmann's "The Church and State in Mexico: American Mediation."

On the critical situation the Church faced after the 1929 settlement and the eventual winding down of animosities, see Kenneth Grubb's "Political and Religious Situation in Mexico," Earle K. James's "Church and State in Mexico," and especially Lyle C. Brown's excellent synopsis, "Mexican Church-State Relations, 1933–1940."

It is understandable that most literature on the Cristero rebellion is polemical, given the high feelings the clash engendered and the fact that most who have written about it were either personally involved or associated with people who were. Protagonists have argued their positions largely in terms of their reading of history. Emilio Portes Gil, in *The Conflict between the Civil Power and the Clergy*, justifies the revolutionary regime's stand by tracing the problem back to the time of Charlemagne. *El problema religioso en México: Católicos y cristianos*, by Ramón J. Sender, and *El clero y el gobierno de México: Apuntes para la historia de la crisis en 1926*, by José González [pseud. Luis Balderrama], are both headlong denunciations of the Mexican ecclesiastical structure. The historical argument for the Catholic cause is most lucidly expounded by Anacleto González Flores; in his *El plebiscito de los mártires*, a posthumous edition of his speeches and writings, he brands the liberals and revolutionists as intruders bent on destroying Mexico's Catholic heritage and, perforce, her nationality.

By far the largest part of the literature is by Catholics, nearly all of them partisans of the militant persuasion. The most prolific was Andrés Barquín y Ruiz, by general acclaim the dean of the school until his death in 1967. His earliest effort, written in company with Giovanni Hoyois and published in Belgium shortly after the settlement, is *La tragédie mexicaine: Sous l'ombre d'Obregon*, which set the norm for most of what followed: glorification of the activists, excoriation of their opponents, and presentation of quantities of documentation. Barquín's *Los mártires de Cristo Rey*, *Hacia la cumbre de la cristianidad*, and *El clamor de la sangre* (published under the pseudonym Joaquín Blanco Gil) are equally passionate and useful for the hard-to-find data they contain. The fire-eating bishop of Huejutla, José de Jesús Manríquez y Zárate, wrote a variety of bellicose pieces in support of the militants; he outdid himself in holy fury in his *¡Viva Cristo Rey! en la hora de suprema angustia*. The historian of the ACJM and Barquín's successor as chief chronicler of the *cristeriada* is Antonio Ríus Facius, whose views parallel Barquín's, but whose work is better organized and written in a more mature and graceful style. Ríus Facius records the rise of the Catholic youth movement in *De Don Porfirio a Plutarco: Historia de la ACJM*, republished in 1963 under the title *La juventud católica y la revolución mejicana, 1910 a 1925*. His *Méjico cristero: Historia de la*

ACJM, 1925 a 1931 carries the story through the rebellion to the eclipse of the ACJM.

In 1945 Miguel Palomar y Vizcarra began editing a series on the conflict called "El caso ejemplar mexicano." His own volume of the same name is a fervent defense of the insurrection and a sweeping denunciation of the revolution and the United States. The third volume in the series, *La trinchera sagrada*, by David G. Ramírez, the priest who was secretary to the intransigent Archbishop González Valencia of Durango, hews faithfully to the collection's no-quarter theme.

The most comprehensive treatment of the religious conflict for the entire period of the Mexican Revolution is Joseph H. Schlarman's *Mexico, a Land of Volcanoes*. It is antirevolution and pro-Church but has a wealth of information and a good bibliography. Antonio J. López Ortega, in *Las naciones extranjeras y la persecución religiosa*, describes some aspects of the part played by U.S. Catholics and the Vatican in the conflict, as well as the LNDLR's activities in Europe. A useful study on the National Catholic party that also discusses the early careers of men prominent in the rebellion is Francisco Banegas Galván's *El por qué del Partido Católico Nacional*. Charles S. Macfarland's *Chaos in Mexico: The Conflict of Church and State* is an even-handed piece of reporting by an American Protestant minister who interviewed leaders on both sides of the question. There are a number of antiquarian-type regional sketches on the rebellion, most of them short, semimemoir accounts. Fairly representative is José Dolores Pérez's *La persecución religiosa de Calles en León, Gto.*

Only a few books on the rebellion have been written by persons sympathetic to the government. Cristóbal L. Rodríguez, in *La iglesia católica y la rebelión cristera en México (1926–1929)*, maintains that the revolt was the work of crazed fanatics nourished on retrograde clericalism. Silvano Barba González's *La rebelión de los cristeros* is in the same vein; the author, who was governor of Jalisco during part of the rebellion, argues that Mexico's religious strife stems from the pernicious nature of Latin Catholicism, which he contrasts with the more responsible variety found in Anglo-Saxon nations.

There are several studies on the 1920's which are not primarily concerned with religion but which nevertheless devote space to the conflict or to events germane to it. John W. F. Dulles, in *Yesterday in Mexico: A Chronicle of the Revolution, 1919–1936*, has some engrossing sketches on the Church-State controversy presented in an entertaining manner. Juan Gualberto Amaya, in *Los gobiernos de Obregón, Calles y regímenes "peleles" derivados del callismo: Tercera etapa, 1920 a 1935*, treats the religious issue in the wider context of intrarevolutionary factionalism. Felipe Islas and Manuel Múzquiz Blanco, in *De la pasión sectaria a la noción de las instituciones*, broaden the context by attempting with some success to relate the conflict to the overall struggle for national cohesion. C. Dennis Ignasias, in "Reluctant Recognition: The United States and the Recognition of Alvaro Obregón of Mexico," discusses the steps leading to the American decision to accept the existence of the revolutionary regime despite U.S. Catholic opposition. Historians of the Catholic church in the United States have little to say about American involvement in the Mexican tangle, but John Tracy Ellis, in *American Catholicism*, gives brief biographical summaries of some Catholic leaders prominent at the time.

Life stories of participants in the struggle abound, but few of them approach scholarly standards. Obregón still awaits his biographer. At present, Mario Mena's *Alvaro Obregón: Historia militar y política, 1912–1929* is perhaps the best biography available, but it is short and somewhat superficial. *Obregón: Aspectos de su vida*, by Rubén Romero et al., is a collection of memorial pieces by acquaintances of the leader. For Calles, Portes Gil, and lesser lights there is little except propaganda poetics and campaign rousers. Students must seek biographical data in such sources as the *Diccionario Porrúa de historia, biografía y geografía de México*, Miguel Angel Peral's *Diccionario biográfico mexicano*, or James A. Magner's *Men of Mexico*. Harold Nicolson's *Dwight Morrow*, although not exhaustive, is a competent effort by a writer who knew the ambassador and had access to inside information.

There is no dearth of biographies of Catholics who figured in the fray. All the works are sympathetic to their subjects, and most are pure adulation. Andrés Barquín y Ruiz's *Bernardo Bergöend, S.J.* is a treatise on Catholic activism built around the life and thought of the ACJM's founder. *Luis Navarro Origel: El primer cristero*, by Alfonso Trueba [pseud. Martín Chowell], canonizes the leader of the Michoacán insurgents, and Barquín y Ruiz's *Luis Segura Vilchis* comes close to doing the same with the young zealot who tried to kill Obregón in 1927. Antonio Gómez Robledo's *Anacleto González Flores: El Maestro*, although uncritical in its approach, is a rounded exposition of the ideology of the resistance movement's chief theoretician. Father Miguel Pro Juárez, next to Obregón the conflict's best-remembered victim, has been the object of growing interest for forty years. The most detailed scrutiny of the young priest, by a fellow Jesuit whose aim may have been to hasten the beatification proceedings currently in progress, is Antonio Dragón, S.J.'s *Vida íntima del Padre Pro*. María Elena Sodi de Pallares's *Los cristeros y José de León Toral* is a compassionate account of Obregón's assassin written by the daughter of his defense attorney.

Most of the bishops who were prominent at the time of the conflict have been memorialized in books by admirers. Alberto María Carreño's *El arzobispo de México, excmo. Sr. Dr. D. Pascual Díaz y el conflicto religioso* is a painstaking defense of that prelate by his secretary and closest friend. Díaz's Catholic critics have disputed Carreño's version of events but are hampered by not having access to materials Carreño had at his disposal. Eduardo J. Correa has written a laudatory biography of another of the conciliators, *Mons. Rafael Guízar Valencia: El obispo santo, 1878–1938*. Andrés Barquín y Ruiz's *José María González Valencia: Arzobispo de Durango* and Ramón Moreno's *Excmo. y Revmo. Sr. Dr. Dn. Miguel de la Mora, 5° obispo de Zacatecas y 5° de San Luis Potosí: Breves apuntes biográficos* are useful but heavily weighted in favor of the two prelates' activist views; the first is rabidly antipathetic to Díaz and Ruiz y Flores and must be used as gingerly as Carreño's work on the opposite side. Francisco Orozco y Jiménez merits a competent study. All that is currently available, aside from some short *homenajes,* is Vicente Camberos Vizcaino's *Francisco el Grande: Francisco Orozco y Jiménez,* which avoids much of the controversy surrounding the archbishop and smacks of authorized biography. Besides the *Diccionario Porrúa* and Peral guides, two good references for names and dates on the Mexican hierarchy are José Bravo Ugarte, S.J.'s *Diócesis y obispos de la iglesia mexicana, 1519–1965* and Emeterio Valverde y Téllez's *Bio-bibliografía eclesiástica mexicana (1821–1943).*

MATERIALS CITED

Alamán, Lucas. *Disertaciones sobre la historia de la República megicana, desde la época de la conquista que los Españoles hicieron, a fines del siglo XV y principios del XVI, de la islas y continente americano, hasta la independencia.* 3 vols. Mexico City: Impr. de J. M. Lara, 1844–1849.

————. *Historia de Méjico desde los primeros movimientos que prepararon su independencia en el año de 1808, hasta la época presente.* 5 vols. Mexico City: Impr. de J. M. Lara, 1849–1852.

Amaya, Juan Gualberto. *Los gobiernos de Obregón, Calles y regímenes "peleles" derivados del callismo: Tercera etapa, 1920 a 1935.* Mexico City, 1947.

Annals of the American Academy of Political and Social Science. Philadelphia, 1917.

Archive of the National League for the Defense of Religious Liberty. Departamento de Investigaciones Históricas, Instituto Nacional de Antropología e Historia. Mexico City.

Archivo General de la Nación (Archivo de los Presidentes, Obregón–Calles). Mexico City.

Balderrama, Luis. *See* González, José.

Bancroft, Hubert Howe. *History of Mexico.* 6 vols. San Francisco: A. L. Bancroft and Company, 1883–1888.

Banegas Galván, Francisco. *El por qué del Partido Católico Nacional.* Mexico City: Editorial Jus, 1960.

Barba González, Silvano. *La rebelión de los cristeros.* Mexico City, 1967.

Barquín y Ruiz, Andrés. *Bernardo Bergöend, S.J.* Mexico City: Editorial Jus, 1968.

———— [pseud. Joaquín Blanco Gil]. *El clamor de la sangre.* 2d ed. Mexico City: Editorial Jus, 1967.

————. *Hacia la cumbre de la cristianidad.* Guadalajara: Editorial "Rex-Mex," 1945.

————. *José María González Valencia: Arzobispo de Durango*. Mexico City: Editorial Jus, 1967.

————. *Luis Segura Vilchis*. Mexico City: Editorial Jus, 1967.

————. *Los mártires de Cristo Rey*. 2 vols. Mexico City: Editorial "Criterio," 1937.

————, and Giovanni Hoyois. *La tragédie mexicaine: Sous l'ombre d'Obregon*. Louvain: Ed. Rex, 1929.

Berbusse, Edward J., S.J. "The Unofficial Intervention of the United States in Mexico's Religious Crisis, 1926–1930." *The Americas* 23 (July 1966): 28–62.

Blanco Gil, Joaquín. *See* Barquín y Ruiz, Andrés.

Bravo Ugarte, José. *Diócesis y obispos de la iglesia mexicana (1519–1965)*. 2d ed. Mexico City: Editorial Jus, 1965.

Brinton, Crane. *Ideas and Men: The Story of Western Thought*. 2d ed. Englewood Cliffs: Prentice-Hall, 1963.

Brondo Alvarez, Felipe. Memoirs. 1932. Unpublished manuscript in possession of its author.

Brown, Lyle C. "Mexican Church-State Relations, 1933–1940." *A Journal of Church and State* 6 (Spring 1964): 202–222.

Calcott, Wilfrid Hardy. *Church and State in Mexico, 1822–1857*. Durham: Duke University Press, 1926.

————. *Liberalism in Mexico, 1857–1929*. Stanford: Stanford University Press, 1931.

Camberos Vizcaino, Vicente. *Francisco el Grande: Francisco Orozco y Jiménez*. Mexico City: Editorial Jus, 1966.

Carreño, Alberto María. *El arzobispo de México, excmo. Sr. Dr. D. Pascual Díaz y el conflicto religioso*. 2d ed., rev. Mexico City: Ediciones Victoria, 1943.

Catholic Archives of Texas. Austin.

Ceniceros y Villarreal, Rafael. "Historia de la L.N.D.R." 1931(?) Un published manuscript in possession of Antonio Ríus Facius.

Cházaro, Gabriel. "El caso de la Madre Conchita: Texto revisado por ella misma." *David* 5, no. 110 (September 22, 1961): 220–221.

Chowell, Martín. *See* Trueba, Alfonso.

"Cómo nació la Liga, su escudo y su lema." *David* 5, no. 109 (August 22, 1961): 198–199.

Correa, Eduardo J. *Mons. Rafael Guizar Valencia: El obispo santo, 1878–1938*. Mexico City: Editorial Porrúa, 1951.

Cosío Villegas, Daniel, ed. *Historia moderna de México*. 7 vols. Mexico City: Editorial Hermes, 1955–1965.

"Los cristeros de Parras, Coahuila: La verdad sobre los fusilamientos de 1927." *David* 2, no. 30 (January 22, 1955): 81–82.

Cuevas, Mariano, S.J. *Historia de la iglesia en México*. 5 vols. Mexico City: Editorial Patria, 1946–1947.

Cumberland, Charles C. *Mexican Revolution: Genesis under Madero*. Austin: University of Texas Press, 1952.

———. *Mexican Revolution: The Constitutionalist Years*. Austin: University of Texas Press, 1972.

———. *Mexico: The Struggle for Modernity*. New York: Oxford University Press, 1968.

Current History. 1931.

"Datos biográficos del General Lauro Rocha G." *David* 7, no. 157 (August 22, 1965): 207–208.

David: Revista mensual ilustrada, órgano oficial de la Legión de Cristo Rey y Santa María de Guadalupe—veteranos de la Guardia Nacional (Cristeros). 1952–1969.

Degollado Guízar, Jesús. *Memorias de Jesús Degollado Guízar, último general en jefe del ejército cristero*. Mexico City: Editorial Jus, 1957.

Díaz y Barreto, Pascual. *Informe que rinde al V. Episcopado Mexicano el Obispo de Tabasco Pascual Díaz en relación con las actividades de la Liga Nacional Defensora de la Libertad Religiosa en los Estados Unidos de América*. New York, 1928.

Diccionario Porrúa de historia, biografía y geografía de México. 2d ed. Mexico City: Editorial Porrúa, 1965.

Dragón, Antonio, S.J. *Vida íntima del Padre Pro*. Translated (into Spanish) by Rafael Martínez del Campo, S.J. 3d ed. Mexico City: Editorial Jus, 1961.

Dulles, John W. F. *Yesterday in Mexico: A Chronicle of the Revolution, 1919–1936*. Austin: University of Texas Press, 1961.

Ellis, John Tracy. *American Catholicism*. Chicago: University of Chicago Press, 1956.

Ellis, L. Ethan. "Dwight Morrow and the Church-State Controversy." *Hispanic American Historical Review* 38 (November 1958): 482–505.

Excélsior. Mexico City daily. 1925–1929.

García Gutiérrez, Jesús. *Acción anticatólica en Méjico*. 2d ed. Mexico City: Editorial Jus, 1939.

——— [pseud. Félix Navarrete], ed. *La persecución religiosa en Méjico desde el punto de vista jurídico: Colección de leyes y decretos relativos a la reducción de sacerdotes*. Mexico City, 1939(?).

García Naranjo, Nemesio. *Memorias de García Naranjo*. 10 vols. Monterrey: Talleres de "El Porvenir," 1963.

Gibson, Charles. *Spain in America*. New York: Harper and Row, 1966.

Gilson, Etienne, ed. *The Church Speaks to the Modern World: The Social Teachings of Leo XIII*. Garden City: Doubleday, 1954.

Gómez Robledo, Antonio. *Anacleto González Flores: El Maestro.* 2d ed. Mexico City: Editorial Jus, 1947.

González, José [pseud. Luis Balderrama]. *El clero y el gobierno de México: Apuntes para la historia de la crisis en 1926.* 2 vols. Mexico City: Editorial "Cuauhtémoc," 1926–1927.

González Flores, Anacleto. *El plebiscito de los mártires.* Mexico City, 1930.

González Navarro, Moisés. *El porfiriato: La vida social.* Mexico City: Editorial Hermes, 1957. (Vol. 6 of *Historia moderna de México,* edited by Daniel Cosío Villegas.)

Grubb, Kenneth. "Political and Religious Situation in Mexico." *International Affairs* 14 (September 1935): 674–699.

Gruening, Ernest. *Mexico and Its Heritage.* New York: Appleton-Century Company, 1929.

Gutiérrez Gutiérrez, José. "El General Degollado Guízar: Breves apuntes histórico-biográficos sobre la noble figura." *David* 3, no. 63 (October 22, 1957): 235–240.

Hale, Charles A. *Mexican Liberalism in the Age of Mora, 1821–1853.* New Haven: Yale University Press, 1968.

Haring, Clarence H. *The Spanish Empire in America.* New York: Harcourt, Brace and World, 1947.

Iglesias, Eduardo, S.J., and Rafael Martínez del Campo, S.J. [pseud. Aquiles P. Moctezuma]. *El conflicto religioso de 1926: Sus orígenes, su desarrollo, su solución.* 2 vols. 2d ed. Mexico City: Editorial Jus, 1960.

Ignasias, C. Dennis. "Reluctant Recognition: The United States and the Recognition of Alvaro Obregón of Mexico, 1920–1924." Ph.D. dissertation, Michigan State University, 1967.

El Imparcial. Mexico City daily. 1926.

Islas, Felipe, and Manuel Múzquiz Blanco. *De la pasión sectaria a la noción de las instituciones.* Mexico City, 1932.

James, Earle K. "Church and State in Mexico." *Foreign Policy Reports* 11 (July 3, 1935): 106–116.

El jurado de Toral y la Madre Conchita (lo que se dijo y lo que no se dijo en el sensacional juicio): Versión taquigráfica textual. 2 vols. Mexico City: Editores Alducín y de Llano, n.d.

Kestenbaum, Justin L. "The Question of Intervention in Mexico, 1913–1917." Ph.D. dissertation, Northwestern University, 1963.

Lara, J. Andrés, S.J. *Prisionero de callistas y cristeros.* 2d ed. Mexico City: Editorial Jus, 1959.

Lara y Torres, Leopoldo. *Documentos para la historia de la persecución religiosa en México.* Mexico City: Editorial Jus, 1954.

Lippmann, Walter. "The Church and State in Mexico: American Mediation." *Foreign Affairs* 8 (January 1930): 186–207.

López Ortega, Antonio J. "A propósito del archivo de la 'V.I.T.A.-MEXICO' en Roma, Italia." *David* 8, no. 175 (February 22, 1967): 101–104.

———. *Las naciones extranjeras y la persecución religiosa.* Mexico City, 1944 .

McDevitt, Philip, Papers. University of Notre Dame.

Macfarland, Charles S. *Chaos in Mexico: The Conflict of Church and State.* New York: Harper and Brothers, 1935.

Magner, James A. *Men of Mexico.* 2d ed. Milwaukee: Bruce Publishing Company, 1943.

Manríquez y Zárate, José de Jesús. *¡Viva Cristo Rey! en la hora de suprema angustia.* El Paso: Imprenta de la *Revista Católica*, 1928.

Márquez, Octaviano, ed. *Obras selectas de Don Trinidad Sánchez Santos.* 2d ed. 2 vols. Mexico City: Editorial Jus, 1962.

Martínez Camarena, Rafael. "Rectificando al Mayor Heriberto Navarrete." *David* 5, no. 120 (July 22, 1962): 388–391.

Mecham, John Lloyd. *Church and State in Latin America.* 2d ed., rev. Chapel Hill: University of North Carolina Press, 1966.

"Memorándum del Excmo. Sr. Francisco Orozco y Jiménez, Arzobispo de Guadalajara, México." *David* 7, no. 155 (June 22, 1965): 168–170.

Mena, Mario. *Alvaro Obregón: Historia militar y política, 1912–1929.* Mexico City: Editorial Jus, 1960.

Mexico. *Diario Oficial.* 1925–1929.

Meyer, Jean A. "La Christiade: Société et idéologie dans le Mexique contemporain, 1926–1929." University of Paris doctoral dissertation, 1971.

Meyer, Michael C. *Huerta: A Political Portrait.* Lincoln: University of Nebraska Press, 1972.

Moctezuma, Aquiles P. *See* Iglesias, Eduardo, S.J., and Rafael Martínez del Campo, S.J.

Mora, José María Luis. *México y sus revoluciones.* 3 vols. 2d ed. Mexico City: Editorial Porrúa, 1965. (First edition, Paris, 1836.)

———. *Obras sueltas.* 2d ed. Mexico City: Editorial Porrúa, 1963. (First edition, Paris, 1837.)

Moreno, Ramón. *Excmo. y Revmo. Sr. Dr. Dn. Miguel de la Mora, 5º obispo de Zacatecas y 5º de San Luis Potosí: Breves apuntes biográficos.* San Luis Potosí, 1947.

Morrow, Dwight, Papers. Amherst College.

Navarrete, Félix. *See* García Gutiérrez, Jesús.

Navarrete, Heriberto, S.J. *"Por Dios y Por la Patria": Memorias de mi participación en la defensa de la libertad de conciencia y culto durante la persecución religiosa en México de 1926 a 1929.* 2d ed. Mexico City: Editorial Jus, 1964.

New York Times. 1925–1932.

Nicolson, Harold. *Dwight Morrow.* New York: Harcourt, Brace and Company, 1935.

Obregón, Alvaro. *Ocho mil kilómetros en campaña: Relación de las acciones de armas efectuadas en más de veinte estados de la República durante un período de cuatro años.* Mexico City: Librería de la Vda. de Ch. Bouret, 1917.

El Obrero. Guadalajara weekly. 1925.

Ochoa, Enrique de Jesús [pseud. Spectator]. *Los cristeros del Volcán de Colima.* 2 vols. 2d ed. Mexico City: Editorial Jus, 1961.

Olivera Sedano, Alicia. *Aspectos del conflicto religioso de 1926 a 1929: Sus antecedentes y consecuencias.* Mexico City: Instituto Nacional de Antropología e Historia, 1966.

Orozco y Jiménez, Francisco. *Memorándum.* East Chicago: Contreras Printing Company, 1929.

Our Bishops Speak: Statements of the Hierarchy of the United States and of the Administrative Board of the National Catholic Welfare Conference, 1919–1951. Milwaukee: The Bruce Publishing Company, 1952.

Palomar y Vizcarra, Miguel. *El caso ejemplar mexicano.* 2d ed. Mexico City: Editorial Jus, 1966.

———. "Gorostieta." *David* 2, no. 39 (October 22, 1955): 233–240.

Parkes, Henry Bamford. *A History of Mexico.* 3d ed., rev. Boston: Houghton Mifflin, 1960.

Parsons, Wilfrid, S.J. *Mexican Martyrdom.* New York: Macmillan, 1936.

Pastoral Letter of the Catholic Episcopate of the United States on the Religious Situation in Mexico, December, 1926. New Haven: Knights of Columbus Supreme Council, 1926.

Peral, Miguel Angel. *Diccionario biográfico mexicano.* Mexico City: Editorial P.A.C., 1944.

Pérez, José. "La muerte del Gral. Ferreira: Quién era este jefe fallecido." *Hoy,* February 19, 1928, pp. 30, 63.

Pérez, José Dolores. *La persecución religiosa de Calles en León, Gto.* 2d ed. León, 1952.

Pérez Lugo, J. *La cuestión religiosa en México.* Mexico City: Centro Cultural "Cuauhtémoc," 1927.

Portes Gil, Emilio. *Autobiografía de la Revolución Mexicana*. Mexico City: Instituto Mexicano de Cultura, 1964.

―――. *The Conflict between the Civil Power and the Clergy*. Mexico City: Press of the Ministry of Foreign Affairs, 1935.

La Prensa. Mexico City daily. 1925–1929.

Quirarte, Martín. *El problema religioso en México*. Mexico City: Instituto Nacional de Antropología e Historia, 1967.

Quirk, Robert E. "The Mexican Revolution and the Catholic Church, 1910–1929: An Ideological Study." Ph.D. dissertation, Harvard University, 1950.

Ramírez, Agustín. "El combate de Tepatitlán: Rectificación a Juan Rizo." *David* 7, no. 178 (May 22, 1967): 163.

Ramírez, David G. *La trinchera sagrada*. El caso ejemplar mexicano, vol. 3. Mexico City: Editorial "Rex-Mex," 1948.

Reyes Heroles, Jesús. *El liberalismo mexicano*. 3 vols. Mexico City: Universidad Nacional de México, Facultad de Derecho, 1957–1961.

Ricard, Robert. *La "conquête spirituelle" du Mexique*. Paris: Institut d'Ethnologie, 1933.

Rice, Elizabeth Ann. *The Diplomatic Relations between the United States and Mexico, as Affected by the Struggle for Religious Liberty in Mexico, 1925–1929*. Washington, D.C.: Catholic University of America Press, 1959.

Ríus Facius, Antonio. *La juventud católica y la revolución mejicana, 1910 a 1925*. Mexico City: Editorial Jus, 1963.

―――. *Méjico cristero: Historia de la ACJM, 1925 a 1931*. 2d ed. Mexico City: Editorial Patria, 1966.

Rivero del Val, Luis. *Entre las patas de los caballos: Diario de un cristero*, 3d ed. Mexico City: Editorial Jus, 1961.

Rodríguez, Cristóbal. *La iglesia católica y la rebelión cristera en México (1926–1929)*. 2 vols. Vol. 1: Mexico City: Editora la Voz de Juárez, 1966; vol. 2: *Cristeros contra cristianos*. Mexico City: Editorial "Revolución," 1967.

Romero, Rubén, et al. *Obregón: Aspectos de su vida*. Mexico City: Editorial "Cultura," 1935.

Ross, Stanley R. "Dwight Morrow and the Mexican Revolution." *Hispanic American Historical Review* 38 (November 1958): 506–528.

―――. "Dwight W. Morrow, Ambassador to Mexico." *The Americas* 14 (January 1958): 373–389.

Ruiz y Flores, Leopoldo. *Recuerdo de recuerdos*. Mexico City: Buena Prensa, 1942.

Ryan, Thomas, S.J. *Murdered in Mexico: Father Michael Anthony Pro, S.J.* Dublin: Press of *The Irish Messenger*, 1928.

Sáenz, Aarón, Fernando Torreblanca, and Joaquín Amaro, eds. *Discursos del General Alvaro Obregón*. 2 vols. Mexico City: Biblioteca de la Dirección General de Educación Militar, 1932.

"Santiago Bayacora, Durango: Memorias de Francisco Campos." *David* 2, no. 33 (April 22, 1955): 130–132.

Scherer García, Julio. "Roberto Cruz en la Epoca de la Violencia," *Excélsior*, October 7, 1961.

Schlarman, Joseph H. *Mexico, a Land of Volcanoes*. Milwaukee: Bruce Publishing Company, 1950.

Schmitt, Karl M. "Catholic Adjustment to the Secular State." *Catholic Historical Review* 47 (July 1962): 182–204.

———. "The Evolution of Mexican Thought on Church-State Relations." Ann Arbor: University of Michigan Microfilms, 1954.

Scott, Robert E. *Mexican Government in Transition*. 2d ed., rev. Urbana: University of Illinois Press, 1964.

Sender, Ramón J. *El problema religioso en Méjico: Católicos y cristianos*. Madrid: Imprenta "Argis," 1928.

Sodi de Pallares, María Elena. *Los cristeros y José de León Toral*. Mexico City: Editorial "Cultura," 1936.

The Southern Messenger. San Antonio weekly. 1917, 1926.

Spectator. *See* Ochoa, Enrique de Jesús.

State of Coahuila Archives. Saltillo.

Tena Ramírez, Felipe, ed. *Leyes fundamentales de México, 1808–1964*. 2d ed., rev. Mexico City: Editorial Porrúa, 1964.

Toro, Alfonso. *La iglesia y el estado en México*. Mexico City: Talleres Gráficos de la Nación, 1927.

Trueba, Alfonso [pseud. Martín Chowell]. *Luis Navarro Origel: El primer cristero*. Mexico City: Editorial Jus, 1959.

United States. National Archives. Adjutant General's Office Records (War Department). Record Group 165.

———. National Archives (State Department). Record Groups 59, 84.

El Universal. Mexico City daily. 1926–1929.

Uroz, Antonio. *La cuestión religiosa en México*. Mexico City, 1926.

Valverde y Téllez, Emeterio. *Bio-bibliografía eclesiástica mexicana (1821–1943)*. Mexico City: Editorial Jus, 1949.

Vargas, Oscar. "Algunos rasgos del Lic. Ceniceros y Villarreal." *David* 2, no. 36 (July 22, 1955): 183–184.

Vasconcelos, José, ed. *La caída de Carranza: De la dictadura a la libertad*. Mexico City: Imprenta de Murguía, 1920.

Velázquez Bringas, Esperanza, ed. *Méjico ante el mundo: Ideología del Presidente Plutarco Elías Calles*. Barcelona: Editorial Cervantes, 1927.

Velázquez López, René. "El problema religioso en México, 1917–1929." M.A. thesis, University of Mexico, 1963.

Wilkie, James W. "The Meaning of the Cristero Religious War against the Mexican Revolution." *A Journal of Church and State* 8 (Spring 1966): 214–233.

———, and Edna Monzón de Wilkie. *México visto en el siglo XX.* Mexico City: Instituto Mexicano de Investigaciones Económicas, 1969.

INDEX

Acevedo, Aurelio R.: 89, 296
Acevedo de la Llata, Concepción
(Madre Conchita): and Cristeros in
Mexico City, 115; arrested in Obregón assassination, 218; trial of, 228–
229; released from prison, 297–298
ACJM: founded, 29–31; program of,
31; early growth of, 31–32; clashes
with revolutionists, 32–33, 34, 38;
national convention of, 39; and National Republican party, 43; and
LNDLR, 54 n., 56; propaganda activities of, 85; members of, contemplate rebellion, 86; members of, executed, 87; members of, in rebellion,
113–118 passim; provides Cristero
leaders, 118, 156, 304; members of,
in attack on Obregón, 166; members
of, oppose Unión Nacional, 210–211;
praised by bishops, 230; opposes
compromise settlement, 276; eclipse
of, 290–291; mentioned, 41, 42, 54,
139, 168, 214
Acuña Rodríguez, Antonio: 113, 115
agrarians: as army auxiliaries, 116,
237 and n., 238 n., 251, 273
agraristas: 89. SEE ALSO agrarians
Agua Prieta, Son.: 48, 244
Aguascalientes: ACJM in, 32; Cristero
activity in, 117, 137, 172 n., 237,
272
Aguirre, Jesús M.: 242, 243
Ajusco, D.F.: 116
Alamán, Lucas: 11
Alcorta, Luis: 294
Alemán, Miguel: 297, 298
Alessio Robles, Miguel: 224
Alvarez, Ricardo: 122
Amaro, Joaquín: directs federal oper-
ations in Jalisco, 136, 154; transfers
cavalry to Colima, 155; urges reli-
gious settlement, 252; and Gorostie-

ta's death, 265; berates clergy, 292;
mentioned, 273
American Board of Home Missions: 72
Amor, Emmanuel: 145, 146
Anaya, Gerardo: 142 n., 260
Anguiano Márquez, Miguel: 162
anticlericalism: defined, 9, 10; appears
in Mexico, 10; in nineteenth century, 10–13; in 1910 revolution, 21,
22–23, 301; in Constitution of 1917,
23–25; enforced by Calles, 49–50,
64, 302. SEE ALSO clergy
apostolic delegate. SEE Cimino, Serafín; Filippi, Ernesto; Fumasoni-
Biondi, Pietro; Holy See; Ruiz y
Flores, Leopoldo
Argentina: 215
Arizona: 244
arms and ammunition: U.S. embargo
on, 100–101, 190, 245; procurement
of, by Cristeros, 138, 162, 215, 236;
mentioned, 135, 161
army: popularity of Obregón with, 35,
220; LNDLR seeks support of, 107;
remains loyal to government, 118,
302–303; and Gómez-Serrano revolt,
164; and Escobar rebellion, 242;
mentioned, 135
Asociación Católica de la Juventud
Mexicana. SEE ACJM
Association Catholique de la Jeunesse
Française: 30
Association of Catholic Women: 29
Atotonilco el Alto, Jal.: 155–156, 264,
265
Avila Camacho, Manuel: 137–138,
297–298

Bajío: 90, 162, 188, 243
Banegas Galván, Francisco: 45, 241,
260